Jörg-Thomas Födisch | Jost Neßhöver | Michael Behrndt | Rainer Roßbach

Porsche 718 + 804

Formel-Abenteuer in der Anderthalbliter-Ära
An adventure into Formula One during the 1.5 litre era

McKLEIN
PHOTOGRAPHY
Verlag Reinhard Klein

Impressum

Idee/Idea: Jörg-Thomas Födisch

Text: Jost Neßhöver (jn), Michael Behrndt (mb)

Übersetzung/Translation: Jost Neßhöver

Lektorat (deutsch)/Editing: Jörg-Thomas Födisch, Juliane Klingele

Lektorat (Englisch)/Editing (English): John Davenport

Bildredaktion/Picture editor: Rainer Roßbach

Design und Layout/Design and layout: Rainer Roßbach

Statistik/Statistics: Michael Behrndt

Bilder/Photography: Archiv Bader, Archiv Födisch, Archiv Geerts, Archiv Illg, Archiv Mehne, Archiv Mitter, Archiv Porsche AG, Archiv Völker/Richartz, Archiv Völker/Barth/Lückel, Archiv Weise, Peter Falk, Manfred Förster, Walter Kotauschek, Dr. Benno Müller, McKlein, Kunibert Söntgerath, Kurt Söntgerath.

Einige Abbildungen sind aus Privathand. Deren Ursprung konnte nicht mehr ermittelt werden. A few images are from private collections where the photographer could not be detected.

Bibliographie/Bibliography:

Zeitschriften/Magazines: auto motor und sport, Motor Revue, Christophorus

Bücher/Books: Auto-Jahr, diverse Ausgaben, Jürgen Barth/Gustav Büsing, Das neue große Buch der Porsche Typen (Stuttgart 2005); Lothar Boschen/ Jürgen Barth, Das grosse Buch der Porsche-Typen. Alle Fahrzeuge von 1948 bis heute. (Stuttgart) 1977; David Hayhoe/David Holland, Grand Prix Data Book 1997 (London, GB 1996); Ferry Porsche/Günther Molter, Ferry Porsche. Mein Leben. (Stuttgart 2004); Ingo Seiff, Das große Porsche Buch. Portrait einer Legende. (Augsburg 1997); Steve Small, Grand Prix Who's Who (Bershire, GB 2000); Frits van Someren, Het leven van Formule 1-coureur Carel Godin de Beaufort 1934 -1964 (AC Zaltbommel, NL 2004).

Besonderer Dank gilt/Special thanks to: Remo Bader, Raf Boone, Peter Falk, Hans Herrmann, Dieter Landenberger, Herbert Linge, Hans Mezger, Gerhard Mitter jun., Nanna Neßhöver, Sangita Popat, Porsche AG, Aimée und Yves Roßbach, Jens Torner, Trips'sche Sortstiftung.

Herausgeber/Editor: Reinhard Klein

Druck/Printing: Ge-druckt GmbH, Gelsenkirchen

Distribution: Racingwebshop

In der Rosenau 19, 51143 Köln, Germany

Fon: +49-(0)2203-9242570, Fax: +49-(0)2203-9242590,

contact@racingwebshop.com, www.racingwebshop.com, www.mcklein.de

2009 – Erste Auflage, 2009 – 1st edition

Publisher: Verlag Reinhard Klein, In der Rosenau 19,

D-51143 Köln, Klein@mcklein.de

ISBN: 978-3-927458-43-7

Inhalt / Content

Das kurze, schnelle Leben des 804

Weder Schlankheitskur noch Krafttraining retten den vielversprechenden Formel-Renner made in Zuffenhausen

The fast but short life of the 804

Weight loss and power gain were not enough to save the promising Formula One racing car from Zuffenhausen

Porsche kann über eins ganz bestimmt nicht klagen: Mangel an rennsportlichen Erfolgen. Vom Start nach dem Zweiten Weltkrieg weg baut das Werk Sportwagen und betreibt fleißig Rennsport. Stets profitiert der eine Zweig vom andern, Siege auf den Pisten dieser Welt sind gut für die Werbung, und was sich im Sport als gut erweist, taugt in der Regel auch für die Serie. Lange Jahre ist Porsche, dessen Dauerläufer 356 ja mit dem unermüdlichen Vierzylinder-Boxer unterwegs ist, somit vor allem eher in den kleinen Klassen erfolgreich – und fährt gelegentlich und immer öfter auch weit potenteren Gegnern vor der Nase her. Später machen dann die gewaltigen Dreiliter-Achtzylinder im 908 und der noch größere Fünfliter-Zwölfzylinder im legendären 917 Furore, bis die Turbos kommen und die unzähligen Elfer und, und, und. Gelegentlich klappt's auch mal nicht gleich mit dem spektakulären Erfolg. Das mit dem 804 ist so eine Episode. Es hätte vielleicht noch etwas werden können aus dem ersten Engagement der Zuffenhausener in der Formel 1. Die einen sagen so, die andern sagen so. Ferry Porsche jedenfalls sagt damals nach einer Saison: Nein. Aber: Der nagelneue Achtzylinder (der später noch einmal von sich reden macht) und das völlig neue Fahrgestell sind eine ganz besondere Herausforderung für Techniker, Ingenieure und Fahrer. Es ist eine spannende

Erster und zweiter Versuch: Der 718/2 (rechts) und der 804 im Werkshof bei Porsche in Zuffenhausen.

First and second try: the 718/2 (on the right) and 804 in the factory yard at Zuffenhausen.

For certain, there is one thing Porsche cannot lament and that is any lack of success in motor sport. From the very beginning, immediately after the Second World War, the firm was building sports cars and using them in racing and rallying. Always one side of the business profited from the other since victories on the world's racing circuits are good promotion and what is good for a racing car generally suits the commercial product as well. For a long time Porsche was very successful in the small categories as their workhorse 356 was powered by the indefatigable and comparatively small four-cylinder engine. Often the fast little cars from Zuffenhausen took much more powerful opponents by surprise. Later the magnificent eight-cylinder engine of the 908 and its successor, the legendary big twelve-cylinder of the 917 caused a furore until the turbocharged cars arrived and the countless variants of the 911 and so on.

But occasionally, Porsche's plans did not work out with the same spectacular success. That was the way it was with the 804. Maybe it would eventually have worked out with an on-going commitment from Porsche in Formula One. No, said Ferry Porsche, after only one season. But the new eight-cylinder engine would make a name for itself later on and both it and the new chassis provided a challenge for the technicians, engineers and

Foto: Porsche

Episode, und – wer weiß? – vielleicht sähe die Formel-1-Welt heute anders aus, wenn … Aber das ist alles Spekulation. Das hier ist die kurze, heftige Geschichte des 804 und seiner Vorläufer aus der Formel 2 und aus dem Sportwagenbau.

Die Vorgeschichte beginnt kurz vor Ende der 50er Jahre. Ganz interessant ist ein Blick nach England, wo sich am 29. Oktober 1958 Fürchterliches tut – zumindest für einige Briten, die sich doch eigentlich ganz behaglich soeben im siebten Himmel eingefunden haben. Das ist an jenem Abend die Zentrale des britischen Royal Automobile Club (RAC) an der piekfeinen Pall Mall in London. An diesem Tag sollen die Meistertitel des Jahres vergeben werden. Es ist die Erfüllung eines Traums: Beide Preise bleiben auf der Insel, Vanwall heimst den für Konstrukteure ein, Mike Hawthorn den für den besten Fahrer. Dann folgt die Ernüchterung: RAC-Pressesprecher Pat Gregory verliest, was die CSI, die Commission Sportive International (CSI), also die Internationale Sportkommission, für 1961 vorhat. Namentlich die Briten sind sauer, CSI-Präsident Auguste Perouse, der das Dokument mitgebracht hat, ist einer Flut von Vorwürfen ausgesetzt. Was ist geschehen? Nun, ganz einfach ausgedrückt: Die aktuelle Formel 2 wird praktisch zur Formel 1 inklusive kleiner 1,5-Liter-Motoren, die großen Zweieinhalbliter, die zuletzt die Großen Preise unter sich ausmachen, haben ausgedient.

Nun schreckt die Briten nicht so sehr die Vorstellung, dass sie jetzt womöglich schleunigst neue Motoren entwickeln müssen. So etwas passiert alle Jahre wieder, wenn zum Beispiel wieder in irgendeiner Motorsportvariante die Regeln geändert werden. Obendrein gibt es für die Konstrukteure von den Inseln wenig Anlass zur Sorge, weil sie bereits die taufrische Formel 2 praktisch

drivers. It was an exciting episode in Porsche's history and, who knows, maybe Formula One would look different today, if … But speculation is pointless. What happened is history and this book is a record of the short and lively story of the 804 and its forerunners in Formula Two and in sports cars.

The Porsche Formula One story began at the end of the 1950s. In England something shocking happened on October 29, 1958 – shocking that was to some British teams who felt that they were comfortably ensconced on Cloud Nine, the Nirvana of Formula One. That evening, the occasion was the awards ceremony of the Formula One Championship at the headquarters of the Royal Automobile Club (RAC) at Pall Mall in London. For most of those present, a dream had come true since, for the first time, both awards remained in the United Kingdom. The constructor's title went to Vanwall and Mike Hawthorn was recognised as World Champion driver. Then came some sobering news. The RAC spokesman, Pat Gregory, read out the CSI's (Commission Sportive International) plans for the Formula One rules that were to apply from the 1961 season onwards. The details were not well received by the Britons who became hopping mad. The CSI President, Auguste Perouse, who had brought the note was faced with a barrage of allegations. What was it that so enraged the current entrants and drivers? Put simply, the current Formula Two would evolve into Formula One and the main feature was to be smaller engines with a displacement of 1,500 cubic centimetres. The big-capacity 2.5-litre engines that had powered the existing cars and were used to dominating the races could now pack up and go home.

The British teams were naturally a little apprehensive that their

Formelrenner: Am 4. August 1957 gehen auf dem Nürburgring die Fahrer der Formel 1 und der Formel 2 gemeinsam an den Start. Rechts liegt Fangio vor Barth im 550 A. Der Porschepilot gewinnt die Formel 2 …

Formula racers: in August 1957 at the 'Ring, the drivers of Formula One and Formula Two shared the track. On the right, Fangio leads Barth in the 550 A. The Porsche driver won the Formula Two category …

… sein Kollege Umberto Maglioli scheidet aus.

… while his colleague Umberto Maglioli retired.

Fotos: Porsche

Monoposto: 1958 testet Porsche den RSK mit neuer Querlenker-Hinterachse und Mittellenkung.

Monoposto: in 1958, Porsche tested the RSK with a new rear axle and central steering.

vom Fleck weg dominiert haben – mit kleineren Motoren. Nein, die – nicht ganz abwegige – Sorge gilt der Attraktivität des Motorsports. Werden Rennen mit Motoren in Mittelklassewagen-Größe, deren mutmaßliche Leistung die mancher Seriensportwagen kaum übertrifft, noch Menschen an die GP-Kurse locken? Na ja, die Geschichte lehrt: Es kommt dann alles ganz anders.

Zunächst aber geht ein Aufschrei durch die britische Sportpresse. Die Franzosen hätten den Coup ausgeheckt, und ganz Kontinentaleuropa habe sich gegen die Briten verschworen. Nun mischen in der Formel 1 ernsthaft eigentlich nur Engländer und die Scuderia Ferrari mit. Ausgerechnet die Italiener sind die einzigen, die an der Seite ihrer Hauptkonkurrenten gegen den CSI-Beschluss gestimmt haben. Frankreich, Deutschland, die Niederlande, Monaco und Belgien finden die neue Formel gut, die Schweden, die Schweizer und Mexiko halten sich raus, und den US-Amerikanern sind ja schon die Zweieinhalbliter viel zu winzig. Sie wollen etwas ganz anderes, sie wollen eine Dreiliter-Klasse.

Zwei Wochen nach dem großen Knall sitzen die Verantwortlichen des RAC-Wettbewerbskomitees zusammen, und Lord Howe kommentiert den ganz offensichtlich enorm antibritischen Vorstoß von jenseits des Ärmelkanals mit den harschen Worten, das sei „nicht unbedingt im Interesse der britischen Rennsportkreise". Das ist deutlich genug. Aus diesem Grund hätten sich die Briten einer Initiative mit Italien und den USA angeschlossen, deren Ziel eine wahrhaft interkontinentale Formel sei, die auch Dreilitermotoren zulasse. Somit wären auch die existierenden Zweieinhalbliter fein raus, weil drin. Dass sie in angemessen modernen Fahrgestellen bestens auch mit Größeren mithalten können, beweisen etwa die neuen Cooper-Wagen, in denen auch die eigentlich unterlegenen Coventry-Climax-Vierzylinder konkurrenzfähig sind.

1959 und 1960 geht denn auch alles nach Wunsch. British Racing Green und gelegentlich Schottisch-blau sind die Farben der Saison, und Lotus und B.R.M. nehmen mit, was Cooper-Climax nicht holt. Nun, es läuft alles bestens, die Zweieinhalbliterformel ist doch herrlich, und die Welt ist schön. Was die Briten da verständlicherweise unter den Tisch fallen lassen, ist die Tatsache, dass außer Ferrari keiner sonst mitmacht von den Berühmten, den Schnellen und den Großen. Außerdem ist es um das Image des Sports gar nicht so gut bestellt. Zahlreiche Todesfälle in den Jahren 1957 und 1958 sind noch in guter Erinnerung, ganz zu schweigen von der Katastrophe in Le Mans 1955, nach dem sich Mercedes komplett aus dem Geschäft zurückgezogen hat. Die Mille Miglia endet 1957. In den USA zieht sich der große nationale Club, die American Automobile Association, aus dem Rennsport zurück. Es ist Zeit für etwas Neues, unter anderem für viel mehr Sicherheit.

Zunächst soll das Tempo raus aus dem Sport. Die Motoren sollen aber noch aus einem weiteren Grund schrumpfen, lange vor der ersten Ölkrise: Geringerer Spritverbrauch macht große oder gar Zusatz-Tanks überflüssig. Außerdem, so spekulieren die Funktionäre, macht die kleine Formel die Autos vergleichbarer, es komme also künftig mehr darauf an, was der Fahrer daraus macht, spannendere Rennen mit häufigeren Positionskämpfen sind das Ziel. Nichts Neues also, Pläne dieser Art gibt es alle Jahre wieder. Das Kuriose Anfang der 60er Jahre: Ausgerechnet die Hauptsorge

engine suppliers would not be able to build and develop new engines as quickly as possible. But in the past regulations had been altered and the British chassis designers had been able to react quickly. Indeed they already dominated the new 1,500 cc Formula Two. Their fear was for the public appeal of the new Formula One. They were concerned that nobody would want to watch racing cars with engines not much more powerful than road-legal sports cars. As it turned out, they were wrong.

But first of all the British sports press protested that the French had played tricks and that continental Europe had conspired against the Britons. Now the only Formula One competitors with any significant standing at that time were the various British constructors and Scuderia Ferrari. And, in fact, the Italians had voted against the CSI's changes. Amongst those supporting the new regulations were France, Germany, the Netherlands, Monaco and Belgium while Sweden, Switzerland and Mexico took a non-committal approach. Last but not least, the Americans considered even a 2.5-litre limit much too small and they had proposed something completely different, namely a three-litre category.

Two weeks after this shock announcement, the RAC's competitions committee held a council of war. Lord Howe said that it was an underhand business and definitely not in the best interests of the British racing community. That was both a supreme understatement as well as being a clear-cut statement of the British position. Thus it was that the Britons had associated themselves with an initiative, along with Italy and the USA, in favour of a truly intercontinental Formula open to three-litre cars – and that would include engines of 2.5 litre displacement. Thanks to their up-to-date chassis, the new Coopers in particular, had already shown themselves to be competitive even using slightly less powerful Coventry Climax engines.

During 1959 and 1960 everything went well. British racing green and Scottish blue were the fashionable colours and Lotus and BRM took what Cooper missed. Everything went well on the surface, the 2.5-litre formula worked well and the world was wonderful. The British kept quiet about the fact that apart from Ferrari, there were none of the big car manufacturers involved in the Formula One circus. And in fact the public image of motor racing was already suffering from the loss of life involved. Many drivers were killed in motor racing accidents during the 1957 and 1958 seasons. The memory was still fresh of the massacre at Le Mans in 1955 when Pierre Levegh died in a crash in which eighty-six spectators lost their lives and which was the reason for the retirement of Mercedes-Benz from active racing. The Mille Miglia had been abandoned for 1958 after the 1957 accident of the Marquis de Portago in which both he and nine spectators were killed, including children. In the USA the big national club, the American Automobile Association also withdrew. The time had clearly come for some new initiative in motor racing, primarily an increase in safety.

First of all, speed was to be restricted by the use of smaller engines. And, long before the oil crisis, the lesser engine displacement would reduce fuel consumption and thus the size of the petrol tank capacity required since fire following impact was a frequent killer. There was also the desire of the governing body to make the cars more equal. Thus the skill of the drivers

der Briten bleibt unbegründet: Spannend bleibt es vor allem zwischen den grünen und den roten Rennern, obwohl es eine kleine Weile so aussieht, als könnte sich etwas Silbernes – leuchtend orangefarben ergänzt – dauerhaft als dritte Kraft dazwischenmogeln.

Für Porsche kommt die Reveländerung eigentlich am wenigsten ungelegen. Die Briten wollen bekanntlich alles so, wie es ist. Obendrein dominieren sie die Formel 2 und müssen sich daher schon einmal gar keine Gedanken machen. In Modena sieht es schon wieder ganz anders aus. Dort entsteht mittlerweile ein hochinteressanter Heckmotorwagen, der auch ganz schnell von sich reden machen wird. Enzo Ferrari hätte bestimmt nichts gegen eine Dreiliter-Formel gehabt, weil er dann einen brutalen Zwölfzylinder hätte bauen können. Immerhin – für die Formel 2 hat er schon ein Eisen ins Feuer gelegt.

Aus Zuffenhausen kommt der hervorragende 718. Der hat eine lange Vorgeschichte. Die geht im Grunde zurück auf die Anfangstage aller Nachkriegsporsche. Den Urahn hat Ferry Porsche, Sohn des Professors, gebaut. Der erste Porsche ist denn auch ein schnelles Volkswagen-Fahrgestell. Rennsportgene sind erfolgreich vererbt, in Ferrys Vaters Vita stehen Legenden wie der Mercedes SSK und die Mittelmotor-Supersportler der Auto Union mit V12 und V16.

Im Verlauf der 1950er Jahre macht Porsche mit dem Modell 550 und der Weiterentwicklung 718 RSK Furore. Klassensieg folgt auf Klassensieg. Trotz der im Vergleich zur Konkurrenz durchweg kleinen Motoren scheinen gar Gesamtsiege nicht unmöglich, Leichtbau, gute Aerodynamik und feine Fahrgestelle plus zuverlässige gutgehende Motoren machen's möglich. Außerdem sitzen die weltbesten Fahrer am Steuer der Flitzer aus dem Schwabenland. Es sieht also gut aus für den kleinen Hersteller. Firmenchef Ferry Porsche ist außerdem klar der Meinung, dass sich der Rennsport sowohl zugunsten der technischen Weiterentwicklung lohne als auch zu Werbezwecken. Immerhin verkauft er schnelle Wagen mit ausgesprochen sportlicher Note.

Mit dem Grand-Prix-Sport hat Porsche allerdings nicht so viel am Hut. Dass sich die Formelrenner Anfang der 60er Jahre immer stärker von dem entfernen, was auch in der Herstellung von Serienautos umsetzbar ist, wird ein Grund dafür sein, warum Ferry Porsche schließlich den Schlussstrich unter das Kapitel Formel-1-Grand-Prix setzt.

Ende der 50er Jahre aber ist ja auch von der Formel 1 überhaupt noch nicht die Rede. 1957 wird die neue Anderthalbliter-Formel 2 eingeführt. Die Formel ist Rennsport pur, Motoren in der Größenordnung von 1,5 Litern sind gleichsam die Spezialität des Hauses, und Rennleiter Huschke von Hanstein ist begeistert. Viel müssen die Porsche-Leute gar nicht machen. Weil die Formel zunächst nicht einmal die später übliche Zigarren-Form der Karosserie vorschreibt, dürfen auch die Spyder mitmischen. In einigen Autos wandern immerhin Fahrersitz und Lenkrad in die Mitte des Autos. Das dient der Übersicht und erlaubt gleich hohe Geschwindigkeiten in beiden Arten von Kurven: links- wie rechtsherum. Ganz nebenbei entsteht so eine Art Sicherheitslenksäule mit Knick. Beim Frontalaufprall bohrt sich die Lenksäule nun nicht gleich wie ein Speer in des Fahrers Brust.

Die „Formel-Sportwagen" sind gut. Es gelingen bedeutende Siege – 1957 etwa beim Großen Preis von Deutschland, 1958 in

was intended to matter more and thus the races were hoped to become more exciting for the public. Viewed from the present day, nothing of this sounds new, since plans like that surface about once a year!

But the British teams in fact had no great cause for concern. Racing remained thrilling particularly thanks to the duels between the green and red cars although there was short time when it looked as if something silvery – with an added touch of orange – might manage to wangle its way into the upper echelons of the Formula One club.

For Porsche, the new regulations seemed to suit perfectly. The British teams would have been happy to maintain the status quo but, in any case, they already dominated Formula Two. Down in Modena things underwent a major change. In the Ferrari workshop, an extremely interesting rear engined car came into being that was going to make a big name for itself. Enzo Ferrari perhaps would not have turned down the chance of racing with a three-litre formula because that would have allowed him to design a big twelve cylinder. Anyway he already had an iron in the fire with his Formula Two car and its V6 engine.

From Zuffenhausen came the excellent 718. It had a long history and its lineage goes back to the days of the first post-war Porsche. Ferry Porsche, son of the Beetle's father, Ferdinand, built its earliest ancestor. The first Porsche was a tuned-up Volkswagen with some additional motor sport DNA. Ferdinand Porsche himself had been responsible for some of the most famous racing cars of all times such as the Mercedes SSK and the mid-engined Auto Union legends with V-twelve and V-sixteen engines.

In the 1950s the Porsche 550s and 718 RSKs caused a sensation with one class victory after another. Despite the comparatively small size of their engines, even overall victories were not out of their reach. Lightweight construction, excellent aerodynamics and a sophisticated chassis were the main ingredients for success, all allied to an engine that gave more than expected for its size. Porsche also had the best drivers from all over the world. Thus things were looking good for the small firm. The boss, Ferry Porsche, considered racing extremely useful for the technical development of his production cars as well as for promotion since he was offering fast cars for sale with a distinctly sporting appeal.

GP racing though was not really his cup of tea. At the beginning of the sixties, the development of GP cars moved further and further away from designs that were relevant to road cars. That could have been one of the things besides the costs that eventually made Ferry Porsche abandon the Formula One project.

During the majority of the 1950s, nobody at Porsche was talking about Formula One. Then in 1957, Formula Two was introduced. It was basic motor sport featuring engines with a displacement of 1.5 litres. Since these were Porsche's specialty, their racing director Huschke von Hanstein was simply delighted. To enter this new formula, there was in fact not too much to do for the Porsche people. Thanks to the fact that the regulations did not rule out bodywork covering the wheels, their Spyders were allowed to enter in these races. And Porsche built the Mittellenker, a Spyder with central steering – and a central

Foto: Porsche

Siegertyp: In Reims lässt Jean Behra 1959 im Mittellenker-RSK Ferrari, Lotus und Cooper hinter sich.

Winner in 1959 at Reims: Jean Behra with the special RSK won ahead of Ferrari, Lotus and Cooper.

Reims. Der Erfolg führt letztlich dazu, dass Ferry Porsche sich bereit erklärt zu einem eigenen Formel-2-Projekt mit der Option, eine Weiterentwicklung Richtung Formel 1 zu wagen. Die neue 61er Formel mit ebenfalls anderthalb Liter großen Motoren ist ja bereits heraus.

Am Althergebrachten müssen die Porsche-Leute nichts ändern. Der luftgekühlte Vierzylinder-Boxer steht gut im Futter, ist zuverlässig – und in jedem Serienporsche auf dem ganzen Globus klang- und kraftvoll unterwegs. Und zwar hinten drin. Das ist praktisch, heckmotorisierten Rennern gehört ohnehin die Zukunft, der umfassende Evolutionsschritt in der Königsklasse steht kurz bevor.

Der neue Formelrenner ist eindeutig ein Bruder des Spyders, auch wenn ihn rein äußerlich auf den ersten Blick wenig mit dem Sportwagen verbindet. Immerhin kommt da ein Monoposto daher. Beim näheren Hinsehen allerdings fällt vor allem die klassische Kurbellenkervorderachse mit Drehstabfederung auf, die der Käfer schon immer hatte, die aber auch die Auto-Union-Boliden hatten. Der Name spricht für sich: 718/2. Im Vergleich zur Konkurrenz sieht der Wagen etwas plump aus. Das liegt aber vor allem am Motor, der breiter baut als die Reihenmotoren der bri-

seat – thus introducing by chance an important safety feature, a steering column with a kink. This meant that in the case of a frontal impact, the column would not pierce the driver's chest like a spear.

The Formula Two "sports cars" were fine racers and Porsche gained some important victories, for instance the German Grand Prix of 1957, and at Reims in 1958. These successes and others like them at last made Ferry Porsche agree to start an open-wheel Formula Two project with the aim of developing a Formula One car as it was already known from the end of 1957 that the new 1.5-litre formula would apply in 1961.

At first, the Porsche technicians did not have too much to modify. Air-cooled flat fours – fit as a fiddle and reliable – were mounted in every Porsche that left the Zuffenhausen works. And they were mounted behind the driver. Thus the engineers were saved the trouble of moving the engine from the front to the rear – unlike their future rivals in Formula One of which many had still to carry out that exercise.

Obviously the new formula racer was a brother of the Spyder though it no longer looked like a sports car. Yet the open wheeler still had the familiar front axle with torsion bar springing that

Foto: Porsche

Monaco 1959: Trips qualifiziert sich mit dem 718/2 in einer Zeit von 1:43,8 Minuten für den zwölften Startplatz.

Just before the exit: Von Trips had been very quick in testing on the ‚Ring and thus was allowed to drive the 718/2 at Monaco where, sadly, he lived up to his nickname of "Count Crash".

tischen Konkurrenz, und der vor allem das bauchige Lüftergehäuse auf dem Rücken trägt. Am hinteren Ende des Rohrrahmens ist die Doppelquerlenker-Achse mit Schraubenfeder angeschlagen. Für den Boxer gibt es ein neues Sechsganggetriebe, das für bessere Sprintqualitäten sorgen soll.

Wolfgang Graf Berghe von Trips, vielfacher Porsche-Pilot, heute bekannt aber vor allem als der Mann im Cockpit des Ferrari 156, qualifiziert sich 1959 mit Leichtigkeit im neuen Monoposto für den monegassischen Grand Prix. Im Rennen allerdings fliegt er gleich in der zweiten Runde raus und macht das Auto ziemlich kaputt.

Der reparierte Porsche kommt dann erst wieder beim Coupe de Vitesse in Reims zum Einsatz, wo er auf den dritten Platz fährt. Allerdings stellt sich auch heraus, dass die Motorverkleidung den Vierzylinder am freien Atmen hindert. Das wird verbessert, und der Formel-Renner geht nach England. Joakim Bonnier erreicht den vierten Rang unter den Platzhirschen aus den britischen Rennställen. In Goodwood probiert dann Stirling Moss den Wagen aus – und fährt damit schneller als mit seinem Cooper. So kommt es, dass Hanstein dem Briten für 1960 einen Werkswagen anbietet, den Rob Walker betreuen soll.

Es wird jetzt immer ernster mit dem Formel-2-Engagement von Porsche – und es läuft auch gut. Das Fahrgestell wird verbessert und leicht verlängert zugunsten größerer Tankkapazität und mehr Platz im Cockpit. Die 1960er Bilanz lässt sich sehen: Sechs Siege in zwölf Rennen, fünf zweite Plätze und fünf dritte. Den Konstrukteurstitel teilt sich Porsche am Ende mit Cooper. Bereits Mitte des Jahres ist klar, dass Porsche in der kommenden Saison auch in der Formel 1 mitmischen will, nachdem es sich in der hubraumgleichen Formel 2 so gut angelassen hat.

Technisch geht das Team gleich zweierlei Wege. Der gut eingeführte 718/2 soll fitgemacht werden für den Einsatz in der Königsklasse, gleichzeitig aber wird das Projekt 804 in Angriff genommen: ein völlig neuer Achtzylinder – luftgekühlt und in Boxer-Konfiguration natürlich – in einem völlig neuen Fahrgestell.

Am pummeligen 718 wird noch allerhand getan. Noch einmal wird die Atmung der Doppelvergaser erleichtert, die Bremsen – nach wie vor Trommeln, die sich außen mit den Rädern drehen – erhalten Magnesiumtrommeln zur Verringerung der ungefederten Massen und großzügige Kühlrippen. 479 Kilogramm bringt der 718/2 schließlich auf die Waage. Das sind 29 mehr als das erlaubte Minimum.

1960 entstehen fünf Wagen, die auch alle in der 61er Saison zum Einsatz kommen. Darunter ist auch der Walker-Wagen, den Carel Godin de Beaufort übernimmt. In seiner Ecurie Maarsbergen, benannt nach seinem Heimatort in der niederländischen Provinz Utrecht, fährt er das enorm zuverlässige Auto mehrere Jahre lang. Der orangefarben lackierte Wagen wird eine bekannte Größe.

Zwei 718/2 und einen 787 setzt Porsche beim Debut in Monaco ein. Der Wagen mit der eigenen Typnummer ist ein erheblich veränderter 718 und soll übergangsweise den Platz einnehmen, der für den 804 reserviert ist. Mangels Achtzylinder erhält er den bekannten Vierzylinderboxer, allerdings mit Kugelfischer-Benzineinspritzung anstelle der dicken Weber-Vergaser. Außerdem ist er der erste Porsche-Renner, der vorn nicht die

could be seen on the Beetle as well as on the earlier Auto Union racers. The new car received a type number of its own: 718/2.

Compared to its competitors, the car looked a little ungainly thanks to the engine that was broader in stature than the slim in-line engines of the British cars. Another contributor to the voluminous rear was the bulbous fan housing and its associated ducting that provided the cooling for the engine. The rear suspension comprised double wishbones with coil springs and dampers. Also the car was equipped was a new six-speed gearbox to give better response over the engine's power band.

Wolfgang Graf Berghe von Trips, nowadays remembered more for driving the Ferrari Dino 156, effortlessly qualified the new open-wheeler Porsche for the Monaco GP of 1959. In the race however, he crashed on the second lap and damaged the car badly. The rebuilt Porsche was then entered in the Coupe de Vitesse at Reims and finished third. However, it turned out that the rear cowling was hindering engine breathing. Improvements were made and the racer went to England where Jo Bonnier finished fourth amid the local heroes. At Goodwood, Stirling Moss tried the Porsche and found it faster than his Cooper. Soon after that Moss was faced with an offer to drive a works Porsche to be entered and run by Rob Walker.

This was where the hard part of the development began – and, on the whole, it went pretty well. The chassis was improved and lengthened to give a bigger tank capacity and a more spacious cockpit. Porsche's racing balance sheet for 1960 showed six victories in twelve races, five second and five third places. The Formula Two constructor's title was awarded equally to Porsche and Cooper. In the middle of the year, it started to become evident that Porsche would have a presence in Formula One as well. Their start in Formula Two with the same capacity engine had been sufficiently promising to make them want to go further.

First of all the well-established 718/2 was prepared for racing in Formula One while simultaneously Porsche started work on the 804 project. This was to comprise an entirely new eight-cylinder, air-cooled boxer engine, in an entirely new chassis. Many improvements were made to the chubby 718. Bigger twin carburettors were fitted and the brake drums were now finned more generously and made of magnesium with the object of reducing un-sprung weight. As a result of all this effort, the 718/2 weighed 479 kilograms, only twenty-nine more than the legal minimum.

The 1960 season saw the construction of five new cars that then raced throughout 1961. Among them was the Rob Walker team car that was later taken over by Carel de Beaufort. Entered by his Écurie Maarsbergen – the name came from his hometown in the Dutch province of Utrecht – this extraordinarily reliable racing car would be used for several years in the Dutch national colours of orange. Porsche turned up at the Monaco GP in 1961 with two 718/2s and a 787. The latter was a significantly altered 718 and was intended to act as an intermediate solution before the introduction of the 804. Instead of the eight-cylinder engine, it was powered by the familiar four-cylinder engine with Kugelfischer injection replacing the fat Weber carburettors. It was the first Porsche without the seemingly inevitable front axle with torsion bar springs springing. The 787 sported a

beinahe unvermeidliche Kurbellenker-Achse führt. Stattdessen kommt am 787 eine Doppelquerlenker-Konstruktion mit Federbeinen zum Einsatz, seinerzeit Stand der Technik im GP-Sport. Gebremst wird per Trommel, die neue Scheibenbremse – die so genannte innenumgriffene, eine Porsche-Neuheit – wird allerdings im neuen Fahrgestell getestet.

Der 787 erfüllt aber leider nicht die Erwartungen. Zwar ist Jo Bonnier in Monaco in zweiter Position unterwegs, allerdings macht ihm ein Malheur mit der Spritzufuhr einen Strich durch die Rechnung. Obendrein erweist sich das Fahrwerk als noch keineswegs ausgereift, und gegen die neuen Climax-Motoren und den V6 von Ferrari sieht der so lange erfolgreiche Vierzylinder mittlerweile etwas alt aus. 1962 fährt noch einmal ein 787, diesmal in oranje für die Ecurie Maarsbergen. Ben Pon gerät aber schon in der zweiten Runde ins Schleudern und fällt aus.

Also müssen die guten alten 718er ran, bis der 804 mit dem so vielversprechenden Achtzylinder endlich fertig ist. Allerdings schrumpfen die Chancen der kaum mehr konkurrenzfähigen Autos immer weiter. Immerhin sorgt Dan Gurney für bemerkenswerte Szenen und einige beachtliche Erfolge. Dreimal noch schafft er es auf Platz zwei, in Reims nach einem atemberaubenden Duell mit Baghetti im überlegenen Ferrari 156.

Immerhin: Die am Ende gar nicht so schlechte Bilanz verschafft Porsche wichtige Punkte für die Konstrukteursmeisterschaft. Platz drei hinter Ferrari und Lotus ist der Lohn. Und wieder hat sich Porsche als die Manufaktur entpuppt, aus der die zuverlässigsten Wagen kommen. Von 22 gestarteten Autos mit dem Stuttgarter Wappen kommen bis auf drei alle auch ins Ziel.

Als der 804 endlich fertig ist, verkauft das Werk die alten Vierzylinder an Privatleute. Kurz trennt sich auch Beaufort von seiner Fahrgestellnummer 01, um ihn dann aber für die kommende Saison wieder zurückzuholen. Immerhin kassiert er noch zweimal Meisterschaftspunkte. Der Niederländer übernimmt außerdem die Fahrgestellnummer 02. Anstatt aber den zweiten Wagen wie geplant zum Ersatzteilspender zu machen, setzt er ihn gar noch einmal in Südafrika ein, wo das Auto allerdings mit defekter Benzinpumpe liegenbleibt.

Beaufort fährt nach dem Rückzug des Werks weiter im GP-Zirkus. Er rennt zwar ohne Siegchance, kämpft aber tapfer mit und erreicht einige ganz respektable Ergebnisse. Gerhard Mitter fährt 1963 seinen Zweitwagen 02 auf dem Nürburgring gar auf den vierten Platz. Dank Beauforts Engagement erlebt der 718/2 tatsächlich eine fünfjährige Rennkarriere. Sie endet, als der Niederländer 1964 beim Training auf dem Nürburgring tödlich verunglückt.

Es gibt allerdings einen zweiten Farbtupfer in der Geschichte der ersten Porsche-GP-Renner. Fahrgestellnummer 03 geht an Giovanni Volpis Scuderia Serenissima SSS Repubblica di Venezia – und wird natürlich rot lackiert.

Nachdem es also 1961 noch nichts ist mit dem schönen neuen Achtzylinder und die Übergangslösung 787 sich mehr oder weniger als Flop erweist, setzt Porsche für 1962 alles auf die Karte 804. Wieder einmal machen die Schwaben einiges anders als die anderen. Nach bester Tradition des Hauses ist der neue Motor luftgekühlt – die Konkurrenz schleppt Wasser mit sich herum. Die Maschine arbeitet selbstverständlich nach dem Boxer-Prinzip – alle anderen setzen auf V-Motoren. Und um dem allem

double wishbone design with suspension struts which in those days were state-of-the-art in GP racing. The brakes still drums, although the new disc brake that was being made especially for the 804 was tested with the new chassis.

Anyway the 787 failed to meet the expectations. At Monaco, Jo Bonnier was driving in second place until failure to get fuel to the engine forced him out. The chassis was also not a complete success while the indefatigable four-cylinder began to look old compared to the new Climax V8 engines and the Ferrari V6. In 1962, a 787, this time painted orange and entered by the Écurie Maarsbergen was raced once again with Ben Pon at the wheel. He lost control of the car on lap two and that was that.

So the good old 718 had to hold the fort until the 804 was ready with its promising eight-cylinder. The fact of the matter is that it was no longer competitive. But least Dan Gurney did well to finish second overall on three occasions including an exciting tussle at Reims against Baghetti in a superior Ferrari F156. There was some consolation in the fact that in the constructor's championship Porsche was placed third behind Ferrari and Lotus and ahead of Cooper and BRM. Once again the German company had turned out to have very reliable cars. Porsche entered twenty-two cars during the season and all but of three of them crossed the finishing line.

As soon as the 804 was ready, the company sold their old four-cylinder cars to private owners. For a short time de Beaufort forsook his old car that carried chassis number 01 only to bring it back for the following season. At least he scored some points on a couple of occasions. The Dutch driver also took over chassis number 02 but instead of turning the second car into a spare parts reservoir as had been planned, he entered it in South Africa. Sadly, the car retired thanks to a faulty fuel pump.

After Porsche's withdrawal from Formula One, de Beaufort was the last driver to race a Porsche in the GP circus. Despite having practically no chance at all of outright success, he appeared at nearly every race and achieved some respectable results. In addition, Gerhard Mitter finished fourth in de Beaufort's second car at the 'Ring. It was almost entirely due to de Beaufort's involvement that the 718/2 enjoyed a five-year racing career that only came to an end when de Beaufort met his death in an accident at the Nürburgring in 1964.

As well as the orange of Holland, there was a second spot of colour in the history of the first Porsche GP racing cars. Chassis number 03 went to Giovanni Volpi's Scuderia SSS Repubblica di Venezia and, naturally, was painted red.

Since during 1961, the eight-cylinder was not ready to race and the interim car, the 787, had turned out to be more or less a flop, Porsche staked everything on the 804 for 1962. Once again Porsche went its own way. Following their traditional practice, the new engine was air-cooled – their rivals had to lug around radiators and gallons of water – and had opposed cylinders while the others preferred engines with their cylinder configured in a "V". On top of all that, their car had torsion-bar springs, though utilised in a different way to the design of the VW Beetle, and disc brakes manufactured in-house by Porsche. Thus Porsche was at no time exposed to the same jibes that Enzo Ferrari levelled at the British teams whom he had nicknamed "garagistes". The Italian was famous for designing every little detail of his

Unschlagbar: Joakim Bonnier hat beim Großen Preis von Deutschland 1960 auf der Nürburgring-Südschleife die Nase vorn.

Unbeatable: Jo Bonnier won the 1960 German Grand Prix on the Nürburgring-Südschleife.

noch eins draufzusetzen, federt der Wagen mittels Drehstäben
– letzte Reminiszenz an alte Käferzeiten, freilich komplett anders
eingebaut. Dazu kommen die selbstentwickelten Scheibenbremsen. Porsche muss sich keinen Moment lang dem Spott Enzo
Ferraris ausgesetzt fühlen. Der andere Große in der Riege der
Alles-Selbst-Macher hat die britischen Chassis-Konstrukteure als
„Garagisten" verspottet, weil sie die Motoren nicht selber bauen,
sondern bei Coventry-Climax und B.R.M. einkaufen.

Der neue Wagen ist erheblich eleganter geraten als der etwas
plumpe 718/2. Dennoch ist die Karosserie merklich breiter,
vor allem als die sehr eleganten britischen Wagen, deren Hülle
nirgendwo breiter ist als die sehr schlank bauenden V8-Motoren.
Geschuldet ist das dem Boxer, der zwar den Schwerpunkt tief
hält, aber eben auch ein wenig pausbackig daherkommt. Die
Achskonstruktion folgt im Großen und Ganzen dem Maßstab,
den Colin Chapman gesetzt hat. Fahrfertig wiegt der Neue 460
Kilogramm, zehn mehr als das vorgeschriebene Mindestgewicht.

Im März 1962 beginnen die Tests. Als Reserveauto wird ein
Chassis für den Vierzylinder vorbereitet, bis klar ist, dass der neue
Achtzylinder läuft. Beide Autos werden mit neuem Motor an
die Piste in den Nordseedünen geschickt. Beinahe bleibt's dabei,
beinahe stoppt Ferry Porsche doch noch den Einsatz, dem er

racing cars himself and had scoffed at the "garagistes" because
they did not even build their own engines but bought them from
Coventry Climax and BRM.

The new Porsche Formula One car was much sleeker than
the somewhat chubby 718/2. Yet the body was still wider than
the elegant British designs with their slim V8 engines. The flat
eight kept the centre of gravity low but it tended to be a little
wider thus forcing the body outwards to accommodate it. Its
suspension was made more or less according to the standard set
by Colin Chapman. The car weighed 460 kilograms, ten more
than the prescribed minimum.

In March 1962, testing of the 804 started in earnest. To
be on the safe side, one chassis was prepared for mounting a
four-cylinder engine until it should become clear that the eight-
cylinder was able to perform adequately. Both cars with new
eight-cylinder engines were sent to the first Formula One race
at Zandvoort. Ferry Porsche very nearly cancelled this debut of
the 804 thanks to his mixed emotions concerning the car. To
him the project was not Porsche-like enough. Formula One was
already a bit too far away from their production cars, and it had
not escaped his notice that the company already spent a significant amount of money on various other racing projects. There

Experimente: Mit liegendem Lüfterrad und viel Feinarbeit am alten Vierzylinder versuchen die Ingenieure, dem unbefriedigenden 787 doch noch auf die Sprünge zu helfen.

Experimental: with a horizontally mounted cooling fan and much engine and chassis tuning, the engineers tried hard to make the unsatisfactory 787 competitive.

mit gemischten Gefühlen entgegensieht. Das Projekt ist ihm zu wenig Porsche-like. Zu weit ist die Formel von der Serie entfernt, zu sehr ist Porsche schon anderweitig im teuren Rennsport engagiert, zu groß ist das Risiko, wertvolles Image mit fahrlässig verspielten Triumphen zu riskieren.

Also stellt der Chef eine Bedingung: Schon im Training müssen die Autos zeigen, dass sie das Zeug zum Sieger haben, sonst gibt es keinen Renneinsatz. Basta. Dan Gurney probiert's und fährt prompt zwei Sekunden schneller als im Vorjahr. Fein, aber wenig beeindruckend. Die Zeiten sind härter geworden. Der Mann aus New York verpasst um weitere zwei Sekunden die Qualifizierung für die dritte Startreihe. Nun, Porsche gibt dennoch grünes Licht. Er soll aber Recht behalten mit seiner Skepsis: Bonnier schafft es auf den siebten Platz – hinter Carel de Beaufort im alten 718/2, Gurney fällt gar aus, nachdem erst sein Schalthebel abbricht und dann das Schaltgestänge den Geist aufgibt.

Eine Pleite ist auch Monaco, wo Gurney gerammt wird und wiederum ausfällt. Spa wird gleich komplett gestrichen, weil viel zu viel am Auto zu tun ist. Auf dem Nürburgring testen die Fahrer – allen voran unermüdlich Herbert Linge mit einer abenteuerlichen Datenaufzeichnung – alles auf Herz und Nieren. Das Fahrwerk wird verstärkt, die Sitzposition des Fahrers verbessert – im neuen Lotus 25, der dem Neuzugang aus Deutschland in Zandvoort die Schau gestohlen hat, liegen die Fahrer mittlerweile fast –, hinten wächst die Spur um etwas mehr als einen Zentimeter, Bilstein liefert neuerdings die Dämpfer. Gurney bleibt optimistisch und legt schließlich auf dem Nürburgring eine Rundenzeit von 8:44,4 hin. Das reicht für Kommendes.

was also the risk of defeat spoiling what was already a winning image.

So he said that the car would race only when it was shown to be a potential winner and that was that. Dan Gurney went out in practice at Zandvoort and at once drove two seconds faster than the previous year. That was not bad but did little to impress anyone since the rival teams had improved as well. It was by two point two seconds that the American lagged behind pole-sitter John Surtees and had to be content with starting eighth fastest from the third row. Anyway Ferry Porsche agreed to let the cars race. But he had been right in his scepticism. Bonnier finished seventh, behind even Carel de Beaufort in the old 718/2 while Gurney retired with gear-change problems.

Next came the Monaco GP and another flop. Gurney, the only 804 to start, qualified fifth but was taken out in a crash at the first bend and then their entry for the Belgian GP at Spa, only a fortnight after Monaco, was cancelled because the cars had to be repaired. Testing at the Nürburgring with both drivers, including the indefatigable Herbert Linge using a rather odd data recording apparatus, put the 804 through its paces. Its chassis was reinforced, the driver's position was altered and the rear track width was widened by one centimetre. And the dampers fitted now came from Bilstein rather than Koni. Gurney remained optimistic since he was able to lap the Nordschleife in 8:44.4 and they all felt this was fast enough to be competitive.

At the French GP at Rouen, Porsche gained its first victory with the new car. Still to this day, it is the one and only victory in a Formula One championship race of a car made entirely by Porsche. It was thanks to Gurney's skills as he drove brilliantly

Knapp: In Reims liefern sich Gurney und Bonnier 1961 ein spannendes Rennen mit Ferrari und dem neuen Talent Giancarlo Baghetti. Mit dem wackeren Vierzylinder verpasst Gurney knapp den ersten GP-Sieg.

A close one: at Reims, Gurney and Bonnier fought against Ferrari and their new star, Giancarlo Baghetti. Thanks to their reliable four-cylinder, Porsche were rewarded with second place.

Foto: Porsche

Foto: Porsche

Prompt gelingt in Rouen der erste Sieg mit dem neuen Auto – es ist bis heute der einzige Formel-1-Sieg in einem Auto durch und durch aus dem Hause Porsche. Zu verdanken ist das Dan Gurneys Leistung, der trotz heftigster Erkältung stetig und schnell ist – und der Tatsache, dass die Konkurrenz gewaltiges Pech hat und Ferrari fehlt. Macht nichts, bei Porsche ist die Laune gut und wird noch besser, als Gurney und Bonnier auf der Solitude bei Stuttgart hintereinander als erste durchs Ziel gehen. Es ist allerdings kein Meisterschaftslauf.

Richtig vielversprechend beginnt der Lauf zum Großen Preis von Deutschland. Gurney fährt den flachen Silberpfeil im einzigen trockenen Trainingslauf auf den ersten Startplatz. In Nässe und Nebel am Renntag führt er vom Start weg. Dann ereignet sich jenes mittlerweile legendäre Malheur, als die Batterie, die gleich neben dem Kupplungspedal untergebracht ist, sich löst. Von nun an muss der US-Amerikaner nicht nur die höllisch anspruchsvolle Eifelstrecke bewältigen, sondern mit dem linken Fuß auch noch den Stromspeicher festhalten, der bloß noch an den Polkabeln hängt. So gelingt es bald Hill im B.R.M. und Surtees im Lola, den Porsche zu überholen. Das lässt sich nicht mehr rückgängig machen, aber Gurney hält zumindest Anschluss und legt einen glänzenden Dritten hin.

Das ist denn auch schon der Höhepunkt der kurzen Laufbahn des 804, der zwischendurch als erster Porsche eine Glasfaser-Kunstoff-Karosserie erhält. In Monza ist noch einmal ein sechster Platz für Bonnier drin, nachdem Gurney mit Getriebeproblemen ausfällt, der Amerikaner fährt in Watkins Glen auf den Fünften. Der Einsatz in Südafrika wird wieder abgesagt. Da ist aber längst klar, dass die 63er Saison ohne den Porsche 804 ablaufen wird.

despite suffering from a bad cold – and thanks to the fact that other teams were unlucky and also that Ferrari had not entered. Anyway, the Porsche people were in high spirits and continued to feel on the top of the world after their one-two victory with Gurney and Bonnier at the Solitude circuit near Stuttgart. Unfortunately this was not a championship race.

The German Grand Prix weekend started in very promising fashion. Gurney put his sleek silver car on pole position. On a race day visited by both rain and fog, he was in the lead from the start. Then came the legendary story concerning the loose battery. In the 804, the battery was mounted next to the clutch pedal and this one broke loose and began to wander around, only held in by the wires to its terminals. Thus Gurney not only had to cope with the extremely demanding Eifel track and the weather, but also had to keep the battery under control with his left foot. Thus both Graham Hill (BRM) and John Surtees (Lola) managed to pass the Porsche and it was a miracle that Gurney was able to keep hard on their heels and finish third.

All this was already the high-water mark of the 804's career. Bonnier finished sixth at Monza, Gurney fifth at Watkins Glen. With declining performance, the trip to the final round in South African was called off. It was becoming clear that the 1963 season would go ahead without the Porsche 804. The project had swallowed up enormous sums and, in spite of some promising successes, Ferry Porsche abandoned the project as too expensive, too exotic and too risky. During the winter of 1962/63, some improvements to the engine and chassis were made but effectively the 804 was headed straight to the Porsche museum. Only four 804s were built and just three of them were raced. But this

Endlich acht Zylinder: In Rouen gelingt Dan Gurney 1962 der erste Porsche-Sieg in der Formel 1.

Eight cylinders at last: in 1962, Dan Gurney took the first Formula One championship victory for Porsche at Rouen.

Das Werk hat Unsummen investiert, aber trotz einiger Erfolge, die mehr möglich scheinen lassen, winkt Ferry Porsche ab. Zu teuer, zu exotisch, zu riskant. Im Winter werden noch ein paar Verbesserungen an Motor und Fahrwerk vorgenommen. Für den 804 – vier werden gebaut, drei fahren auch im Rennen – heißt es: ab ins Museum.

Das gilt allerdings wohlgemerkt nicht für den Motor. Anfangs bringt er erschütternd wenig Leistung, mühsam tasten sich Ingenieure und Techniker an die magische 200-PS-Marke heran, mit der der Wagen überhaupt erst konkurrenzfähig ist. Das Ziel wird erreicht, als das Ende des Projekts schon feststeht. Doch dem Motor ist noch eine Karriere vorbestimmt, die 1968 in jenem berühmten 1-2-3-Finish in Daytona gipfelt, als drei 907 Langheck-Coupés in Formation das 24-Stunden-Rennen beenden. Da hat der Motor freilich schon 2,2 Liter Hubraum, und der neue Dreiliter für den 908, der dann noch ganz anderes leisten soll, steht schon bereit. (jn) ■

was not the end for the eight-cylinder engine. At first it showed a rather mundane performance with the engineers and technicians struggling to get it to reach the magic 200 bhp mark. The car needed that power output to be competitive from the outset, but this tantalising goal was only reached at a time when the end of the project was a foregone conclusion. Anyway the engine was ultimately destined for a successful career in Porsche's sports cars that culminated in the famous one-two-three finish at Daytona in 1968. Three 907 Langheck coupés passed the finishing line in formation and they were powered by the latest 2.2-litre version of the old eight-cylinder Formula One engine. (jn) ■

In Führung: Das Soitude-Rennen beherrscht Gurney im dritten 804 souverän.

In the lead: Gurney dominated the Solitude race in the third 804.

Foto: Porsche

Kärntener Neubeginn, ein transmontanes Experiment und die wunderbare Wandlung eines Sportwagens

Wie man aus einem flachen Flitzer einen Monoposto macht – Porsches Wanderung auf gewundenen Wegen zur Formel 1

Es war schon die Rede davon, dass Porsches Formel-Engagement auf Sportwagen zurückgeht. Undenkbar wäre das Projekt ohne den 718 gewesen, einen reinrassigen Sportwagen und Abkömmling des Ur-Porsche. Und deshalb muss auch ganz von vorn anfangen, wer vom 718 berichten will, der für uns vor allem als der unermüdliche 718/2 interessant ist. Wir müssen nicht ganz zurückgehen bis zum Berlin-Rom-Wagen aus dem letzten Vorkriegsjahr, der formal schon den 356 vorwegnahm und auf Käfer- respektive KdF-Wagen-Plattform daherkam. Die ersten Nachkriegstage müssen es aber schon sein.

1944 ist das Unternehmen vor den Bombardierungen aus Stuttgart ins ländliche Gmünd nach Österreich, in die damals so genannte „Ostmark", umgezogen. Nach Kriegsende hält sich die Belegschaft in Kärnten mit der Reparatur von Autos, vorzugsweise Volkswagen, und Landmaschinen über Wasser, Ferdinand Porsche und Schwiegersohn Anton Piëch haben die französischen Besatzer in Haft genommen. Immerhin hat sich Porsche nicht nur als Renn- und Volkswagenkonstrukteur einen Namen gemacht, sondern auch als einer von Panzern – er galt als nicht gerade unbelastet. Nun wollen die Siegermächte freilich außerdem vom Know-How profitieren. Im Gespräch ist auch die Herstellung des Volkswagens in Frankreich.

Die technische Expertise schätzen noch andere, die freilich weder Kriegsvergangenheit noch Kleinwagen im Sinn haben.

A new beginning in Austria, a transalpine experiment and the miraculous metamorphosis of a sports car

How to change a sleek spider into a monoposto – Porsche finds its way into Formula One

Porsche's presence in Formula One had their roots in Formula Two racing. Indeed, the project would have been unthinkable without the 718 that was a classic sports car and, in its turn, a descendant of the very first Porsche. That is why one has to go back to the very beginning, if you want to tell the 718 story and the gestation of the Porsche Formula One project. It is almost necessary to go all the way back to the Type 64 that was built for the 1939 Berlin-Rome but never used. That car was a kind of grandfather to the 356 and based on the KdF (Strength through Joy) chassis that became the Beetle. But we do have to take a close look at the post-war days.

Back in 1944, the Porsche company had moved to rural Gmünd in Austria – known as the "Ostmark" in Nazi Germany – because Stuttgart was a major target for Allied bombers. After the end of the war, the Porsche personnel kept their heads above water by carrying out maintenance work on cars, especially Volkswagens, and on agricultural equipment. At that time, the French imprisoned Ferdinand Porsche and his son-in-law, Anton Piëch. In the war, Porsche was not famed for making racing and normal cars but tanks. So in some people's eyes he did not have a clean record. Nevertheless, the Allies were keen on profiting from his technical know-how. For a while, it even looked as if the Volkswagen might have been built in France rather than Germany.

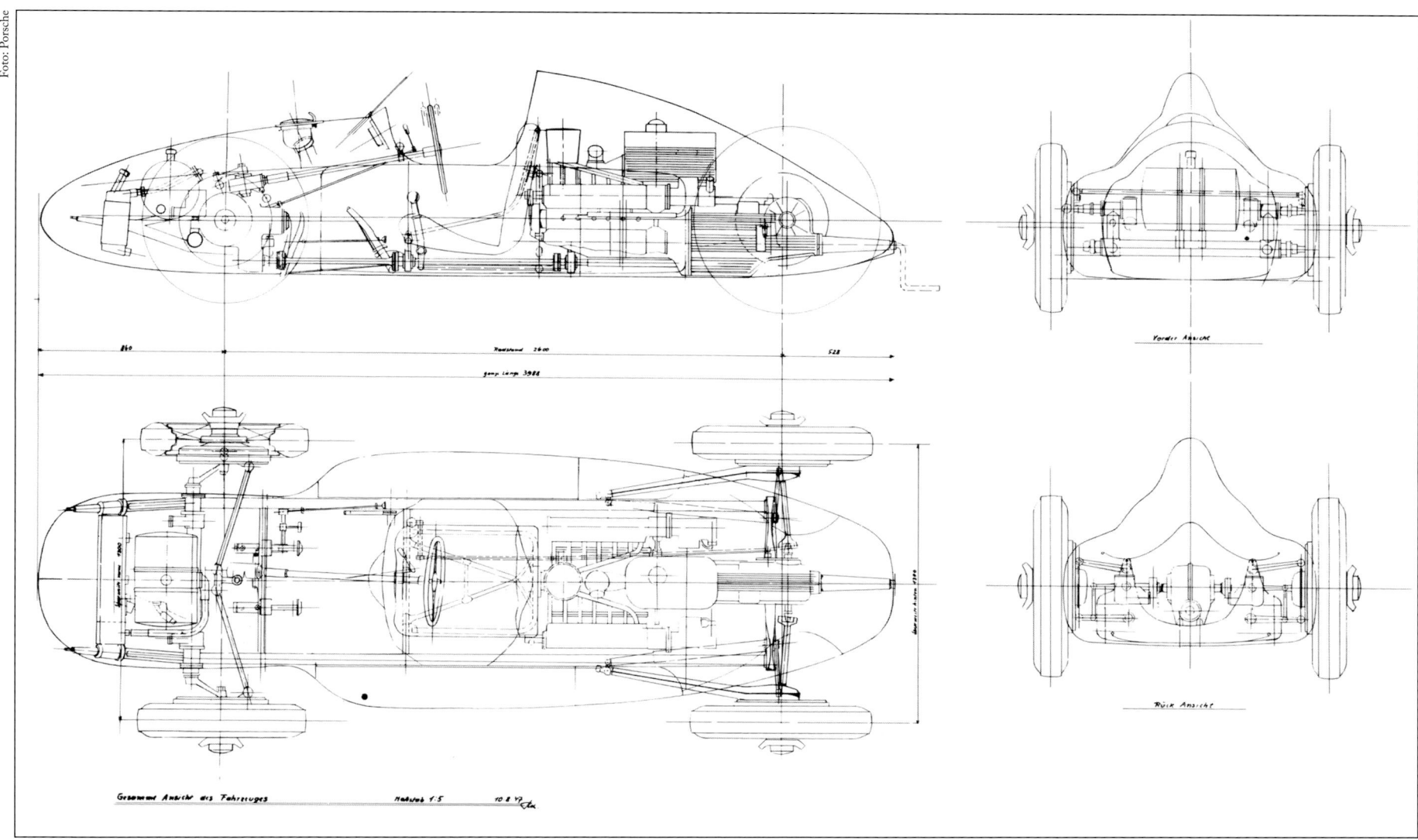

Und das kommt so: Nicht nur dank des Umzugs Richtung Süden gibt es einen transmontanen Kontakt nach Italien. Carlo Abarth, Österreicher von Geburt und mittlerweile nach Italien verzogen – und später vor allem berühmt für seine kleinen, feinen und vor allem schnellen Kreationen auf Fiat-Basis – ist verheiratet mit Anton Piëchs früherer Sekretärin. In Italien herrscht kein Besatzungsstatut, und so können Abarth und der ebenfalls nach Meran gegangene frühere Porsche-Mann Rudolf Hruska südlich der Alpen die Fühler für das Werk ausstrecken. Spätestens jetzt fällt der magische Name Cisitalia. Dahinter steht der von Piero Dusio, Industrieller aus der Fiat-Metropole Turin. Der Mann will einen Rennwagen bauen. Dieser nimmt in Form eines Fiat-Cisitalia bereits Gestalt an. Mit im Boot sind Konstrukteur Piero Taruffi und Giovanni Savonuzzi, der spätere Ghia-Chefdesigner.

Schön, aber was hat das mit Porsche zu tun? Nun, Tazio Nuvolari, Vorkriegs-Rennfahrerlegende und auf der Suche nach vielversprechendem fahrbarem Untersatz, hat Kontakt zu Abarth, und eines Tages kommt auch Giovanni Lurani mit ins Spiel, ebenfalls Rennfahrer und stark engagiert im Nachkriegs-motorsport in Italien – und eng verbunden mit Dusio. Von da ist der Weg nicht mehr weit zu Gesprächen mit den versierten Rennwagenspezialisten aus dem Hause Porsche. Unter der Ägide von Chefingenieur Karl Rabe, so sieht es schließlich ein Vertrag vom Februar 1947 vor, sollen die Gmünder einen kleinen Diesel-schlepper, Typ 323, konstruieren, einen fünfsitzigen Gran Turismo (Typ 370) und eine Wasserturbine (Typ 285) – sowie den Typ 360, einen Rennsportwagen. Es fließt Geld, viel Geld. Vor allem

But there were others who appreciated Porsche's technical expertise away from tanks and small cars. Ferdinand Porsche had good connections with Italy partly thanks to the company's move to Austria. Carlo Abarth, Austrian by birth and now living in Italy – and later renowned for his neat and fast creations based on Fiat cars – was married to Anton Piëch's former secretary. Italy was not an occupied country so Abarth and Rudolf Hruska, a former Porsche employee who had also moved to Merano, were free to travel and to get in touch with Porsche. And then into the picture came Cisitalia (Consorzio Industriale Sportive Italia). The man behind that magic name was Piero Dusio, an industrialist from the Fiat city of Turin, who wanted to build a racing car. There was a project named the Fiat-Cisitalia (D46) based on a Fiat 500 that had already been started and in the team were Piero Taruffi and Giovanni Savonuzzi who later became chief designer for Ghia.

All very nice, but where did Porsche fit in? Tazio Nuvolari, the legendary pre-war racing driver was searching for a drive and had already been in touch with Abarth as well as driving a D46 for Dusio. To complete the trio, there was Count Giovanni (Johnny) Lurani, another driver who was deeply involved in post-war motor sport in Italy. Lurani was in touch with Dusio and from there it was only a short step to the first meetings with the engineers at Porsche. On February 2nd 1947, a contract was signed. Under the auspices of chief engineer, Karl Rabe, the Gmünd team would construct a small diesel tractor (type 323), a five-seater Gran Turismo (type 370) and a water

Wie man einen Monoposto baut: Der Cisitalia hat Mittelmotor, Sitz im Schwerpunkt und seitliche Tanks – und sogar zuschaltbaren Allradantrieb.

How to build a modern racing car: the Cisitalia was mid-engined, had the driving seat located at the centre of gravity and was fitted with laterally mounted tanks – it even had four wheel drive.

fließt es in Form einer Kaution nach Frankreich, wo daraufhin Ferdinand Porsche und Anton Piëch wieder nach Hause entlassen werden. Ferry Porsche ist nach einem Hausarrest im Schwarzwald schon viel früher nach Gmünd zurückgekehrt und hat an den Verhandlungen mit Dusio teilgenommen.

Der Mann, der vor allem einen Rennwagen will, bekommt etwas für sein Geld. Der Monoposto wird ein brillanter und hochmoderner Entwurf. Eigentlich hat der Wagen alles, was einen Formelrenner bis heute ausmacht, vor allem den Motor in bester Schwerpunktlage. Seitlich des Rohrrahmens aus Chrom-Molybdän-Stahl sind die beiden Tanks angeordnet, der Fahrer sitzt ziemlich genau in der Mitte des Autos. An den Motor schließt das synchronisierte Fünfganggetriebe an, und wenig davon ragt über die Hinterachse hinaus, die wie die vordere dreh-stabgefedert ist. Ein Knüller ist das Antriebsaggregat. Wer nun irgendwo ein Gebläse für die an sich doch so Porsche-typische Luftkühlung sucht, kann gleich wieder gehen. Gebläsekühlung ist noch keineswegs Dogma für Renner aus dem Hause Porsche. Immerhin handelt es sich um einen Boxer. Der 1,5-Liter-Motor ist wassergekühlt, verteilt das bisschen Hubraum auf zwölf Zylinder und hat einen herrlich komplexen Ventiltrieb mit vier obenliegenden Nockenwellen. Das jemand aus einem derart kleinen Motor 450 PS holen will, klingt kühn. Ist es auch – so lange man sich die beiden Kompressoren wegdenkt, die der Maschine zu reichlich Luft verhelfen. Ein weiterer Knüller ist die Fortsetzung der Kraftübertragung am anderen Ende des Getriebes. Der 360 hat Allradantrieb – und zwar nach Gusto des Fahrers. Der kann sich während der Fahrt entscheiden, ob er bloß mit Hinterrad-

turbine (type 285) – and, in addition, the type 360, a pure-bred racing car. Cash began to flow, lots of cash, and some of it was transferred to France as bail for Ferdinand Porsche and Anton Piëch. Ferdinand's son, Ferry Porsche, who had been under house arrest in the Black Forest had already returned to Gmünd and took part in the initial meetings with Dusio.

Dusio got his money's worth. The racing car was a brilliant and up-to-date design. It had all the features that are still state of the art today. The engine was centrally mounted. Two fuel tanks were located at the sides of the Chromalloy steel frame and the driver sat virtually in the centre of the car. Mounted behind the engine was a five-speed gearbox with the rear differential integral with it. There were torsion bar springs on both axles. But the real scoop was the engine. There is no point in looking for a cooling fan here just because it is a Porsche design as in 1947 air-cooling was not yet a dogma with the company. However, it was an engine with opposed cylinders, a boxer twelve. This 1.5-litre had water-cooling and a mar-vellously complex valve drive with four overhead camshafts, two on each bank of cylinders. Anyone who proclaimed that he could extract 450 horsepower from an engine of that size would have to face being called an idiot until he happened to mention the two superchargers with which it was fitted.

But on top of all that, there was yet another scoop with this car. The type 360 had four-wheel-drive and the driver could decide how many wheels he wanted to be driven. He had the choice of either rear-wheel or all-wheel-drive – and he was able to switch between them while the car was in motion.

Foto: Porsche

450 PS aus anderthalb Litern: Ganz so viel wird es am Ende zwar nicht, aber der Zwölfzylinder mit doppeltem Kompressor und vier obenliegenden Nockenwellen ist ein technischer Leckerbissen.

1.5 litres and 450 bhp: as it turned out, the Cisitalia was not a roaring success but its twelve-cylinder engine with twin superchargers and four overhead camshafts was an engineer's delight.

Porsche-Rezeptur: Die Kur-
bellenker-Vorderachse soll
sich ziemlich lange auch im
Spitzen-Motorsport halten.
Erst in den Auto-Union-Boliden, dann im Cisitalia, später
in der Formel 2.

The Porsche recipe: their
torsion bar suspension had
a long racing life – first with
the Auto Union racers, then
with the Cisitalia and later in
Formula Two.

Foto: Porsche

oder aber mit Vierradantrieb fahren möchte. Kurioserweise haben die Entwickler die Allradfunktion in erster Linie für den Start vorgesehen. Sie glauben, das Prinzip nutze nur beim Geradeaus-Beschleunigen, wenn es darum geht, die enorme Leistung auf die Straße zu bringen. Mit den 450 PS wird es nichts, die während eines Tests ermittelten rund 380 PS sind dennoch reichlich beeindruckend.

Nuvolari, der einst die Nazi-Funktionäre und die scheinbar unbesiegbaren Mercedes-Leute im Alfa düpierte, und der Cisitalia mit seinen Auto-Union-Genen – das hätte ganz hübsch etwas werden können. Doch es soll nicht sein. Der wegweisende Entwurf bleibt auf halber Strecke stehen, weil das Geld ausgeht.

Curiously the engineers calculated that the four-wheel drive would only be good for the start. They thought that it would be while accelerating on the straights that the four-wheel drive would make the best use of the enormous power of the engine. They never actually achieved 450 hp but the 380 horsepower they did reach in testing was nevertheless impressive.

It could have been a sensation – Nuvolari, who had once outwitted Nazi officials and the apparently invincible Mercedes team with his Alfa, could have been sensational in the Cisitalia with its Auto Union genes. But nothing came of it. This car that pointed the way to the future was stopped halfway thanks to lack of money. Dusio had gone bankrupt and Porsche was

Schade um den schönen 360. Immerhin hat er überlebt. Nachdem Piero Dusio den Offenbarungseid leisten muss, setzt er sich nach Argentinien ab und nimmt das Auto mit. In Südamerika sieht der 360 immer nur kurz die Straße und landet schließlich in einem Lagerhaus. Aus dem holt Ferry Porsche den glücklosen Renner 1959 heraus, lässt ihn nach Stuttgart bringen, restaurieren und schließlich ins Museum stellen. Dass es noch einen zweiten 360 gibt, ist dem Umstand zu verdanken, dass sich in der Dusio-Konkursmasse noch allerhand Teile finden. Die sichert sich Anfang der 1970er Jahre die Donington-Formel-1-Sammlung von Porsche und stellt zumindest den größten Teil eines gleichsam fabrikneuen Cisitalia zwar nicht auf die Räder, aber doch immerhin zusammen.

It was a shame about the type 360 but at least it did survive. After Piero Dusio's business went into administration, he left the country to go to Argentina and took the car with him. In South America, the 360 raced a couple of times and finally ended up in a warehouse. From there, Ferry Porsche brought it out in 1959, shipped it to Stuttgart, restored it and finally put it into the Porsche museum. But there also exists a second type 360 thanks to the fact that there were many parts for a second car in Dusio's bankrupt estate. They were taken over in the early seventies by Tom Wheatcroft's Donington Formula One Collection. The Donington team managed to assemble almost a complete new Cisitalia.

Foto: Porsche

Transmontanes Projekt: Italiens Rennstar Tazio Nuvolari (mit Haube) hätte den Cisitalia zu großen Siegen fahren sollen. Foto: Porsche

A project across the Alps: it was hoped that the star Italian driver, Tazio Nuvolari (with cap and goggles), would win many victories with the Cisitalia.

Nazi-Propaganda: Der Berlin-
Rom-Wagen sollte Reklame
fürs Regime und für
den KdF-Wagen Verkauf
machen. Es wurde dann aber
etwas Besseres aus ihm: der
Urahn der Porsche-Sport-
wagen und somit auch des
Formel-2-Wagens.

Nazi propaganda: the Berlin-
Rome-Wagen was built as a
public relations exercise for
the regime and also as a sales
promotion for the KdF-Wagen,
ancestor of the Beetle. Finally
it grew into something much
better which was the prototype of the Porsche sports car
and thus also the FormulaTwo
racing car.

Dusio hat sich verhoben. Und Porsche stemmt das Projekt nicht alleine. Im Gegenteil – die Firma setzt zwar weiter auf das sportliche Pferd, verlegt sich aber von den hochgezüchteten auf die eher robusten Linien. Porsche will verkaufen, seien es Ideen oder seien es ganze Autos. Mit beidem lässt sich nur dann Geld verdienen, wenn es in ausreichend großen Zahlen produziert wird. Nun, die Ideen sind den Porsche-Entwicklern noch immer nicht ausgegangen, und dass sich mit vielen guten Sportwagen richtig viel Geld verdienen lässt, das machen sie auch noch immer vor.

Vorhang auf für den Porsche-Seriensportwagen. Der heißt bekanntlich 356, hat wiederum Gene aus Vorkriegstagen – diesmal vom Volkswagen – und soll auf Umwegen tatsächlich auf seine Weise zum ersten richtigen Formel-1-Einsatz der – Zuffenhausener führen.

Und das geht so: Am Anfang schaffen die Gmünder den 356. Nein, ganz so Genesis-artig geht das dann doch nicht vonstatten. Es ist ja schon vieles da, und vielversprechend ist es auch. Da wäre einmal die Käfertechnik als recht moderne, gut entwickelte Basis. Da wäre weiterhin der legendäre Berlin-Rom-Wagen, mit dem die Nazis Propaganda machen wollten, und der ja auch schon reichlich sportlich war inklusive Stromlinienkarosserie. Und da wäre schließlich die reiche Motorsporterfahrung des Hauses. Immerhin ist der Name Porsches eng mit den sagenhaften Auto-Union-Boliden verbunden. Nur ein kleines Beispiel: Jedem Käferkenner werden gleich die charakteristischen Kurbellenker-Vorderachsen mit Drehstabfederung an den Zwölf- und Sechzehnzylindern auffallen.

Die Porsche-Volkswagen-Connection ist ja nun naturgemäß so alt wie das Werk. Was also liegt näher, als sich der reichlich vorhandenen und leicht lieferbaren Technik zu bedienen. In

unable to keep the project alive on its own. The company went on to build fast cars that were sturdy rather than highbred. Porsche have always been keen to sell their expertise no matter whether that was ideas or complete cars incorporating those ideas. Both will only sell well when being produced in large enough numbers. To this day Porsche has not run out of ideas and consequently they make a lot of money with them. Meet their first effort, the first Porsche production sports car. Its name was 356, its genes came from pre-war days – the Volkswagen – and in a roundabout way it was to lead to the first real Formula One project of the team based in Zuffenhausen.

In the beginning, the Gmünd people made the 356. No, stop, it was not quite as in the Book of Genesis. Much already existed from the pre-war days. There was the design for the Beetle that already provided a reasonably modern and well-developed basis. Then there was the legendary Berlin-Rome type 64, Nazi propaganda material maybe but pretty sportive and with a streamlined body. And then there was Porsche's rich experience in racing from the time when Porsche was involved in the development of the famous Auto Union racers. If you know the Beetle well, you will know its characteristic axle with torsion bar springs was also found at the front end of the twelve and sixteen-cylinder Auto Unions. The Porsche-Volkswagen connection is as old as the firm itself. Obviously the engineers working on the new car made good use of freely available parts. In a relatively short time, a sports car based largely on Volkswagen elements emerged. The first cars sported bodywork in aluminium, tailored by Erwin Komenda but the later cars were in steel. Fifty cars were built at Gmünd before

Fotos: Porsche

Der erste Speedster: In Gmünd entstehen die frühen Porsche, darunter das schicke offene Mittelmotorauto.

Speedster: the first Porsches were made at Gmünd in Austria, and amongst them was this neat open mid-engined car.

relativ kurzer Zeit entsteht so der Sportwagen auf Käferbasis. Die ersten Autos haben gar edle Aluminiumkleider, geschneidert von Erwin Komenda. Es entstehen rund 50 Stück in Gmünd, bevor Porsche 1949 nach Stuttgart umzieht und – ab sofort mit Stahlblech-Karosserien – die Serienherstellung so richtig ins Laufen kommt.

Der neue Serien-356 kommt erheblich gefälliger daher als die handgedengelten Alu-Coupés, auf denen Porsche dann auch prompt sitzenbleibt. Macht nichts, die Autos sind leichter als ihre jüngeren Brüder, und ein bisschen flacher. Da wäre es: Porsches Erfolgsrezept Nummer eins: Leichtbau macht auch schlappere Autos munter. Und: Recht windschlüpfrig sind die Coupés schon von Haus aus dank der Erbschaft vom Stromlinienwagen – Erfolgsrezept-Zutat Nummer zwei. Mit kleinen Motoren lässt sich da ganz gut leben, und das wird lange, lange so bleiben in der Rennabteilung.

Klein fängt es denn auch an – mit Elfhunderter-Motörchen und 46 PS, aber weich und windschlüpfrig gerundet und dank Aluminium schön leicht. Klein, aber fix. Und nicht bloß irgend-

Porsche moved back to Stuttgart in 1949 where serial production on larger scale began.

The new production 356 was prettier than the handmade aluminium coupés. But the older cars were considerably lighter then their younger brothers and they were narrower. This was an expression of Porsche's recipe for success, which was that lightweight construction gets even underpowered cars going quickly. On top of that, the coupés were originally streamlined thanks to their racing car roots and that also became an ingredient for success. Small engines were no problem at all and that would not change for decades in the racing department.

So the big story began on a small scale with a tiny 1,100 cubic centimetre engine and forty-six horsepower mated to a smoothly rounded and streamlined body of light aluminium. Small but fast and to prove it, at Le Mans in 1951, Porsche's French importer, Auguste Veuillet, and Edmond Mouche crossed the finishing line in twentieth place and won their class. It was the first such class victory for Porsche in what was to become a seemingly never-ending list.

Leichtbau: Die Coupés aus Gmünd hatten Aluminiumkarrosserien – eine gute Voraussetzung für den ersten Einsatz plus den ersten von vielen Klassensiegen in Le Mans 1951.

Lightweight construction: the first Gmünd coupés had aluminium bodies which made them a first choice for competition purposes, for example, at Le Mans where in 1951 Porsche gained the first of many class victories.

Motor mit Namen: Nach seinem Erbauer hieß der Viernockenwellen-Dauerläufer 547 auch der „Fuhrmann"-Motor.

An engine with a name: the four-camshaft 547 was christened the „Fuhrmann" engine after its designer.

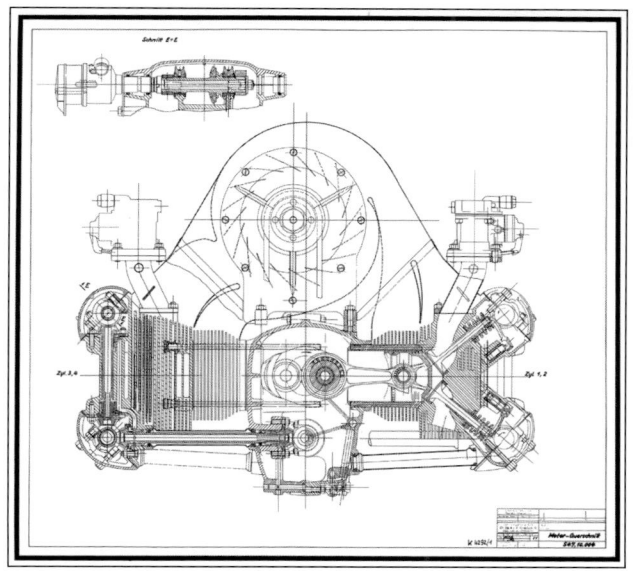

wo, sondern gleich in Le Mans. Importeur Auguste Veuillet und Edmond Mouche fahren den Porsche auf Platz 20 im Gesamtklassement und machen den Klassensieg klar – den ersten in einer nicht enden wollenden Reihe.

Der 356 erweist sich schnell als ziemlich brauchbare Basis für eine Art automobilen Breitensports – durchaus schon für betuchtere Kreise. Allerdings ist das Coupé doch eher ein schneller kleiner Reisewagen als ein reinrassiger Renner. Dennoch machen Enthusiasten in aller Welt – schon vor dem Erscheinen des potenten „Fuhrmann"-Motors mit vier obenliegenden Nockenwellen und Königswellenantrieb, danach aber erst recht – mit viel Phantasie und noch mehr technischem Geschick aus den sportlichen Coupés veritable Rennmaschinen, oft in Form offener Zwei- oder Einsitzer. Ferry Porsche kennt indes die Grenzen des 356 gut. Als junger Mann hat er als einer der ersten am Steuer eines der legendären Grand-Prix-Wagen mit den vier Auto-Union-Ringen Platz genommen. Dann war da der Cisitalia. Bei po-

The 356 very quickly turned out to be a pretty useful basis for general automobile sport, though admittedly for the somewhat more affluent competitor. In fact the coupé was more a fast little Gran Turismo than a thoroughbred racer. Nevertheless enthusiasts all over the world turned these sports cars into serious racing machines, sometimes in the form of open one or two-seaters. That was even before the time of the mighty "Fuhrmann" engine with four overhead camshafts driven directly from the crankshaft .

In all kinds of races, rallies and hill climbs, and especially in the United States where the "America Roadster" was very successful, the 356 was a popular choice for the motor sport enthusiast. In Europe the coupés, had shown themselves to be very capable in long distance events. But the first to make the step to a pure racing car was an automobile dealer from Frankfurt, Walter Glöckler. He was successful with a creation of his own with a Volkswagen basis powered by a Porsche engine

Schön, schnell, kernig: Der America Roadster von 1952.

Beautiful, fast, and full of go : the America Roadster of 1952.

Foto: Porsche

pulären Straßenrennen, in Rallyes und in den USA – dort unter anderem dank der Erfolge des „America Roadster" – ist der 356 nicht ohne Grund beliebt. In Europa haben die Coupés überdies ihr Langstreckentalent beeindruckend unter Beweis gestellt.

Die ersten Schritte zum reinen Rennwagen mit dem Porsche-Signet unternimmt dann allerdings ein anderer: Walter Glöckler ist Autohändler in Frankfurt und reüssiert mit einer Eigenkreation auf VW-Basis mit Porschemotor, den er allerdings vor der Hinterachse einbaut. Der offene Flitzer hat einen Leiterrahmen und eine Alu-Karosserie, die schon ein wenig wie die der kommenden Spyder aussieht. 1950 wird er deutscher Meister in der 1100er-Sportwagenklasse. Glöckler wendet sich an Porsche und hofft auf Hilfe – und wird, weil erfolgreich, der erste in einer langen Reihe von Renn-Unternehmern, die als Quasi-Werksteam für Porsche den Lorbeer ernten.

1951 tragen die Glöckler-Wagen den Porsche-Namenszug, und das Werk ist in aller Munde. Allmählich entstehen auch im Zuffenhausener Werk die ersten Renner à la Glöckler. Längst hat sich gezeigt, wie werbewirksam Rennerfolge auch für die Serienfertigung sind, und zu jener Zeit macht sich auch der Einfluss Huschke von Hansteins bemerkbar, Leiter der Presseabteilung und mit den denkbar besten Kontakten zur internationalen Rennsportszene überreichlich gesegnet.

Die Rennerei hat sich zu gut angelassen, als dass Porsche sich jetzt nach so kurzer Zeit schon auf ein bequemes Lorbeerpolster zurückziehen könnte. Das geht auch gar nicht, weil andere besser werden. OSCA etwa heißt die Konkurrenz, in Deutschland reden Borgward und EMW in der Anderthalbliter-Klasse ein vernehmliches Wörtchen mit. Zweierlei soll die Schwaben im Gespräch halten: Ein Motor namens 547 und ein Auto mit der Typnummer 550. Beide entstehen unter der Ägide von Karl Rabe. Basis des Wagens ist ein Stahlrohr-Leiterrahmen, der Motor die bestfrisierte Version des 1500er-Stoßstangenmotors, der mittlerweile

which he installed in front of the rear axle. The open sports car had a ladder frame with aluminium body and a strong resemblance to the later Porsche Spyder. In 1950 he drove this car to become German champion in the 1,100 sports car category. With that achievement in his pocket, Glöckler asked Porsche for help and became the first in a long line of racing entrepreneurs who won laurels for Porsche as semi-works teams.

In 1951, Glöckler's cars wore Porsche badges and the firm became the talk of the pits. Gradually the first racing cars à la Glöckler were built at Zuffenhausen. In the meantime, it became evident that these motor sport victories were good publicity for Porsche and their press officer, Huschke von Hanstein, made best use of this fact.

Porsche had no time to rest on its laurels since its rivals in the small capacity class were becoming stronger every day. These included OSCA (effectively Maserati) and the Germany companies, Borgward and EMW all of whom were competing in the 1.5 litre class. To counter this threat Porsche came up with a car with type number 550 and the 547 engine. Both of them were built under the aegis of Karl Rabe. The car came first and had a steel tubular frame while until the arrival of the 547, its engine was the best-prepared derivative of the original 1,5 litre pushrod engine and, as with the 356 Super, it was also installed behind the rear axle. In the first 550, Walter Glöckler's cousin, Helm, was victorious in the Eifel Races on May 31st 1953 at the Nürburgring. At Le Mans Richard von Frankenberg and Paul Frère won their class in the second 550 while Helm Glöckler and Hans Hermann finished a hairsbreadth behind them in the Eifel-winning car.

But it was the new engine that finally made the new racing cars from Zuffenhausen really successful. The old engine with pushrods and a single central camshaft that went back to the Volkswagen power plant had reached its limits and it was not

auch im Heck des 356 (Super) röhrt. Walter Glöcklers Vetter Helm siegt mit dem allerersten 550 beim Eifelrennen auf dem Nürburgring 1953. Den Le-Mans-Klassensieg holt sich der zweite 550 mit Richard von Frankenberg und Paul Frère am Steuer.

So richtig schnell werden die neuen Rennsportwagen aus dem Hause Porsche allerdings erst mit dem neuen Motor. Aus den Stoßstangenmotoren mit zentraler Nockenwelle – nach wie vor im Herzen reine Käfermaschinen – haben die Ingenieure herausgeholt, was herauszuholen ist: Zum Schluss sind das mit 40er Doppelvergasern, einer Verdichtung von sagenhaften 12,5:1 und Alkoholgemisch fast 100 PS. Bei 6000 Touren aber ist fürchterlich viel Masse in Form der massiven und langen Stößelstangen in Bewegung, die von der Motormitte aus in den weit entfernten Zylinderköpfen bei den Kipphebeln anklopfen. Auch die Federn haben allerhand zu tun, die Ventile so schnell wie möglich nach dem Ansaugen und dem Auspuffen wieder an Ort und Stelle zu drücken. Steuerzeiten lassen sich da kaum mehr fahrplanmäßig einhalten.

Nun lässt sich Hubraum ab einer gewissen Leistung eben wirklich nur noch durch eins ersetzen: noch mehr Hubraum. Geht aber nicht. Weil: Eine 1500-Kubik-Klasse bleibt eine 1500-Kubik-Klasse. Turbo ist noch nicht, den macht Porsche erst 20 Jahre später salonfähig. Also bleibt nur ein Weg: Der Motor muss schneller drehen. Kann er aber nicht, wie wir soeben ganz leicht und wie es einige Käferfans einst schmerzvoll erfahren haben.

Die vorigen Sätze haben Kenner und Ingenieure natürlich schon mit wissendem Grinsen im Gesicht gelesen und freuen sich auf ein technisches Gourmetstück, das bis heute Hobbyschrauber

possible to squeeze anything more out of it. Thanks to the use of 40mm twin Solex carburettors, a compression ratio of 12.5 to 1 and alcohol based fuel its maximum output was around 100 bhp. But the limit was reached at about 6,000 revs. When the engine was revving that high, the inertial weight of the valve gear with its long pushrods and rocker arms became self-destructive. Also the springs had to work exceptionally hard to keep these oscillating masses under control. Beyond 6,000 revs there was no control. To get more power, you can always increase the capacity of the engine but that solution is not open to you when you race in a class with limitation of 1.5 litres. Turbo technology was still a long way off and Porsche would make it fashionable twenty years in the future. So there was only one way left open to the Porsche engineers. The engine simply had to rotate faster.

The type 547 engine was Porsche's elegant solution to the problem and it made the engineer Ernst Fuhrmann famous. Among other things, Fuhrmann was responsible for camshaft development at the Porsche works. It is interesting to note that Hans Mezger, who developed the equally famous twelve-cylinder 917 engine, also began his career as a camshaft specialist in Zuffenhausen. Earlier, Fuhrmann had taken part in the Cisitalia 360 project and the type 547 engine had something in common with that earlier project, namely camshafts driven by shafts directly from the crankshaft and called "Königswelle".

There are many ways to open and close valves. For example you can have pushrods working on rocker arms from a central camshaft, or chains or belts driving overhead camshafts that

Berühmte Namen: Hans Herrmann fährt für Porsche legendäre Siege ein, und der bei der '54er Carrera Panamericana führt zu einem der wenigen Eigennamen für Sportwagen aus Zuffenhausen.

A famous name: Hans Herrmann gained some remarkable victories for Porsche as, for example, the 1954 Carrera Panamericana, a victory that lead to the name "Carrera" being adopted for extra-fast Porsches.

Foto: Porsche

in den Wahnsinn und notgedrungen bald zum nächsten Fachbetrieb treibt. Dem Kundigen aber ist die Lösung des Drehzahlproblems Herausforderung und Leckerbissen zugleich. Landauf, landab ist der Motor mit der Typnummer 547 – einer der erfolgreichsten überhaupt – mit dem Namen dessen verbunden, der für das Projekt bei Porsche zuständig war: Ernst Fuhrmann. Der war unter anderem Nockenwellen-Spezialist (übrigens begann auch Hans Mezger, der nächste der ganz großen Motorenleute bei Porsche und verantwortlich unter anderem für den sagenhaften Zwölfzylinder des 917 mit Nockenwellen) und hatte sich seine Sporen schon beim Cisitalia-Projekt verdient. Mit dessen Motor hat der neue Boxer auch jene Spezialität gemein, die ihn von den bisherigen Porsche-Serienmaschinen signifikant unterschied: den Königswellenantrieb.

Es gibt allerlei Möglichkeiten, die Ventile zum Öffnen und Schließen zu bewegen. Da wären etwa die bekannten Stößelstangen, wenn Kraft von der Nockenwelle in der Nähe des Kurbeltriebs abgenommen wird; wie eben beim Käfermotor. Das ist eine saubere und bewährte Lösung. Da gibt es überdies Ketten und Zahnriemen, die – wenn es die Nockenwelle schon in den Zylinderkopf geschafft hat – die Kraft schon viel spielfreier an den Ort des Geschehens liefern. Das ist dann schon die hohe Schule. Ganz schick aber sind die oben- und beim Boxer eben seitlich liegenden Nockenwellen, die per Königswelle am Laufen gehalten werden. Beim 547 sind das übrigens gleich vier – je eine pro Einlass- und Auslassseite am Kopf beider Zylinderbänke.

lie in the cylinder head. But the best solution by far is to have overhead camshafts – which in the case of a boxer engine are on the sides of the engine – driven by shafts. In the Fuhrmann engine, there are four of them – two of each for the inlet and the exhaust camshafts. Correctly designed and assembled with the all the right tolerances, this system of directly driving the camshafts gave very precise results and enabled high revs and was thus the first choice for a racing engine.

The pushrod engine with its Beetle ancestry had many strengthened parts and was of a very strong and reliable construction. But the new Fuhrmann engine had some specialties of its own. For example, there was a new high performance fan that took air from the front as well as from the back of the housing. Thus it doubled the quantity of cooling air available to the cylinders. Also the oil system was significantly refined. The engine might have looked to a casual observer as if it could have been a Volkswagen engine on steroids but the similarities were limited to the fact that they were both air cooled, both were boxer fours and both were mounted behind the rear axle. In fact, the latter resemblance was soon obsolete as the Spyder was a mid-engined racing car and that is what is most important for this Formula One history.

During the development of the formula racing car, the 547 engine took several steps forward including an increase of around twenty-five horsepower. And it is this four-cylinder engine that will accompany us right to the end of the story.

Superleggera: Der 550 A hat einen Rohrrahmen und ist somit noch einmal leichter geworden. Trips fährt ihn im 1000-Kilometer-Rennen 1956 auf dem Nürburgring mit Umberto Maglioli auf den vierten Platz.

Superleggera: the 550 A had a tubular chassis frame and thus was even lighter than its predecessor. Von Trips drove one in the 1,000-kilometre race at the 'Ring.

Sauber eingestellt und gut gefertigt, ist das sehr präzise, sehr drehzahlfest und ziemlich schwingungsfrei – allererste Wahl also für den Rennsport, wo die Wartungsfreundlichkeit ein ganz klein wenig zurückstehen darf. Toppen lässt sich das Ganze allenfalls noch mit einer Zwangssteuerung der Ventile, das wäre jetzt aber ein bisschen viel verlangt.

Wie viele Komponenten des Stoßstangenmotors zwar noch dem Käferprinzip folgten, aber längst in modifizierter und stark verbesserter Ausführung gebaut wurden, weist natürlich auch der „Fuhrmann"-Motor allerhand Spezialitäten auf, die ebenfalls großen Anteil an der neuen Potenz der Porsche-Boxer haben. Das neue Hochleistungsgebläse – zweistufig: es saugt von vorn und von hinten an – gibt doppelt so viel Luft an raffiniert verrippte Köpfe und Zylinder ab, der Ölkreislauf ist erheblich verfeinert. Ernst Fuhrmann hat zwar rein äußerlich etwas gebaut, was vielleicht auch aus Wolfsburg stammen könnte, aber die Gemeinsamkeiten beschränken sich längst auf: luftgekühlt, Boxerprinzip, hinten eingebaut. Letzteres ist im Spyder bald auch nicht mehr der Fall, da haben wir es dann mit dem Mittelmotor zu tun, und der interessiert uns ja hier vor allem.

Nun sind wir dem Formelwagen schon ein Riesenstück und zunächst rund 25 PS nähergekommen. Der Vierzylinder, der am Ende fast schon an der 190-PS-Grenze kratzt, soll uns bis zum Schluss begleiten. Zunächst wird er das Herz des ganz neuen 550. Dessen neuer Leiterrahmen birgt vorn wie hinten die klassischen Torsionsstäbe. Die Drehstabfederung der Hinterräder aber ist

Eventually it will deliver about 190 bhp in 1.5 litre form.

At first it was to become the heart of the brand new type 550. Its ladder frame bore the familiar axles with torsion bar springs. The novelty here was the mounting of the rear axle with the torsion bars now located in front of the axle. Earlier conversions to a mid-engine configuration had made it necessary to turn the whole engine, gearbox and axle arrangement around. The result had been that trailing arms showed forward thus leading to positive wheel camber. Now with the newly arranged axle, this was eliminated. The Spyder had now its classic look for Erwin Komenda had designed a neat body around the new innards. The doors were real doors and the silhouette showed a smooth but smart wasp waist along with small tailfins incorporating the taillights. It was the prototype of all the Spyders that were to follow.

The 550 and its derivative the 1500 RS, were pretty successful. Hans Herrmann for example carried the day on the 1954 Carrera Pan Americana. In the same year, Herrmann and Herbert Linge were victorious in the Mille Miglia in the 1500 class. During the event, Herrmann made the memorable manoeuvre of driving his low-slung car under some closed railway-crossing gates because he had not managed to slow down in time. Again this was a private entry. As usual the Porsche people serviced the car and in all but name it was a works entry. But the company preferred to enter as if it were a privateer entry.
In the winter of 1955, the Spyder matured yet further. A lot went

Spitzentrio: Ferry Porsche (rechts) mit seinen langjährigen Mitarbeitern Karl Rabe (links) und Erwin Komenda 1956. Erwin Komenda (1904-1966) war als Karosseriekonstrukteur seit 1931 maßgeblich an vielen grundlegenden Porsche-Konstruktionen wie dem Volkswagen (Porsche Typ 60), dem Auto-Union-P-Rennwagen (Porsche Typ 22) und dem Porsche 356 beteiligt.

The top three: Ferry Porsche (on the right) and his long time staff members Karl Rabe (left) and Erwin Komenda seen together in 1956. Komenda (1904–1966) in his role as body designer, took part in the development of many famous cars like the Volkswagen (Porsche type 60), the Auto Union P (type 22) and the 356.

Foto: Porsche

endlich vor der Achse angeordnet. Frühere Umbauten zum Mittelmotorprinzip hatten gleichsam die Drehung des Aggregats samt Getriebe und Achse bedeutet – mit der Folge, dass die Hebelarme der Federung nun geschoben statt gezogen wurden. Das hatte sich nicht unbedingt zugunsten der Straßenlage ausgewirkt. Nun ist die alte Ordnung wiederhergestellt, und die Hinterräder entwickeln beim Ausfedern nicht länger den unerwünschten starken positiven Sturz.

Außerdem sieht der Spyder jetzt so aus, wie ihn die meisten kennen: Eine sehr flott (wiederum von Erwin Komenda) gezeichnete Karosserie umhüllt die feine neue Technik. Die Türen verdienen nun ihren Namen, die Seitenlinie hat einen sanften flotten Hüftschwung, und am Ende trägt der 550 dezente Heckflossen mit kleinen Rückleuchten in den abgerundeten Spitzen. Im Prinzip wird diese Form den Spydern weitgehend erhalten bleiben.

Der 550 und seine Variante 1500 RS sind erfolgreich. Einer der berühmtesten Siege ist der von Hans Herrmann bei der Carrera Panamericana 1954, als er seine Klasse klar dominiert. Im gleichen Jahr siegen Herrmann und Herbert Linge in der 1500er-Klasse bei der Mille Miglia – es ist jenes berühmte Rennen, in dem Herrmann, weil er nicht mehr bremsen kann, den flachen Renner mit eingezogenem Kopf kurzerhand unter den bereits geschlossenen Schranken eines Bahnübergangs hindurchsteuert. Es handelt sich übrigens wieder einmal um eine „private Meldung" zum Rennen. Wie

on between its two axles. A filigree tube frame replaced the ladder design. The distinguishing marks for this car were two service hatches with vents on the flanks. They replaced the former hinged rear that had opened as a whole. For maintenance that went beyond mere carburettor tuning or a spark plug change, the rear bodywork was still removable. The result was a remarkably light and more rigid car. And the new geometry for the independent swing axle considerably improved the car's handling. All this paid off and Porsche's series of class wins continued.

In 1956, there was an interesting episode with a car christened "Micky Maus". It was so nicknamed because of its capricious comportment on the road. The car was a Spyder that had been reduced in size and was given a type number of its own. This type 645 was intended to replace the 550 and to be even more streamlined, lighter and possess even better road holding. The triangular trailing arms that later worked well in the 804 were obviously not really compatible with Micky Maus. After only two months this chapter of Porsche's development was closed. This speedy race mouse's career came to violent end on September 16th when Richard von Frankenberg survived by a mere hairsbreadth a spectacular accident at the Avus circuit. In the north curve the car went into a skid, got airborne and crashed blazing into the paddock. Rescuers found the unconscious but barely hurt driver in the bushes near the track. He had been thrown out of the car and the undergrowth had cushioned his fall.

Im alten Fahrerlager: Herbert Linge sitzt 1957 am Steuer des 718 RSK Spyder, der schon alles für die Formel 2 hat.

In the old Nurburgring paddock: in 1957, Herbert Linge sits behind the wheel of the 718 RSK Spyder prepared for Formula Two racing.

Foto: Porsche

üblich betreuen zwar Porsche-Leute das Auto, und es handelt sich selbstverständlich in Wahrheit auch um einen Werkseinsatz, auf dem Papier aber tritt die Firma hinter einen anderen Namen zurück.

Im Winter 1955/56 wird der Spyder erneut ein Stück erwachsener. Zwar gibt es nach wie vor die Rohre für die Torsionsstäbe vorn und hinten, dazwischen und drumherum aber wird alles anders. Ein filigraner Rohrrahmen bildet das Skelett des neuen Autos. Äußerlich ist der 550 A, der allerdings bekannter ist unter dem Kürzel RS, vor allem an den beiden seitlichen Wartungsklappen mit Lüftungsschlitzen zu erkennen, die das aufklappbare Heck als Motorhaube ersetzen. Geht es um größere Operationen als Vergasereinstellung und Zündkerzenwechsel, lässt sich nun das Heck als Ganzes abnehmen. Das Ergebnis: Der Wagen wird leichter und trotzdem viel stabiler.

Die neue Geometrie der hinteren Pendelachse lässt ihn wesentlich besser beherrschbar werden. Das alles zahlt sich aus, und Porsches Serie der Klassensiege bei den namhaften Rennen setzt sich fort.

Interessant ist übrigens eine kleine Episode namens „Micky Maus". Den Spitznamen erhält er wegen seines kapriziösen Fahrverhaltens. Das Auto ist ein in fast allen Dimensionen verkleinerter Spyder mit eigener Typnummer. Der 645 soll eigentlich den 550 ablösen, noch leichter, noch windschlüpfriger soll er sein und vor allem besser auf der Straße liegen. Dazu erhält er eine überaus fortschrittliche neue hintere Radaufhängung. Dreieckslenker finden sich später im 804 wieder, wollen aber zu „Micky Maus" offenbar gar nicht passen. Das Experiment aus dem Jahr 1956 ist schon nach zwei Monaten wieder beendet. Die Karriere der schnellen, aber unberechenbaren Rennmaus endet am 16. September spektakulär, als Richard von Frankenberg einen haarsträubenden Unfall auf der Berliner Avus wie durch ein Wunder überlebt. Der Wagen bricht in der Nordkurve aus, fliegt aus ihr heraus und kracht brennend ins Fahrerlager. Den bewusstlosen, aber kaum verletzten Piloten finden Helfer erst Minuten später im Unterholz am Streckenrand. Er war aus dem Auto herausgeschleudert und vom Bewuchs des Erdwalls aufgefangen worden.

Dennoch hat „Micky Maus" gezeigt, dass noch einiges drin ist, etwa bei der Verbesserung der Aerodynamik und des Fahrwerks. Der nächste Schritt aber ist der RSK. Den dritten Buchstaben im Kürzel hat er von der Form des Rahmenvorderteils, das aussieht wie ein liegendes „K". Es ist Teil einer neuen Vorderachskonstruktion, die zwar weiter nach dem Kurbellenkerprinzip funktioniert, die Radführung aber erheblich verbessert. So erhalten die Vorderräder nun beim Einfedern leicht negativen Sturz. Der neue Rahmenbug erlaubt auch eine neue Karosserienase. Sie ist länger, angedeutet schaufelförmig und der der „Micky Maus" nicht ganz unähnlich.

Ein interessantes Detail am Rande: Die vordere Haube birgt ein feines Leitungssystem, durch das heißes Motoröl zirkuliert. So dient die Klappe als Oberflächenkühler. Außerdem wird mit einer so genannten Jetkühlung experimentiert. Der Trick: Die mit Macht nach hinten abgeführten Abgase sollen einen gezielten Sog erzeugen, der kühlende Luft herbei- und um die heißen Motorteile führt. Das funktioniert zwar, macht aber vor allem sehr viel Krach und kommt deshalb nicht zum Einsatz.

Mittlerweile hat sich der 550 nun allerdings derart stark verändert, dass er endlich einen neuen Namen bekommt. Ab

At least the Micky Maus experience informed the team in no uncertain fashion that they had not yet exhausted the fields of aerodynamics and chassis development. The next step was the RSK, so named because that third letter resembled the shape of the front end of the car's frame, a "K" that was lying on its side. This was part of a new front axle design that gave the wheels a slightly negative camber. Because of the layout, the body got a new nose that recalled the front end of the "Micky Maus".

An interesting detail was that a part of the oil system was integrated into the front bonnet. The hot oil from the engine circulated through tiny pipes in the bonnet and thus the bonnet itself worked as a cooler. Another invention that was tried was called jet cooling. The drag of the exhaust gas was intended to generate suction that was used to draw in cool air and to take it to the hot engine. In fact it did work after a fashion but it also made a lot of noise and was thus abandoned.

Meanwhile the 550 had turned into something completely different and thus received a new type number. Meet the 718.

The most significant change was the disappearance of the old swing axle at the rear. Suspension struts replaced the torsion bars and a Watts linkage was introduced as a lateral guide for wheel movement. In addition, two struts connected to the car and its suspension by ball joints supported each wheel. By contrast, the front wheels were kept in place by the familiar Porsche uprights without adjustable camber. The four-camshaft engine was still competitive. Version number three delivered more than 140 horsepower thanks to king-size 46 mm carburettors and higher lift camshafts. Maybe the new RSK still needed some fine-tuning but a third and a fourth place at Le Mans 1958 (overall – their class victory was by now taken for granted) assured Porsche that the team was on its way to the top. During the season the engine output was increased and on both sides of the Atlantic, many private teams entering the RSK were successful.

By March 1959, Wolfgang Graf Berghe von Trips and Jo Bonnier were driving the new RSK at Sebring. It had the third version of the rear axle where double wishbones had replaced the old oscillating devices. From then on the wheel camber was adjustable and longer springs could be used that permitted increased wheel movement. The newly designed rear end of the chassis frame made engine maintenance much easier including the ability to change gear ratios without having to remove the entire gearbox.

In May 1959, Porsche gained its first overall victory in the World Sports car championship. This was achieved with a model from the previous year driven by Edgar Barth and Wolfgang Seidel. Von Trips and Bonnier both retired with cars employing the new double wishbone system.

The success was short-lived for at Le Mans in June, Porsche suffered their worst nightmare. For the first time, all their cars that were entered retired, although it was Ferry Porsche himself – with the championship title within reach – had given the go-ahead for the use of high-lift, high-performance camshafts. A little later, von Trips won a 1.5-litre sports car race at the Avus against some very fast privately entered RSK models. But it was also a tragic event. Jean Behra, a very successful

sofort – also 1957 – heißt der Porsche-Rennsportwagen 718. Signifikantes tut sich zunächst im Heck. Es ist das Ende der alten Pendelachse. Federbeine ersetzen die Drehstäbe, ein Watt-Gestänge führt die Räder in der Lotrechten. Dazu werden pro Rad zwei Streben mit Kugelgelenken verwendet. Vorn hingegen werden wieder herkömmliche Achsschenkel ohne variablen Sturz montiert. Die Pendelachse schmiegt sich gleichsam im Bogen um die Antriebswellen.

Dass der Viernockenwellenmotor immer noch gut im Futter steht, beweist seine Ausführung Nummer drei, die unter anderem dank fetter 46er Vergaser plus schärferer Nockenwellen nun knapp über 140 PS leistet. Der neue RSK muss zwar noch in allerhand Details verbessert werden, ein dritter und ein vierter Platz im Gesamtklassement in Le Mans 1958 – der Klassensieg ist ohnehin ausgemacht – lassen aber erkennen, dass Porsche auf dem besten Weg nach ganz oben ist. Im Laufe der Saison steigt die Motorleistung weiter, und in Europa wie in den USA haben auch die mittlerweile recht zahlreichen Privatfahrer viel Erfolg im RSK.

Im März 1959 gehen Wolfgang Graf Berghe von Trips und Joakim Bonnier in Sebring mit dem ganz neuen RSK an den Start. Zum Einsatz kommt die dritte Hinterachse in diesem Modell. Von nun an ist Schluss mit der Pendelei. Doppelquerlenker führen die Räder – ganz ähnlich wie im Formel-1-Lotus. Die neue Achsgeometrie mit Dreieckslenkern erlaubt die Einstellung des Sturzes und diese die Verwendung längerer Federn. Überdies ist das Rahmenheck nun einfacher konstruiert. Es erleichtert die

driver who had suggested many improvements on Porsche racing cars, was killed in the race. Rather like the previous accident involving von Frankenberg, he lost control in the north curve and crashed into an old concrete pedestal that had been erected in wartime as an anti-aircraft gun turret. Behra was thrown out of the car and smashed into a flagpole. Carel de Beaufort was lucky things did not turn out in a similar fashion when he crashed at the same meeting. The Dutchman also shot off the track but managed to make his way through the undergrowth straight into the paddock – and then rejoined the race. Nevertheless a couple of laps later, the officials black flagged him once they realised what had happened.

Racing at Avus that day, we thus have two names that were deeply involved in the efforts of Porsche to break into formula racing. No one used a Porsche open-wheeler longer than Beaufort. And Behra paved the way for the Porsche formula racing car in various ways.

After a three-year break, Formula Two was reintroduced in 1957 as a category for up-and-coming drivers. Regulations were kept within reasonable limits and the use of small 1.5-litre engines with no forced induction seemed to be tailor-made for Porsche. To top it all, the regulations did not even stipulate that the cars had to have open wheels. Thus in the beginning, fully dressed sports cars were entered in the races including, of course, cars from Porsche. There had been plans to send an RSK to Reims but they were dashed when the car was demol-

Foto: Porsche

Gipfelstürmer: Der RSK 1958 in einem Lauf zur Europa-Bergmeisterschaft. Trips am Gaisberg.

Road to the top: the RSK during a heat of the European Hillclimb Championship in 1958.

Otto Mathés Fetzenflieger

Otto Mathé's "Goes-like-blazes"

Foto: Porsche

Es gibt schon einen Porsche-Monoposto, bevor das Werk aus dem Sport- einen Grand-Prix-Wagen macht. 1953 setzt der Österreicher Otto Mathé, der Ölzusätze unter seinem Namen herstellt, einen pfiffigen Eigenbau ein. Vor allem in Eisrennen auf zugefrorenen Seen ist der „Fetzenflieger" unschlagbar. Er besteht zu je rund einem Drittel aus Volkswagen- und aus Porscheteilen sowie allerhand Selbstgebasteltem. Vorn führt eine Käferachse die Räder, hinten röhrt ein 1500er Porschemotor. Die Motor-Getriebe-Kombi hat Mathé umgedreht, die Achse aber in herkömmlicher Position belassen. Sie sitzt freilich weiter vorn und erhält, wie der 550, verlängerte Hebelarme. Vor dem Motor sitzt der Tank und vor diesem in Wagenmitte der Fahrer. Obwohl Mathé nur noch einen Arm hat, düpiert er seine Gegner reihenweise und meistens im gekonnten

Je ein Drittel VW, Porsche und Selbstgemachtes: Ein Monoposto Marke Eigenbau. Bahnrennen, Baden, 1955.

Drift. Beim Schalten stemmt er sich mit der Schulter gegen das Lenkrad. Vom Prinzip her ist das bereits der Monoposto, mit dem Porsche 1959 in der Formel 2 antritt. Der Leichtbau-Mathé ist sensationell agil, selbst nach dem Einbau eines Viernockenwellenmotors plus Porschebremsen und -rädern bringt er weniger als 400 Kilogramm auf die Waage. Noch 1959 schlägt der „Eiskönig" zwei Spyder, die von Frankenberg und von Hanstein lenken.

DIY for cars: this open wheeler was made from one third VW, one third Porsche, plus some homemade bits.

Before Porsche turned their successful Spyder into a GP racer, there had been another Porsche open wheeler. In 1953 Austrian Otto Mathé, a maker of oil additives, created a smartly designed racing car. Especially in races on frozen lakes, the Fetzenflieger ("Goes like Blazes") turned out to be unbeatable. It was made from equal shares of Volkswagen, Porsche and homemade parts. The front axle was from a Beetle while its earthy roar came from a 1,500cc Porsche engine at the rear.

Mathé had turned the engine-gearbox unit round but left the rear axle roughly where it was, only moving it a bit forward and lengthening the trailing arms. The fuel tank was mounted in front of the engine and the driver sat in the middle of the car. Mathé was handicapped by virtue of having lost an arm but he still outran nearly every competitor and his normal style was to drift his car in a breathtaking manner. When he had to change gear, he pressed his shoulder against the steering wheel to keep it steady. Thus Mathé built a monoposto before Porsche made an open-wheeler and he anticipated the principle long before Zuffenhausen entered their car in Formula Two in 1959. The Mathé lightweight racer was sensationally agile and weighed less than 400 kilograms. It kept that weight even when he installed a Fuhrmann engine plus Porsche brakes. As late as 1959, the "Ice King" beat two Spyders driven by von Frankenberg and von Hanstein.

Wartung des Motors erheblich und gestattet unter anderem das Ändern der Gangabstufung bei eingebautem Getriebe.

Mit einem Vorjahresmodell gelingt 1959 bei der Targa Florio der erste Porsche-Gesamtsieg in einem Rennen zur Markenmeisterschaft. Barth und Seidel gewinnen, nachdem die führenden Trips und Bonnier im Querlenker-Wagen ausfallen.

Was sich da so vielversprechend anlässt, ist nicht von Dauer. In Le Mans fallen erstmals alle Autos aus, nachdem Ferry Porsche, nun den Titel vor Augen, sogar den Einsatz sehr scharfer Nockenwellen erlaubt hat. Trips gewinnt dann aber ein 1,5-Liter-Sportwagenrennen auf der Avus, in dem die privat eingesetzten RSK den Werksautos mächtig Dampf machen. Es ist ein tragisches Rennen. Jean Behra, der so manche Idee zur Verbesserung der Porscherenner beigetragen hat und ein sehr erfolgreicher Fahrer ist, kommt bei einem Unfall ums Leben. Er rutscht wie Frankenberg aus der Nordkurve und prallt in seinem Wagen gegen einen alten Betonsockel, auf dem während des Zweiten Weltkrieges eine Fliegerabwehrkanone montiert war. Behra wird gegen einen Flaggenmast geschleudert.

Glück im Unglück hat Carel de Beaufort. Der Niederländer, der bald den Formelrenner unermüdlich Saison für Saison einsetzt, bis er selbst ums Leben kommt, rutscht ebenfalls über den

ished at Le Mans. Thus Christian Goethals entered his own 550A as a private entry and finished fifth. The sports car body proved to be no disadvantage and in fact proved to be very stable especially on the faster tracks.

Finally, Porsche entered two 550A in August 1957 when their Formula Two cars raced together with the Formula One cars in the German Grand Prix. Edgar Barth won the Formula Two section, Umberto Maglioli retired but Carel de Beaufort finished third in his privately entered Porsche. By the following year at Reims, Formula Two was well established and Porsche invested more time and money into the project. The RSK seen there was the previous year's model but it had the new rear axle – and they had fitted the steering wheel in the centre of the car. It was called the Mittellenker. The cockpit was covered apart from a small opening to accommodate the driver and behind the neat windscreen on this occasion sat Jean Behra. There were two little tailfins and spats covered the rear wheels. The bodywork over the engine sported three characteristic bumps, two for the carburettors while the big one in the middle worked as a streamlined headrest. With this special RSK, Behra beat Ferrari, Lotus and Cooper. But there was better to come since at the 'Ring, Edgar Barth also won Formula

Kurvenrand, holpert aber durchs Grün hinunter ins Fahrerlager – und setzt tatsächlich das Rennen fort. Nach einigen Runden winken ihn aber die Rennoffiziellen heraus, nachdem sie gewahr werden, was da geschehen ist.

Nun sind zwei Namen im Spiel, die eine große Rolle in der Geschichte von Porsches Formelengagement spielen. Beaufort setzt seine orangefarbenen Wagen am längsten ein, Behra ebnet dem Formelrenner in den anderthalb Jahren vor seinem Tod gleich in mehrfacher Hinsicht den Weg.

Die Formel 2 scheint fast auf Porsche zugeschnitten. Fast das Schönste: Es sind nicht einmal freistehende Räder vorgeschrieben. So fahren anfangs auch Spyder mit, allen voran ein Porsche. Pläne, den RSK beim ersten großen Formel-2-Termin in Reims an den Start zu bringen, scheitern, als der Wagen in Le Mans demoliert wird. So startet Christian Goethals im eigenen 550 A als einziger Porschefahrer und wird Fünfter. Die Sportwagenkarosserie ist nicht nur kein Nachteil, sondern erweist sich auf den schnellen Passagen als sehr stabil.

Gleich zwei 550 A stellt Porsche im August 1957 an den Start, als im Großen Preis von Deutschland auch die Formel-2-Renner fahren. Edgar Barth gewinnt, Umberto Maglioli scheidet aus, den dritten Platz aber erreicht Carel de Beaufort im privaten Porsche.

Two in his similar car, but this time without the spats and tailfins. What was special was he was sixth overall amongst all the Formula One cars. A '58 model was sent to Reims in 1959 in which von Trips finished fifth. Colin Davis drove a second Mittellenker, one of four cars prepared by Porsche individually for customers with different arrangements for pedals and steering. The three other drivers were Wolfgang Seidel, Christian Goethals and Carel de Beaufort. The cars gave a good account of themselves but soon it became evident that there was still work to do as the Formula Two opposition became faster and faster. The big temptation lay with the new regulations that had been announced for Formula One. The adoption of the 1.5-litre formula from 1961 meant that the current Formula Two cars were suitable for first class racing provided that they were open-wheelers and weighed at least 500 kilograms. Decisions like that are seldom made on just a whim. In the background, the Germans had been beating the drum for a 1,500 cc formula – and von Hanstein had the right connections within the sport to make that opinion widely known. So it was no wonder that the Porsche racing department got working on an open-wheeler very shortly after the news had broken. The Formula Two 718 came into being along the RSK during the winter of 1958/9 and was soon renamed 718/2.

Überführungsnummer: Edgar Barth beim Großen Preis von Deutschland.

Trade plates: in 1957, Edgar Barth at the Nürburgring with a Spyder.

Foto: Porsche

Nächstes Jahr, Reims. Die neue Formel 2 hat sich gut einge-führt, und Porsche steckt etwas mehr Zeit und Geld ins Projekt. Der RSK ist zwar vom Vorjahr, hat aber bereits die neue Hin-terachse – und Mittellenkung. Das Cockpit wird abgedeckt und lässt nur dem Fahrer, es ist Jean Behra, eine kleine Öffnung hinter einer Windschutzscheibe. Zwei kleine Heckflossen gibt es und Abdeckungen vor den Hinterrädern. Unter den tropfenförmigen Ausbuchtungen der Motorhaube verbergen sich die Vergaser, die dicke mittlere ist die Kopfstütze. Behra lässt im RSK Ferrari, Lotus und Cooper hinter sich und siegt.

Es kommt noch besser. Auf dem Nürburgring kommt Barth mit dem um Heckflossen und Radabdeckungen erleichterten Wagen als Sechster ins Ziel – unter lauter Formel-1-Rennern.

Einen RSK des Jahrgangs 1958, wiederum in Mittellenker-Konfiguration, bringt Porsche 1959 in Reims an den Start. Trips wird Fünfter. Colin Davis fährt in Reims einen weiteren Mit-tellenker. Es ist eins von vier Autos, die das Werk in jenem Jahr auf Kundenwunsch mit Halterungen für Pedale und Lenkung in Mittelposition versieht. Weitere Käufer sind Wolfgang Seidel, Christian Goethals und Carel de Beaufort.

So gut die RSK sich schlagen – es ist absehbar, dass noch einiges getan werden muss. Die Formel 2 wird immer schneller. Vor allem wird klar, dass auch die Königsklasse, die Formel 1, in

In fact the new racer became a little bit more than just a 718 without its wheels covered. The transmission had six gears but no reverse. A starter motor was considered unneces-sary weight and a bump-start would do as well. Its brakes and engine came from the Spyder as well as the dimensions of the tyres and wheelbase. At the front of the car, the torsion arms had to be taken further to the outside thanks to the adoption of a shorter torsion bar housing that was designed to allow the nose of the car to be a little more slender. Apart from the cock-pit the bodywork had only three openings. A slot in the nose provided airflow to the oil cooler. The two lateral "ears" behind the cockpit supplied the carburettors and the cooling fan. The mirrors were mounted next to the suspension strut brackets and its 547/3 engine delivered 155 hp. The Zuffenhausen mu-nicipal scales, which Porsche used to weigh its cars, showed the car to be just less than 500 kilograms. When the car was ready, Herbert Linge and Hubert Mimler drove it in April 1959 at Malmsheim and they considered it to be fast.

Now the racer was supposed to race and the plan said that it should be at the Monaco GP on May 10. But Ferry Porsche had made a stipulation that must to be fulfilled first as he definitely wanted a good result on its major debut. The 718/2 would only be allowed to start at Monaco if it could be shown that it could

Batmobil: Mit Heckflossen geht der Mittellenker in Frank-reich an den Start.

Batmobile: for France, the Mit-tellenker was equipped with tail fins.

Foto: Porsche

Sachen Hubraum stark abspeckt. Vereinfacht ausgedrückt, sind ab 1961 alle aktuellen Formel-2-Wagen auch tauglich für die Formel 1, sofern sie freistehende Räder haben und mindestens 500 Kilogramm auf die Waage bringen.

Derartige Entscheidungen treffen Rennsportfunktionäre selten aus dem Bauch und einer plötzlichen Laune heraus. Außerdem hatten die deutschen Vertreter kräftig für die 1,5-Liter-Formel getrommelt, und Hanstein hatte sowieso die erforderlichen Kontakte. So nimmt es nicht Wunder, dass in der Rennabteilung schon an einem Monoposto gebastelt wird, als die neuen Formelelemente verkündet werden. So entsteht der Formel-718 praktisch parallel zum RSK und soll ja auch bloß 718/2 heißen.

Allerdings wird der Renner dann doch etwas mehr als bloß ein 718 mit freistehenden Rädern. Das Getriebe hat sechs Gänge, darunter freilich keinen zum Rückwärtsfahren. Einen Anlasser haben die Ingenieure ebenfalls nicht eingeplant, der Wagen wird eben einfach angeschoben. Bremsen und Motor übernimmt der

lap the Nürburgring Nordschleife in under 9:30 minutes. That was very demanding target since going round in less than 9:30 would mean driving the fastest ever lap of the 'Ring in a 1.5-litre. On a wet track Barth, Linge and von Trips did the first test drives with the object of tuning the chassis. Then, as the track dried out, von Trips became faster and faster and managed to turn in a lap of 9:29.8. Thus the condition was met and, a couple of days later down in Monaco, the young man from Horrem near Cologne was on twelfth place on the grid, ahead of all the other Formula Two cars and even in front of some Formula One cars. In the race he had some difficulties with the gear change, perhaps because there was no gate change. But the car's debut was short for, though "Count Crash" was fast, he was sometimes a bit too fast. He flew off into the wall at the Sainte Dévote curve and took two Formula Two competitors with him.

A second Porsche made by Colotti at Modena and which was much more elegantly tailored than the works cars was also

Foto: Porsche

Schnell, aber glücklos: Mit dem ersten 718/2-Monoposto wird Trips 1959 in Monte Carlo in einen Unfall verwickelt.

Fast, but unlucky: von Trips totalled the first 718/2 open-wheeler at the Monte Carlo GP.

Formelwagen vom Spyder, ebenso die hydraulische Kupplung und die Maße für Spur und Radstand. Vorn müssen allerdings die Achsschenkel etwas nach außen verlängert werden, weil die Drehstabgehäuse zugunsten der schmaleren Nase verkürzt werden. Der Prototyp hat außer dem Cockpit nur drei Öffnungen. Der Schlitz im Bug lässt Luft an den Ölkühler, die beiden seitlichen Ohren gleich hinter dem Cockpit an Vergaser und Gebläse des mittlerweile 155 PS leistenden 547/3. Die beiden Hutzen neben den Stoßdämpferaufnahmen bergen die Spiegel. Die städtische Waage von Zuffenhausen, auf der Porsche seine Fahrzeuge wiegt, zeigt ein Trockengewicht von knapp unter 500 Kilogramm an. Ende April 1959 ist das Auto fertig. Herbert Linge und Hu-

there in Monaco but took no part in the race. This was Jean Behra's car. The Frenchman had bought an RSK and turned it into an open wheeler. Despite having the old axle and the same bulky engine, the car was much sleeker than the Porsche design. Some former Maserati mechanics made an effort to prepare the car and get it right for the race but neither Maria-Teresa de Fillipis nor Edgar Barth managed to qualify with it. The Behra Porsche still exists after a career in the USA where it was owned by, among others, Lloyd Casner and his Casner Motor Racing Division Camoradi. In 1963 Vic Meinhardt won the SCCA title in the unlimited class using that car. After Trips' accident at Monaco the technicians repaired his

bert Mimler fahren es im April 1959 in Malmsheim und finden es schnell.

Nun soll der Renner auch rennen. Am 10. Mai steht Monaco auf dem Tourneeplan. Ferry Porsche aber stellt eine Bedingung, schließlich will er, dass der neue Hoffnungsträger möglichst von vornherein vorn mitfährt. Sollte der 718/2 auf der Nordschleife des Nürburgrings Zeiten unter 9:30 einfahren, darf er auch in Monte Carlo an den Start. Das ist viel verlangt. Gelingt es, wäre der Wagen der schnellste Anderthalbliter aller Zeiten in der Eifel. Barth, Linge und Trips machen auf noch nasser Straße Testfahrten, die vor allem der Einstellung des Fahrwerks dienen. Trips fährt auf schließlich trockener Strecke immer schneller und schafft am Ende tatsächlich 9:29,8. Knapp, aber die Bedingung ist erfüllt.

Der junge Mann aus Horrem steht dann auch wenige Tage später an der Mittelmeerküste auf dem zwölften Startplatz – vor den übrigen Formel-2-Kandidaten und noch vor einigen Formel-1-Rennern. Im Rennen tut er sich gelegentlich schwer mit der kulissenlosen Schaltung. „Count Crash" ist aber schnell und gelegentlich gar zu schnell. In der Sainte-Dévote-Kurve fliegt er raus und nimmt gleich noch zwei weitere Formel-2-Konkurrenten mit.

Im Rennen fehlt ein zweiter Porsche, den Colotti in Modena weitaus eleganter verpackt hatte als die Porsche-Designer. Es ist das Auto von Jean Behra. Der Franzose hat einen RSK gekauft

car and, at Reims, Jo Bonnier drove it. He eventually placed third behind Hans Herrmann and Stirling Moss but he had encountered problems with the carburettors on his car. It turned out that the lateral intakes did not work properly at high speed. The air jammed itself up in front of the opening and the airflow was thus interrupted. Vents soon replaced the intakes and their rear opening enabled the air to flow properly to the engine.

For test purposes, Porsche sent the 718/2 and Jo Bonnier to Great Britain. On August 29 at Brands Hatch they started in the Formula Two race for the Kentish Trophy. Bonnier finished the first fifty-mile heat in third place and in the second heat he was fourth. The only cars to beat him were Coopers fitted with Climax and Borgward engines and the Lotus-Climax. This was not a bad result and Stirling Moss became curious. Soon his curiosity turned into enthusiasm after he tested the Porsche at Goodwood and discovered that it was four-tenths of a second faster than his Cooper-Borgward. It was the beginning of a rather extraordinary relationship. Suddenly there was a Porsche in the Scottish blue with white stripe of the Rob Walker team to which Moss belonged. The result was two Porsche semi-works teams on the track for 1960, Porsche's own and the one belonging to the Scotsman. That meant a lot of work for the racing department at Zuffenhausen. Over the winter, extensive tests took place at Hockenheim and, with the new Formula

Blaues Wunder: Colin Davis fährt in Behras Porsche-Variation in Reims auf den neunten Platz.

Blue racer: at Reims, Colin Davis finished ninth in the unique Behra Porsche.

Foto: Porsche

Regenrennen: Moss fährt 1960 in Brüssel die schnellste Runde.

A race in the rain: in 1960, Moss recorded the fastest lap at the Brussels GP.

und ihn zum eigenen Monoposto umgebaut. Trotz der alten Pendelachse und des voluminösen luftgekühlten Motors kommt der in der Spur vorn wie hinten schmalere Behra-Porsche viel schnittiger daher als der Werkswagen. Ex-Maseratileute mühen sich, den Wagen noch rechtzeitig für Monaco fertigzubekommen. Leider wird nichts aus dem Renneinsatz, weil sich weder Maria-Teresa de Fillipis noch Edgar Barth qualifizieren.

Der Behra-Porsche existiert immer noch, nachdem er in den USA durch mehrere Hände gegangen ist, unter anderem durch die von Lloyd Casner und seiner Casner Motor Racing Division (Camoradi). Vic Meinhardt gewann 1963 damit den SCCA-Titel in der freien Klasse.

Nach dem Unfall in Monte Carlo haben die Porsche-Techniker Trips' Auto wieder aufgebaut. Der Wagen wird in Reims Dritter hinter denen von Herrmann und Moss. Bonnier hat Probleme mit den Vergasern. Es erweist sich, dass die seitlichen Hutzen bei hohem Tempo zur Belüftung ungeeignet sind. Die Luft staut sich zu stark und kann nicht sauber zu den Ansaugtrichtern fließen. Schlitze ersetzen die Hutzen, hintere Öffnungen verbessern den Durchfluss.

Vor allem zu Testzwecken schickt Porsche den 718/2 und Joakim Bonnier nach Großbritannien. In Brands Hatch geht es am 29. August um die Kentish Trophy. In den beiden 50-Meilen-Läufen fährt der Schwede auf Platz drei respektive auf Platz vier. Schneller sind nur Cooper-Climax und -Borgward sowie Lotus-Climax. Das ist ziemlich gut, und Stirling Moss wird neugierig. Bald schlägt die Neugier in Begeisterung um, nachdem er in

One almost in sight, the new cars were prepared for the challenge by incorporating modifications.

Firstly the wheelbase was increased by ten centimetres up to 2,200mm that gave more room for the driver and anticipated the need for larger fuel tanks in Formula One. To keep the front trailing arms outward from the bodywork and thus plenty of clearance for the wheels, the engineers decided to angle the tubes carrying the torsion bar springs slightly to the rear near the centre of the car. This meant that the front torsion bars had to be split at their centres and that two height adjusting screws had to be fitted in the middle rather than the normal single screw. To achieve the correct camber, the torsion bar tubes were also angled slightly up towards the wheels.

Outwardly little was changed with just minor alterations to the nose of the car and the rear bodywork. The opening at the front for the oil cooler was made smaller and placed as low as possible. The rearmost cover with four openings was removable as was the engine cover immediately behind the cockpit with its smaller headrest. The cars put on weight slightly and back on those municipal scales, they found that it had crept up to 465 kilograms.

In July 1960, the last two 718/2s were built which meant that the crowd at Stuttgart's Solitude circuit were able to watch all five Formula Two racers performing not far from the factory where they had been constructed. Butzi Porsche, Ferry Porsche's son, had redesigned one of them to make it a little sleeker. Its windscreen and the engine cover, now open at the

Goodwood heimlich den Porsche testet und gleich vier Zehntel schneller ist als im Cooper-Borgward.

Es ist der Beginn einer eher außergewöhnlichen Ehe. Bald fährt ein Porsche im edlen Schottischblau mit dem weißen Nasenring des Rennstalls von Rob Walker, für den Moss verpflichtet ist. Das bedeutet für die 1960er Saison, dass Porsche gleichsam zwei Werksteams auf der Strecke hat: das eigene und das des Schotten. Das bedeutet für die Rennabteilung auch jede Menge Arbeit. Im Winter beginnen umfangreiche Tests in Hockenheim.

Weil die Formel 1 in Sicht ist, werden die neuen Autos schon für die neue Herausforderung vorbereitet. Zunächst wächst der Radstand um zehn auf 220 Zentimeter. Außerdem werden die Kurbellenker der Vorderachse weiter ausgestellt. Das lässt sich am einfachsten bewerkstelligen, indem man die Drehstab-Gehäuserohre anwinkelt. Zeigen die Enden der Rohre in Fahrtrichtung gesehen nach vorn, zeigen automatisch die nach hinten gerichteten Kurbellenker weiter nach außen. Damit das auch auf beiden Seiten funktioniert, müssen die Drehstab-Rohre geteilt werden. In der Mitte verbunden, weisen sie also nun einen Knick auf, genauer, ein breites „V" mit nach vorn geöffneten Armen. Schrauben für die Federvorspannung finden sich nun individuell für jede Seite gleich im Doppelpack.

Äußerlich werden die Nase und die Konstruktion der hinteren Hauben behutsam modifiziert. Die Eintrittsöffnung für den vorderen Ölkühler wird verkleinert und so tief wie möglich in der Frontpartie angebracht, die Heckverkleidung reicht nicht mehr bis zu den Radaufhängungen hinunter, die nun hinter eigenen Abdeckblechen liegen. Das komplette Heckteil mit vier Luftöffnungen lässt sich abnehmen, ebenso die Motorabdeckung hinter dem Cockpit, das eine weniger massive Kopfstütze aufweist. Das Gewicht steigt kaum merklich um wenige Kilogramm auf 465 Kilo.

rear, were connected in a streamlined design. The frontal area was a little smaller than the normal 718/2's but the car was also a little heavier. Also at Solitude were the first signs of the cars that Porsche would have to beat in the forthcoming Formula One season. There was the new Lotus, the first to have a rear engine, and there was also the Ferrari F156 with its fine V6 engine.

All in all, the 1960 season went pretty well for the open-wheeler racing cars from Swabia. Thus Porsche started the 1961 season with confidence that the new downsized Formula One was an arena in which they could succeed. Maybe the Zuffenhausen team was a bit too optimistic as their rivals were not sleeping. Porsche of course was counting on the fact that they had a lot of experience with small high-performance engines. But that changed all of a sudden. There was Ferrari with its new V6 racer and the British teams with their excellent chassis soon to be equipped with V8 engines.

The four-cylinder 547 was starting to reach its limits. But Porsche had more than one iron in the fire in the matter of engines. Unfortunately their promising eight-cylinder engine with its accompanying chassis was long in gestation and was slowed up by all kinds of things some of which were beyond Porsche's control.

So Porsche started into the new 1961season with the modestly modified 718/2. The cars had small rollover bars to protect the driver, a starter motor and grilles on the intakes to comply with the regulations. At Brussels, a non-championship race, Bonnier won the first of three 100-kilometre heats. However, in the second heat he was pushed off the track but generally the car had performed well. But at a race at Syracuse, Porsche had to deal with the Ferrari 156 in full Formula One array and was soundly beaten.

Im Juli sind die beiden letzten 718/2 fertig. Das Publikum des Solitude-Rennens bei Stuttgart sieht dann alle fünf Formel-2-Wagen am Start. Den fünften hat übrigens Butzi Porsche umgestaltet. Er ist ein wenig flotter gezeichnet, die Cockpitscheibe geht in die hinten offene Motorverkleidung über. Die Stirnfläche ist ein wenig kleiner als beim normalen 718/2, dafür wiegt er zehn Kilogramm mehr. Die Konkurrenz tritt schon in Formel-1-Trimm an. Da ist der neue Lotus, der erste mit Heckmotor, und da ist der Ferrari F156 mit dem feinen V6.

Alles in allem gerät die 1960er Saison dennoch ganz brauchbar für die neuen Monoposti aus dem Schwabenland. So geht Porsche denn auch recht zuversichtlich in die entscheidende Saison 1961 mit der neuen kleinen Formel 1. Die Zuffenhausener sind ein wenig zu optimistisch, denn die Konkurrenz hat nicht geschlafen. Zwar hat Porsche seinen Bonus der größeren Erfahrung mit den kleineren Motoren und deren Reife ausspielen können. Das ändert sich schlagartig, als die vermeintlich Kleinen plötzlich die Größten sind. Bestes Beispiel ist Ferrari mit dem neuen V6-Renner. Aus Großbritannien kommen überdies nun die schlanken Flitzer mit brillanten Fahrwerken. Schön, Porsche kann auf erprobte Vierzylinderrenner setzen, deren Grenzen sich aber bald abzeichnen. Das zweite, noch interessantere Eisen im Feuer ist der vielversprechende Achtzylinderboxer, der aber ebenso wie das Chassis für die Zukunft viel zu spät in Fahrt kommt und von vielerlei Hürden aufgehalten wird. Also geht Porsche mit kaum veränderten 718/2 in die neue Saison. Die Autos haben

Then came the time for the Monaco Grand Prix. Three Porsches were entered with Dan Gurney at the wheel of Bonnier's Syracuse car while the two other cars featured changes to try to keep the 718/2 competitive. Bonnier drove a highly modified car with a lengthened chassis that was intended ultimately to receive the awaited flat-8. That car then received a unique type number, 787. Herrmann at last received a 718/2 that was also a kind of intermediate version. It retained the normal chassis length but, like Bonnier's car, benefited from the new front suspension free from any Beetle ancestry. Double wishbones and suspension struts were expected to improve road holding significantly.

The fuel tank was no longer at the front. There were tanks mounted behind the driver and alongside the cockpit all of which was intended to eliminate the shift of the centre of gravity as a result of fuel being consumed. Also new was the Kugelfischer fuel injection fitted to the engines. It did not increase the power output significantly but the torque was noticeably increased and the spark plugs were less likely to oil up on low revs. Everything went fine at first but, of all things, it was the fuel system that thwarted Bonnier's plans. Every time he braked hard, the fuel sloshed away from the pick up in the tank and the engine stopped.

With the next GP close at hand, the technicians prepared a second 787 with baffles in the tanks and new electrical fuel pumps. Gurney took over Bonnier's Monaco car and the

Foto: Porsche

T wie Testwagen: Michael May vor dem 1961er Rennen in Monaco.

T for test car: Michael May during the 1961 Monaco GP practice.

Hans Herrmann ärgert sich

Hans Herrmann is upset

„Um Gottes willen, sieht das schlecht aus. Da hätt' ich besser aufgehört." Als Hans Herrmann im Frühjahr 2008 – kurz nach seinem 80. Geburtstag – noch einmal in der Statistik der '61er Saison blättert, schüttelt er den Kopf und in seinem Gesicht wechseln nach wie vor stabile Enttäuschung und ein gewisses Amüsement nach all den Jahren einander ab. „Das war wirklich ein Jahr, wo ich aufhören wollte", sagt der Mann, der erst neun Jahre später, nach einer langen großartigen Rennfahrerkarriere und nach dem heißersehnten Gesamtsieg in Le Mans im Porsche 917 seinen Abschied nimmt. In jenem ersten Jahr der 1,5-Liter-Formel leidet er unter dem verhältnismäßig schwachen Porsche. „Er kam überhaupt nicht mit den Engländern mit." Oft sind es

Dünenrennen: Beaufort hinter Herrmann in Zandvoort 1961.

Dune race: De Beaufort behind Hans Herrmann during the Dutch GP 1961.

Kleinigkeiten, die den schnellen Schwaben ausbremsen. „Das war manchmal nur so ein ganz kleiner Mist, da haben die mich ganz schön geärgert." Die Bilanz der kurzen Episode im Porsche-Formelrenner fällt eindeutig aus: „Es war nur Mist. Ausgefallen oder nix – das war das 61er Jahr."

"For heaven's sake, this looks really bad. I should really have quit at that time!" Shortly after his 80th birthday in the Spring of 2008, Hans Herrmann was looking through the race statistics from 1961 and shaking his head as he remembered that awful time. In his face, disappointment was mixed with

a kind of wry amusement. "That was indeed a year when I was certain that I should quit." This was being said by the man who did say goodbye to motor racing but only nine years later after a very successful driving career and his overall victory at Le Mans in a Porsche 917. In that first year of the 1.5-litre Formula One, he suffered behind the wheel of a 718/2 that, apart from anything else, was down on power compared with its rivals. "It couldn't keep up with the Englishmen at all." Often it was just minor things that frustrated the fast Swabian in his efforts to get it to perform. "Sometimes it was just a pesky nuisance." The racing balance sheet was certainly short of results for this talented driver "Damn it. Retire or nothing – that was it in the year 1961."

jetzt kleine Überrollbügel und einen Anlasser und tragen Schutzgitter über den Ansaugstutzen. In Brüssel – das Rennen bringt keine Formel-1-Punkte – gewinnt Bonnier den ersten von drei 100-Kilometer-Läufen. Zwar wird er im zweiten von der Strecke gedrängt, das Auto hat aber eine ziemlich gute Figur gemacht. In Syrakus bekommt Porsche es aber dann mit dem F156 im vollen Formel-1-Trimm zu tun und wird prompt auf die Plätze verwiesen.

Dann kommt Monaco 1961. Es sind drei Porsches am Start. Dan Gurney sitzt am Steuer von Bonniers Syrakus-Auto. Den beiden weiteren Wagen hat die Rennabteilung Verbesserungen mitgegeben, die den 718/2 konkurrenzfähig halten sollen. Bonnier steuert ein Auto, das erheblich modifiziert ist und daher auch eine eigene Typnummer erhält: 787. Herrmann schließlich bekommt einen 718/2, der so eine Art Zwischenstufe darstellt. Tatsächlich hat er vor allem den etwas kürzeren, herkömmlichen Radstand. In Bonniers Auto ist das Motorenabteil verlängert worden, um dem Achtzylinder Platz zu schaffen, der schließlich irgendwann kommen soll. Beide haben eine neue Vorderradaufhängung, die nun endgültig keinerlei Käferteile mehr hat. Doppelquerlenker und Federbeine sollen die Bodenhaftung der Räder entscheidend verbessern.

Das Benzin ist nun nicht länger vorn untergebracht, sondern hinter dem Fahrer und seitlich von ihm. Das soll ebenfalls die Straßenlage verbessern, weil sich der Gewichtsunterschied

Swede received the new 787 while Herrmann stuck with the modified 718/2 and was entered for the Zandvoort race by the Écurie Maasbergen of Carel de Beaufort who drove a further 718/2 himself. If Monaco had been a letdown, then the Dutch GP was a disaster. Gurney and Bonnier came tenth and eleventh respectively, while Herrmann and Beaufort were the last cars to finish, the Swabian finishing even behind the older car of the Dutchman.

As a result of the Zandvoort debacle, Porsche put the 787 to one side. The brave 718/2 carried on throughout the whole season but it was not enough to win the reward of even one first place. Then came 1962 and finally the eight-cylinder was ready and thus all those at Porsche hoped that things would improve.

By then, the 718/2s were faster than before as they had profited from some of the development of the new eight-cylinder. Newly designed combustion chambers and valves pushed the power output up to around 165 hp and indeed some individual engines were even stronger. Soon Beaufort was back on the scene, once again in his old number 01. At the championship races at Zandvoort and Rouen, he finished sixth and thus scored points. In 1963, the Dutchman also bought Schiller's car. It turned out to be a good decision especially since he was able to call on the services of a new recruit to Formula One, Gerhard Mitter. One year after Porsche retired from Formula

Reims 1961: Bonnier, Gurney und Baghetti (v.l.).

Reims 1961: Bonnier, Gurney and Baghetti.

zwischen leerem und vollem Tank nun nicht mehr unangenehm weit vor dem Schwerpunkt bemerkbar machen soll. Neu ist auch die Kugelfischer-Benzineinspritzung mit Vierstempeltechnik. Die bringt zwar kaum Mehrleistung, aber einen gleichmäßigeren Drehmomentanstieg und Schonung für die Kerzen bei niedrigen Drehzahlen.

Das klappt auch bestens, allerdings macht just die Gemischaufbereitung Bonnier einen Strich durch die Rechnung. Vermutlich, weil beim starken Bremsen der Restsprit im Tank aus der Reichweite des Ansaugschlauchs schwappt, bleibt das Auto mit Luft in der Leitung stehen.

Für Zandvoort stellen die Techniker einen zweiten 787 bereit, Schwallbleche im Tank und neue elektrische Benzinpumpen sollen das unerwünschte Luftholen der Motoren verhindern. Gurney übernimmt Bonniers Monaco-Auto, der Schwede erhält den neuen. Herrmann bleibt beim modifizierten 718/2 und startet für die Ecurie Maarsbergen von Carel de Beaufort, der einen 718/2 fährt. War Monaco schon eine Enttäuschung, wird Holland ein Desaster. Gurney und Bonnier werden Zehnter respektive Elfter, Herrmann und Beaufort bilden das Ende des Feldes, wobei der Schwabe noch dem älteren Wagen des Niederländers den Vorrang lassen muss. Hans Herrmann hat auch für diesen Tag ein paar kräftige Ausdrücke parat und wundert sich immer noch, wenn er die Resultate jener Saison nachliest.

Am Ende wird der 787 abgestellt. Tapfer fahren die 718/2 die gesamte Saison hindurch Rennen um Rennen, doch für den ersten Platz will und will es nicht reichen. Dann kommt das neue Jahr 1962. Endlich ist der Achtzylinder fertig, und endlich soll es klappen.

Die 718/2 sind übrigens schneller geworden. Die Entwicklung des neuen Achtzylinders wirft auch Erkenntnisse für die alten Motoren ab. Neue Brennräume und Ventile lassen die Leistung auf standfeste 165 PS steigen, einzelne Motoren sind noch kräftiger. Bald ist auch Beaufort wieder mit dabei – erneut in

One racing, Mitter finished fourth in the German Grand Prix at the Nürburgring.

Carel de Beaufort seemed to be somewhat stubborn by sticking to his old racing car that gradually became more and more eclipsed by the rest of the Formula One field. 1963 he scored some points once again by finishing at Spa and Watkins Glen. In an attempt to be more competitive, he even subjected himself to a diet. If there were no possibilities remaining to lighten the car, then the driver had to bite the bullet. This private owner with his famous orange racer was rightly considered as an old hand among the professional drivers. Unfortunately he lost his life one year later while qualifying for the GP at the Nürburgring. On August 3 he died of his serious injuries in a hospital at Koblenz. And it was with the end of his life that the racing life of the 718/2 also ended.

Earlier the engineers had attempted to make the four-cylinder engine more powerful and the 787 more pleasing to drive. Thus they experimented with a horizontally mounted cooling fan and disc brakes that they had developed for the 804. At the Solitude race, Barth had been frustrated with the car's performance and it was rapidly abandoned. From then on Porsche put all its eggs in one basket – a basket named the 804 – and turned over a new leaf. We now do the same thing and pass to the next chapter of our story. (jn) ■

Gebrauchtwagen

Die 718er sind 1962 noch nicht ganz aus dem Rennen. Porsche verkauft zum Stückpreis von 50.000 Mark die Nummer 02 an den Genfer Heinz Schiller, der das Auto in der Ecurie Nationale Suisse einsetzt, und die Nummer 03 an Giovanni Volpi und dessen Scuderia SSS Repubblica di Venezia. Beaufort trennt sich ebenfalls – vorübergehend – von seiner Nummer 01. Der neue Besitzer, Wolfgang Seidel, Schiller und Bonnier im 03 treten mit den Veteranen im April 1962 in Brüssel an und werden Neunter, Achter und Zweiter.

Foto: Porsche

Privatfahrer: Beaufort, Rouen 1962.

Second-hand cars

In 1962, the 718 had not yet disappeared forever from the tracks. Porsche sold serial number 02 for a unit price of 50,000 Marks to Heinz Schiller of Geneva, who then entered the car under the flag of the Écurie Nationale Suisse. Number 03 went to Giovanni Volpi and his Scuderia SSS Repubblica di Venezia while de Beaufort temporarily rested his chassis number 01. Wolfgang Seidel, Schiller and Jo Bonnier drove 718s in the Brussels GP in April 1962 and finished ninth, eighth and second overall respectively after the three heats.

Privat entry: Beaufort, Rouen 1962.

Reservelösung

Der Vierzylinder muss 1961 noch einmal ran, weil der nagelneue Formel-Achtzylinder immer noch auf sich warten lässt. Seine Tage sind jedoch gezählt. Als klar ist, dass sich das Werk dennoch mit dem Viernockenweller von Ernst Fuhrmann behelfen muss, versucht Ferry Porsche es unter anderem mit einem Mann, dessen zukunftsweisende Spoilerversuche mit einem Spyder einige Jahre zuvor mit Unverständnis, Ärger und bestenfalls Gelächter quittiert worden waren. Der Schweizer Michael May hat unterdessen bei Mercedes an Einspritzanlagen gearbeitet und ist Rennfahrer. May soll dem glücklosen 787 auf die Sprünge helfen. Er nimmt das liegende Lüfterrad, setzt bei der Einspritzanlage auf Bosch statt auf Kugelfischer, stülpt hohe Kunststoffstutzen auf die Einlasskanäle und verpasst denen auch gleich eine neue Form. Im Motor geht es weiter, neue Kolbenböden und eine pfiffigere Anordnung der Einspritzdüsen machen aus dem alten 547er-Motor ein Aggregat, das für vielleicht 185 PS gut sein könnte. Das wären dann nur noch 15 weniger als sich Porsche vom Achtzylinder erhofft. Nun, für die 61er Saison kommt auch der May-Motor zu spät. Im März 1962 geht es zu Tests auf den Hockenheimring, wo auch der Achtzylinder erprobt wird. Ein Test im echten Rennen und mit May am Steuer platzt, vor allem wegen einiger interner Querelen bei Porsche, in deren Verlauf der Schweizer das Werk wieder verlässt. Dennoch gibt es einen Renneinsatz. Der 24

Jahre alte Ben Pon, Sohn des niederländischen VW- und Porscheimporteurs, startet mit dem improvisierten Wagen in Zandvoort, rutscht aber auf einer Sandverwehung weg und beschädigt das Auto. Die beiden 787 werden 1964 verschrottet, der May-Motor kommt aber just in jenem Jahr noch einmal zu Ehren – im Elva-Porsche, aber das ist eine andere Geschichte.

Halbe Portion: Michael May soll dem Vierzylinder im 804 noch einmal Beine machen. Liegendes Lüfterrad, ordentliche Trichter und eine Bosch-Einspritzung kommen aber nur in Zandvoort zum Einsatz.

Spare Engine

Half measure: Michael May was asked to get more power from the four-cylinder fitted in the 804 chassis. With its horizonzally mounted fan, tall inlet tracts and fuel injection, it was used only once at Zandvoort.

In 1961, the four-cylinder was pressed into service due to the fact that the new eight-cylinder was still a long way off completion. But its days were numbered. When it became obvious that the team had to manage with the original "Fuhrmann" engine on its carburettors, Ferry Porsche called in Michael May. This Swiss engineer had received a lack of understanding, annoyance and even laughter for his spoiler-bearing Spyder some years earlier. Meanwhile he had worked on injection systems for Mercedes and he still drove racing cars. The intention was for May to give the unlucky 787 an adrenalin injection. He took a Bosch injection system instead of the Kugelfischer and put long plastic intake stacks on top of the re-engineered intake ports. This plus new piston crowns and a smart new arrangement of the injection nozzles turned the old 547 engine into a power plant capable of delivering 185 bhp, a mere fifteen horsepower less than the estimated 200 bhp of the long-awaited eight-cylinder. Anyway the May engine development came too late for the 1961 season. In March 1962 it was tested at the Hockenheimring – along with the eight-cylinder. A test in a real race with May behind the wheel was cancelled due to an internal quarrel at Porsche and the subsequent departure of May. Nevertheless the car was raced once. The twenty-four year-old, Ben Pon, son of the Dutch VW and Porsche importer, entered the car at Zandvoort. He lost control on one of the many places where sand from the dunes had blown on the circuit and skidded off the road, damaging the car too badly to continue. Both 787s were scrapped in 1964. At least the May engine earned some reputation that year in the Elva-Porsche – but that is another story.

Oranje außen: Gerhard Mitter wird im zweiten Auto von Beauforts Rennstall im Solitu-de-Rennen Fünfter.

Orange exterior: driving de Beaufort's second car, Gerhard Mitter finished fifth in the Solitude race.

seiner alten Nummer 01. In Zandvoort und in Rouen schafft er es jeweils auf den sechsten Platz und somit in die Punkte. Der Niederländer wird im Jahr darauf noch ein zweites Auto haben, weil er auch Schillers Wagen übernimmt. Eine gute Entscheidung, die sich als noch besser erweist, als er voll auf den Formel-1-Newcomer Gerhard Mitter und den in sein neues altes Auto setzt. Im Jahr nach dem Rückzug Porsches aus der Formelrennerei fährt Mitter den Vierzylinder beim Großen Preis von Deutschland auf dem Nürburgring auf Platz vier.

Der Niederländer scheint fast stur in seinem nicht nachlassenden Engagement mit dem immer unterlegeneren alten Porscherenner. 1963 fährt er selbst noch einmal Punkte ein, wird Sechster in Spa und in Watkins Glen. Er unterzieht sich gar einer Diät, um, wenn schon nicht den Wagen, so doch sich selbst noch ein wenig leichter zu machen. Längst ist der Privatier ein Routinier zwischen den Profis. Doch im Jahr darauf verliert er das Leben, als er sich auf dem Nürburgring erneut mit dem mittlerweile berühmten orangefarbenen Wagen für den Grand Prix qualifizieren will. Am 2. August erliegt er in einem Koblenzer Krankenhaus seinen schweren Verletzungen, und mit seinem Leben endet auch die Renngeschichte des 718/2.

Unterdessen unternehmen die Ingenieure noch einige Versuche, den Vierzylinder schneller und den 787 fahrbarer zu machen. So experimentieren sie mit einem liegenden Lüfterrad, außerdem gibt es Tests mit der speziellen innenumgriffenen Porsche-Scheibenbremse. Auf der Solitude erlebt Edgar Barth mit dem Auto eine Enttäuschung, zu weiteren Einsätzen kommt es gar nicht mehr. Also setzt Porsche alles auf die Karte Achtzylinder und schlägt ein neues Kapitel auf. Wir tun das auch. (jn) ■

Graf de Beaufort starb nach Sturz auf dem „Ring"

BILD 64   Köln, 4. August

Ein Schatten fällt über den so glanzvollen 26. „Großen Preis von Deutschland": Graf Carel Godin de Beaufort, Hollands einziger Grand-Prix-Fahrer, erlag in der Universitätsklinik von Köln seinen Verletzungen, die er sich bei einem Sturz im Training zugezogen hatte.

Graf de Beaufort hatte im „Bergwerk" auf dem Nürburgring die Gewalt über seinen alten Vier-Zylinder-Porsche verloren. Der Wagen überschlug sich. Der Holländer wurde aus dem Wagen geschleudert. Im Koblenzer Krankenhaus stellten die Ärzte einen doppelten Schädelbruch und eine Querschnittslähmung fest. Er wurde nach Köln transportiert und verstarb dort kurz nach seiner Ankunft.

Der 30jährige Holländer galt als ein besonnener, sicherer Fahrer. Besonders aber wurde von seinen Kameraden die heitere Gelassenheit geschätzt, die ihn umgab. Er kümmerte sich nicht allzuviel um seine Besitzungen in Maarsbergen. Sein Leben war der Motorsport. Sein Leben — und nun sein Tod.

Edgar Barth, der den blonden Grafen aus Holland unter seine Fittiche genommen und ihn zu einem Klassefahrer hatte reifen lassen zu diesem tragischen Todesfall: „Das kann doch nicht wahr sein! Das kann ich mir nicht vorstellen. Carel war das Leben in seiner heitersten Form selbst!"

Eine Saison, ein Sieg und ganz viel Pech

Die Karriere des 804 endet vor der Zeit –
Dan Gurney ist der Mann der Stunde – Ein Achtzylinder mit
Anlaufschwierigkeiten und die ersten GFK-Teile

Alles Tüfteln und Forschen und Testen bringt irgendwann nichts mehr – am Ende der 1961er Saison ist klar, dass der alte Vierzylinder zwar eine tolle Figur als Lückenbüßer gemacht hat. Es muss aber dringend etwas Neues her, will Porsche der fortgeschrittenen Konkurrenz Paroli bieten.

Die Formel 1 wird immer schneller, und wer da mithalten will, muss mehr bieten. Die Konkurrenz setzt aus gutem Grund längst auf Motoren mit mehr Zylindern. Die sind schlicht drehfreudiger, weil sie den Hubraum auf mehrere Zylinder verteilen. Dem Vierzylinder ließe sich mehr Leistung nur mit höheren Drehzahlen entlocken, weil an eine Hubraumvergrößerung wegen der Reglementierung nicht zu denken ist. Höhere Tourenzahlen aber würden den alten Motor ziemlich sicher seine Zuverlässigkeit kosten – sein größtes Kapital.

Was die Porsche-Leute nun auf die Beine stellen, lässt sich sehen. Es wird ein technisch anspruchsvoller und eleganter Achtzylinder-Boxer, selbstverständlich mit Gebläsekühlung und ein paar Schmankerln für Technik-Fans. Es steckt auch durchaus Potential im neuen Triebwerk – allein es will im Wortsinn nicht gleich anspringen. So sind es vor allem die Schwierigkeiten mit dem neuen Motor 753, die den 804 daran hindern, ganz vorn mitzumischen im Formel-1-Zirkus. Immerhin: Langsam, aber sicher bringen die Ingenieure der Maschine Manieren bei. Der

One season, one victory and lots of bad luck

The 804 project ended early – Dan Gurney was the right
driver for Porsche – the eight-cylinder got off to a slow start
– and the first fibreglass parts

All the tinkering and researching and testing on the type 547 engine simply could not perform a miracle. By the end of the 1961 season, one thing was completely clear. The old four-cylinder was acceptable as a stopgap but something on an entirely new level would be needed to conquer Porsche's rivals. Formula One racing was becoming faster and faster and anyone who tried to keep pace needed to offer more in the way of performance. The other teams had long since placed their bets on engines with more than four cylinders. These were able to use higher revolutions thanks to the fact that the 1.5-litres of swept volume was distributed among more cylinders. The Porsche four-cylinder could have been forced to rev higher, but it would certainly have cost it its reliability, which, up to that point at least, had been its most valuable quality.

What the Porsche people came up with to address this problem was an impressive piece of technical achievement. Their new flat-eight type 753 was a sophisticated and elegant design that featured, of course, air-cooling and some tasty titbits for the engineering connoisseur to appreciate. This engine did in fact possess enormous potential, but it sadly failed to realize this in the beginning of its existence. Thus it was that initial problems to deliver the performance expected from the new engine spoiled Porsche's hopes of success in Formula One.

Foto: Porsche

Da geht die Sonne auf: Das sind knapp 200 schlummernde PS in einem Anderthalbliter-Achtzylinder mit sehr vielen beweglichen Teilen.

Sunshine for a winner : this is a 1.5-litre eight-cylinder engine with 200 hp and many, many moving parts.

Hoffnungsträger soll es aber nicht alleine richten. Fehlt noch das adäquate Fahrgestell. Es wird gleichsam um den Achtzylinder herum konstruiert, und es wird für Porsche etwas geradezu Revolutionäres. Als im Januar 1962 Hans Tomala neuer Leiter von Werk, Versuch und Konstruktion wird, ist der 804, der Hoffnungsträger für den zweiten Jahrgang der 1,5-Liter-Formel, endlich fertig – fast: Ende Februar ist das erste Auto fahrbereit.

Im Vergleich zu den etwas eigenwilligen und pummeligen 718/2 und namentlich zu den recht improvisiert wirkenden 787 kommt der 804 schon fast als Schönheit daher. Gegen die superschlanken britischen Renner wirkt er zwar immer noch etwas füllig, die Linie aber ist klar, dynamisch und straff. Die Stirnfläche misst nur 0,72 Quadratmeter, fast die Hälfte geht auf Kosten der Räder. Die leicht nach unten gezogene Nase birgt hinter einer schmalen Öffnung den Ölkühler, hinten umschließen die Bleche oval den Motor und münden in eine fast scharfkantig wirkende Öffnung, aus der zwei der vier Auspuffendrohre weiter hervorragen. Schmucklos und wenig elegant sind wieder die beiden

Slowly but surely the engineers managed to teach the engine manners and extract adequate performance from it. But their great white hope, the type 753 engine did not have to make it entirely on its own since there was also a new, and for Porsche revolutionary, chassis frame that had been designed around the new eight-cylinder. When in January 1962 Hans Tomala became the new technical director of the "Versuch" (research) and design department, the 804, Porsche's great hope for the second year of the 1.5-litre formula, was almost completed and at the end of February it was ready for testing.

Compared with the somewhat peculiar and chubby 718/2 and especially to the improvised appearance of the 787, the 804 was a veritable beauty. If compared with the super sleek British racers it still looked a little portly, but the overall design was clean, dynamic and smooth. Its frontal area measured only 0.72 square metres, half of which was due to the wheels and tyres. The slightly dropped nose shrouded the oil cooler behind a narrow opening to admit cooling air. At the rear, the body panels fitted

Porsche quetscht übrigens doch einmal einen Vierzylinder-Boxer ins knappe Kleid des 804. Das gelingt so gerade eben, weil der neue Renner maßgeschneidert ist für den kompakten Achtzylinder. Hintergrund ist die Sorge, dass der nur mühsam das Laufen lernende 753 am Ende gar nicht gehen könnte. Für alle Fälle soll also eine Reserve in Form des ja gar nicht so schlecht im Futter stehenden Vierzylinders geschaffen werden. Dafür bedienen sich die Techniker des von Michael May präparierten Aggregats mit den langen Ansaugstutzen. Um das Triebwerk in den Rahmen zu bringen, müssen zwei Längsträger verlegt und gleichsam zwischen die Nockenwellengehäuse des Motors gequetscht werden. Eventuellen Stabilitätsverlusten lässt sich dadurch beikommen, dass hinter dem kürzeren Vierzylinder Platz für Verstärkungen bleibt. Dass der 804-02 mit dem May-Motor optisch mindestens so gestreckt daherkommt wie der erste Wagen mit Achtzylinder, verdankt er dem liegenden Gebläse, das den hohen Lüfterkasten des 547 ersetzt. Die vier Ansaugtüten sehen überdies viel frecher aus als die biederen Ansauggehäuse vom 01. Schließlich wird aber der 753 doch fertig und scheint viel zu versprechen. So kommt der Vierzylinder-804 nicht zum Einsatz, sondern erhält bald den neuen Motor. Mit dem startet dann Dan Gurney erstmals in Zandvoort – zur großen Überraschung des Publikums, das nach verdächtig langer Funkstille aus dem Werk schon fest mit dem Vierzylinderersatz gerechnet hat.

At one point, Porsche squeezed a flat-four engine into the narrow body of the 804. It was not easy as the new racer was tailor-made for the more compact eight-cylinder. The reason for this exercise was the fear that perhaps the slow-starting 753 could indeed fail to achieve its targets. Thus the reliable and reasonably powerful four-cylinder was considered as a reserve power unit for the new chassis should their fears be confirmed. The technicians used the engine that had been prepared by Michael May that was fitted with the Bosch direct fuel injection system. To make this engine with its ultra-long intake stacks fit into the chassis, the two side members of the frame had to be relocated and fitted tightly between the valve covers of the engine. In the event that the frame might have lost any of its torsional stiffness, there was sufficient space left behind the engine that could be used for reinforcement. This 804-02 was able to keep its sleek look because of the horizontally mounted cooling fan that replaced the bulbous vertical fan shroud familiar from the 718/2. On top of the engine cover, the four intake stacks looked much cheekier than the simple intake bulges of number 804-01. But finally the 753 engine was finished and its initial running was promising. Thus the four-cylinder 804 was never actually raced and the chassis of 804-02 was fitted with the new engine. With it Dan Gurney took the start at Zandvoort – surprising the crowds who were expecting to see him in the stopgap four-cylinder.

Foto: Porsche

Innenumgriffen: Der 804 – hier mit dem May-Motor – hat eigens entwickelte Scheibenbremsen an speziell präparierten Trommeln.

Porsche Design: the 804, shown here with the May engine, had specially developed disc brakes with the calipers inside them.

Sauger: Das zentrale Lüfterrad zwischen den beiden Ansaugbrücken hebt den Porsche aus der Reihe der Konkurrenten hervor.

Unique: the central fan between the two rows of air intakes on the eight-cylinder.

Abdeckungen der Ansaugstutzen geraten. Dazwischen fällt das filigran wirkende Lüfterrad mit seinen 17 Schaufeln auf.

Auffallend ist aber neben der völlig Porsche-untypischen Form vor allem das völlig Porsche-untypische Fahrwerk. Keine Kurbellenker mehr, keine Pendelachse, keine massiven Teile, vorn und hinten – oha – Scheibenbremsen, natürlich nach hauseigenem Spezialrezept, und selbstverständlich auch keine Drehstabfederung. Im Ernst? Von wegen! Nach den ersten Federbeineskapaden nutzt auch der 804 wieder die Elastizität langer Stahlstangen zum Federn. Man kann sie nur nicht mehr sehen, weil die Torsionsstäbe sich nunmehr komplett unter der Karosserie verbergen und obendrein längs zur Fahrtrichtung angeordnet sind.

Die oberen Querlenker übertragen die Auf- und Abbewegungen der Räder auf die waagerecht gelagerten Drehstäbe, die Stoßdämpfer sind fast senkrecht montiert und verschwinden zugunsten kleinerer Luftwiderstands ebenfalls unterm 25 Kilogramm schweren Alukleid. Hinten verlaufen die Drehstäbe

snugly around the engine and terminated in a sharply cut open stern with four exhaust pipes of which the two uppermost pipes protruded beyond the body. Again the intake bulges were simple and lacked elegance while between them the mesh-covered cooling fan with its seventeen vanes could be seen.

Besides the unique Porsche body design, the completely unique Porsche suspension also attracted attention. There were no more "Kurbellenker", no swing axles, no heavy parts, but there were double wishbones front and rear as well as disc brakes fitted all round that were made in the Porsche factory. As for the springs, the Porsche engineers had returned to torsion bars after their flirtation with coil springs and struts. The novelty was that they were hidden now by being fitted longitudinally and were completely covered by the bodywork.

The upper wishbones transferred the up-and-down movements of the wheels to the horizontally mounted torsion bars. The shock absorbers were mounted nearly vertically and, to

knapp unterhalb der oberen Ventildeckel parallel zum Motor. Die Radaufhängungen werden in den klassischen verschweißten Stahlrohrrahmen montiert. In den beiden seitlichen Unterzügen, den längsten der Rohre, fließt das Öl vom Motor zum Öltank im Bug und wieder retour. Ein Ventil öffnet oberhalb der kritischen Öltemperatur von knapp unter 90 Grad Celsius den Weg zum Kühler.

Der Rahmen bringt 38 Kilogramm auf die Waage und hat hinten einen demontierbaren Querträger, der den Motorausbau erleichtert. Radstand und Spur vorn, 230 respektive 130 Zentimeter, entsprechen den Werten des 787, die hintere Spur ist mit 1,33 Metern um sechs Zentimeter breiter.

Viel Wert haben die Ingenieure darauf gelegt, das zwangsläufig nach und nach kleiner werdende Gewicht des Sprits nicht zum Problem werden zu lassen. Liegt etwa der Tank im Bug, wird das Wagenvorderteil immer leichter, je mehr Benzin im Verlauf des Rennens verbraucht wird. Das kann sich enorm auf die Fahreigenschaften auswirken. Der Haupttank ist daher hinter und neben dem Fahrersitz untergebracht. Er fasst 75 Liter.

Die restliche Benzinmenge von 40 Litern passt in den vorderen Tank, der neben dem Öltank eingebaut ist. Auf dass im Wagenbug stets das gleiche Gewicht herrsche, sorgt eine elektrische Pumpe dafür, dass der vordere Tank so lange gefüllt bleibt, bis

reduce drag, mounted within the aluminium bodywork. At the rear, the torsion bars were mounted alongside and underneath the upper valve covers. The frame was made of welded steel tubes and the two lower lateral tubes served as oil pipes carrying oil to and from the engine to the oil cooler in the car's nose. A thermostatic valve opened the oil circulation when the temperature had reached the 90°C mark. The whole chassis frame weighed 38 kilograms and possessed a removable tubular element just behind and on top of the engine to facilitate engine changes. The wheelbase and front track were the same as on the 787, namely 230 cm (90.5 inches) and 130 cm (51.2 inches) respectively, while the rear track was wider at 133 cm (52.4 inches).

The engineers had made quite an effort to solve the problem of balance in the type 804. The longer a racing car ran, the lighter it became thanks to the consumption of the fuel. With the fuel tank mounted only in the nose of the car, the front end would become progressively lighter thus negatively influencing the steering characteristics of the car. To avoid this, the engineers placed the main fuel tank of 75-litre capacity behind and alongside the driver's seat. An additional tank with a capacity of 40 litres was mounted next to the oil cooler in the nose of the car. In order to keep the car balanced, the front tank was only brought into use when the rear tank ran short of fuel. In this way, the engineers

Anschauungsobjekt: Am unverkleideten Auto lassen sich die Radaufhängungen samt längsliegender Drehstäbe, das filigrane Rahmenwerk und die wegen des Boxers etwas breitere Auslegung gut erkennen.

All is revealed: with the bodywork removed, one can see the suspension including the longitudinal torsion bars as well as the delicate tubing of the chassis frame.

Foto: Porsche

Nach der Brigitte-Diät: Leichter, schneller und eleganter sieht der 804 im Vergleich zu seinem Vorgänger 718/2 aus.

Before and after: the 804 was lighter, faster and sleeker than the 718/2.

hinten das Benzin knapp wird. So soll die Gewichtsverteilung von 46 zu 54 Prozent so lange wie möglich erhalten bleiben.

Anfang 1962 wird es langsam Zeit. Ein Jahr zuvor hat Porsche den neuen Achtzylinder angekündigt, die gesamte Vorjahressaison aber mühen sich die Fahrer, mit den 718/2 Ehrenrettung zu betreiben. Aus dem Werk ist seither kaum etwas zu hören, von den regelmäßig erneuerten und ebenso regelmäßig verworfenen internen Absichten, alles aufzugeben, dringt nichts nach draußen. Mittlerweile geht die Öffentlichkeit davon aus, dass ein neues Auto, so es denn kommt, wohl eher mit dem bewährten Vierzylinder laufen wird.

Umso größer ist dann das Aufsehen, als am 20. Mai 1962 in Zandvoort gleich zwei 804 mit Achtzylinder am Start stehen. Bis zuletzt ist auch gar nicht sicher, dass sie überhaupt starten. Ferry Porsche hat verfügt, dass zumindest die beste Trainingszeit des Vorjahres unterboten werden muss. Das sind 1:35,7. Weder Bonnier noch Gurney kommen an die Zeit heran. Es liegt weniger daran, dass der Motor vielleicht zu wenig leistet, sondern am bockigen Fahrwerk, das die Kurvenjagd in den Dünen erschwert. Immerhin gelingt es Gurney schließlich, die Zeit knapp um eine Sekunde zu unterbieten. Er absolviert die Runde in 1:34,7, und Porsche gibt grünes Licht.

Leider ist die Konkurrenz viel schneller, der Erstplatzierte braucht nur 1:32,5. Bonnier ist im 804 nur um ein Zehntel

tried to keep the front-to-rear balance of 46 to 54 per cent for as long as possible in a race.

At the beginning of 1962, things were getting awkward on the public relations front. A year previously Porsche had announced their intention to build a new eight-cylinder but, during the whole of a season in which the drivers made sterling efforts to vindicate Porsche's honour with the 718/2, Porsche remained silent. Nothing was heard of the occasional attempts to stop the project or of the equally frequent attempts to carry on with it. As a result, the public had the expectation that if the new car ever started a race, then the well known four-cylinder would be the most likely engine to power it.

Thus it caused quite a stir when on May 20th 1962, there appeared at Zandvoort not just one but two of the new racers with the mysterious eight-cylinder. Until the very last moment, it was by no means certain that the two cars would race at all. Ferry Porsche had ordered that the cars at the very least had to be faster than the best qualifying time from the previous year at Zandvoort, which was 1:35.7 minutes. Neither Bonnier nor Gurney could manage that at first and the reason was not the new engine but difficulties with the suspension. At last, Gurney lapped one second faster than the crucial time. He drove 1:34.7 and Ferry Porsche finally agreed to let the two cars start the race.

Unfortunately their competitors were much faster and indeed the fastest of them lapped in 1:32.5 while Bonnier in his 804 was

schneller als im Vorjahr mit dem 718/2. Im Rennen hält sich der Amerikaner tapfer und schafft es mit Wagen 02, dem einstigen Vierzylinder-Ersatzwagen, auf die dritte Position. Dann löst sich der Schalthebel. Er muss in der Box befestigt werden. Nach der Zwangspause hat Gurney keine Chance mehr, am Ende hat er auch noch Probleme mit dem Schaltgestänge. Bonnier kämpft mit ungünstiger Getriebe-Übersetzung und beendet das Rennen als Siebter mit fünf Runden Verspätung auf die Spitze – und eine Runde hinter Carel de Beaufort, der nach wie vor im 718/2 unterwegs ist.

Nach der Enttäuschung von Zandvoort werden die Stimmen wieder laut, die den Abbruch des Projektes fordern. Offenbar ist es Hanstein und vor allem Gurney zu verdanken, der sich mit aller Kraft an der Vorbereitung des 804 für Monaco beteiligt, dass Ferry Porsche die Meldung für das nächste Rennen aufrechterhält. Dan Gurney hängt sich richtig rein und bringt den einzigen fertigen 804 in Monte Carlo auf den dritten Startplatz – und hat dann sagenhaftes Pech. In Richie Ginthers B.R.M. klemmt das Gaspedal, leider in Vollgasstellung. Der Amerikaner rammt einen Lotus und schiebt den mit Wucht ins Heck von Gurneys Porsche. In Belgien fehlt Porsche daraufhin. Wieder konzentrieren sich die Techniker auf Verbesserungen. Sie betreffen vor allem das Fahr-

only one tenth of a second faster than he had been in the 718/2 a year previously. In the race, Gurney drove bravely and finally found himself and number 804-02, the former four-cylinder car, in third place. Then the gearshift came loose and he had to come into the pits to have it fixed. He re-joined with little chance to catch up and finally retired with the gearshift inoperative again. Bonnier struggled with a poorly chosen set of gear ratios – he was over-revving in top gear – and finished seventh overall and with a five lap deficit to the winner. To top it all, he crossed the finishing line one lap behind Carel de Beaufort in his old 718/2.

After the Zandvoort debacle, the demands for abandoning the project were heard once again in the corridors at Zuffenhausen. Apparently it was von Hanstein and Gurney who managed to persuade Ferry Porsche to stick to the plan and enter for the next race at Monaco. Gurney threw himself into the exercise even helping to prepare the car himself. When he got to Monaco, he had his reward by taking the car round to qualify third fastest – Gurney, Bruce McLaren and Willy Mairesse all posted equal times and Gurney was actually fifth on the grid. However, that was to be the end of his luck for, at the first bend after the start, Richie Ginther's BRM had the throttle paddle jam wide open so that he hit the rear of Innes Ireland's Lotus so hard that it hit

Verpatzte Premiere: Der erste Einsatz zweier 804 im Jahr 1962 in Zandvoort geht völlig daneben.

Messed-up debut: the first race for the two 804s at Zandvoort in 1962 was not a roaring success.

Glückspilz und Pechvogel: Erst kommt Dan Gurney in Rouen nicht an Jack Brabham vorbei, dann hat der Lotus-Pilot Probleme mit der Hinterachse und muss an die Box – und Gurney siegt.

A lucky guy and a jinx: first Dan Gurney could not pass Jack Brabham at Rouen, but later the Lotus driver suffered a problem with his rear axle and had to go to the pits thus leaving the victory to Gurney.

werk. Es wird an mehreren Stellen verstärkt, dazu kommen neue Bilsteinstoßdämpfer und hinten eine Spurverbreiterung um zwei Zentimeter. Außerdem lässt Helmuth Bott die Cockpits umbauen. Im Porsche sitzen vor allem großgewachsene Fahrer viel zu aufrecht im Wind. So wird unter anderem der Haupttank modifiziert, damit die Piloten weiter nach hinten gelehnt sitzen können. Es folgen lange Tests auf der Süd- wie auf der Nordschleife des Nürburgrings. Herbert Linge und Dan Gurney fahren unermüdlich, bis dem Amerikaner die Rekordzeit von 8:44,4 auf der langen Nordschleife gelingt.

Das ist endlich einmal eine angemessene Vorbereitung, auch wenn noch immer nicht alles hundertprozentig gerichtet ist. Der nächste Renntermin ist Rouen, und der Tag dort endet mit Jubel bei Porsche. Auf der Strecke von Les Essarts erreicht Dan Gurney das langersehnte Ziel: den ersten Porsche-Sieg in der Formel 1. Wieder fahren der Amerikaner und Joakim Bonnier die beiden Renner mit den Fahrgestellnummern 01 und 02. Gurney, den die Grippe plagt, steht in Startreihe drei, der Schwede eine Reihe dahinter.

Im Rennen hält sich Gurney auf Position sechs. An seinem Vordermann Jack Brabham kommt er kaum vorbei, weil der auf der Geraden ein gutes Stück schneller ist. Dann aber schlägt das Schicksal gleich mehrfach zu, und stets zugunsten des Porschepiloten. Brabhams Hinterachse streikt, der Lotus muss an die Box. Vor Gurney fahren nun Graham Hill im B.R.M., dann Jim Clark im Lotus, John Surtees im Lola und Bruce McLaren im Cooper. Der Neuseeländer dreht sich, und Gurney zieht an ihm vorbei,

Gurney's Porsche with such force that it moved the Porsche's engine forward 10 cm (4 inches) and broke the chassis frame.

Thus Porsche did not turn up at the Belgium GP with the 804s. Again the technicians concentrated on numerous improvements especially concerning the suspension. The wishbones were reinforced to eliminate flexing, Bilstein shock absorbers were used in place of the harsher Konis and the rear track was widened by two centimetres. Also Helmuth Bott got the technicians to redesign the cockpit as he had noticed that the upright seating position in the Porsche exposed especially tall drivers too much to the slipstream. And Dan Gurney was 1.9 metres (6 ft 3 in) tall. Thus the main gas tank was altered to allow the driver to adopt a lower, more laid-back position. Then came a long period of testing on both circuits at the Nürburgring. Tirelessly Linge and Gurney drove lap after lap until the American reached the record time of 8:44.4 on the long Nordschleife.

For once their preparations seemed to be at least adequate even if not every problem had been fully addressed. The next date was the French GP at Rouen and that day in France ended in pure delight for Porsche. At Les Essarts, Dan Gurney achieved the goal of Porsche's first victory in Formula One. The American and his teammate Jo Bonnier again drove the racing cars with serial numbers 01 and 02. Gurney, plagued by a bout of influenza, started from the third row and the Swede from one row behind him.

In the race Gurney was running sixth behind Jack Brabham who was too fast for him, especially on the straights, and thus Gur-

Schade, keine WM-Punkte: Im Solitude-Rennen geht für Gurney und Porsche alles nach Plan, und der Sieg ist sicher.

Sorry, no World Championship points: at least at the Solitude race, everything went well for Gurney and thus Porsche's victory was a safe bet.

dann muss Surtees an die Box, und schließlich wird Hill vor einer Kurve gerammt. Das bringt nun Jim Clark nach vorn, aber der Schotte hat bald Schwierigkeiten mit dem Fahrwerk. Nun liegt Gurney auf der zweiten Position, knapp eine halbe Minute hinter Hill. Das kaum Glaubliche geschieht: Auch der offenbar angeschlagene B.R.M. wird immer langsamer, Gurney überholt und fährt den 804 möglichst schonend nach Hause.

Bonnier hat hingegen Pech im Rennen und kommt als Beifahrer wieder zurück. Gurney liest ihn in der Ehrenrunde dort auf, wo sein Wagen mit Schäden an Benzinpumpe und Schaltgestänge stehengeblieben ist. Dennoch wird der Schwede als Zehnter und Letzter gewertet.

Dass es mit dem 804 auch gegen intakte (und vorhandene – Ferrari fehlte in Rouen) Konkurrenz geht, zeigt Gurney bald darauf beim Solitude-Rennen. Jim Clark stellt zwar seinen Lotus auf die Pole Position, der Amerikaner überholt ihn aber im mittlerweile dritten 804 und gibt die Führung auch nicht mehr ab. Ihm gelingt sogar ein neuer Rundenrekord. Der nächste Grand Prix ist der britische in Aintree, wo Gurney wie Bonnier technische Probleme haben und Jim Clark im Lotus nicht zu schlagen ist.

Jetzt erwarten alle mit Spannung den großen Tag in der Eifel. Es steht der Große Preis von Deutschland an, und auf dem Nürburgring schafft es der unbestrittene 804-Star Dan Gurney erneut auf die Pole Position. Bonnier steht auf dem sechsten Startplatz und setzt im Rennen dummerweise auf Dunlop SP, weil die in der Aufwärmrunde auf noch nasser Strecke gut passten. Im Rennen trocknet der Ring dann, und alle anderen freuen sich über die neuen D12-Allwetterreifen. Der Schwede fällt gar auf den siebten Rang zurück.

Weiter vorn aber geht es hoch her. Die Pole Position verteidigt Gurney zunächst erfolgreich, bis es Graham Hill im B.R.M. in der dritten von 15 Runden schafft, vorbeizuziehen. Dass dieses

ney was not able to pass. Then fate played its part and decided that the Porsche driver would be the lucky guy of the day – and it did it more than once. First Brabham's rear axle went on the blink and his Lotus had to return to the pits. Leading then was Graham Hill in a BRM, followed by Jim Clark in a Lotus, John Surtees in a Lola and Bruce McLaren in his Cooper and then Gurney. The Kiwi got into a slide thus allowing Gurney to pass him. Then Surtees had to stop at the pits while Hill was rammed passing a back-marker, which put Clark up front. But the new leader was soon in trouble with his suspension when a front-ball joint failed and he had to retire. Now Gurney was lying second, about half a minute behind Hill. It seemed incredible, but the BRM was suffering from damage suffered in the earlier accident and was slowing down. Once Gurney had passed Hill and inherited the lead, it was enough to drive carefully to the finish especially when Hill was slowed yet further when his throttle linkage failed.

Jo Bonnier on the other hand was unlucky in the other Porsche and returned as a passenger on the winner's car with Gurney picking him on his lap of honour. Bonnier had experienced double trouble first with his fuel pump and then with his gearshift mechanism. Despite all that, Bonnier was still classified as tenth overall and the last finisher.

The next race at Solitude showed that the 804 was able to win against top competition as well as in the presence of Ferrari who had not been competing at Rouen. Though Jim Clark put his Lotus on pole position, Gurney, driving the now-completed third 804, passed Clark and then defended his lead successfully through to the end of the race. He also recorded the fastest race lap.

The next Grand Prix was the one at Aintree where Gurney as well as Bonnier suffered technical problems and Jim Clark was simply unbeatable.

Now everyone in the Porsche world looked forward to the German Grand Prix with eager anticipation. At the 'Ring, the

Foto: Porsche

Besser am Berg: Einen Rekord stellt Bonnier 1962 in Ollon-Villars in der Schweiz auf.

Success in the mountains: in 1962, Bonnier set a new record at the Ollon-Villars hill climb in Switzerland.

Manöver anschließend auch Lola-Fahrer Surtees gelingt, hat einen Grund, den außer Gurney bis zum Ende niemand kennt – der ihn aber scheußlich in Atem hält: Die Batterie, die vorn im Cockpit untergebracht ist, hat sich aus ihrer Befestigung gelöst. Nun muss der Porsche-Pilot nicht bloß auf dem höllisch anspruchsvollen Eifelkurs seinen dritte Position hinter Klassefahrern verteidigen. Nein, mit dem linken Fuß muss er obendrein die Batterie daran hindern, ihm zwischen die Füße zu kippen oder sich gar von den Polkabeln zu lösen. Es ist kaum zu glauben, aber der Parforceritt plus Balanceakt gelingt. Er gelingt derart gut, dass Gurney, Surtees und Hill die restlichen zwei Drittel des Rennens in pfeilschneller geschmeidiger Formation absolvieren. Der dritte Platz ist mehr als respektabel und das Rennen längst legendär.

Vor dem nächsten großen Rennen in Monza fährt Bonnier noch zweimal den 804-01. In Karlskoga wird er Dritter, und beim Bergrennen Ollon-Villars in der Schweiz stellt er mit einem Schnitt von 107,5 Stundenkilometern einen neuen Rekord auf. Doch aller Augen sind auf den Großen Preis von Italien gerichtet. Jetzt wird enorm viel Feinarbeit geleistet. Unter anderem experi-

undisputed 804 star, Dan Gurney, started from pole position while Bonnier qualified sixth. Sadly, the Swede made an unlucky gamble by choosing to race on Dunlop SPs because these tyres felt perfect on the wet track during the warm up. However, during the race the track dried out and everyone except Bonnier was happy with having chosen the new D12 all-weather tyres. Having started sixth, Bonnier was fortunate to only fall back one place to finish seventh.

Meanwhile among the leading group, a real thriller was in progress. The combatants were Graham Hill, John Surtees and, of course, Dan Gurney. Nobody knows how the race would have ended if the battery of Gurney's car had not come loose thus causing him to deal not only with the demanding track and his rivals but with the wandering battery which he had to restrain with his foot. At least he finished third which was, in the circumstances, a major achievement.

Before the Italian Grand Prix, the Porsche technicians again made a lot of fine-tuning on the 804. Among other things that they experimented with was a cooling fan that could be disen-

mentieren die Techniker mit dem auskuppelbaren Gebläserad, das eine Handvoll PS mehr bringen soll, sich aber nicht als nützlich erweist. Dann geht es an die Aerodynamik. Augenfälligste Veränderungen sind die großen individuell lackierten Radkappen, die das Auto aussehen lassen, als habe es Radscheiben. Erstmals hält glasfaserverstärkter Kunststoff Einzug in den Rennkarosseriebau bei Porsche. So bestehen bald die Nase und die Heckabdeckungen aus dem leichten Wundermaterial, das sich in praktisch jeder Form herstellen lässt und so erstaunlich wenig wiegt. GFK-Verkleidungen sollen auch die Querlenker strömungsgünstiger machen.

Vor allem aber sollen die Autos leichter werden. Grund dafür ist das vergrößerte Tankvolumen, dass den Einsatz in Monza ohne Stopp möglich machen soll. Der vordere Tank und jener, der bei der Cockpitveränderung zusätzlich an der Schottwand eingebaut worden war, wachsen um ein paar Liter. Das, sowie Rahmenverstärkungen und einige Modifikationen am Fahrwerk machen die Autos schwerer. Also muss anderswo Material weg. Überall dort, wo es nicht allzu sehr auf Stabilität ankommt, schneiden die Techniker Scheiben aus dem Metall, etwa aus den Lenkradspeichen.

Es nutzt leider alles nichts. An B.R.M. kommt in Italien niemand vorbei. Mindestens ein dritter Platz scheint aber möglich zu sein, bis Bonnier mit rutschender Kupplung auf Position 6 zurück- und Gurney mit fressendem, weil ausgelaufenen Differential ausfällt. Nicht viel besser geht es im Oktober in Watkins Glen aus. Gurney startet aus dritter Position, fällt aber wegen malader Ventilfedern auf Platz fünf zurück. Bonnier kommt bald vom neunten Startplatz aus eins weiter, rutscht aber auf Öl aus,

gaged from its drive. This idea was quickly abandoned as soon as it was proved to be unsuitable. The next thing to be looked at was the aerodynamics. At Monza, the cars were fitted with individually painted hubcaps that made the cars look as if they had disc wheels. And for the first time, fibreglass reinforced plastic was used for a Porsche racing car's bodywork. The nose and the rear covers of the cars were made of this miraculous material that was so easy to mould into almost any shape and was so fantastically light. Fibreglass covers were also used as streamlined covers for the wishbones.

It was decided that the cars had to be made lighter. Bigger fuel tanks made that a necessary operation before Italy as the Monza race was scheduled to be a non-stop event without pit stops for refuelling. To accommodate this requirement, both the front mounted tank and the fuel tank that had been devised during the reshaping of the cockpit grew by a couple of litres. All this plus some necessary reinforcement for the chassis frame meant more weight. But weight cost speed. So the technicians cut and drilled away non-essential material wherever it was possible to do so. Thus it was, for instance, that the spokes of the steering wheel first received their holes.

But it was all for nothing. In Italy, the BRMs were simply unbeatable. For a while, a third place seemed to be possible until Bonnier was slowed with a slipping clutch and then Gurney retired with a complaining differential after some of its oil had leaked out. It did not look any better in the USA at Watkins Glen where Gurney started from fourth place on the grid but then his engine suffered from broken valve springs. Bonnier started from ninth, reached eighth, but then skidded on someone else's oil and

Ohne Schnickschnack: Werbefrei, unverspoilert und schlicht steht der 804 im Jahr 1962 auf dem Nürburgring am Start.

No frills: lacking both advertising and spoilers, the 804 showed itself as a sleek racer at the 'Ring in 1962.

Startbereit in der Eifel: Beim Großen Preis von Deutschland steht Dan Gurney auf der Pole Position.

Ready for racing in the Eifel: Dan Gurney gained pole position in the German GP.

muss in die Box und findet den Anschluss nicht mehr. Ja, und das war's. Wenn nach diesem 7. Oktober 1962 noch einmal ein Porsche bei einem Formel-1-Rennen antritt, dann ist es entweder Carel de Beaufort im guten alten 718/2 oder kein reiner Porsche mehr, an dem bis auf die Reifen und ein paar Kleinigkeiten alles hausgemacht ist.

Es gibt kein offiziell verkündetes Ende des Abenteuers Formel 1. Allerdings tritt Porsche schon zum GP in Südafrika, dem letzten der Saison, nicht mehr an. Zwar wird noch eine Zeitlang weitergearbeitet an der Technik, die Entscheidung gegen den sündhaft teuren Einsatz in der Königsklasse aber ist gefallen. Porsche zieht sich wieder auf den Sportwagenbau und auf die Sportwagenrennerei zurück. (jn) ∎

damaged the car. He had to visit the pit and, though he re-started, he failed to catch up again and finished thirteenth.

Thus it came about that, after October 7th 1962, if ever there was a Porsche entered in a Formula One race, it was either Carel de Beaufort with his good old 718/2 or otherwise it was not a pure bred Porsche with everything, except perhaps the tyres and some minor things, manufactured in Zuffenhausen.

The end of Porsche's engagement in the great adventure of Formula One was never officially announced. Their retirement from this particular branch of motor sport became obvious when the Silver Arrows were withdrawn from the South African Grand Prix and then later their drivers released from their contracts. For a short while, the Porsche engineers carried on working on the cars, but the decision to withdraw from what had turned out to be a shockingly expensive essay into the world of Formula One was already made. Porsche went back to making sports cars – and, of course, racing them. (jn) ∎

Die Rennen

Chronik der Porsche-Renneinsätze in Formel-2- und
Formel-1-Rennen von 1957 bis 1964

Reims 1961.

Foto: Porsche

Reims 1961.

The Races

A chronicle of the Porsche racing involvement in Formula Two
and Formula One from 1957 until 1964

Nach dreijähriger Pause wird 1957 die Formel 2 wieder eingeführt. Sie ist als Nachwuchsklasse gedacht. Mit schmalen Regelwerk und der Begrenzung auf nicht aufgeladene und höchstens anderthalb Liter große Motoren ist sie fast wie auf Porsche zugeschnitten. Nicht einmal freistehende Räder sind vorgeschrieben. So fahren auch Spyder mit – und allen voran Porsche.

Noch vor dem ersten Werkseinsatz startet Umberto Maglioli mit einem Porsche 1500 RS beim Grand Prix von Neapel 1957. Das Rennen wird in Posillipo ausgetragen, dem wohl schönsten und exklusivsten Stadtteil Neapels. Den Kampf um den ersten Platz machen die Ferrari-Werkspiloten Peter Collins und Mike Hawthorn unter sich aus, sie kommen in dieser Reihenfolge auch ins Ziel. Luigi Musso, er pilotiert einen neuen Sechszylinder-Formel-2-Ferrari, sieht als Dritter die Zielflagge und lässt vier Maserati 250F hinter sich. Achter und Zweiter der Formel-2-Wertung wird Maglioli auf seinem Porsche.

Die Coupe Internationale de Vitesse in Reims wartet im Juli mit einem vollem Programm auf. Am Samstag erfolgt um 24 Uhr der Start zum 12-Stunden-Rennen für Sportwagen, sonntags werden um 14 Uhr ein Formel-2- und um 16 Uhr ein Formel-1-Rennen ausgetragen. Gerüchte in den Wochen vor dem Rennen, Porsche würde werksseitig mit einem RSK und dem neuen Einspritzmotor am Formel-2-Wettbewerb teilnehmen, bestätigen sich leider nicht. Nachdem drei Wochen zuvor ein von Umberto Maglioli gefahrener RSK-Spyder bei einem Unfall in Le Mans

After a three-year break, Formula Two was reintroduced in 1957. It was aimed at up-and-coming drivers, had regulations kept within reasonable limits and seemed to be tailor-made for Porsche thanks to its limitation to 1.5-litre engines without forced induction. Thus Porsche's Spyders were allowed to compete under these rules.

Even before the first works entry was made, Umberto Maglioli qualified with a Porsche 1500RS for the 1957 Grand Prix at Naples. The race was held at Posillipo, in maybe the most beautiful and expensive quarter of Naples. Peter Collins and Mike Hawthorn fought for pole position and they also finished the race in the same order. Luigi Musso in the new six-cylinder Formula Two Ferrari finished third and left four Maserati 250Fs trailing behind him. Eighth overall and second in the Formula Two category was Maglioli in his Porsche.

The Coupe Internationale de Vitesse at Reims came with a jam-packed programme. At midnight on Saturday there was the start of the twelve-hour sports-car race, on Sunday a Formula Two race got under way at 2 pm and a Formula One race at 4 pm. Rumours that Porsche would take part in the Formula Two race with an RSK with the new fuel injection turned out to be wrong. Three weeks before Reims, Maglioli's RSK Spyder was destroyed in an accident at Le Mans and the works thus refrained from making an entry in the Formula Two race at Reims. Much to the crowd's pleasure, French Ferrari driver, Maurice Trintignant, finished first in front of his fellow coun-

Fangio schon wieder Meister: Sieht aus wie ein herrliches Bild aus der Frontmotor-Ära. Ist es auch, im Hintergrund aber eilen zwei Werks-550 in der Formel-2-Wertung auf dem Nürburgring 1957 ums Eck. Barth gewinnt sie – und Fangio natürlich die Formel-1-Wertung.

Fangio champion again: this looks like a nice picture from the era of front-engined Formula One. In fact it is, but also in the background one can see two works Formula Two 550s at the Nürburgring in 1957. In the race, Barth won Formula Two while Fangio naturally won Formula One.

Foto: Porsche

Fotos: Porsche

Formel Kotflügel: Edgar Barth (Startnummer 21) und Umberto Maglioli (20) rasen am 4. August 1957 im Spyder durch die Eifel.

All-enclosed Formula Two: on August 4th 1957 Edgar Barth (21) and Umberto Maglioli (20) took part in the race on the Nürburgring.

zerstört worden war, verzichtet das Werk auf den Formel-2-Einsatz. Zur Freude der Zuschauer siegt der französische Ferrari-Pilot Maurice Trintignant vor seinem Landsmann Jean Lucas auf Cooper. Auf Rang fünf kommt der Belgier Christian Goethals auf einem Porsche 550 RS ins Ziel.

Einen Monat später erleben die Zuschauer an der Nürburgring-Nordschleife in mehrfacher Hinsicht Motorsportgeschichte. Juan Manuel Fangio holt sich an diesem 4. August 1957 nach furioser Aufholjagd den wohl eindrucksvollsten Sieg seiner Laufbahn und sichert sich damit seinen fünften WM-Titel. Im Feld der Formel-2-Rennwagen, die zeitgleich mit der Formel 1 auf die Reise gehen, befinden sich zwei Werkswagen aus Zuffenhausen. Porsche hat für Umberto Maglioli und Edgar Barth zwei 550 Spyder in die Eifel gebracht, bei denen der Beifahrersitz sowie das Reserverad ausgebaut sind. Eine weitere Änderung ist die schmalere Windschutzscheibe. Edgar Barth liefert sich ein hartes Duell mit Roy Salvadori auf Cooper. Im Gegensatz zu dem englischen Monoposto ist der Porsche den Nürburgring-Strapazen gewachsen. Salvadori fällt in der elften von 22 Runden aus und Barth kommt als Zwölfter der Gesamtwertung und Sieger des Formel-2-Wettbewerbs ins Ziel. Zwar hat Maglioli das Rennen mit Motorschaden in Runde 13 aufgeben müssen, aber der Triumph beim ersten Werkseinsatz ist für die Porsche-Mannschaft sehr ermutigend, in diese Richtung weiter zu arbeiten.

Während bis zum nächsten Werkseinsatz fast ein Jahr vergehen wird, tauchen Zuffenhausener Produkte trotzdem in den Formel-2-Ergebnislisten auf. So findet auf dem Stadtkurs von Pau am Ostermontag 1958 ein Formel-2-Rennen statt, das Maurice Trintignant auf einem Cooper des Rob-Walker-Teams für sich entscheiden kann. Der Franzose Auguste Veuillet und der Schweizer Heinz Schiller schlagen sich mit ihren privaten Porsche 1500 RS achtbar und belegen mit zwei Runden Rückstand die Plätze fünf und sechs.

Beim Großen Preis von Holland 1958 können die Piloten des englischen B.R.M.-Teams erstmals auf Podiumsplätze fahren. Harry Schell und Jean Behra kommen hinter Stirling Moss im Vanwall auf die Plätze zwei und drei. Während etwa beim Grand Prix von Monaco jeder Bewerber an der Qualifikation teilnehmen muss, sind in Zandvoort nur Teams am Start, die eine Einladung des Veranstalters haben. Ein Startplatz ist somit für alle anwesenden Piloten garantiert, natürlich auch für Lokalmatador Carel Godin de Beaufort, der mit seinem Porsche RSK vom letzten Startplatz aus ins Rennen geht. Mit sechs Runden Rückstand kommt er als Elfter und Letzter ins Ziel.

1958 ist Reims erneut Schauplatz einer Motorsport-Mammut-Veranstaltung. Neben dem 12-Stunden-Rennen für Sportwagen und dem Formel-2-Rennen steht bei der Coupe Internationale de Vitesse in diesem Jahr gar der französische Grand Prix auf dem Programm. Der Formel-1-WM-Lauf wird überschattet vom tödlichen Unfall des Italieners Luigi Musso, so dass auf dem Siegerpodest bei Mike Hawthorn, Stirling Moss und Graf Berghe von Trips keine Freude aufkommt. Das hat bei dem vor diesem tragischen Ereignis ausgerichteten Formel-2-Rennen noch ganz anders ausgesehen. Porsche stellt sich mit einem Werks-RSK, umgebaut zum Einsitzer und Mittellenker, der gesamten europäischen Formel-2-Elite, darunter Peter Collins im Werks-Ferrari und Stirling Moss sowie Jack Brabham auf Cooper. Der von Jean

tryman, Jean Lucas in a Cooper. Fifth was the Belgian Christian Goethals in a Porsche 550 RS.

A month later the crowds witnessed motor-sport history at the Nürburgring. On August 4th 1957, Juan Manuel Fangio gained the most impressive victory of his career, and ensured his fifth world championship title, after a rousing drive through the field to catch up lost time. Among the Formula Two entries that raced together with the Formula One cars were two works cars from Zuffenhausen. Porsche had entered two 550 Spyders for Umberto Maglioli and Edgar Barth. The co-driver's seats were removed from these sports cars as well as the spare wheels. Along with those modifications, a narrower windscreen was fitted. Edgar Barth fought a duel with Roy Salvadori in a Cooper. Unlike the British monoposto, the Porsche was able to make the most of the demanding Eifel track. Salvadori retired during the eleventh of the twenty-two laps and Barth came in twelfth overall and first in the Formula Two contest. Maglioli had to retire on lap thirteen thanks to engine failure. However, being triumphant with their first works entry in Formula Two encouraged the Porsche team to carry on down the road on which they had just set out.

The next works entry for Porsche was to be nearly one year ahead but cars made in Zuffenhausen regularly turned up in the finishing lists in the various Formula Two races. On Easter Monday in 1958, a Formula Two race was held on the city track at Pau. Maurice Trintignant finished first in a Cooper entered by Rob Walker while Frenchman Auguste Veuillet and Swiss Heinz Schiller both in Porsches finished fifth and sixth respectively, two-laps down on the leader.

At the Dutch Grand Prix in 1958, Harry Schell and Jean Behra gained the first places on the victory rostrum for the British BRM team. They finished second and third respectively behind Stirling Moss in his Vanwall. Whereas at Monaco, every participant had to qualify to be able to start, for the race at Zandvoort the teams were merely invited by the organiser. Thus all of the drivers got to start the race including of course local hero, Carel Godin de Beaufort who placed his RSK at the back of the grid. With six laps down he finished eleventh and thus last.

In 1958 Reims was again venue of a big motor sport event on July 6th. There was a twelve-hour sports car race, a Formula Two race and the French Grand Prix, the Coupe Internationale de Vitesse. The Formula One race was overshadowed by the fatal accident involving the Italian, Luigi Musso, who was killed when his Ferrari 246 rolled on the exit to the Gueux corner. Thus the spirits of Mike Hawthorn, Stirling Moss and Wolfgang von Trips on the victory rostrum were not as cheerful as they could have been.

Everything had been all right in the Formula Two race held before that. Porsche took on the whole European Formula Two elite, among them Peter Collins in the works Ferrari and Stirling Moss and Jack Brabham with their Coopers. Jean Behra drove an RSK with tailfins and with the headlights removed. The shape of the windscreen plus spats on the rear wheels and a covered filler cap improved aerodynamics. Already during the first lap, Behra took the lead. Just once Moss managed to pass him but then soon fell back again due to the fact that the

Fotos: Porsche

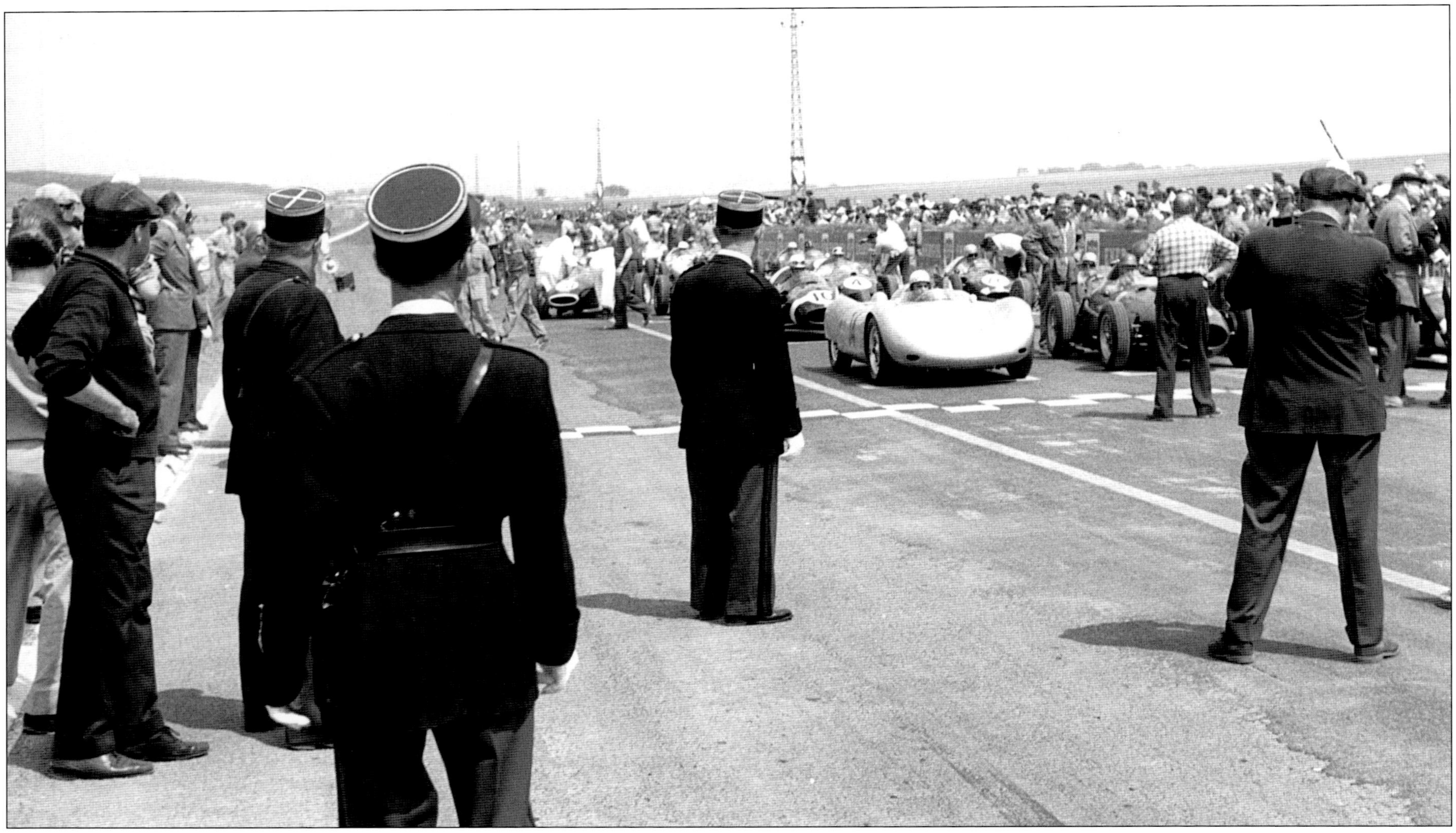

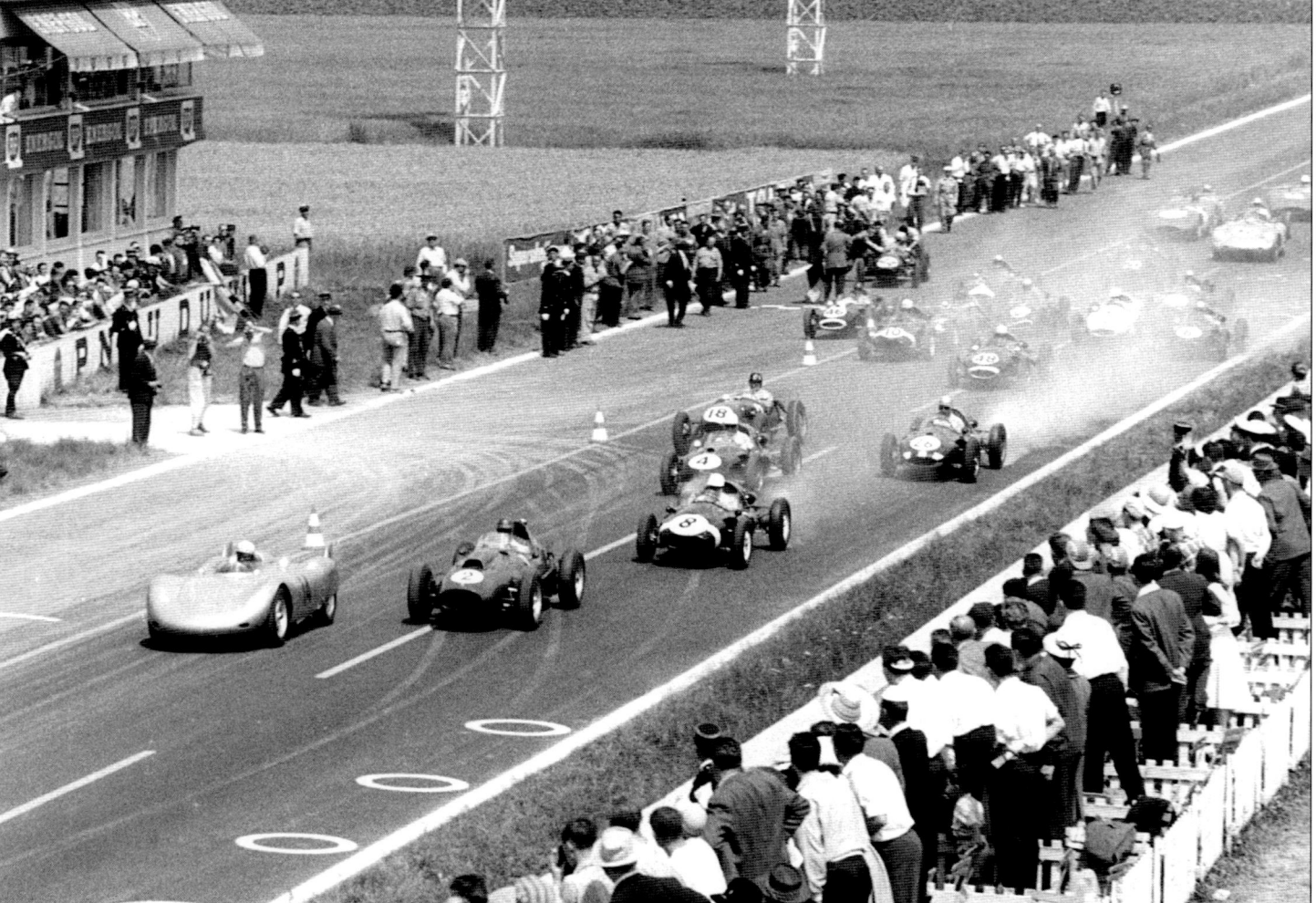

Sportwagen-Monoposto: Jean Behra am Start zur Coupe Internationale de Vitesse 1958 in Reims.

Sportscar against open-wheelers: Jean Behra at the start of the 1958 Coupe Internationale de Vitesse at Reims.

Gut weggekommen: Behra muss die Führung in Reims 1958 nur einmal kurz an Moss abgeben und siegt souverän.

Perfect start: at Reims, Behra had to give the lead to Moss only once and that for just a short time. Finally, he won the race in style.

Foto: Porsche

Man trägt Kopfbedeckung: Behra freut sich höchstwahrscheinlich mehr über seinen Sieg als darüber, dass er den härtesten Hut am Platz trägt.

A matter of hats: Behra was more likely to have been pleased about his victory than the fact that he had to wear the hardest hat of the day.

Behra pilotierte RSK ist mit Heckflossen und einer Fahrzeugfront ausgestattet ohne Scheinwerfer ausgestattet. Eine halbrunde Windschutzscheibe und die Abdeckung der Hinterräder sowie des Tankstutzens verbessern die Aerodynamik des Porsche. Schon in der ersten Runde übernimmt Behra die Spitze und muss sie nur einmal kurz an Moss abgeben. Nicht zuletzt wegen der aerodynamischen Vorteile des Porsche auf dem Hochgeschwindigkeitskurs von Reims muss Moss den Franzosen ziehen lassen und scheidet nach elf Runden mit sinkendem Öldruck aus. Auch Collins im Ferrari kann Behra nicht gefährden, mit 20 Sekunden Vorsprung fährt der Franzose den Porsche-Triumph sicher nach Hause.

Mit einem umfangreichen Rennprogramm wird am 27. Juli 1958 unweit von Clermont-Ferrand die neue Rennstrecke „Circuit de Montagne d'Auvergne" eröffnet. Erneut gewinnt Maurice Trintignant im Cooper von Rob Walker das Rennen. Claude Storez belegt bei der Trophée D'Auvergne in einem Porsche 1500 RS den fünften Rang.

Wie schon beim Rennen in Reims liegen auch beim Großen Preis von Deutschland auf dem Nürburgring Triumph und Tragik dicht beieinander. Dieses Mal wird das Formel-1-Rennen vom tödlichen Unfall des englischen Ferrari-Piloten Peter Collins überschattet, der am Pflanzgarten von der Strecke abkommt und gegen einen Baum prallt. Tony Brooks siegt auf Vanwall vor Roy Salvadori auf Cooper. Den parallel zum Grand-Prix ausgetragenen Formel-2-Wettbewerb kann Bruce McLaren im Cooper für sich entscheiden. Er wird hart bedrängt von Edgar Barth, der im Mittellenker-Porsche Zweiter wird. Der erneut vom Werk eingesetzte Siegerwagen aus Reims startet in der Eifel ohne Heckflossen und Hinterradverkleidungen. Zu Beginn des Rennens hat sich auch Carel Godin de Beaufort auf seinem 550 RS in der Spitzengruppe der Formel 2 halten können, fällt dann aber mit defekter Vorderradaufhängung aus. Erneut macht die

Zweiter beim GP in der Eifel: Die Formel-2-Wertung entscheidet 1958 Bruce McLaren im Cooper für sich, Edgar Barth (Startnummer 21) bleibt ihm aber hart auf den Fersen und wird Zweiter. Carel de Beaufort (18) fällt aus.

Second at the 'Ring: in 1958, Bruce McLaren finished first in Formula Two. Edgar Barth (21) finished second while Carel Godin de Beaufort (18) retired.

streamlined Porsche was able to pull away on the high-speed track. Moss also had problems with a lack of oil pressure. Collins in his Ferrari was no danger to Behra who, with a twenty second lead, ensured Porsche's triumph.

The new "Circuit de Montagne D'Auvergne" near Clermont-Ferrand was inaugurated on July 27th 1958. Once again Maurice Trintignant in a Cooper entered by Rob Walker was victorious. Claude Storez in a Porsche 1500RS finished fifth in the Tropheé D'Auvergne.

In the German Grand Prix at the 'Ring on August 3rd, the British Ferrari driver Peter Collins lost his life when he crashed into a tree. Vanwall driver Tony Brooks finished first in the race ahead of Roy Salvadori in a Cooper. Cooper driver Bruce McLaren won the Formula Two race that was run simultaneously with the Grand Prix. He was hustled all the way to the flag by Edgar Barth who finished second with his "Mittellenker" (central steering) Porsche. It was the Reims car without spats and tailfins. Carel de Beaufort in his 550RS stuck with the Formula Two leaders until a broken front suspension forced him to retire. Again the motoring press encouraged Porsche to carry on with the Formula Two programme. The German magazine "auto motor und sport" wrote: "One can imagine how much of a

Fachpresse dem Stuttgarter Werk nach diesem Rennen Mut, das Engagement auszuweiten. „auto motor und sport" schreibt: „Und man kann sich vorstellen, welchen Wirbel es in der Formel-2-Klasse geben würde, wenn Porsche einen echten Einsitzer bauen würde!"

Auf ein volles Programm können sich die Zuschauer des Großen Preises von Berlin am 21. September 1958 freuen. Neben zwei Gran-Turismo-Klassen gehen Sportwagen bis 1500 ccm und bis 2000 ccm an den Start. Das Rennen der Formel 2 ist zugleich ein Lauf zur englischen Meisterschaft, so dass alle englischen Spitzenfahrer in Berlin anwesend sind. Der jeweils zweite Lauf der Sportwagen und der Formel 2 wird gemeinsam über eine Distanz von 40 Runden ausgetragen. Neben der Wertung in den Klassen wird der Sieger dieses gemeinsamen Rennens den Großen Preis von Berlin erhalten. Porsche setzt seine Werkswagen zweigleisig ein. Während Jean Behra und Edgar Barth bei den Sportwagen bis 1500 ccm an den Start gehen, pilotiert der Amerikaner Masten Gregory einen RSK in der Formel-2-Wertung. Mit dem Ergebnis des Renntages können die Zuffenhausener durchaus zufrieden sein. Huschke von Hanstein gewinnt die GT-Wertung bis 1600 ccm, Jean Behra bei den Sportwagen bis 1500 ccm, was dem Franzosen auch den Großen Preis von Berlin beschert. Masten Gregory gewinnt die F2-Wertung und holt sich den dritten Rang in der Gesamtwertung. Pech hat de Beaufort. Er überquert im Rennen der Sportwagen bis 2000 ccm als Erster die Ziellinie, wird aber nach einem Protest der Scuderia Centro Sud disqualifiziert. Das Rennen ist für Sportwagen von 1500 bis 2000 ccm ausgeschrieben, de Beaufort hat jedoch nur den regulären Spyder-Motor mit 1498 ccm im Heck.

Ende 1958 wird das neue, ab 1961 gültige Reglement für Formel-1-Rennwagen bekannt gegeben. Es sieht folgende Eckdaten vor:
- Der Hubraum darf nicht kleiner sein als 1300 Kubikzentimeter und nicht größer als 1500. Aufladung ist verboten, und der Einsatz handelsüblichen Benzins ist vorgeschrieben. Die Güte des Kraftstoffs bestimmt die FIA, die Fédération Internationale de l'Automobile. Das bedeutet eine ROZ (Research-Oktanzahl) von 100, das entspricht der Klopffestigkeit von Flugbenzin.
- Die Autos müssen mindestens 450 Kilogramm wiegen. Gewogen werden sie in fahrfertigem Zustand, also inklusive Öl und Kühlmittel, aber mit trockenen Tanks.
- Ein Anlasser ist vorgeschrieben. Der Fahrer muss vor dem Start und nach jedem Boxenstopp den Motor mit Bordmitteln vom Sitz aus anlassen können. Die Energie – also etwa eine Starterbatterie – muss mitgeführt werden.
- Die Autos müssen einen elektrischen Hauptschalter besitzen, der entweder automatisch funktioniert oder sich vom Fahrer bedienen lassen muss.
- Der Fahrersitz muss derart gestaltet sein, dass der Fahrer Platz nehmen kann respektive das Auto verlassen, ohne eine Tür oder Klappe oder ähnliches öffnen zu müssen.
- Für den Einbau von Sicherheitsgurten müssen Befestigungspunkte vorgesehen sein. Der Gebrauch von Gurten ist allerdings nicht vorgeschrieben.
- Ein Überrollbügel ist vorgeschrieben. Er muss folgende Bedingungen erfüllen: Er soll den Kopf des Fahrers überragen,

stir it would cause if Porsche were to build a real single seater!"

On September 21st 1958, the crowds at Berlin were anticipating an exciting race programme. Not only were there two GT races for cars up to 1,500 cc and 2-litres respectively but the Formula Two race was also a round of the British championship and thus all of the British top drivers had come to Berlin. The sports car race and the Formula Two race were held together over a distance of forty laps. The winner would receive the "Großer Preis von Berlin". Porsche hedged its bets so that Jean Behra and Edgar Barth participated in the 1,500 sports car division, while the American, Masten Gregory, drove an RSK in Formula Two. The Zuffenhausen staff could be very satisfied with the result. Jean Behra won the 1,500 sports car class plus the Berlin Grand Prix, Masten Gregory won the Formula Two category by finishing third overall, and Huschke von Hanstein finished first in the 1600 GT division. De Beaufort was unlucky. In the two-litre sports car race he finished first but was disqualified after the Scuderia Centro Sud had protested his engine. It was a matter of a mere two cubic centimetres too few as the regulations had stipulated engines from 1,500 to 2,000 cc. De Beaufort's regular Spyder engine displaced only 1,498 cubic centimetres.

At the end of 1958 the new Formula One regulations for the 1961 season were published. The relevant parts read like this:
- Engine displacement should not be less than 1,300 cc and not bigger than 1,500 cc. Supercharging was forbidden and fuel from commercial pumps had to be used. The FIA, the Fédération Internationale de l'Automobile, would control the fuel quality. That meant an octane number no higher than 100 with the same rating as aviation fuel.
- The cars had to weigh at least 450 kg. They were to be weighed in ready-to-drive condition with oil and coolant but without fuel.
- A starter had to be mounted. The driver should be able to start the engine before the race and after each pit stop without external help and while being seated. The necessary power for the starter, the battery, had to be onboard.
- The cars had to have a main circuit breaker operated either automatically or by the driver.
- The driver's seat had to be constructed in a way that the driver was able to get in and out of the car without opening a door or hatch or similar device.
- Fixing points for safety belts had to be mounted although the use of belts was not compulsorily prescribed.
- A roll-over bar was obligatory. It had to reach above the driver's head and be at least as broad as his shoulders while he was seated in the car. The roll-over bar should not impede the driver in any way.
- The cars had to be open wheelers. No piece of the body should cover the wheels even when the steering wheel was turned fully to one side or the other.
- Dual-circuit brakes were prescribed. They had to be operated by one single pedal. In case of leakage or any kind of brake failure, as a minimum requirement, the front brakes had to retain their full function.
- The fuel filler caps were not allowed to project from the body. The filler neck had to be wide enough to allow ventila-

ihn aber nicht behindern, und er soll mindestens so breit sein wie die Schultern des Fahrers, wenn er hinterm Steuer Platz genommen hat.

- Die Räder müssen freistehen. Kein Stück der Karosserie darf sie decken, auch nicht bei voll eingeschlagenen Vorderrädern.
- Die Bremsen müssen ein Zweikreis-System sein. Bedient wird es über ein einziges Pedal. Im Falle eines Leitungslecks oder sonstigen Bremsenversagens müssen mindestens die Vorderräder bremsbar bleiben.
- Die Tankdeckel dürfen nicht aus der Karosserie herausragen. Die Öffnungen müssen ausreichend groß sein, damit bei Druckbetankung Luft entweichen kann. Die Tankentlüftung muss derart konstruiert sein, dass keinerlei Kraftstoff austreten kann.
- Im Verlauf des Rennens darf kein Öl nachgefüllt werden. Die Einfüllstutzen für Öl und Wasser müssen mit Befestigungspunkten für Siegel versehen sein. Ist ein Siegel am Öltank verletzt, führt das zur Disqualifikation. Die Siegel am Wasserkühler dürfen bei jedem Boxenstopp entfernt werden.

Porsche begrüßt dieses Reglement, ist es doch den aktuellen Formel-2-Bestimmungen sehr ähnlich. Vereinfacht ausgedrückt, sind ab 1961 alle aktuellen Formel-2-Wagen auch tauglich für die Formel 1, sofern sie freistehende Räder haben und mindestens 500 Kilogramm auf die Waage bringen.

Noch im Winter 1958/59 beginnen die Techniker in Zuffenhausen mit der Entwicklung eines Wagens, der in der laufenden Formel 2 Erfahrungen ermöglichen soll. Der neue Monoposto entspricht in seinem Aufbau im Wesentlichen dem Typ 718 RSK, dessen Produktion nun ausläuft.

Während die Porsche-Techniker Testfahrten auf dem Nürburgring vorbereiten, trifft sich die Formel-2-Elite am 25. April 1959 beim Grand Prix von Syrakus. Stirling Moss gewinnt das Rennen auf einem Cooper, der erstmals mit einem 1,5-Liter-Motor von Borgward ausgerüstet ist. Seine Durchschnittsgeschwindigkeit von 160,477 km/h liegt nur knapp unter dem Formel-1-Durchschnittswert vom Vorjahr, der 161,31 km/h betrug. Der Deutsch-Brasilianer Christian Heinz nimmt mit einem Porsche RSK an dem Rennen teil und belegt einen guten sechsten Rang.

In der Eifel schlägt für den Porsche 718-2/01 die Stunde der Wahrheit. Porsche-Rennleiter Huschke von Hanstein hat diese Ereignisse für die Porsche-Zeitschrift Christophorus beschrieben:

„Abstimmungen der Federn, der Stoßdämpfer, kleine Änderungen der Sitzposition unter Assistenz von Edgar Barth und Herbert Linge füllten den Tag voll aus, und als am Morgen des 5. Mai die Morgensonne eine fast trockene Strecke bescherte, startete Graf Trips zum ersten Probegalopp um den Ring. 9:47 für die erste Runde – 9:39 für die zweite (schnellste Porsche-Zeit bisher im Mittellenker von 1958 Edgar Barth mit 9:42) – 9:29.8 für die dritte Runde.

Da Herr Porsche uns mit einem ‚wenn ihr 9:30 fahrt, können wir auch über Monte Carlo reden‘, auf die Reise geschickt hatte, war nunmehr die Voraussetzung für ein erstes Auftreten des Wagens in der Öffentlichkeit gegeben. Nur wer jemals selbst einen Wagen für ein Rennen vorbereitet hat, wird ermessen können, welches Maß an Arbeit vom ersten Schnaufer eines neuen Wagens bis zum rennfähigen Einsatz für Monte Carlo noch zu bewältigen war, – und die 1000 km Anreise mußten ja schließlich

tion during fast refuelling. The tank ventilation had to be constructed in a way that no fuel should be able to come out of it.

- Topping up the engine oil during the race was forbidden. The filler necks for oil and water had to be provided with brackets for mounting seals. A damaged oil tank seal meant disqualification. The seals for the water-cooling system could be removed at each pit stop.

Porsche welcomed these new regulations as they were very similar to the then current Formula Two rules. Expressed simply, the existing Formula Two racing cars were just right for the new Formula One as long as they were open-wheelers and weighed at least 500 kilograms.

During the winter of 1958/59, the Zuffenhausen technicians started designing a car for the new formula into which they hoped to incorporate all they had learned from the current Formula Two. The new open wheeler's design essentially resembled the 718 RSK, which at that time was no longer being produced.

While the Porsche technicians prepared to test the car at the Nürburgring on April 25th 1959, the Formula Two elite met at the Grand Prix at Syracuse. Stirling Moss won the race in a Cooper with a 1.5-litre Borgward engine. His average speed of 160.477 kph was even slightly better than the average Formula One speed set during the 1958 race, which was 161.31 kph. Christian Heinz entered a Porsche RSK and finished sixth.

In the Eifel, the 718/2, as the Formula Two car was designated, encountered its moment of truth. Porsche's racing director Huschke von Hanstein wrote thus in the Porsche magazine "Christophorus":

"Nearly all of our time on the first day was taken up with tuning the suspension and dampers, and then small adjustments to the position of the driver in the car with the assistance of Edgar Barth and Herbert Linge. When on the morning of May 5th, the morning sun blessed us with a nearly dry track, Count von Trips started his first test run around the 'Ring. He recorded 9:47 for the first lap then 9:39 for the second (fastest Porsche time until then in the Mittellenker was made by Edgar Barth in 1958 who lapped in 9:42) and 9:29.8 for the third lap."

"As Herr Porsche sent us on our test mission with the comment that 'If you drive a lap in 9:30, we can talk about entering Monte Carlo' we already had the prerequisite for the car's first public appearance. Only if one has ever prepared a car for a race by himself can he imagine how much work had to be done from the first outing of a new car to achieve the race-ready status for Monte Carlo. And the 1,000 km journey from Germany also had to be achieved somehow. In the Porsche racing department, nobody slept much for the following two nights and every single man threw himself into the task to be able to present the youngest offspring of the house of Porsche at the Monte Carlo Grand Prix."

"The challenge that awaited us there was considerable as not less than twenty Formula One and eight Formula Two cars were entered in the Monte Carlo Grand Prix and they all had to fight for the sixteen best lap times in qualifying as no more than sixteen cars were allowed to race on the narrow, twisty track. Thus the members of the world's motor racing elite were all present even at the first practice sessions on Thursday. On

Foto: Porsche

auch irgendwie heruntergespult werden. Jedenfalls hat man in der Porsche-Rennabteilung in den folgenden zwei Nächten nicht viel Schlaf gekannt und jeder einzelne Mann hat sich wieder einmal voll eingesetzt, um den jüngsten Sproß des Hauses Porsche in Monte Carlo zu präsentieren.

Die Aufgabe, die uns dort erwartete, war nämlich nicht gerade leicht, denn nicht weniger als 20 Formel-1- und acht Formel-2-Wagen standen in der Nennliste für den Grand Prix von Monte Carlo und mußten während des Trainings um die 16 besten Rundenzeiten kämpfen, da mehr Autos auf der engen und kurvenreichen Strecke nicht zugelassen werden. Die Weltelite war daher schon beim Donnerstag-Training vollzählig am Start. Schon beim Freitag-Training erfüllten Wagen und Fahrer die in sie gesetzten Hoffnungen: Graf Trips konnte sich als 12. des Klassefeldes mit einer Zeit von 1:44,6 als bester Formel-2-Wagen klassifizieren. Beim letzten Training am Sonnabend wurde dann noch einmal von allen Fahrern und Werken die letzten Reserven eingesetzt. Die Zeiten wurden von Stunde zu Stunde schneller. Trotzdem konnte Graf Trips mit einer Zeit von 1:43,8 = 109 km/h seinen 12. Platz behalten, womit er sich in der Startaufstellung sogar noch vor McLaren und Graham Hill auf den neuen Cooper- bzw. Lotus Formel-1-Wagen sowie den bei den noch zum Rennen qualifizierten Formel-2-Wagen – dem Ferrari von Allison und

Raucherzone: Man qualmt noch so ungeniert wie in Werner Höfers „Frühschoppen", als es 1959 zu Testfahrten auf den Nürburgring geht.

Smoking area: in 1959 nobody complained when just about everybody used to smoke cigarettes during trials at the Nürburgring.

Friday the car and driver met the raised hopes of the team as von Trips managed to qualify twelfth within the elite field with 1:44.6 and best Formula Two car. In the final session on Saturday, the last reserves of all the drivers and of all the works teams were mobilized once again. Times were getting faster and faster from one moment to the next. Nevertheless von Trips managed to keep his twelfth position with a time of 1:43.8 thus positioning himself even in front of McLaren and Graham Hill in the new Cooper and Lotus Formula One cars, and in front of the other Formula Two cars such as Cliff Allison's Ferrari and Bruce Halford's Lotus. As a yardstick for this performance, it should be noted that in the years of the triple Mercedes Benz triumphs, between 1935 and 1937, Caracciola drove the best lap at Monaco with 1:46.5 and that in 1955 Fangio in a Mercedes lapped in 1:42.4 in practice. As evidence of the titanic struggle for

Erst in die Eifel, dann ans Mittelmeer: Ferry Porsche will gute Ergebnisse, und Trips muss zuvor auf dem Nürburgring zeigen, was der 718/2 kann, bevor er in Monaco starten darf.

First the Eifel, then the Mediterranean: Ferry Porsche wanted good results. Thus von Trips had to show the 718/2's performance at the 'Ring, before he was given the green light for a Monaco GP entry.

dem Lotus von Halford – placiert hatte. Als Vergleich mag dienen, daß in den Jahren des dreifachen Mercedes Benz-Triumphes 1935 bis 1937 die beste Runde von Caracciola mit 1:46,5 gefahren wurde, und daß im Jahre 1955 Fangio auf Mercedes im Training 1:42,4 erreichte. Als Beispiel, mit welcher Erbitterung um die Qualifikation gerungen wurde, mag die Tatsache dienen, daß zwischen den besten Formel 1 – Moss auf Cooper – und dem besten Formel 2 – Trips auf Porsche – nur 4.2 Sekunden Differenz lagen.

Damit war die kurze, aber brillante Karriere des Porsche Formel 2 aber auch fast zu Ende, denn im Rennen selbst geriet Graf Trips kurz nach der ersten Runde auf eine rutschige Stelle, prallte gegen die recht stabile Kaimauer und die beiden hinter ihm liegenden Formel-2-Wagen von Allison und Halford donnerten in ihn hinein, wobei alle drei Wagen stark beschädigt wurden, ohne daß gottlob einem der Fahrer etwas passierte.

Für alle Beteiligten war der Verlust des neuen Wagens äußerst schmerzhaft. Es existierte nur dieses eine Fahrzeug, weil es sich ja nur um einen technischen Versuch gehandelt hat. Immerhin konnte man sehen, daß wir mit unseren Aggregaten in der heutigen Formel 2 – der künftigen Formel 1 – mitmischen können. Von der technischen Seite gesehen verlief der Versuch positiv, von der Erfolgsseite gesehen müssen wir uns in Geduld fassen, nachdem unsere Rennabteilung bei der vielen Arbeit in der Hauptsaison kaum dazu kommen wird, diesen Prototyp kurzfristig wieder einsatzfähig zu machen."

Im Rennen fehlt ein zweiter Porsche, den Colotti in Modena weitaus eleganter verpackt hatte als die Porsche-Designer. Es ist das Auto von Jean Behra. Der Franzose hat einen RSK gekauft und ihn zum eigenen Monoposto umgebaut. Trotz der alten Pendelachse und des voluminösen luftgekühlten Motors kommt der in der Spur vorn wie hinten schmalere Behra-Porsche viel schnittiger daher als der Werkswagen. Ex-Maseratileute mühen sich, den Wagen noch rechtzeitig für Monaco fertigzubekommen. Leider wird nichts aus dem Renneinsatz, weil sich weder Maria-Teresa de Fillipis noch Edgar Barth dafür qualifizieren können.

Das Rennen in Monaco gewinnt der Australier Jack Brabham auf Cooper, der damit den Grundstein für den ersten seiner drei WM-Titel legt.

Das Echo in der deutschen Fachpresse fällt vernichtend aus. So schreibt Günther Molter in „auto motor und sport":

„Wir sind um eine große Hoffnung ärmer. Der erste Start des neuen Porsche-Rennwagens endete an einer Mauer der Sainte-Devote von Monte Carlo, bevor der Grand Prix des monegassischen Fürstentums überhaupt erst richtig in Gang gekommen war. Man kann dies dem kleinen Zuffenhausener Werk, das es gewiß nicht mehr notwendig hat, durch sportliche Erfolge für die Qualität seiner Erzeugnisse zu werben, nicht hoch genug anrechnen. Wir sind uns darüber hinaus bewußt, daß die Konstrukteure, Ingenieure und Mechaniker des Hauses Porsche sehr viel Begeisterung für die Sache aufbringen mußten, damit der Monoposto überhaupt noch rechtzeitig fertig wurde. Sie alle waren sich sicher klar darüber, daß es mehr als nur ein Rennwagen war, was da entstand: es war neuer Anfang schlechthin, ein Vorläufer und Versuchsträger für die neue, ab 1961 gültige Formel. Das alles hätte sich auch Graf Trips überlegen sollen, als man ihm den neuen Porsche anvertraute. Damit war ihm eine Verantwortung aufer-

qualification, the fact is that between the best Formula One car – Moss in a Cooper – and the best Formula Two car – von Trips in the Porsche – there was only a difference of 4.2 seconds."

"But the brilliant career of the Formula Two Porsche was shortly to come to an end as, in the race, von Trips lost control on a slippery part of the track and crashed into the extremely solid quayside. To make matters worse, the two following Formula Two cars of Allison and Halford thundered into him. The three cars were all severely damaged but, thank God, none of the drivers was hurt."

"To all persons concerned, the loss of the new Porsche was particularly painful. At that instant, only this one car existed as it was a prototype. But at least it was possible to realise that we were competitive with our cars in the current Formula Two – the future Formula One. From a technical point of view, the result of the appearance at Monaco was positive, while it is clear that from the point of view of obtaining success that we have to have patience since our heavily occupied racing department will hardly be able to make the prototype race-ready again for some time."

A second Porsche failed to start in the Monaco race. This was one that Colotti had tailored in a much more elegant fashion than that of the Porsche designers. The car was Jean Behra's. The Frenchman had bought an RSK and turned it into an open wheeler in his own style. Despite the old swing axle suspension and the voluminous air-cooled engine, the Porsche-Behra was much sleeker than the works car. Some of the former Maserati mechanics had worked hard to prepare the car in time for Monaco but unfortunately it did not race because neither Maria-Teresa de Fillipis nor Edgar Barth managed to qualify with it. The winner of the Monaco race was the Australian, Jack Brabham, in his Cooper. This was to be the season of the first of his three World Championship titles.

Articles in the German press on the Porsche showing at Monaco amounted to severe condemnation. Günther Molter wrote in "Auto Motor und Sport":

"Our great hope has been dashed. The first entry of the new Porsche racer ended in the wall at Sainte-Devote before the Monte Carlo Grand Prix really got under way. One's appreciation for the small Zuffenhausen firm is boundless and certainly they have no shortage of race successes. Nevertheless, we are aware that the managers, the engineers and the mechanics of Porsche had to summon up every iota of enthusiasm to get the open-wheeler ready for this race. All of them were well aware that it was more than just another racing car. It was a new beginning and, as such, a forerunner and a test bed for the new 1961 Formula One."

"All of this von Trips should have had in his mind when he was entrusted with the new Porsche. A great responsibility was placed on his shoulders and it turned out that he was not up to it. Without doubt it would have been better to let him drive in the Junior Grand Prix and instead invest some money to engage a top class driver, no matter whether he came from England or from America. Again it turned out that, in a Grand Prix, it is sport that really counts and it needs a mature personality matched to the obligatory driver's skills who does not lose sight of the main issue. Think of how many years Moss needed to

Foto: Porsche

legt worden, der er sich leider nicht gewachsen zeigte. Zweifellos wäre es besser gewesen, Graf Trips in Monte Carlo im Junior-Grand-Prix fahren zu lassen und nach der Mühe, die für den Bau des Monoposto aufgewendet wurde, einmal tief in die Tasche zu greifen und einen Fahrer der Spitzenklasse zu verpflichten, ob er nun aus England oder Amerika stammt. Es hat sich eben wieder einmal gezeigt, daß der Grand Prix-Sport das absolute Kriterium ist und neben dem selbstverständlichen fahrerischen Können vor allem eine ausgereifte Persönlichkeit erfordert, die keinen Augenblick das Gesamtziel aus dem Auge verliert. Wie viele Jahre hat allein ein Moss gebraucht, bis er das wurde, was er heute ist. Das sollte man sich auch bei Porsche in Zukunft überlegen."

Beim Grand Prix von Pau geht Jean Behra am 18. Mai 1959 erstmals selbst mit seinem Behra-Porsche an den Start. Der Franzose liegt nach dem Start hinter Masten Gregory aussichtsreich auf Platz zwei, als er in der dritten Runde einen Bordstein des Stadtkurses streift, was den Vorderreifen platzen lässt. Der fällige Boxenstopp dauert fünf Minuten, denn die Boxencrew ist nicht auf einen Reifenwechsel vorbereitet und muss sich Vorderräder an de Beauforts Box ausleihen!

Mit zwei Runden Rückstand jagt Behra dem Feld hinterher, holt noch eine Runde auf und belegt schließlich den fünften Platz. Maurice Trintignant profitiert von Behras Pech und gewinnt das Rennen auf einem Cooper. Wolfgang Seidel, de Beaufort und Christian Goethals werden von technischen Problemen an ihren RSK zur Aufgabe gezwungen. Nur der Amerikaner Harry Schell bringt seinen Porsche über die Distanz und wird am Ende Achter.

Nicht qualifiziert: Marie-Thérèse de Filippis tritt zwar in Monaco im Behra-Porsche an, schafft es aber nicht bis an den Start.

Not qualified: Marie-Thérèse de Filippis took part in the practice session at Monaco in 1959 but failed to qualify.

become what he is today. At Porsche, they should be aware of that for the future."

On May 18th 1959, Jean Behra entered his own Behra-Porsche for the first time with himself as a driver. At Pau it was looking good for the Frenchman as, right after the start, he found himself in second position behind Masten Gregory. Unfortunately in lap three he touched a kerb and a tyre burst. He lost five minutes in the pits. The pit crew was not prepared for a wheel change and, to top it all, had to borrow a spare wheel from de Beaufort's crew. With two laps down, Behra tried to catch up. He managed to make up a lap and finally finished fifth. Maurice Trintignant profited from Behra's bad luck and won in his Cooper. RSK drivers Wolfgang Seidel, Carel Godin de Beaufort and Christian Goethals retired due to mechanical problems. Only American Harry Schell managed to get his Porsche across the finishing line and did so in eighth place.

Local hero, Carel Godin de Beaufort of course entered his RSK in the 1959 Dutch Grand Prix at Zandvoort. During practice, the Dutch driver offered his car to Stirling Moss for

Beim Grand Prix von Holland darf Lokalmatador de Beaufort auch 1959 nicht fehlen. Erneut bringt er seinen RSK mit nach Zandvoort. Während des Trainings bittet der Niederländer Stirling Moss darum, einige Runden mit dem Porsche zu fahren. Nach einer Runde von 1:45,1 Minuten kehrt der Engländer an die Box zurück und erklärt, dass maximal eine um zwei Sekunden schnellere Zeit möglich sei. Mit 1:44,5 ist de Beaufort dann tatsächlich schneller als Moss, steht aber dennoch in der letzten Startreihe. Am Renntag wird der holländische Graf Zehnter, während sich der Schwede Joakim Bonnier auf B.R.M. über seinen ersten Grand-Prix-Sieg freuen kann.

Nach dem Unfall in Monte Carlo haben die Porsche-Techniker Trips' Auto wieder aufgebaut, es wird bei der Coupe de Vitesse am 5. Juli 1959 in Reims eingesetzt. Als Pilot haben die Schwaben den frischgebackenen Grand-Prix-Sieger Joakim Bonnier aus Schweden verpflichtet. Er hat aber Probleme mit schwer atmenden Vergasern.

Graf Trips geht auf einem Werks-RSK mit der Fahrgestellnummer 718 007 an den Start. Der Wagen ähnelt Behras Siegerwagen des Vorjahres, hat aber eine höhere Windschutzscheibe und kleine Lufteinlassschlitze an der Vorderseite der Heckauswölbungen. Colin Davis pilotiert den RSK von Jean Behra. Es ist eines von vier Autos, die das Werk in jenem Jahr auf Kundenwunsch mit Halterungen für Pedale und Lenkung in Mittelposition versieht. Weitere Käufer sind Wolfgang Seidel, Christian Goethals und Carel de Beaufort.

Seinen Formel-2-Porsche vertraut Behra Hans Herrmann an, der den Wagen auf den dritten Startplatz stellt. Das Rennen entwickelt sich zu einem spannenden Zweikampf zwischen

a trial run. After having lapped it in 1:45.1 the Briton returned to the pits and proclaimed that it would not be possible to drive more than two seconds faster. De Beaufort in fact was faster than Moss and did a lap in 1:44.5. At least that meant a position on the last row of the grid. In the race, de Beaufort finished tenth while Swede, Jo Bonnier, enjoyed his first GP victory with his BRM P25.

After the Monte Carlo accident the Porsche technicians had successfully rebuilt von Trips's car. It was then entered in the Coupe de Vitesse at Reims on July 5th 1959. The driver on this occasion was the newly distinguished race-winner, Jo Bonnier. Unfortunately the car suffered from difficulties with its carburettor and air supply. Von Trips took the start in a works RSK with serial number 718 007. The car resembled the previous year's victorious Behra racer though it featured a higher windscreen plus little vents on the front of the rear bulges. Colin Davis drove Behra's RSK. It was one of four cars that Porsche had modified in accordance with customers' wishes. They were fitted with adjustable brackets for the pedals and a central steering position. The other customers were Wolfgang Seidel, Christian Goethals and Carel Godin de Beaufort.

Behra entrusted his Formula Two Porsche to Hans Herrmann who qualified third. The race soon turned into a duel between Stirling Moss (Cooper) and Herrmann in the Behra-Porsche. The man from Stuttgart led the race initially but finally had to admit defeat. One thing to cheer up the German contingent was the fact that a Borgward engine powered Moss's Cooper. Bonnier finished third just a minute down, and von Trips fifth.

Brausen: Lokalmatador de Beaufort unterm knalligen Limonadenplakat wird 1958 in Zandvoort mit dem RSK Elfter.

Local hero: RSK driver, Godin de Beaufort, finished eleventh in his home race at Zandvoort in 1958.

Stirling Moss auf Cooper und Herrmann im Behra-Porsche. Der Stuttgarter liegt sogar zeitweise in Führung, muss sich aber am Ende knapp geschlagen geben. Aus deutscher Sicht ein kleiner Trost: Der Cooper von Stirling Moss wird auf seiner Siegesfahrt wieder von einem Borgward-Motor angetrieben. Erfreulich auch die Platzierungen der Werks-Piloten. Mit einer knappen Minute Rückstand kommt Bonnier als Dritter ins Ziel, Graf Trips wird Fünfter.

Im Training zum Grand Prix von Rouen-Les-Essarts 1959 kann sich Hans Herrmann im Behra-Porsche zwar die Pole Position sichern und zu Beginn des Rennens auch in der Spitzengruppe halten, aber in der siebten Runde wird er durch einen Getriebeschaden gestoppt. Damit ist der Weg frei für Stirling Moss, der auf seinem Cooper-Borgward mit einer halben Minute Vorsprung vor Harry Schell die Ziellinie überquert.

Der diesjährige Grand Prix der Avergne wird am 26. Juli 1959 auf dem neuen Kurs von Clermont-Ferrand ausgetragen. Der

At Rouen-Les Essarts, Herrmann in the Behra-Porsche started from pole position but on lap seven he retired with gearbox failure. So Stirling Moss had a clear run and, with his Cooper-Borgward, finished half a minute ahead of Harry Schell.

The Auvergne Grand Prix was held on July 26th 1959 on the new track near Clermont-Ferrand. It had been opened just two years previously and the drivers called it the "little Nürburgring". Again Jean Behra drove his Formula Two Porsche, cut a fine figure and, yet again, was deprived of the fruits of his labour. First he got a bad start and finished the first lap in seventh position. But then he gradually caught up, passing one competitor after the other until he was only eleven seconds down on the leader, Stirling Moss. Then mechanical problems forced him into pit lane where repairs cost him ten minutes and that was that. Thus Moss drove unhindered to another victory in his Cooper-Borgward. Behra finished twelfth while de Beaufort in

Variationen eines Themas: In Reims waren 1959 außer dem Behra-Porsche, den Hans Herrmann fuhr, zwei RSK und ein 718/2 am Start. Trips wurde im voll karossierten Wagen mit der Nummer 42 Fünfter, Bonnier im 718/2 (44) wurde Dritter.

Variations on a theme: in 1959, two RSK and a 718/2 were entered at Reims besides the Behra-Porsche in which Hans Herrmann finished second. Von Trips finished fifth in the RSK number 42 while Bonnier came in third in the open-wheeler number 44.

Sieht schnell aus, war auch schnell: Hans Herrmann im Behra-Porsche wurde 1959 Zweiter in Reims.

Looks fast, was fast: in 1959 Hans Herrmann finished second in the Behra-Porsche at Reims.

von den Fahrern auch gerne als „kleiner Nürburgring" bezeichnete Kurs war erst zwei Jahre zuvor eröffnet worden. Jean Behra fährt erneut seinen Formel-2-Porsche, setzt sich damit groß in Szene und wird, wieder einmal, um die Früchte seiner Arbeit gebracht. Nach einem schlechten Start kommt er als Siebter aus der Startrunde und überholt in den folgenden Runden einen Konkurrenten nach dem anderen, bis er nur noch elf Sekunden hinter dem führenden Stirling Moss liegt. Technische Probleme zwingen den Franzosen in der 15. Runde an die Box. Sein Stopp dauert zehn Minuten, was ihm natürlich alle Chancen auf eine gute Platzierung nimmt. Stirling Moss fährt so ungefährdet zu einem weiteren Sieg im Cooper-Borgward, Behra wird Zwölfter. De Beaufort kommt mit seinem RSK nicht in die Wertung. Überschattet wird das Rennen durch zwei schwere Unfälle. Bruce Halford aus England zieht sich einen Beckenbruch zu, sein Landsmann Ivor Bueb erliegt eine Woche später den schweren Kopfverletzungen, die er sich bei seinem Sturz zugezogen hatte.

Der Große Preis von Deutschland findet 1959 erstmals seit 1926 wieder auf der Berliner Avus statt. Der veranstaltende Automobilclub von Deutschland (AvD) will auf diese Weise die

his RSK was not classified. The race was over-shadowed by two severe accidents in the first of which Bruce Halford broke his pelvis, while in the second, his countryman Ivor Bueb sustained severe head injuries and died one week after the race.

For the first time since 1926, the German Grand Prix of 1959 was held at the Berlin Avus track. The promoter was the Automobilclub von Deutschland (AvD). By using Avus, the club saved the enormous track fee for the Nürburgring and could confidently expect more spectators, especially in the case of bad weather. Last but not least, they enjoyed a guarantee of 50,000 Marks to cover any loss offered by the city of Berlin. Entered in the Formula One race were Jean Behra with his homemade Porsche and von Trips in a works 718. The car looked slightly different here as it had new vents and the mirrors were mounted onto the windscreen. For the first time the car carried the Porsche name on its body. Unfortunately the Grand Prix, which was won by Tony Brooks with a Ferrari, was held without either of these two drivers. Both von Trips and Behra participated in a sports car race held prior to the Grand Prix. It had rained and in the banked turn, Behra got into a skid

Fotos: Porsche

Die Avus-Tragödie: Nachdem Jean Behra tags zuvor im Sportwagenrennen bis 1500 ccm ums Leben gekommen ist, zieht Porsche die Nennung für den Großen Preis von Deutschland, der 1959 in Berlin ausgetragen wird, zurück. Trips (14) geht nicht an den Start.

The Avus tragedy: after Jean Behra was killed in an accident during the preceding sports car race, Porsche cancelled its entry for the German GP which was held at Berlin in 1959 which meant that von Trips (14) did not race.

hohen Kosten für die Streckenmiete des Nürburgrings umgehen, rechnet in Berlin, gerade bei schlechtem Wetter, mit mehr Zuschauern und freut sich zudem über eine Ausfallbürgschaft der Stadt über 50.000 Mark. Für das Formel-1-Rennen sind auch Jean Behra mit seinem Porsche-Eigenbau und Graf Trips im Werks-718 gemeldet. Am Werkswagen sind beide Lufteinlässe verändert und die Rückspiegel an die Windschutzscheibe verlegt worden. Erstmals ziert der Porsche-Schriftzug den Wagen. Leider geht der Grand Prix, den Tony Brooks auf Ferrari gewinnt, ohne diese beiden Fahrer über die Bühne. Sowohl Trips als auch Behra nehmen an dem zum Rahmenprogramm gehörenden Sportwagenrennen um den Großen Preis von Berlin teil. Während dieses Wettbewerbs kommt Behra mit seinem RSK in der regennassen Steilkurve ins Schleudern, dreht sich mehrfach und prallt mit dem Porsche gegen einen Betonsockel. Dabei wird der Franzose aus seinem Wagen und gegen einen Fahnenmast geschleudert. Er ist sofort tot. Graf Trips gewinnt das Sportwagenrennen. Als nach dem Zieleinlauf das volle Ausmaß der Tragödie bekannt wird, zieht Porsche die Nennung für den Grand Prix zurück.

Im englischen Brands Hatch schickt Porsche den 718 Ende August in den letzten Werkseinsatz des Jahres 1959. Joakim Bonnier soll beim Kentish 100 im Vergleich mit der europäischen Elite noch einmal eine Standortbestimmung vornehmen. Er kommt hinter Jack Brabham (Cooper), Graham Hill (Lotus) und Stirling

Ein Porsche in Berlin: Trips im leicht modifizierten 718/2 auf der Avus.

A Porsche at Berlin: Von Trips in the slightly modified 718/2 on the Avus.

and crashed into a concrete post. The Frenchman was thrown out of his car and against a flagpole. He was killed instantly. When the race was finished and the full scale of the tragedy became clear, Porsche withdrew its entry from the Grand Prix.

The last works entry from Porsche in 1959 was at a non-championship race at Brands Hatch. Jo Bonnier faced Europe's top drivers in the Kentish 100.

He finished behind Jack Brabham (Cooper), Graham Hill (Lotus) and Stirling Moss (Cooper-Borgward). This was not at all a poor result considering that the 718 was still approximately 50 kg overweight and probably needed between fifteen and twenty more horsepower to put it on a par with its British-made competition.

There was no Formula Two race when the Tourist Trophy was held at Goodwood one week later. However the 718 was still in the race truck of the Porsche team so Stirling Moss was invited to try the car and he surprised them all by lapping in 1:29.6. That was faster than his own Formula Two track record

Foto: Porsche

Moss (Cooper-Borgward) auf Rang vier. Fazit des Einsatzes: Der 718 ist noch um rund 50 Kilogramm zu schwer oder brauchte 15 bis 20 PS mehr, um gegen die britischen Konstruktionen bestehen zu können.

Bei der Tourist Trophy in Goodwood steht eine Woche später zwar kein Formel-2-Rennen auf dem Programm. Dennoch hat das Porsche-Team den 718 vom Renneinsatz des vorhergehenden Wochenendes noch im Transporter. Stirling Moss bekommt die Gelegenheit zu einem Test und überrascht mit einer Rundenzeit von 1:29,6 Minuten. Damit unterbietet er seinen eigenen F2-Rundenrekord von 1:30,0 Minuten und ist nur geringfügig langsamer als die Formel 1, deren Bestzeit bei 1:28,8 liegt.

Am 23. September 1959 sind drei Porsche RSK für den Formel-2-Lauf beim Flugplatzrennen in Zeltweg gemeldet: Porsche Österreich schickt Lokalmatador Ernst Vogel ins Rennen, Wolfgang Seidel startet unter eigener Bewerbung und Carel de Beaufort für sein eigenes Team. Schon im Training wird deutlich, dass die Porsche-Piloten nicht ernsthaft um den Sieg kämpfen können. Fast zwei Sekunden trennen sie von der Pole Position. Während Seidel ausfällt und de Beaufort als Sechster ins Ziel kommt, überrascht Ernst Vogel mit einem phantastischen Rennen. Mit nur 19 Sekunden Rückstand wird er Dritter und lässt sogar Lucien Bianchi hinter sich, der auf seinem Cooper die schnellste Runde des Rennens fährt.

Nachdem aus Testfahrten auf dem Nürburgring im September nichts wird, erprobt Porsche den 718/2 in Hockenheim. Mit at the circuit of 1:30.0 and only slightly slower than the Formula One record there of 1:28.8.

On September 23rd, 1959, three Porsche RSKs were entered for the Formula Two race at Zeltweg at Austria. Porsche-Austria's driver was local hero Ernst Vogel. Wolfgang Seidel started for the Scuderia Colonia and Carel Godin de Beaufort entered his own car. During the practice, it became obvious that the Porsche drivers were going to be uncompetitive as they were two seconds down on the pole position time. Seidel retired and de Beaufort finished sixth. Only Vogel drove impressively. With just nineteen seconds down on the leaders, he finished third overall and at one point even passed Lucien Bianchi who drove the fastest lap of the race in his Cooper.

September testing on the Nürburgring was cancelled and so Porsche went to Hockenheim instead. Woollen threads attached to the rear of the car were used to analyse its aerodynamic qualities. Edgar Barth and Hans Herrmann did the driving accompanied by von Hanstein, Hubert Mimler, Zora Arkus-Duntov and Heinz Ulrich Wieselmann.

Among the nineteen drivers who took at the start of the USA Grand Prix at Sebring in December was one with a Porsche. The American, Harry Blanchard, started from sixteenth position on the grid and finished seventh overall thanks to a whole string of retirements. He was four minutes down on New Zealander, Bruce McLaren in a Cooper T51-Climax, who gained his first Grand Prix victory at this race.

Wollfäden am Heck werden Strömungsversuche unternommen. Neben Edgar Barth und Hans Herrmann kommen auch von Hanstein, Hubert Mimler, Zora Arkus-Duntov und Heinz Ulrich Wieselmann zum Einsatz.

Unter den 19 Fahrern, die im Dezember in Sebring am Start zum Großen Preis der USA stehen, befindet sich mit dem Amerikaner Harry Blanchard auch ein Porsche-Pilot. Er geht vom 16. Startplatz ins Rennen und wird, begünstigt durch zahlreiche Ausfälle, am Ende sogar Siebter. Sein Rückstand auf den Neuseeländer Bruce McLaren, der in Sebring seinen ersten Grand-Prix-Sieg holt, beträgt fast vier Minuten.

Auf einer Pressekonferenz in München informiert Porsche-Rennleiter Huschke von Hanstein über die personelle Zusammensetzung des Porsche-Teams für die Saison 1960. Graham Hill, Joakim Bonnier und Edgar Barth sind für die Sportwageneinsätze sowie für einige Formel-2-Rennen vorgesehen. Zudem sind gelegentliche Einsätze von Stirling Moss geplant. Damit entspricht Porsche im Grunde genommen genau den Empfehlungen, die nach dem Großen Preis von Monaco 1959 und dem Unfall von Graf Trips geäußert worden waren.

Nun aber stellt die „auto motor und sport" fest: „In dieser Diskussion tauchte natürlich auch die Frage auf, warum man bei Porsche sich nicht intensiver mit dem deutschen Nachwuchs beschäftige und stets ausländische Fahrer engagiere."

Im Winter 1959/60 wird ein zweiter Prototyp gebaut, und für die Saison 1960 sollen insgesamt vier weitere Fahrzeuge (718/2-02 bis 05) entstehen.

Bei Testfahrten mit dem noch unlackierten Fahrzeug (718/2-01) in Hockenheim sind wieder Wollfäden aufs Heck geklebt,

In a press conference in Munich, Porsche racing director Huschke von Hanstein introduced the works team for the coming 1960 season. Graham Hill, Jo Bonnier and Edgar Barth were chosen to drive in the sports car races plus some Formula Two races. It was announced that Stirling Moss would occasionally drive for Porsche. All this met more or less the recommendations that had been made in the press after the Monaco Grand Prix and von Trips's crash. But it could not satisfy everyone. This time "Auto Motor und Sport" still had a complaint: "The question arises in this matter why Porsche does not pay enough attention to German up-and-coming drivers and instead hires foreign drivers."

During the winter of 1959/1960, a second prototype was built and it was planned to make four more for the 1960 season. These were to be numbers 718/02 through to 718/05.

Again for testing at Hockenheim, more woollen threads were mounted to the still unpainted original car. In addition, the mechanics mounted a pressure gauge in front of the rear vents. While Hubert Mimler was driving round Hockenheim, Rob Walker's chief mechanic, Alf Francis, was there watching and participating. It was the beginning of an extraordinary partnership. Rob Walker, the Scottish whisky heir, would enter a Porsche in Formula Two with Stirling Moss during the 1960 season. That meant a lot of work for the small Competition Department at Zuffenhausen as from now on there would be two works teams to keep supplied.

Porsche did not turn up at the Argentine Grand Prix on February 7th 1960. However Masten Gregory drove the Behra-Porsche that had been taken over by the American Camoradi

Angeblasen: Auf Wiegebalken steht der Renner 1960 im Windkanal. Wollfäden zeigen den Verlauf der Strömung.

In the wind tunnel: in 1960, this Porsche racer was tested for aerodynamic qualities by attching woollen threads to indicate the direction of the airflow.

Foto: Porsche

an den Heck-Luftöffnungen befindet sich ein Druckmanometer. Als Mimler seine Runden dreht, ist auch der Chefmechaniker des Rob-Walker-Teams, Alf Francis, anwesend. Es ist der Beginn einer eher außergewöhnlichen Partnerschaft. Der schottische Teamchef wird 1960 einen Porsche für Stirling Moss einsetzen. Das bedeutet für die 1960er Saison, dass Porsche gleichsam zwei Werksteams auf der Strecke hat – jede Menge Arbeit für die kleine Rennabteilung der Schwaben.

Beim Grand Prix von Argentinien am 6. Februar 1960 ist Porsche werksseitig nicht präsent, aber Masten Gregory nimmt mit dem Behra-Porsche an dem Rennen teil. Der Wagen war nach Behras Tod vom amerikanischen Camoradi-Team übernommen worden, und sein amerikanischer Pilot qualifiziert sich als 16. von 23. Startern. Die Saison beginnt, wie die vorgehende aufgehört hat: mit einem Sieg des Neuseeländers Bruce McLaren auf Cooper. Gregory kommt mit vier Runden Rückstand als Zwölfter ins Ziel.

In den Farben des schottischen Rob-Walker-Teams, blau mit einem weißen Querstreifen an der Front, präsentiert sich der Formel-2-Porsche bei seinem ersten offiziellen Auftritt 1960. Porsche-Rennleiter Huschke von Hanstein und Renningenieur Hild sind beim Grand Prix von Syrakus am 19. März 1960 ebenfalls an Ort und Stelle, auch wenn es sich offiziell um einen Einsatz des englischen Teams handelt. Den Wagen fährt Stirling Moss, der damit beide Trainingssitzungen dominiert und sich die Pole Position sichert. Im Rennen übernimmt er sogleich die Führung, die er bis zur 27. Runde unangefochten inne hat. Ein Ventilschaden stoppt seine bravouröse Fahrt. Der Spion am Drehzahlmesser spricht ihn von jeder Schuld frei. Bemerkenswert: Moss fuhr mit 5,50- anstelle der 6,00-Zoll-Reifen. Aus deutscher Sicht ist das Ergebnis des Rennens trotzdem erfreulich: Graf Trips gewinnt auf Ferrari.

Das Auto von Moss wird in Stuttgart repariert und wieder nach Dorking zu Rob Walker verschifft. In dessen Werkstatt baut Chefmechaniker Alf Francis eine Schaltkulisse ein, die aus einem Maserati 250F stammt. Derart präpariert steht Moss neben Bonnier am 10. April ganz vorn im Starterfeld beim Großen Preis

team after Behra's death. The American driver qualified sixteenth among the twenty-three starters. The Formula One season started the same way that the previous one had ended with the victory of New Zealander Bruce McLaren in his Cooper T45-Climax. Gregory finished twelfth and was four laps down on the leader.

The first appearance in public of the Formula Two Porsche was thus in the colours of the Rob Walker team, dark blue with a white band on the nose. Porsche's racing director Huschke von Hanstein together with engineer Wilhelm Hild attended the Syracuse Grand Prix on March 19th though it was officially just an entry from the Walker team. Stirling Moss was the driver and he dominated both of the two practice sessions and started from pole position. He kept the lead up to lap twenty-seven when a broken valve stopped him, but the telltale on the rev-counter exonerated him from any suggestion that he had over-revved the engine. Incidentally, Moss drove using 5.5 inch tyres instead of the more usual 6 inch items. Winner of the race was Wolfgang Graf Berghe von Trips (Ferrari).

Moss's car was repaired at Stuttgart and shipped back to Rob Walker at Dorking. There Alf Francis mounted a gate change for the gear lever taken from a Maserati 250F.

On April 10th, Moss started next to Bonnier on the front of the grid at Brussels. Two Porsches on the front row were a promising start.

Moss won the first heat in style, Bonnier retired after thirty laps due to clutch failure. Before the second heat it had drizzled with rain and the track was slippery. However in Moss's car, first gear jumped out at the start and after the first lap he found himself in eleventh position. But he struggled to catch up, again drove the fastest lap, and was soon back with the leading

Porsche in schottisch-blau: 1960 nimmt Moss in Syrakus selbst hinterm Steuer des 718/2 Platz. Er liegt in Führung, bis ihn ein kaputtes Ventil stoppt.

A Porsche in Scottish blue: in 1960, Moss drove a 718/2 at Syracuse where he led until a valve broke.

Belgische Pralinen: Moss (links) und Bonnier (rechts) stehen in Brüssel 1960 auf den beiden vordersten Startplätzen. Der Brite gewinnt den ersten Lauf, wird aber wegen des schlechteren Ergebnisses im zweiten Durchgang nur Zweiter in der Gesamtwertung.

Belgian Chocolates: at Brussels, Moss (on the left) and Bonnier (right) put their cars on the front row of the grid. Moss won the first heat but then finished second overall on the combined results with the second heat.

von Brüssel. Zwei Porsche auf den ersten beiden Startplätzen – das ist ein vielversprechender Auftakt für die Zuffenhausener. Moss gewinnt den ersten von zwei Läufen überlegen, sein ärgster Konkurrent, Bonnier auf Porsche, muss nach 30 Runden mit Kupplungsschaden aufgeben.

Vor dem Start zum zweiten Lauf hat es leicht geregnet, die Strecke ist dementsprechend rutschig. Als Moss beim Start der Gang herausspringt, liegt er nach der ersten Runde nur auf Platz elf. Mit einer imposanten Aufholjagd, bei der er auch im zweiten Lauf die schnellste Runde fährt, kämpft sich Moss in die Spitzengruppe zurück. In der 23. Runde liegt er bereits hinter Jack Brabham und Maurice Trintignant an dritter Stelle. In der vorletzten Runde ist Moss schon Zweiter, leistet sich aber bei der Jagd auf den führenden Australier einen Dreher, der ihn wieder auf Platz drei zurückwirft.

In der Addition beider Läufe hat Moss zwar die schnellste Gesamtzeit erzielt, gewertet werden aber die Platzierungen. Mit einem zweiten Platz im ersten Lauf und dem Sieg im zweiten hat Jack Brabham die Nase vorn. Moss wird durch die Plätze eins und drei in den zwei Läufen „nur" Zweiter.

Der Grand Prix von Pau, auch in diesem Jahr als Formel-2-Rennen ausgetragen, führt am 18. April 1960 über eine Distanz von 90 Runden. Die drei Trainingsschnellsten, Jack Brabham und Maurice Trintignant auf Cooper sowie Olivier Gendebien auf Porsche 718/2, überqueren nach einem Rennen ohne Positionskämpfe an der Spitze in dieser Reihenfolge auch die Ziellinie.

group. By lap twenty-three, he was third behind Jack Brabham and Maurice Trintignant. In the lap before last he managed to get by passed Trintignant but then skidded, was re-passed and finally finished third.

In both heats Moss had been the fastest driver but sadly what counted were the actual finishing positions. Thanks to a second place in the first heat and the victory in the second, Jack Brabham was one step ahead, and Moss came second when the results were combined.

The Pau Grand Prix on April 18th was again held as a Formula Two race over ninety laps. Jack Brabham, Maurice Trintignant (both in Coopers) and Olivier Gendebien (Porsche 718/2) crossed the finishing line in the same order in which they had qualified.

Spectators expected a return match at the Goodwood Lavant Cup on April 18th. Moss put his 718/2 on the front row but pole position went to Innes Ireland in the new Lotus 18. This startling rear engined design by Lotus boss Colin Chapman was significantly lighter than any other car. For example, the Porsche weighed approximately 50 kg more than this Lotus. Though Moss took the lead after the start, he had to make room for Ireland during the third lap so that Ireland won in style with Moss taking second place

Four Porsches were entered for the British Automobile Racing Club's Formula Two race, the Aintree International 200 on April 30th. Besides Moss in the Walker car, there were works

Dritter hinter zwei Cooper:
Olivier Gendebien kommt in
Pau hinter Jack Brabham und
Maurice Trintignant ins Ziel.

Third behind two Cooper:
at Pau, Olivier Gendebien
crossed the finishing line
behind Jack Brabham and
Maurice Trintignant.

Beim Lavant Cup am 18. April 1960 in Goodwood rechnen die Zuschauer mit einer Revanche von Stirling Moss. Er stellt den 718/2 auch prompt in die erste Startreihe, muss aber die Pole Position Innes Ireland im neuen Lotus 18 überlassen. Die filigrane Heckmotor-Konstruktion von Lotus-Chef Colin Chapman ist wesentlich leichter als alle anderen Wagen, der Gewichtsunterschied zwischen dem Lotus und dem Porsche wird auf 50 Kilogramm geschätzt. Moss geht beim Start zwar in Führung, muss Ireland aber in der dritten Runde ziehen lassen, der einem ungefährdeten Sieg entgegenfährt. Moss und Porsche müssen erneut mit Rang zwei vorlieb nehmen.

Zum Rennen des British Automobile Racing Club am 30. April 1960 treten gleich vier Porsche an. Neben Stirling Moss sind die Werks-Piloten Graham Hill und Joakim Bonnier am Start, zusätzlich Masten Gregory im Behra-Porsche, dieses Mal eingesetzt von der Scuderia Centro Sud.

Moss fährt Trainingsbestzeit vor Jack Brabham (Cooper) und Hill. Bonnier qualifiziert sich auf Rang sieben. Beim Start hat Moss erneut Probleme. Brabham schießt vor Salvadori und Ireland in Führung, der Rob-Walker-Porsche kommt erst als siebtes Fahrzeug aus der ersten Runde. Zur Hälfte des Rennens hat sich Moss auf Rang drei vorgekämpft und dabei auch die Werks-Porsche hinter sich gelassen. Eine Runde später führt der Engländer sogar, Brabham und Salvadori sind zeitgleich wegen technischer Probleme an die Box gefahren. Bonnier und Hill rücken auf die Plätze zwei und drei vor und können diese Positionen auch gegen den heranstürmenden John Surtees verteidigen. Der Engländer dreht mit seinem Cooper zwar noch die schnellste Runde, kann aber den Dreifach-Erfolg von Porsche nicht mehr verhindern.

drivers Graham Hill and Jo Bonnier plus Masten Gregory in the Behra-Porsche, entered by the Scuderia Centro Sud.

In practising, Moss was faster than Jack Brabham (Cooper) and Hill while Bonnier qualified in seventh position. Again Moss was to suffer problems at the start. Brabham jumped into the lead, followed by Roy Salvadori (Cooper) and Ireland (Lotus). The Walker-Porsche came round in seventh place at the end of the first lap but by half distance in the race Moss had made it back up to third and had even passed the two works Porsches. One lap later the Briton was in the lead thanks to the fact that both Brabham and Salvadori had to retire due to mechanical problems. Bonnier and Hill finished second and third respectively after resisted the attentions of John Surtees in another Cooper Climax who set the fastest lap in pursuit but failed to spoil the triple success for Porsche.

The Porsche technicians made good use of the break before the next race and shipped the car to the Nürburgring for further testing. John Surtees, Hans Herrmann and Edgar Barth drove a full GP distance in order to be well prepared for the German Grand Prix.

At Chimay in Belgium on June 5th, thanks to a clash with the Dutch Grand Prix, Hans Herrmann in the Behra car and Christian Goethals were the only Porsche drivers entered in the Belgian Grand Prix des Frontières. Herrmann started from the front row and immediately took the lead but Jackie Lewis passed him in the first lap. Hermann managed to stick to the leading group for a while but later retired with gearbox failure. Goethals in an RSR finished seventh, one lap down on the winner.

Die Pause bis zum nächsten Rennen nutzen die Porsche-Techniker zu Testfahrten auf der Südschleife des Nürburgrings. John Surtees, Hans Herrmann und Edgar Barth absolvieren eine Grand-Prix-Distanz, um für den Großen Preis von Deutschland auf dem Nürburgring gerüstet zu sein.

Hans Herrmann im Behra-Porsche und Christian Goethals sind die einzigen Porsche-Piloten beim Grand Prix des Frontières, der am 5. Juni 1960 im belgischen Chimay ausgetragen wird. Herrmann startet aus der ersten Reihe und übernimmt nach dem Start auch gleich die Führung, muss aber noch in der ersten Runde Jack Lewis im Cooper ziehen lassen. Der Stuttgarter hält sich noch eine Weile in der Spitzengruppe, gibt dann aber mit Getriebeproblemen auf. Goethals kommt mit seinem RSR nach zuverlässiger Fahrt mit einer Runde Rückstand auf den siebten Platz.

Im Juli 1960 sind die nächsten beiden Wagen fertig. Während die Fahrgestellnummer 718/02-04 ein Schwesterfahrzeug der Nummern 1, 2 und 3 ist, erhält 05 eine andere, von Butzi Porsche entwickelte Karosserie. Eine niedrigere Nase, flache Karosserieseiten, ein kantiger Aufbau über dem Motor, der vorn in die Windschutzscheibe übergeht und nach hinten offen ist, verleihen dem Monoposto eine ansprechende Form, die mit elf Kilogramm Mehrgewicht erkauft wird.

Im Juli stehen erneut Testfahrten auf der Südschleife an, Bonnier und Herrmann absolvieren die nächste Grand-Prix-Distanz. So gerüstet, tritt die Porsche-Mannschaft am 24. Juli 1960 mit fünf Wagen zum Großen Preis der Solitude an. Stirling Moss fehlt, er hat sich bei einem Unfall beim Großen Preis von Belgien in Spa schwere Verletzungen zugezogen. Rob Walker verpflichtet den mehrfachen Motorrad-Weltmeister John Surtees als Ersatzmann.

Das Rennen nahe Stuttgart ist aus deutscher Sicht natürlich auch wegen des bevorstehenden Duells zwischen den Porsche-Piloten und Graf Berghe von Trips in seinem Ferrari interessant. Daneben aber wird das Rennen zur Sternstunde eines jungen Schotten, der den Rennsport der sechziger Jahre prägen soll: Jim Clark auf Lotus. Seinen Sieg in der Formel Junior empfinden die Zuschauer noch als normal, sind doch die Formel-Junior-Renn-

In July 1960 the next two cars were built. While serial number 718/2-04 was similar to numbers one, two and three, number 05 received a new body designed by Butzi Porsche. The nose was sharper and lower while the flanks of the body were flatter. The engine cover was open to the rear and its sides went alongside the driver and were faired into the windscreen. The car looked sleeker than its predecessors but was in fact eleven kilograms heavier.

In July, testing was again scheduled on the Nürburgring's Südschleife. Bonnier and Herrmann between them drove the next practice GP distance. Thus, well prepared, the team entered five cars for the "Großer Preis der Solitude" on July 24th. Stirling Moss did not turn up as he had suffered severe injuries in an accident at the Belgian Grand Prix while driving Rob Walker's Lotus. As a result, Walker hired multiple motorbike World Champion, John Surtees, to drive his Porsche while Dan Gurney, Hans Herrmann, Jo Bonnier and Graham Hill drove the other four.

The race outside Stuttgart was eagerly anticipated especially concerning the expected duel between the Porsche drivers and von Trips who was now driving for Ferrari. Besides this, the meeting turned out to be a turning point of his career for a young Scotsman in a Lotus, Jim Clark, who would go on to set the benchmark in motor racing for the 1960s. His victory in the Formula Junior race was not rated that highly as the British Formula Junior cars were well known for their excellent design and high performance. But in the Formula Two race, Clark went away from the whole Formula Two field and only a broken head gasket at half distance stopped him. Only then did the race turn into the expected duel between von Trips in the new Ferrari and Herrmann in the Porsche 718/2. Hans Herrmann gave his memories of this race in his autobiography "Ein Leben für den Rennsport" (A Life in Racing)

"Now Count Trips catches up in his Ferrari and we lapped several times with our wheels almost touching. It is obvious that the two of us will have to sort it out between ourselves. All of our teammates are far behind. I can see the spectators are delighted with the fight on the track. The Ferrari is lighter than

Solitude 1960: In der ersten Startreihe stehen (v.l.) Herrmann, Trips und Clark. In der zweiten Bonnier und Gurney.

Solitude 1960: First row: Herrmann, Trips and Clark. Second row Bonnier and Gurney.

Fotos: Porsche

Solitude-Zwischenstand: Bonnier vor Graham Hill und Hans Herrmann.

Solitude's intermediate result: Jo Bonnier ahead of Graham Hill and Hans Herrmann.

Deutsch-britische Kombi: Graham Hill und Motorrad-Star John Surtess fahren vor den Toren Stuttgarts 1960 Porsche.

Anglo-German combinations: Graham Hill and motorbike star John Surtees in Porsches outside Stuttgart.

Sieht gut aus für Porsche: Hans Herrmann vor Wolfgang Graf Berghe von Trips, der am Ende aber vor dem Schwaben durchs Ziel rollt.

It is looking good for Porsche: Hans Herrman ahead of Wolfgang Graf Berghe von Trips who will finally finish first.

wagen aus Großbritannien bekannt leistungsstark, und Clark ist zu diesem Zeitpunkt auch schon kein Anfänger mehr. Der Schotte fährt dem gesamten Formel-2-Feld davon und wird erst von seinem überhitzten Motor gestoppt. So wird das Rennen zum Duell zwischen Trips im neuen Ferrari und Herrmann im 718/2. Nach dem Boxenstopp von Clark liefern sich die beiden ein spannendes Rennen. Hans Herrmann berichtete über dieses Rennen in seiner Autobiografie „Ein Leben für den Rennsport": „Jetzt rückt Graf Trips mit dem Ferrari auf, und wir umrunden den Kurs mehrmals fast Rad an Rad. Das Rennen wird zwischen uns entschieden werden, meine Stallgefährten liegen deutlich zurück. Ich sehe, wie die Zuschauer mit Begeisterung diesen Kampf verfolgen. Der Ferrari ist leichter, und der Motor leistet 20 bis 25 PS mehr als das Porsche-Triebwerk. Doch der kurvenreiche Kurs bietet nur wenige Möglichkeiten zum Überholen, die günstigste für meinen Verfolger ist noch die Gerade vom Steinbachsee zur Schattenkurve. Sein Wagen ist aber nicht so überlegen, dass er auch da nach Belieben vorbeiziehen könnte. Ich hätte die Möglichkeit, ihn dort durch entsprechenden Spurwechsel aufzuhalten. Nach den Szenen zu schließen, die sich heutzutage immer wieder in der Formel 1 abspielen, scheint das jetzt für die Fahrer naheliegend, wenn nicht selbstverständlich zu sein. Damals herrschte unter uns

Und noch ein Zwischenergebnis: Herrmann vor Trips und Bonnier.

Another intermediate result: Herrmann ahead of von Trips and Bonnier.

the Porsche and the engine delivers 20 or even 25 horsepower more than my own. But the twisty track offers only a few opportunities to pass one's opponent. For von Trips that place is the straight between Steinbachsee and Schattenkurve. However his car was not so much better than mine that he could pass just as he liked. By changing my line, I could easily have delayed him there. Behaviour of that kind seems to be okay for some of the drivers today, but in the past there was a different spirit. And though I would have loved to gain the victory on my home track, I refrained from dirty tricks and let him pass. Thus he crossed the finishing line ahead of me by a margin of four seconds. The Porsche convoy Bonnier-Hill-Gurney was more than half a minute behind us. After the presentation ceremony, Wolfgang and I were driven round the track in an open car that had to clear its way through thousands of cheering spectators." Behind von Trips and Herrmann, Bonnier, Hill and Dan Gur-

noch ein anderer Geist. Obwohl ich auf meiner Hausstrecke gerne wieder gewinnen würde, verzichte ich auf Behinderungstricks und lasse mich überholen. So geht er mit vier Sekunden Vorsprung als Sieger durchs Ziel, während der Porsche-Pulk Bonnier-Hill-Gurney über eine halbe Minute zurückliegt. Wolfgang und ich werden nach der Siegerehrung im offenen PKW um den Kurs gefahren, und der Wagen muß sich eine Gasse durch Tausende von Zuschauern bahnen, die uns zujubeln."

Hinter Trips und Herrmann kommen Bonnier, Hill und der Amerikaner Dan Gurney ins Ziel. Motorradstar John Surtees, der den von Walker geliehenen fünften Wagen fährt, verschaltet sich und scheidet aus.

Ein Jahr nach dem gescheiterten Berlin-Abenteuer findet der deutsche Grand Prix am 31. Juli 1960 wieder auf dem Nürburgring statt. Schauplatz ist die Südschleife, fahrerisch ebenso anspruchsvoll wie die legendäre Nordschleife. Der deutsche Grand Prix wird in diesem Jahr nur für Rennwagen der Formel 2 ausgetragen und zählt deshalb nicht zur Fahrer-WM. Punkte gibt es nur für den FIA-F2-Pokal.

Porsche meldet eine Flotte von vier Werkswagen, und als Ferrari überraschend einen Rückzieher macht, vertrauen die Zuffenhausener Graf Trips ein fünftes Auto an. Eigentlich soll Hans Herrmann den Behra-Porsche für das Camoradi-Team fahren. Aufgrund seines guten Ergebnisses auf der Solitude stellt ihm das Werk den Wagen von Rob Walker zur Verfügung, da Stirling Moss weiterhin pausieren muss. Weil Herrmanns Nennung aber über das Camoradi-Team eingereicht worden war, trägt sein Porsche auch einen entsprechenden Schriftzug des amerikanischen Teams.

Starker Regen verhindert einen pünktlichen Start. Die Wasserschlacht über 32 Runden à 7,7 Kilometer steht im Zeichen des Schweden Joakim Bonnier, der von der Pole Position ins Rennen geht und die Führung nur für zwei Runden an Trips abgeben muss. Abgeschlagen geht der amtierende F1-Weltmeister Jack Brabham als Dritter über die volle Distanz. Damit ist der Australier der Einzige, der in die Porsche-Phalanx eindringen kann, die neben den beiden ersten Plätzen mit Hans Herrmann und Edgar Barth auch die Ränge vier und fünf heimfährt.

ney crossed the finishing line in third, fourth and fifth places while John Surtees missed the correct gear, damaged the engine and retired.

One year after its visit to Berlin, the German Grand Prix was again held at the Nürburgring on July 31st 1960. The venue was the Südschleife that in many ways was almost as demanding as the legendary – and longer – Nordschleife. The German Grand Prix that year was held exclusively for Formula Two cars and thus did not form part of the World Drivers Championship. Points awarded here were only for the FIA Formula Two Cup.

Porsche originally entered a team of four works cars. As Ferrari unexpectedly backed out of the race after a disagreement with the AvD, the Zuffenhausen team offered von Trips a car bearing the Porsche badge. Actually Hans Herrmann was supposed to drive the Behra-Porsche for the Camoradi team but as he had been so successful at the Solitude race, he got the Walker car as Moss was still not able to drive.

Heavy rain spoilt a punctual start. The race itself was in fact a very wet affair over 32 laps of 7.7 kilometres each. Jo Bonnier took the lead from pole position but had to let von Trips past on the eighth lap only to take the lead again on the tenth lap. Formula One champion, Jack Brabham, was running third and finished in that position. Indeed, only the Australian managed to intrude on the finishing phalanx of Porsches who were first (Bonnier), second (von Trips), fourth (Herrmann) and fifth (Barth).

Idealline: Edgar Barth erklärt irgendetwas mit Kurven und wartet (linkes Bild) geduldig darauf, bis er neben Bonnier, Herrmann und Trips (von links) von Günther Jendrisch interviewt wird.

Perfect line x 2: in the photo on the right, Edgar Barth was evidently sorting out the line through a curve and, in the one on the left, was waiting patiently in line with Bonnier and Herrmann until von Trips had been interviewed.

Grüne Idylle: Unterhaltung für die ganze Familie bietet der Nürburgring mit angedeuteter Streckensicherung, als 1960 Trips vorüberdriftet.

Green idyll: at the Nürburgring, there was entertainment for the whole family on the – hopefully – safe side of the rather basic safety barrier. Here von Trips comes drifting around the bend.

Regenrennen: Grau in grau und nur ein paar rote Farbtupfer – obwohl Ferrari nicht dabei ist. Daher ist Trips frei für Porsche – und holt prompt hinter Bonnier den zweiten Platz.

A race in the rain: everything is grey with just a few spots of red colour – and Ferrari was not even present. Thus the way was open for von Trips to finish second behind Bonnier.

Report concerning the German Grand Prix
from Wolfgang von Trips

Porsche, Formula Two

The vehicle is equipped, as we know, with a six-speed transmission that is not always easy to operate. On my vehicle, it was easy to lock a wheel while braking hard. Its comportment on the road is comparable with the rear-engined Ferrari with the distinction that its front axle keeps perfect contact to the ground and the car consequently tends to oversteer. During the practice sessions, the front wheels tended to skip sideways but, after replacing the dampers with ones having a higher degree of hardness, the effect vanished. To me, the steering of the car seemed to be a little less direct than the one in our car [the Ferrari] as I had to shuffle the steering wheel through my hands in several bends to get sufficient lock. The engine is very flexible and seems to have torque enough over a pretty wide range of engine revolutions. WOT is at 8,200 rpm but we were allowed to let the engine go to between 8,500 rpm and 8,600 rpm for short periods. During the first practice day, we had dry weather conditions while on the second day and again on race day it was wet. During the race we were using Dunlop radial-ply tyres that are clearly the best choice for wet tracks. It is pretty much impossible to compare all the cars at this race since the Lotus cars and some of the Coopers were fitted with standard cross-ply tyres and thus were severely handicapped.

Let me emphasize that, in comparison with the British formula cars, the seating position in the Porsche is remarkably upright. It should be possible to recline the driver further thus lowering the position of one's head by 20 to 30 centimetres.

I could not discern any outstanding characteristic features setting the vehicle apart from our car. Besides, the very special characteristics of the track made it difficult to clearly identify such differences.

```
                    B e r i c h t
                         über
              Großer Preis von Deutschland

Porsche, Formel II

Das Fahrzeug ist, wie bekannt, mit 6-Ganggetriebe ausgerüstet, welches
nicht immer leicht zu schalten ist. An meinem Fahrzeug trat öfters
bei zu scharfem BREMSEN Blockierwirkung an den Forderrädern auf.
Die Straßenlage ist sehr ähnlich dem Ferrari Heckmotor Wagen mit dem
Unterschied, daß die Forderachse völlig fest am Boden liegt und der
Wagen eher eine Übersteuerungstendenz aufweist. Während des Trainings
sprang das Fahrzeug auch mit den Vorderrädern seitlich weg, nach aus-
wechseln der Stoßdämpfer (Einbau eines höheren Härtegrades) verschwand
dieser Effekt. Die Steuerung schien mir etwas weniger direkt zu sein,
wie bei unserem Wagen, wenigstens mußte ich in mehreren Kurven umgreifen.
Der Motor ist sehr elastisch und scheint eine sehr gleichmäßige Brems-
kurve zu haben. Höchstdrehzahl liegt bei 8,2. Es wurde uns für kurze
Momente eine Drehzahl von 8,5 bis 8,6 frei gegeben. Das Training war
nur am ersten Tag trocken, während des 2. Trainingstages und Rennen
war es naß. Während des Rennens fuhren wir mit Dunlop-Gürtel-Reifen,
die einen enormen Vorteil bei nasser Fahrbahn mitbringen. Ein wirklicher
Vergleich zwischen allen Wagen auf dieser Strecke läßt sich nicht an-
stellen, da die Lotuswagen und manche Cooper mit Normalreifen fahren
fahren mußten, so also ein großes Handikap hatten.

Hervorheben möchte ich auch, daß, genau wie bei englischen Formel-
wagen, auch bei Porsche die Sitzposition des Fahrers stark abge-
schrägt ist, so daß seine Kopfhöhe um 20 - 30 cm gesenkt werden konnte.

Hervorstechende Merkmale, die das Fahrzeug von unserem Wagen unter-
scheiden, konnte ich nicht bemerken. Außerdem ist es bei der völlig
anderen Streckencharakteristik auch schwer, einen ganz klaren Unter-
schied heraus zu arbeiten.
```

Wolfgang Graf Berghe zu Trips: Protokoll zum Großen Preis von Deutschland 1960.

Wolfgang Graf Berghe zu Trips: Report concerning the German Grand Prix 1960

Erst am 28. August 1960, bei den Kentish 100 in Brands Hatch, sitzt Stirling Moss nach seinem schweren Unfall wieder am Steuer des F2-Porsche. Er fährt im Training die zweitbeste Zeit, muss aber schon zu Beginn des Rennens mit Vergaserproblemen die Box aufsuchen. Bonnier und Hill drehen dagegen zuverlässig ihre Runden, können Jim Clark und Dan Gurney in den neuen Lotus 18 aber nicht bedrängen. Mit zehn Sekunden Rückstand belegen sie am Ende Rang drei und vier.

Monza als Austragungsort des italienischen Grand Prix ist nicht ungewöhnlich, die Wahl der Streckenvariante für das Rennen an diesem 4. September 1960 hingegen schon. Die Streckenführung mit den beiden Steilwandkurven soll nach dem Willen des Veranstalters genutzt werden und zusätzlich Zuschauer anlocken. Zahlreiche Teams sehen Probleme hinsichtlich der Bodenfreiheit ihrer Fahrzeuge, insbesondere wegen der Unebenheiten zwischen den einzelnen Betonsegmenten der Steilwandkurven. Als sich die Italiener auch nach langen Diskussionen nicht von dieser Planung abbringen lassen, boykottieren die englischen Teams das Rennen. Damit ist der Weg frei zum ersten Ferrari-F1-Triumph des Jahres, den Phil Hill für die Scuderia sicherstellt. Auch die Formel-2-Wertung geht an das italienische Team, und wieder ist es Graf Trips, der die Porsche-Piloten Hans Herrmann und Edgar Barth auf die Plätze zwei und drei der F2-Wertung verweist.

Trips profitiert von der Ferrari-Teamorder. F1-Pilot Willy Mairesse gibt dem deutschen Grafen auf Geheiß von Rennleiter Tavoni mehrere Runden Windschatten, um sich von den beiden Porsche absetzen zu können.

Das Rob-Walker-Team ist am 11. September 1960 beim

The Kentish 100 on August 28th 1960 was Moss' first race in the Formula Two Porsche after his Belgian accident. In practising he finished second but soon after the start of the race, he had to return to pits with carburettor problems. Bonnier and Hill drove steady and fast but did not manage to hinder Jim Clark and Dan Gurney, both driving the new Lotus 18 who finished first and second. The Porsche drivers finished ten seconds down on the leaders in third and fourth places.

At Monza the promoter tried to attract more spectators by using the steep banked turns for the Grand Prix of Europe on September 4th. Many of the teams worried about the ground clearance of the new cars especially since the concrete segments of the steeply banked curves made the track very bumpy where the down force was highest. But even after a long discussion, the Italians refused to alter their plans. Thus the British teams boycotted the race. That helped to pave the way for the first Ferrari victory of the season in Formula One. Phil Hill finished first with his team mates Ritchie Ginther and Willy Mairesse second and third. The Formula Two points also went to the Italian team as it was von Trips back at the wheel of a Dino 156P who beat Herrmann and Barth into second and third respectively. In fact, von Trips profited from Ferrari's stratagem of allowing him to slipstream Mairesse's Formula One car for several laps, thus allowing him to consolidate his lead over the other Formula Two cars.

The Rob Walker team entered for the Danish Grand Prix on September 11th 1960. The race at the Roskildering was overshadowed by a fatal accident to New Zealander, George Lawton, who somersaulted in the first heat and was thrown out

Vor dem Start in Monza 1960: Fred Gamble nimmt Platz in Nummer 28, Hans Herrmann sitzt schon (Nummer 26).

Coming up to the start at Monza, 1960: Fred Gamble was driving number 28 with Herrmann behind the wheel of number 26.

Foto: Porsche

Im Windschatten: In Monza ist Hans Herrmann Edgar Barth dicht auf den Fersen.

In the slipstream: at Monza, Hans Herrmann took the opportunity to get a tow from Edgar Barth on the long straight.

Grand Prix von Dänemark am Start. Das Rennen am Roskilde-ring wird überschattet durch den tödlichen Unfall des Neuseelän-ders George Lawton, der sich mit seinem Cooper im ersten Lauf überschlägt und dabei aus dem Wagen geschleudert wird. Vor dem Hintergrund dieses Ereignisses wird die Rundenzahl aller Läufe gekürzt. Stirling Moss hat mit seinem Porsche zwar die Trainingsbestzeit erzielt, muss aber einmal mehr den Siegeslor-beer Jack Brabham auf Cooper überlassen, der vor den Lotus-Pi-loten Innes Ireland und Graham Hill gewinnt. Ein mit Getriebe-problemen kämpfender Moss wird nur Vierter.

Eine Woche später reist Porsche mit drei Wagen zum Flug-platzrennen von Zeltweg nach Österreich. Moss fährt wieder für Rob Walker, die Werkswagen pilotieren Hans Herrmann und Edgar Barth. Die schnellste Trainingszeit gelingt Jack Brabham auf seinem Cooper, der den Porsche-Piloten in der laufenden Saison ja schon mehrfach das Nachsehen gegeben hatte.

Edgar Barth erwischt den besten Start, Herrmann kommt we-gen durchdrehender Antriebsräder schlecht ins Rennen, kämpft sich aber rasch an die Spitzengruppe heran, in der mehrfach die Führung wechselt. Tony Marsh auf Lotus, Drittschnellster im Training, liegt zeitweise an der Spitze, aber ab der zehnten Runde wird Moss immer schneller. Brabham folgt direkt dahinter, schiebt sich beim Anbremsen auch mal neben den Engländer, ist aber nicht in der Lage, das Rennen von der Spitze aus zu kont-rollieren. In der 38. Runde kommt für den Australier das Aus, ihn stoppt eine defekte Benzinpumpe. Damit ist der Weg für Porsche frei. Moss fährt den Sieg sicher nach Hause, Herrmann wird

of his car. After the accident the number of laps for the fol-lowing heats was reduced. Again Stirling Moss was the fastest driver in practice but had to leave the laurels to Jack Brabham. The Cooper driver came in ahead of Lotus drivers Innes Ireland and Graham Hill while Moss finished fourth after struggling with gearbox problems in the Porsche.

One week later Porsche entered three cars for the airport track race at Zeltweg in Austria. Moss started for the Walker team while Hans Herrmann and Edgar Barth drove the works cars. Fastest in practice was Jack Brabham in his Cooper. At the start, Edgar Barth shot away while Herrmann accelerated too hard and was delayed by wheel spin but he soon caught back the deficit. Lotus driver Tony Marsh who had started from third position was in the lead for some time but from lap ten onwards there was no resisting Moss. Brabham followed hard on his heels and was often driving neck-to-neck with Graham Hill. Eventually on lap 38 the Australian's Cooper stopped with fuel pump failure. Thus the way was open for Porsche to shine. Moss won in style with Herrmann finishing second just 0.7 seconds behind, followed by Edgar Barth in third place.

Because of the shortness of the track, only twelve cars were allowed to enter the Formula Two race at Modena on October 2nd 1960. As drivers for Scuderia Ferrari, von Trips and Richie Ginther were naturally local heroes. Stirling Moss drove a Lotus for Reg Parnell team, while Jo Bonnier, Hans Herrmann and Edgar Barth were entered for Porsche. Bonnier started the race from pole position and had a long duel with von Trips and

mit 0,7 Sekunden Rückstand Zweiter vor Edgar Barth, der mit seinem dritten Rang den Triumph komplett macht.

Zwischen den Rennen treibt man bei Porsche die Entwicklung für 1961 voran. Ende Oktober erzielt der 718/2-05 bei Windkanalmessungen im Vergleich mit dem 718/2-04 sowie dem 718 GT in zwei Ausführungen den besten Cw-Wert.

Für das Formel-2-Rennen um den Grand Prix von Modena sind am 2. Oktober 1960 wegen der Kürze der Strecke lediglich zwölf Starter zugelassen. Graf Trips und Richie Ginther sind als Ferrari-Piloten die Lokalmatadoren, Stirling Moss fährt einen Lotus des Reg-Parnell-Teams, Joakim Bonnier, Hans Herrmann und Edgar Barth starten für Porsche. Bonnier geht von der Pole Position ins Rennen und liefert sich lange Zeit einen Dreikampf mit Trips und Moss. Als Moss in Runde 21 wegen eines Ventilschadens aufgeben muss, wird daraus ein Duell, das bis zur 90. Runde dauert. Dann zwingen nachlassende Bremsen Trips zu einer langsameren Gangart, die ihn auch noch den zweiten Platz kostet. So gewinnt Bonnier vor Ginther, Trips, Herrmann und Barth. Auch die schnellste Rennrunde geht auf das Konto des Schweden, der sich diese Ehre aber mit Trips teilen muss.

Dann stehen erneut Testfahrten auf dem Hockenheimring an. Hubert Mimler fährt an zwei Tagen fast 200 Runden auf dem 7,725 Kilometer langen Kurs.

Beim Preis von Tirol auf dem Innsbrucker Alpenflughafen fehlen zahlreiche Teams, so dass Hans Herrmann als einziger Porsche-Pilot mit klaren Vorteilen ins Rennen geht. Während er an der Spitze zuverlässig seine Bahnen zieht, entbrennt um den zweiten Platz ein harter Kampf zwischen Gerry Ashmore im Cooper und Graf Trips, der ebenfalls auf einem Cooper unterwegs ist. Schaltprobleme bei Ashmore entscheiden dieses Duell, und Trips wird hinter Herrmann Zweiter.

Porsche nutzt die beiden letzten Formel-2-Rennen des Jahres 1960 und schickt Stirling Moss und Joakim Bonnier mit Werkswagen zum Cape Grand Prix und zum Großen Preis nach Südafrika. Die Porsche-Piloten entscheiden das Rennen am Ende

1-2-3-Sieg auf dem Flugplatz: In Zeltweg siegt am 18. September 1960 Moss im blauen Walker-Wagen knapp vor Herrmann. Dritter wird Barth.

One-two-three on the airfield: Moss won on September 18th, 1960 at Zeltweg driving the blue Walker car to finish ahead of Herrmann while Barth came in third.

Moss. Moss retired on lap 21 thanks to a damaged valve but the neck-and-neck fight between von Trips and Bonnier lasted until lap 90 when fading brakes slowed the Ferrari. Finally he finished third with Bonnier winning the race ahead of Ginther, von Trips, Herrmann and Barth. Bonnier and von Trips shared the honour of having driven the fastest lap.

Next step for Porsche were further tests on the Hockenheimring. Hubert Mimler drove 200 laps on the 7.725-kilometre track in the space of just two days.

Only a small number of teams were entered for the Tyrolean Cup on Innsbruck's Alpenflughafen circuit and Herrmann was the only Porsche driver. While he was out in front, lapping fast and imperturbably, Cooper drivers Gerry Ashmore and von Trips fought fiercely for second. Problems with the gear shift slowed Ashmore and thus, at the finish, von Trips was second behind Herrmann

For the last two Formula Two races of the year, Porsche shipped works cars to South Africa. Stirling Moss and Jo Bonnier were entered for both the Cape Grand Prix and the South African Grand Prix. The Porsches were superior at the Cape. Moss finished first just two metres in front of Bonnier who was credited with the fastest lap.

In the second race, the results were practically identical. Moss finished first with a fourteen second lead over Bonnier and, this time it was he who set the fastest lap. This series of

Erst Drei-, dann Zweikampf: Bonnier (rechts, mit Huschke von Hanstein) liefert sich in Modena ein spannendes Rennen mit Moss im Lotus und Trips im Ferrari. Moss erleidet Ventilschaden, Trips lassen schlappe Bremsen schließlich auf Platz drei zurückfallen.

A thrilling race: at Modena, Bonnier (right, with Huschke von Hanstein) fought with Moss (Lotus) and von Trips (Ferrari) until the Briton broke a valve and von Trips suffered from fading brakes that put him down to third.

klar für sich und fahren mit einem Abstand von zwei Metern über die Ziellinie. Moss gewinnt, und Bonnier darf sich über den zweiten Platz und die schnellste Runde des Rennens freuen.

Auch das zweite Rennen in Südafrika ist eine klare Angelegenheit für die Porsche-Mannschaft. Moss setzt sich erneut gegen Bonnier durch und siegt mit 14 Sekunden Vorsprung, dieses Mal eindeutig. Auch die schnellste Rennrunde geht auf sein Konto. Die Serie von fünf Siegen bei den letzten fünf Starts lässt die Crew aus Zuffenhausen optimistisch in die Zukunft blicken, ist es

five victories in five races naturally encouraged the Zuffenhausen team. It was a fine result for their new open-wheel racing car.

Thus Porsche entered the new and important 1961 season with confidence. It was the first year of the new downsized Formula One. But Porsche entered the contest with the well-known but barely improved 718/2 with its boxer 4-cylinder engine. By then, their rivals were one step ahead of them. Ferrari had their new Dino 156 V6 racer while the British had their sleek Coventry Climax FPF 4-cylinder engined cars with superior suspension.

Fotos: Porsche

doch alles in allem eine ordentliche Bilanz für die neuen Monoposti aus dem Schwabenland.

So geht Porsche denn auch zuversichtlich in die entscheidende Saison 1961, das erste Jahr mit der neuen kleinen Formel 1 – freilich mit dem kaum veränderten 718/2. Die Konkurrenz hat längst völlig Neues zu bieten: Ferrari den neuen V6-Renner, die Briten ihre schlanken V8 mit feinen Fahrwerken.

Die Formel-1-Saison wird mit zwei nicht zur Weltmeisterschaft zählenden Rennen in Pau und Brüssel eröffnet. Während Porsche dem Rennen in Pau fern bleibt, gehen die Zuffenhausener am 9. April 1961 in der belgischen Hauptstadt mit Joakim Bonnier und Dan Gurney in ihr erstes Formel-1-Rennen. Am ersten Trainingstag fährt Gurney auf der regennassen Piste Bestzeit, auf trockener Strecke dominiert dann Bonnier. Mit anderthalb Sekunden Vorsprung holt er sich vor Bruce McLaren auf Cooper und Gurney im zweiten Porsche die Pole Position.

The 1961 season began with two non-championship races at Pau and Brussels. Porsche did not turn up at Pau so that Jo Bonnier and Dan Gurney drove the first Formula One race for the Zuffenhausen team on April 9th in the Belgian capital. On the first day of practice, Gurney was fastest on a wet track while Bonnier lapped fastest of anyone when it became dry. He was one and a half seconds ahead of both Bruce McLaren with a Cooper and Gurney in the second Porsche.

Bonnier won the first of three heats in style finishing ahead of Roy Salvadori's Cooper. Gurney retired early in the race due to a broken gear-change. Bonnier also led in the second heat though he was being hard-pressed by John Surtees in his Cooper. On lap eleven, Surtees touched the leading Porsche and both cars spun. After all three heats, Jack Brabham emerged as the winner overall ahead of Bruce McLaren, the second-fastest Cooper Climax driver.

Gute Laune in südlichster Sonne: Die Porsche gehen gut am Kap der guten Hoffnung. Moss siegt und fährt die schnellste Runde, Bonnier wird Zweiter.

Good mood under the southern Sun: the Porsche racers were in great form at the Cape of Good Hope. Moss won and recorded the fastest lap with Bonnier second.

Das Rennen wird in drei Läufen ausgetragen, von denen Bonnier den ersten souverän vor Roy Salvadori auf Cooper gewinnt. Für Gurney ist der Renntag wegen eines gebrochenen Schaltgestänges schon früh beendet. Auch im zweiten Lauf führt Bonnier, der sich jedoch harter Attacken durch John Surtees auf Cooper ausgesetzt sieht. In der elften Runde berührt Surtees den vor ihm liegenden Porsche, beide Wagen kreiseln ins Aus. In der Addition aller drei Läufe gewinnt Jack Brabham vor Bruce McLaren, beide auf Cooper-Climax.

Das Duell zwischen John Surtees und den Porsche-Piloten findet am 25. April 1961 beim Großen Preis von Syrakus eine Fortsetzung. Nach dem Start geht der Engländer in Führung, duelliert sich einige Runden mit Gurney und fällt dann mit Motorschaden aus. Sowohl beim Amerikaner als auch bei Bonnier stellen sich vermehrt Probleme mit der Schaltung ein. Die Übertragung zwischen Schalthebel und Getriebe macht den Fahrern, wie schon im Jahr zuvor, zu schaffen. So haben sie dem Werks-Ferrari mit Giancarlo Baghetti am Steuer nichts entgegen zu setzen. Der italienische Nachwuchsfahrer siegt überlegen und

Da war das Atomium drei Jahre alt: In Brüssel gehen die Zuffenhausener in ihr erstes Formel-1-Rennen. Bonnier (30) gewinnt den ersten Lauf, Gurney (38) hat technische Probleme, am Ende gewinnt Brabham im Cooper-Climax.

The Atomium was only three years old then: at Brussels, the Zuffenhausen team raced for the first time in Formula One. Bonnier (30) won the first heat while Gurney (38) suffered a technical mishap. Finally Brabham won overall with his Cooper-Climax.

The contest between Surtees and the Porsche drivers was continued on April 15th at the Syracuse Grand Prix. After the start, the Briton gained the lead, duelled with Gurney for a couple of laps, but finally retired with engine failure. Gurney and Bonnier both suffered problems with the Porsche's gear-change mechanism. Just as it had done the previous year, the linkage between the gear lever and the gearbox was causing a lot of trouble. Thus they failed to challenge the works Ferrari driven by Giancarlo Baghetti who won confidently, thus adding weight

bestätigt die Einschätzung der Experten, dass 1961 ein Ferrari-Jahr werden könnte. Mit einem zweiten Platz für Gurney und einem dritten Rang von Bonnier endet das sizilianische Abenteuer für Porsche dennoch versöhnlich.

Der erste WM-Lauf des Jahres, der Grand Prix von Monaco, beginnt für die Porsche-Truppe mit einem Handicap. Auf der Fahrt nach Monaco hat der Renntransporter einen Schaden an der Bremsölleitung, die beiden Werks-Piloten können daher nicht am Donnerstag-Training teilnehmen. Aus den Transportern rollen nicht die erwarteten neuen Achtzylinder, sondern die Vierzylinder-Wagen mit Benzineinspritzung. Im Rennen kommt neben den Stammpiloten Gurney und Bonnier auch Hans Herrmann zum Einsatz, im Training dreht auch Michael May einige Runden. Der fehlende Trainingstag macht sich im Porsche-Team bemerkbar.

Dan Gurney sitzt am Steuer von Bonniers Syrakus-Auto. Bonnier steuert ein modifiziertes Auto mit eigener Typnummer 787, Herrmann einen 718/2 mit dem etwas kürzeren, herkömmlichen Radstand.

Bonnier hat Pech mit der neuen Technik, die Spritversorgung macht ihm einen Strich durch die Rechnung.

Das ist eine Schande, ist er doch aus der vierten Startreihe auf Platz zwei vorgedrungen. Zwar überholen ihn dann noch zwei Ferraris, aber Platz vier scheint sicher, bis in der 59. Runde an der Hafenschikane das Spritmalheur passiert. Gurney im „alten" 718/2 wird Fünfter und holt so die ersten Punkte, Herrmann hat einen schlechten Tag – an den er sich bis heute nur mit Bitterkeit und deftigen Worten erinnert – und wird Neunter.

to the experts' opinion that 1961 would become Ferrari's year. At least the Sicilian adventure ended up with some consolation for Porsche thanks to a second place for Gurney and a third for Bonnier

The first championship race of the season was the Monaco Grand Prix on May 14th and it began with a handicap for Porsche. On the journey to Monte Carlo their race transporter was delayed with a broken brake pipe. Thus the two works drivers were not able to participate in practice on the Thursday. On top of that, they were not driving the expected new eight-cylinder engined car but four cylinder cars now fitted with indirect fuel injection. In the race Hans Herrmann was the third works driver with Jo Bonnier and Dan Gurney.

The young engineer and driver, Michael May, who was to join Porsche in July, drove a couple of laps in practice. In the race, Dan Gurney drove Bonnier's Syracuse car while the Swede drove the long wheelbase car with the new type number 787, and Herrmann received a 718/2 retaining the slightly shorter wheelbase.

Bonnier was unlucky with the new design and suffered problems with its fuel feed. It was a shame as he had gone from starting fourth on the grid up to second place. Then two Ferraris passed Bonnier but the fourth place seemed to be secure for him until the fuel mishap occurred at the harbour chicane where he coasted to a halt. Gurney in the "old" 718/2 finished fifth and thus received the first points for Porsche. Herrmann was in a bad mood and finished ninth – and still remembers this race today with some bitterness and bad words.

Der Achtzylinder lässt auf sich warten: Weil der Renntransporter verpätet in Monaco eintrifft, fällt das erste Training für Porsche aus, und die Vierzylinder von Bonnier (2), Gurney (4) und Herrmann (6) haben keinen Erfolg.

The race transporter reached Monaco too late for practice and the four-cylinder cars driven by Bonnier (2), Gurney (4) and Herrmann (6) had no success at all.

Im Nordseebad Zandvoort, am 22. Mai 1961 Schauplatz des Großen Preises von Holland, stellen die Techniker einen zweiten 787 bereit. Schwallbleche im Tank und neue elektrische Benzinpumpen sollen das unerwünschte Luftholen der Motoren verhindern. Gurney übernimmt Bonniers Monaco-Auto, der Schwede erhält den neuen. Herrmann bleibt beim modifizierten 718/2 und startet für die Ecurie Maarsbergen von Carel de Beaufort, der ebenfalls einen 718/2 fährt. War Monaco schon eine Enttäuschung, wird Holland ein Desaster. Während Graf Berghe von Trips im Ferrari 156 für den ersten deutschen Grand-Prix-Sieg nach dem Krieg sorgt, können sich die Werks-Porsche auf dem Dünenkurs nicht in Szene setzen. Dan Gurney hat im Training den sechsten Startplatz erkämpft, kommt aber im Rennen nicht über den neunten Rang hinaus. Schließlich muss er auch Tony Brooks noch ziehen lassen und kommt vor Bonnier als Zehnter ins Ziel. Hans Herrmann klagt über einen Motor, der nicht die volle Leistung abgibt, und wird Letzter hinter de Beaufort. Das Beste, was sich für Porsche sagen lässt, ist, dass alle Wagen ankommen, wie übrigens das gesamte Starterfeld. (The best to say all of the Porsches finished (as did all cars entried).)

Das Porsche-Debakel in Holland hat Konsequenzen. Während Herrmann bei Testfahrten in Hockenheim Modifizierungen des Fahrgestells erprobt, kommen beim Grand Prix von Belgien am 18. Juni 1961 statt des Einspritzmotors nun wieder die Ver-

At the seaside resort of Zandvoort, Porsche entered the second 787 variant for the Dutch Grand Prix on May 22nd. Its fuel tanks were fitted with baffles and a small intermediary swirl-pot fed by new electrical fuel pumps were fitted to these fuel-injected cars in order to avoid any fuel feed problems. Gurney drove the car that Bonnier had driven at Monaco while the Swede received a new one again with the long wheelbase. Herrmann stayed with the modified 718/2 and was entered by the Écurie Maarsbergen of Carel Godin de Beaufort who himself raced a 718/2. If Monaco had been a disappointment for Porsche, the Dutch race was a disaster. While Ferrari driver Wolfgang von Trips took the first GP victory for a German driver since the end of World War II, the works Porsches did not cut a fine figure in the dunes of Zandvoort. Dan Gurney qualified in sixth but fell back to ninth in the race. Finally he had to let Tony Brooks in the BRM pass him and thus finished tenth just one place ahead of Bonnier. Hans Herrmann complained about a flagging engine and finished last even behind Beaufort. The best thing one can say about all this was that all the Porsches finished (as in fact did all of the fifteen cars entered in the race).

The Dutch debacle had consequences. While Herrmann was testing the suspension at Hockenheim, Porsche entered carburettor-engined cars for the Belgian Grand Prix at Spa of June 18th 1961. Ferry Porsche was putting his money on reli-

Debakel in den Dünen: Weit abgeschlagen enden 1961 in Zandvoort Gurney (7), Bonnier (6), Beaufort (9) und Herrmann (8).

Debacle in the dunes: Gurney (7), Bonnier (6), Beaufort (9) and Herrmann (8) finished far behind the others in the 1961 Zandvoort GP.

Fotos: Porsche

Sicher ist sicher: In Belgien gehen die Renner wieder mit Vergasern an den Start. Gurney (20) wird Sechster, Bonnier Siebter und de Beaufort Elfter.

Better safe than sorry: for Belgium, the Porsches were re-equipped with carburettors and Gurney (20) finished sixth, Bonnier seventh and Godin de Beaufort eleventh.

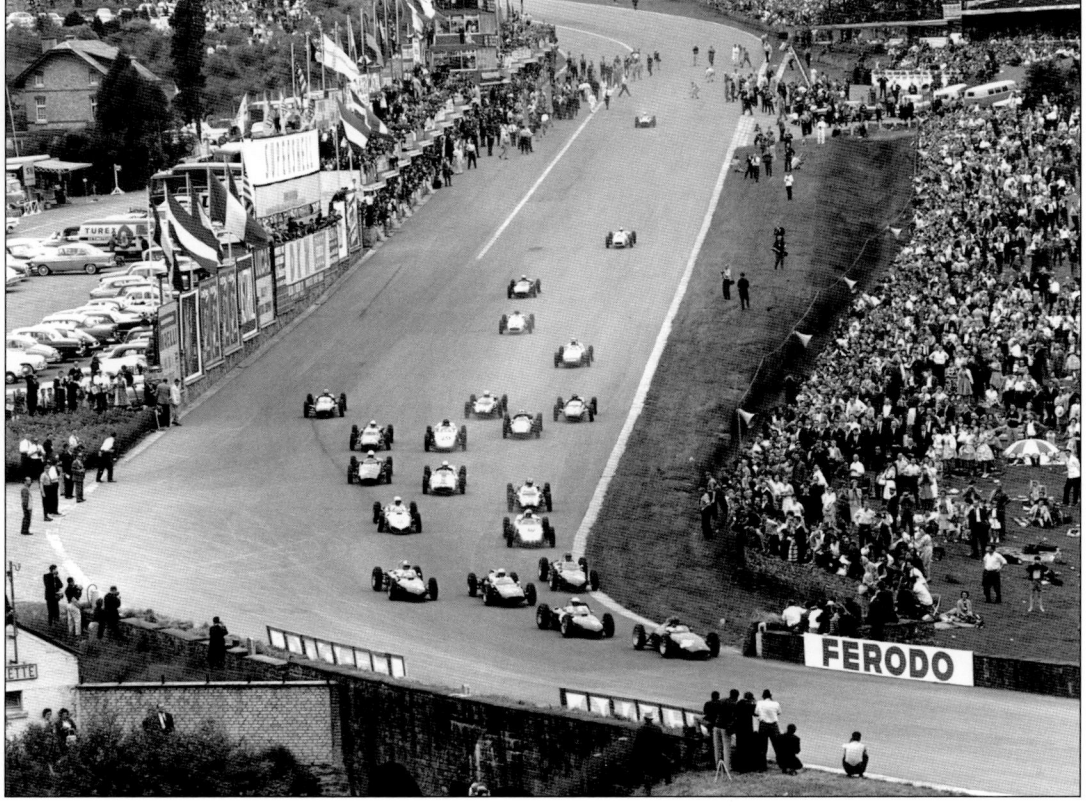

gaser-Triebwerke zum Einsatz, die sich in den ersten Rennen der Saison bewährt hatten. Diese Wagen will Ferry Porsche so lange einsetzen, bis der neue Achtzylinder-Motor rennreif ist. Zwar sind die beiden Zuffenhausener Werkswagen, wie zahlreiche andere Fabrikate auch, nicht in der Lage, den Ferrari gefährlich zu werden, aber Gurney holt mit Platz sechs wenigstens einen WM-Punkt. Bonnier, der zum Ende des Rennens mit sinkendem Öldruck zu kämpfen hat, wird Siebter, de Beaufort Elfter.

Die Stimmung ist denkbar schlecht in Zuffenhausen, Hanstein und die Mannschaft möchten am liebsten aufstecken. Doch ausgerechnet Ferry Porsche denkt nicht ans Aufgeben. Der Chef, der im Jahr darauf dann doch den Schlussstrich ziehen wird, macht weiter. Weitermachen heißt: Die 718/2 der alten Machart mit den bewährten großen Vergasern auf den Viernockern bleiben heiße Eisen im Feuer, der enttäuschende 787 mit dem eigenwilligen Heckdesign und den „Öhrchen" über den Ansaugstutzen wird abgestellt.

Also bleibt nun alles praktisch an drei Autos hängen. Die Fahrgestellnummern 03 und 04 übernehmen Gurney und Bonnier, Carel de Beaufort kauft Nummer 01.

Mit ausgiebigen Testfahrten auf der Nordschleife des Nürburgrings versuchen Bonnier und Gurney, den Wagen zu verbessern. Mit 18 Runden legen sie mehr als eine Grand-Prix-Distanz zurück und klagen über Probleme mit der Übersetzung

Die Ferrari-Fahrer gehen natürlich auch als Favoriten in den Grand Prix von Frankreich, der am 2. Juli 1961 auf der Hochgeschwindigkeitsstrecke von Reims ausgetragen wird. Phil Hill, Graf Trips und Richie Ginther sichern sich erwartungsgemäß die drei besten Startplätze, auf Startposition zwölf steht Giancarlo Baghetti, der auf Ferrari sein Grand-Prix-Debüt gab. Für

able carburettor systems until the new eight-cylinder engine was race-ready. Though neither of the two Porsche works cars nor other competitors were able to beat Ferrari who took the first four places, Gurney at least scored one championship point in sixth place. Bonnier, who suffered from a faltering oil pressure, finished seventh and de Beaufort came in eleventh.

Morale was naturally bad at Zuffenhausen. Von Hanstein and the team were ready to chuck it all in. Of all people, at this point it was Ferry Porsche who did not contemplate giving up. The boss, who would announce the single-seater project was to be stopped just one year later, was determined to carry on. The old style 718/2 with the well tried "Königswellen" engine fitted with big bore carburettors was to be used from now on while the disappointing 787 chassis with its obstinate rear design and those "ears" on top of the rear bodywork was abandoned

So there were only three race cars left. Serial numbers 03 and 04 were taken over by Gurney and Bonnier while number 01 was sold to de Beaufort. Number 02 was kept as a test car.

By carrying out extensive testing on the Nordschleife of the 'Ring, Bonnier and Gurney tried to improve the car. After no fewer than eighteen laps of the long circuit, more than the distance driven in a GP, their complaints centred mainly on the gear ratios.

The Ferrari drivers of course were odds-on favourites at the French Grand Prix held on July 2nd at the high-speed track at Reims. Phil Hill, Wolfgang von Trips and Richie Ginther put their cars, as expected, at the front of the grid. Back in twelfth place was Giancarlo Baghetti making his Grand Prix debut in a Ferrari. Gurney and Bonnier had qualified in ninth and thirteenth places respectively. The first half of the race ran as

Ferrari-Phalanx: In Reims stehen drei rote Renner ganz vorn. Am Ende siegt Newcomer Baghetti (Ferrari 156), der von Position 12 aus ins Rennen gegangen war, vor Gurney.

Ferrari phalanx: at Reims, three red cars started from the front row. Finally Baghetti won the race ahead of Gurney who had started from twelfth position.

Schnelles Rennen: Bonnier (10) und Gurney (12) fahren in der Champagne ein tolles Rennen, bis am Ende Baghetti ganz knapp gewinnt.

A fast race: Bonnier (10) and Gurney (12) drove well at the Champagne circuit where Baghetti won by a hairs-breadth.

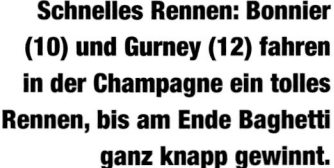

Foto: Porsche

Das Fahrerlager in Aintree: Nummer 56 ist der 718/2 von Carel de Beaufort.

In the paddock at Aintree: number 56 was the 718/2 of Carel Godin de Beaufort.

die Startplätze neun und dreizehn qualifizieren sich Gurney und Bonnier. Die erste Hälfte des Rennens verläuft erwartungsgemäß, Hill und Trips wechseln sich an der Spitze ab, auf Rang drei folgt Ginther.

Als Trips in der 21. Runde wegen Steinschlags am Kühler die Box ansteuert, Ginther wenig später ebenfalls aufgeben muss, Spitzenreiter Phil Hill sich in der Thillois-Kurve dreht und dabei den Motor abwürgt, ist das Rennen wieder völlig offen. Um die Spitze kämpfen nun der einzig verbliebene Ferrari-Pilot Baghetti und die beiden Werks-Fahrer aus Zuffenhausen. Als Bonnier in den letzten beiden Runden langsamer wird, muss die Entscheidung zwischen Gurney und Baghetti fallen. Der italienische Neuling macht seine Sache ausgesprochen clever. Er bleibt bis 300 Meter vor dem Ziel in Gurneys Windschatten und nutzt den PS-Vorteil seines Ferrari dann aus, um rechtzeitig vor dem Ziel am Amerikaner vorbeizuziehen und das Rennen mit einer Zehntelsekunde Vorsprung zu gewinnen.

Der britische Grand Prix, ausgetragen am 15. Juli 1961 in Aintree, ist wieder eine sichere Beute der Ferrari-Piloten. Aus deutscher Sicht besonderes erfreulich: Graf Trips sichert sich seinen zweiten Grand-Prix-Sieg und geht in der WM-Wertung in Führung. Sein härtester Widersacher, der Amerikaner Phil Hill, wird Zweiter, Richie Ginther kommt auf Rang drei ins Ziel. Unter diesen Umständen bleiben für die anderen Teams nur hintere Plätze, von denen sich Bonnier den fünften und Gurney den siebten erkämpfen. De Beaufort sieht die Zielflagge in Aintree als Sechzehnter.

Im Heimrennen auf der Solitude setzt die Porsche-Mannschaft gleich vier Werkswagen ein. Außer den Stammpiloten Bonnier und Gurney sitzen Hans Herrmann und Edgar Barth am Steuer. Da Ferrari den geplanten Einsatz von Graf Trips kurzfristig absagt, sind die Werkteams von Lotus und Cooper die härtesten Gegner der Zuffenhausener. Bonnier und Gurney fahren im Training die schnellsten Zeiten, Herrmann wird Sechster und Barth, der eine Weiterentwicklung des erstmals in Monaco eingesetzten Wagens pilotiert, Zehnter.

expected with Hill and von Trips taking turns at the front followed by Ginther. But the race was thrown wide-open after von Trips had to retire to the pits after a stone punctured his Ferrari's radiator. Soon after that Ginther also had to retire while the leader, Phil Hill, spun at the Thillois hairpin and stalled his engine. Thus fighting for the lead were now the last remaining Ferrari driver, Baghetti, and the two works drivers from Zuffenhausen. Bonnier dropped back in the closing laps to finish seventh, and the race turned into a duel between Gurney and Baghetti. The young Italian was clever. He stayed in the slipstream of Gurney's car until the finish was just 300 metres away. Then he made the best use of his more powerful engine to pass the American and take the win by a single tenth of a second.

The British Grand Prix of 1961 was held at Aintree on July 15th and the Ferrari drivers fought it out between themselves. Von Trips gained his second GP victory and thus put himself into the lead of the championship and his strongest opponents at Aintree were team mates Phil Hill, who came in second, and Richie Ginther third. Bonnier finished fifth, Gurney seventh, and de Beaufort finished sixteenth.

At home, Porsche entered four works cars for the nonchampionship Solitude Grand Prix. Their drivers were Bonnier and Gurney plus Hans Herrmann and Edgar Barth. Ferrari had cancelled the planned entry of von Trips at the last minute so that Lotus and Copper were the main competitors facing the Porsche team. Bonnier and Gurney proved to be fastest in practice, and behind them Herrmann put his car in sixth place and Barth, driving a derivative of the Monaco car fitted with a horizontally mounted fan that was eventually due to be used in the eight-cylinder engine, was tenth.

After the first lap, Lotus driver Innes Ireland led ahead of Bonnier, Gurney, McLaren and Brabham. The five drivers wowed the spectators with one of the most exciting races ever seen on the Solitude circuit. In the heat of the battle, Brabham nudged Bonnier's Porsche and forced him to slide onto the grass. However the Swede managed to catch up and even gain

Solitude-Rennen 1961: Edgar Barths Auto wird zum Start geschoben.

Solitude 1961: Edgar Barth's car was pushed to the start.

Risikofaktor Eifelwetter: Vier Porsche sind am Start, darunter Herrmann (11) und Bonnier (8). Dan Gurney (9) schafft die beste Wertung für die Zuffenhausener mit Rang sieben.

Eifel weather was always a risk factor: five Porsches were entered, amongst them the cars of Herrmann (11) and Bonnier (8). Dan Gurney (9) got the best result for Porsche by finishing seventh.

Nach der ersten Runde führt Lotus-Pilot Innes Ireland vor Bonnier, Gurney, McLaren und Brabham. Diese fünf Fahrer werden mit ihren Duellen die Zuschauer begeistern und eines der spannendsten Rennen auf der Solitude liefern. In der Hitze des Gefechts berührt Brabham Bonniers Porsche am Heck und zwingt ihn zu einem kurzen Ausflug in die Wiese. Aber der Schwede kämpft sich in die Spitzengruppe zurück und liegt eine Runde vor Schluss sogar in Führung. In der letzten Runde aber schiebt sich Ireland noch an dem Porsche vorbei und gewinnt mit einer Zehntelsekunde Vorsprung vor Bonnier. Nur weitere zwei Zehntelsekunden zurück passiert Gurney die Ziellinie. Hans Herrmann, in den Anfangsrunden kurzzeitig sogar bestplatzierter Porsche-Pilot, fällt mit Bremsproblemen zurück und wird Sechster.

Beim Großen Preis von Deutschland am 6. August 1961 tritt Porsche nach zwei weiteren Testtagen in der Eifel wieder mit drei Wagen an. Auf der fahrerisch anspruchsvollen Nordschleife des Nürburgrings kommt der Leistungsvorteil der Ferrari weniger zur Geltung als auf anderen Strecken. Zwar steht Phil Hill auf der Pole Position, aber mit Jack Brabham im Cooper, Stirling Moss auf Lotus und Joakim Bonnier im Porsche stehen gleich drei Fahrzeuge zwischen ihm und Graf Trips, der im Training nur die fünftschnellste Zeit gefahren war. Gurney folgt auf dem siebten, Herrmann auf dem elften und de Beaufort auf dem siebzehnten Startplatz.

Am Renntag regnet es zunächst, was dem beim Start in Führung gegangenen Jack Brabham zum Verhängnis wird. Er rutscht schon im Streckenabschnitt Hatzenbach von der Piste. Während

the lead on the penultimate lap. Then on that last lap, Ireland made his move, passed Bonnier and finished first by just one tenth of a second. And only two tenths later, Gurney crossed the finishing line in third. Hans Herrmann, who had been in the lead for a short time early on, was slowed with a braking problem and finished sixth.

For the German Grand Prix on August 6th, Porsche entered three cars after carrying out two further test sessions on the Nordschleife. On this demanding track, the Ferrari drivers found it difficult to make good use of their better engine performance. Though Phil Hill took pole position, in front of von Trips in the next red racer there were Jack Brabham (Cooper), Stirling Moss (Lotus) and Jo Bonnier (Porsche). Gurney started from sixth position, Herrmann from eleventh and de Beaufort from seventeenth.

On the day of the race, at first it rained and that sealed Brabham's fate for, after taking the lead soon after the start, he slid off the road at Hatzenbach. While Moss finished the first lap ahead of Hill and Herrmann, Bonnier had already returned to the pits as one of the Porsche's rear wheels had to be changed. After the second lap, Moss was still leading and von Trips had passed Herrmann. As the Porsche driver fell back with clutch trouble, for the Ferrari drivers the hunt was on to catch up with the leading Lotus. Under normal circumstances, Ferrari would have won in style. However the Eifel has laws of its own concerning the weather. Towards the end of the race it once again began to rain heavily and Moss gained his second GP victory of the season. To the public's delight, von Trips made it

Autos lieben Shell
BOSCH
Autos lieben Shell
Mobiloil
HEINPREUSSEN

Moss als Erster vor Phil Hill und Hans Herrmann aus der Startrunde kommt, fährt Bonnier bereits an die Box: Ein Hinterrad muss gewechselt werden. Nach der zweiten Runde, noch immer liegt Moss vorne, kommt Trips bereits vor Herrmann bei Start und Ziel vorbei. Als der Porsche-Pilot mit Kupplungsproblemen nun immer weiter zurückfällt, machen die Ferrari Jagd auf den führenden Lotus. Unter regulären Bedingungen hätten sie das Rennen wohl gewonnen, aber die Eifel hat bekanntlich in punkto Wetter eigene Gesetze. Zum Ende des Rennens setzt erneut starker Regen ein, und Moss holt sich den zweiten Grand-Prix-Sieg der Saison. Zur Freude der Zuschauer kann sich Trips noch auf den zweiten Platz verbessern und damit seine Führung in der WM-Wertung ausbauen. Bester Porsche-Pilot ist Dan Gurney auf Rang sieben.

Bei den folgenden, nicht zur WM zählenden Rennen ist Porsche nur bei Bonniers Heim-Rennen in Schweden werksseitig vertreten. Zuvor wird am 17. August 1961 der Große Preis von Dänemark in Roskilde ausgetragen. Stirling Moss triumphiert in allen drei Durchgängen und entscheidet die Gesamtwertung klar für sich. Einziger Porsche-Pilot im Feld ist de Beaufort, der im ersten Lauf als Elfter ins Ziel kommt. Nach einem Reifenschaden im zweiten Durchgang tritt er zum letzten Lauf nicht mehr an.

Weil Stirling Moss am Samstag noch bei der Tourist Trophy in Goodwood startet und diese auch gewinnt, trifft er erst kurz vor Start des Kannonloppet-Formel-1-Rennens in Karlskoga ein. Der Veranstalter erlaubt ihm den Start auch ohne Training, allerdings muss Moss aus der letzten Startreihe ins Rennen gehen. Dennoch liegt der Engländer nach der ersten Runde bereits in Führung, die er bis ins Ziel nicht mehr abgibt. Mit zwölf Sekunden Rückstand wird Bonnier Zweiter vor John Surtees auf Cooper.

Mit Testfahrten in Monza beginnt für die Porsche-Mannschaft der Abstecher nach Italien. Eine Woche vor dem Großen

into second place and thereby managed to increase his lead in the championship. The best Porsche driver was Gurney who finished seventh.

In the ensuing non-championship races, Porsche only turned up at Bonnier's home circuit in Sweden. Before that, the Danish Grand Prix was held at Roskilde on August 17th. Stirling Moss was triumphant in all three of the heats and thus won in style. The only Porsche present was de Beaufort. He finished eleventh in the first heat but suffered a punctured tyre in the second and thus did not enter for the third.

Because Stirling Moss was racing in the Tourist Trophy at Goodwood on Saturday (and won it), he arrived at Sweden's Karlskoga circuit only shortly before the Kannonlopet Formula One race. The organizer permitted him to start without having practised, but of course he had to start from the back of the grid. Anyhow Moss managed to catch up in his usual style and took the lead before the first lap was over. There he stayed until the finish and won the race by twelve seconds from Bonnier who was followed by John Surtees (Cooper).

One week before the Italian Grand Prix all the top drivers gathered at Modena for the Modena Grand Prix. Only Ferrari did not send any cars as he preferred to save his efforts for the following weekend. Bonnier and Gurney wowed the crowds with their skill but finally had to surrender as, once again, Moss in the Lotus proved to be unbeatable. At the start, Bonnier shot off in the lead only to fall back soon afterwards when he lost fifth gear. On lap twelve, Moss took the lead while Gurney had to defend his second place against Surtees. After Surtees retired, Gurney was then attacked by Bonnier who had caught up and now passed Gurney on lap fifty-nine. The drivers crossed the finishing line with Moss first ahead of Bonnier, Gurney, Clark and Brabham.

Modena mal ohne Ferrari: Dan Gurney und Joakim Bonnnier (3.v.r.) machen 1961 in Norditalien eine gute Figur. Den Sieg trägt freilich Moss davon.

Modena with no Ferraris: Dan Gurney and Jo Bonnier (third from right) cut fine figures at the 1961 race but eventually it was Moss who took the victory.

Preis von Italien findet sich die Grand-Prix-Elite in Modena ein, nur Lokalmatador Ferrari fehlt. Bonnier und Gurney liefern den zahlreichen Zuschauern in ihren Porsche eine tolle Show, müssen sich am Ende aber wieder einmal Stirling Moss beugen. Während Gurney das Rennen vom Start bis zur zwölften Runde anführt, fällt Bonnier schon zu Beginn weit zurück, weil sich der fünfte Gang nicht mehr einlegen lässt. In der zwölften Runde übernimmt Moss die Führung, Gurney muss seinen zweiten Platz nun gegen Surtees verteidigen. Nach dem Ausfall des Engländers bekommt Gurney Konkurrenz aus dem eigenen Team. Bonnier hat sich an die Spitze zurück gekämpft und überholt seinen Teamgefährten in der 59. Runde. An dieser Reihenfolge ändert sich bis zur Zielankunft nichts mehr, Moss gewinnt vor Bonnier, Gurney, Clark und Brabham.

Als Dan Gurney am 10. September 1961 die Ziellinie beim Großen Preis von Italien als Zweiter hinter dem neuen Weltmeister Phil Hill überquert, kommt keine Freude auf, zu grausam ist bei diesem Rennen die Kehrseite des Motorsports zu Tage getreten. Der tödliche Unfall von Graf Berghe von Trips, der in der zweiten Runde mit Jim Clark kollidiert und bei dem folgenden Überschlag aus seinem Ferrari geschleudert worden war, kostet auch fünfzehn Zuschauer das Leben. Vor diesem Hintergrund wird der Rennverlauf, ja selbst die Entscheidung im WM-Titelkampf zugunsten des Amerikaners Phil Hill, zur Nebensache. Das betrifft auch de Beaufort, der sich einen tollen siebten Platz erkämpft und nur knapp einen WM-Punkt verfehlt.

Eine Woche später bleibt Ferrari dem Flugplatz-Rennen in Österreich fern, alle anderen Hersteller sind in Zeltweg vertreten. Neben de Beaufort geht auch Bonnier ins Rennen, dessen

A week later, there was little elation shown when Dan Gurney crossed the finishing line in second place of the 1961 Italian Grand Prix on September 10th behind the winner and new World Champion, Phil Hill. The race had been overshadowed by the fatal accident of Wolfgang Graf Berghe von Trips. On only the second lap he had collided with Jim Clark's Lotus causing his Ferrari to flip over, throw him out and killing him. The car then crashed into the crowd, killing fifteen spectators. That incident totally degraded what had been a thrilling race and relegated the matter of who had won the championship into the background. For the record, de Beaufort finished seventh and missed a point by just a hair's breadth behind Roy Salvadori's Cooper.

One week later Ferrari did not turn up at the non-championship race in Austria but all of the other main competitors entered the race at Zeltweg. There was of course de Beaufort again but Bonnier's Porsche arrived only in time for the second practice session. Lotus drivers Jim Clark and Innes Ireland and Cooper drivers John Surtees and Jack Brabham put their cars on the first four grid positions and then competed in a neck-and-neck race. Bonnier followed them in fifth place and benefitted when Clark and Surtees both retired. Thus the Swede finished third behind Ireland and Brabham. Nine drivers finished the race with de Beaufort finishing sixth.

At the US Grand Prix at Watkins Glen on October 8th, Ferrari was also absent from the line up. Thus the American crowds missed seeing "their" world champion, Phil Hill, in action. Jack Brabham put his car on pole position and fought hard for the lead with Stirling Moss. On lap fifty-seven, Brabham

Im Tiefflug: Das Flugplatzrennen am 17. September in Zeltweg beendet Bonnier als Dritter.

Low-level flight: in the race at Zeltweg airport on September 17th, Bonnier finished third.

Foto: Porsche

108

Porsche allerdings erst zum zweiten Training eintrifft. Die vier Trainingsschnellsten, Jim Clark und Innes Ireland (beide Lotus) sowie John Surtees und Jack Brabham (beide Cooper), liefern sich ein abwechslungsreiches Rennen. Bonnier folgt ihnen auf Rang fünf und profitiert davon, dass Clark und Surtees ausfallen. Der Schwede kommt so hinter Ireland und Brabham als Dritter ins Ziel. Insgesamt werden neun Fahrer gewertet, unter ihnen de Beaufort auf einem guten sechsten Rang.

Ferrari fehlt auch beim Grand Prix der USA in Watkins Glen, das amerikanische Publikum bekommt „seinen" Weltmeister somit nicht auf der Piste zu sehen. Jack Brabham sichert sich die Pole Position und kämpft lange mit Stirling Moss um die Führung. In der 57. Runde muss Brabham wegen Überhitzung seines Motors aufgeben, nur zwei Runden später stellt auch Moss seinen Lotus mit einem verbrannten Kurbelwellenlager ab. Die Führung des Rennens erbt Lotus-Pilot Innes Ireland, der dem Lotus-Team den ersten Grand-Prix-Sieg sichern kann. Zwar hat Moss bereits zwei WM-Läufe auf Lotus gewonnen, für das Werks-Team aber ist es der erste ganz große Erfolg. Zweiter wird Dan Gurney, der dank sechs WM-Punkten in der Tabelle noch zu Moss aufschließt und die WM als Dritter beendet. Das gute Ergebnis in den USA komplettiert Bonniers sechster Rang.

Ausgerechnet ein Italiener beschert Porsche den ersten Formel-1-Triumph des Jahres 1961. Bei der Coppa Italia in Vallelunga sind am 12. Oktober 1961 nur italienische Piloten am Start, darunter Giancarlo Baghetti in einem Porsche 718/2, den die Scuderia Sant Ambroeus gemeldet hat.

Hinter Nino Vaccarella auf einem Cooper qualifiziert sich Baghetti als Zweiter. Der Porsche-Pilot gewinnt beide Läufe des Rennens und somit auch die Gesamtwertung vor Ernesto Prinroth (Lotus) und Vaccarella.

In einem Interview mit der Süddeutschen Zeitung, das am 22. November 1961 erscheint, dämpft Huschke von Hanstein die Erwartungen hinsichtlich des neuen F1-Wagens: „Noch sind wir längst nicht soweit. Hockenheim brachte wohl ordentliche Resultate, aber der Motor noch nicht die für dieses Versuchsstadium erhoffte Leistung. 180 PS sind jedenfalls noch nicht drin. Die Weiterentwicklung wird zusätzlich erschwert, da wir oftmals an die langen Fristen der Lieferfirmen gebunden sind. So müssen wir auf neue Kolben bzw. Zylinderköpfe etwa zwei Monate warten. Eines steht jedenfalls unabdingbar fest: Der Achtzylinder-Rennwagen startet nur mit voller Rennreife in die nächste Saison. Zum Hinterherfahren haben wir keine Lust. Falls es notwendig sein sollte, können wir auch ein Jahr pausieren."

Er verweist auch auf die begrenzten personellen Ressourcen: „Die Rennabteilung ist nur eine kleine Zelle im Hause. Mehr als 20 Mann lassen sich von der 1200-köpfigen Belegschaft für spezielle Rennaufgaben nicht abzweigen. Wir müssen uns nach der Decke strecken."

Nicht unumstritten sind seine Aussagen zu Hans Herrmann: „Wenn alles gut läuft, können wir in der nächsten Saison zwei neue Achtzylinder einsetzen. Bonnier und Gurney wollen gern weiter bei uns fahren. Weitere Angebote namhafter Ausländer liegen vor. Mit Hans Herrmann können wir kaum noch rechnen. Es mangelt ihm an der unerbittlichen Härte, um vornehmlich mit den „hungrigen" Engländern mitzuhalten. Ein junger deutscher Ersatzmann für ihn ist weit und breit nicht zu sehen."

had to retire with an overheating engine and then, with only two laps to go, Moss had to park his Lotus after the crankshaft bearings gave up the ghost. Thus the Lotus driver, Innes Ireland, inherited the lead and gave the Lotus team its first championship Grand Prix victory. Though Moss had already won two non-championship races, this was the first really big success. Dan Gurney finished second in the race and the six points that he scored enabled him to catch up with Moss and they tied for third place in the World Championship. A sixth place for Bonnier completed a good result for Porsche in the USA.

Of all people, it had to be an Italian who provided Porsche with its first Formula One victory of the season. Only Italian drivers took part in the Coppa Italia at Vallelunga. Giancarlo Baghetti drove a Porsche 718/2 entered by the Scuderia Sant Ambroeus and he qualified it second fastest behind Nino Vaccarella (Cooper). The Porsche driver then won both heats and thus the race overall ahead of Ernesto Prinroth (Lotus) and Vaccarella.

Huschke von Hanstein gave an interview to the renowned daily newspaper "Süddeutsche Zeitung". It was published on November 22nd and Hanstein dampened expectations concerning their new Formula One car: "In fact we are far from reaching our aim. Hockenheim no doubt brought good results, but the engine is performing far short of expectations at this trial stage. As yet, one hundred and eighty horsepower are simply not available. Moreover, further development is impeded by long delivery times from the component suppliers. For example, we have to wait about two months for new pistons or cylinder heads. One thing is for certain: our eight-cylinder racer will not start in the next season before it is absolutely ready to race competitively. We are surely not doing all this just to drive behind other people. If it turns out to be necessary, we will even hold fire for another year."

Von Hanstein also made reference to the small size of the Porsche team. "The racing department is just a small unit within the main body of the company. We cannot afford to draw more than twenty men from our 1,200 employees for the specific racing job. As a company, we do have to make both ends meet."

More controversial were his comments about Hans Herrmann: "If everything goes well, we will enter two new eight-cylinder cars for next season. Bonnier and Gurney have confirmed that they would like to drive for us. There are more proposals from other renowned foreigners. But I fear that we cannot count on Hans Herrmann. He lacks that hard edge that is needed to keep up especially with the 'hungry' Englishmen. And there is no up-and-coming young German driver in sight at present."

Thus came the break-up between Porsche's racing director and Hans Herrmann. It lasted until 1966 when Ferdinand Piëch brought Herrmann back into the fold – a clever move as it turned out for the fast Swabian gained many victories for Porsche, among them the first overall victory at Le Mans in 1970.

At the end of the year, Porsche sent Bonnier and Barth with their 1961 racing cars to South Africa and the so called Christmas races. The first race was the Rand Grand Prix at Kyalami. The ship bringing the Porsche racing cars to South Africa was

Weihnachtsrennen: Edgar Barth und Jo Bonnier gehen Ende 1961 nach Südafrika.

A race at Christmas: Edgar Barth and Jo Bonnier were entered in the South African series at the end of 1961.

So kommt es 1961 zum Bruch zwischen dem Porsche-Rennleiter und Herrmann, ein Schritt, den erst Ferdinand Piëch 1966 korrigiert. Er holt den schnellen Schwaben ins Team zurück, der es ihm mit zahlreichen Erfolgen, darunter dem ersten Porsche-Gesamtsieg im 24-Stunden-Rennen von Le Mans, dankt.

Zu den so genannten Weihnachtsrennen schickt Porsche Jo Bonnier und Edgar Barth mit den 1961er Modellen nach Südafrika. Das erste Rennen, der Rand Grand Prix in Kyalami, wird eine sichere Beute für die Lotus-Piloten Clark und Taylor, die außer dem drittplazierten Bonnier das gesamte Feld überrunden. Bonnier fährt zwar die schnellste Runde des Rennens, liegt im Ziel aber mehr als zwanzig Sekunden zurück. Edgar Barth wird Vierter.

Während der daheimgebliebene Teil des Teams zu Testfahrten nach Hockenheim aufbricht, wird die Südafrika-Tour mit dem Natal Grand Prix in Westmead fortgesetzt. Das Rennen bezieht seine Spannung aus dem Duell zwischen Jim Clark und Stirling Moss. Zwar kann sich der Schotte am Ende durchsetzen und mit 32 Sekunden Vorsprung gewinnen, aber er war auch von der Pole Position ins Rennen gegangen. Moss hingen muss, da er nicht am Training teilgenommen hat, vom Ende des Feldes starten. Ohne dieses Handicap wäre das Rennen für ihn wohl anders ausgegangen. Bonnier kann in den Kampf um die Spitze nicht eingreifen und wird mit einer Runde Rückstand Dritter. Eine weitere Runde zurück landet Barth auf Rang vier. Drei Tage vor Weihnachten wird ein erneuter Test in Hockenheim absolviert.

Die Rennen in Südafrika finden mit dem Grand Prix am 26. Dezember 1961 und dem Cape Grand Prix am 2. Januar 1962 ihren Abschluss. Auf dem Siegerpodest des Großen Preises von Südafrika bietet sich das gleiche Bild wie in Westmead. Clark und

late and they only got to the circuit an hour of so before the start of the race. The Lotus drivers Clark and Taylor fought it out at the front and, though Bonnier drove the fastest lap, he finished twenty seconds behind in third with Edgar Barth fourth.

Back at home in Stuttgart, the team hit the road for further testing at Hockenheim, while the South African trip continued with the Natal Grand Prix at Westmead. This was a duel between Jim Clark and Stirling Moss. The Scot finished first with a thirty-two second lead, but then he had started from pole position while Moss had had to start from the last row thanks to the fact that he had not taken part in practice. Maybe the race would have ended in a different way without that handicap. Bonnier finished third one lap down and Barth came in fourth.

Three days before Christmas there was yet further testing at Hockenheim as the engineers sought for the answers they needed for the 1962 season.

The last two races in the southern hemisphere were the South African Grand Prix on December 26th and the Cape Grand Prix on January 2nd. Clark and Moss started the South African GP side by side from the first row and again it was the Scot who won through in impressive fashion with pole position, fastest race lap, and victory. Bonnier finished one lap down and Barth was fifth.

Lotus also won the last race at the Cape GP making it four-in-a-row. This time Trevor Taylor beat Clark by 0.6 seconds. Bonnier again finished third but this time only six seconds down. Masten Gregory (Lotus) was next followed by Tony Maggs (Cooper) and then by Barth who finished one lap down on the leaders.

Fotos: Porsche

Startbahn Süd: Bonnier hat es zwar beim Start am Kap 1961 in die erste Reihe geschafft, kann sich aber gegen die modernere Konkurrenz nicht durchsetzen. Fotos: Porsche

Cape contest: though Bonnier made it onto the front row in the 1961 Cape GP, he had no chance against the more up-to-date competitors.

Moss stehen dieses Mal beide in der ersten Startreihe und erneut setzt sich der Schotte knapp, aber eindrucksvoll durch. Pole Position, schnellste Rennrunde und der Sieg gegen Moss zeigen, über was für ein Fahrtalent der Schotte verfügt. Bonnier liegt im Ziel wieder eine Runde zurück, Barth wird mit zwei Runden Rückstand Fünfter. Auch das letzte Rennen dieser Serie wird eine Beute des Lotus-Teams. Dieses Mal gewinnt Trevor Taylor, der Clark um 0,6 Sekunden hinter sich lässt. Bonnier wird wieder Dritter, liegt im Ziel aber nur sechs Sekunden zurück. Hinter Masten Gregory und Tony Maggs kommt Barth als erster überrundeter Fahrer auf Rang sechs.

Better news came from Malmsheim, where Bott, Linge and Mimler had tested the 804 on the local airstrip. The notes from March 14th 1962 record that: "All of the drivers achieved thirty-three seconds for three laps on the 60-metre circle at their first go. This is the best result ever achieved despite the fact that the surface conditions were not very good – slightly wet and slippery."

The 1962 Formula One season started on April 1st with the Brussels Grand Prix on the Heysel circuit in Belgium. Three Porsches were entered, all of them by private teams. Wolfgang Seidel drove de Beaufort's car from the previous year and the

Ermutigende Signale bringen Probefahrten, die Bott, Linge und Mimler mit dem 804 am 14. März 1962 auf dem Flugplatz von Malmsheim unternehmen. Im Protokoll heißt es: „Alle Fahrer erreichen auf Anhieb 33 Sekunden für 3 Runden auf dem 60-Meter-Kreis. Das ist beste Zeit, die je gefahren wurde, trotzdem die Bodenverhältnisse nicht sehr günstig waren – schmierig und etwas nass."

Mit dem Grand Prix von Brüssel beginnt am 1. April 1962 die europäische Formel-1-Saison. Drei Porsche stehen am Start, alle von privaten Teams gemeldet. Wolfgang Seidel pilotiert den Vorjahreswagen von de Beaufort, der Schweizer Heinz Schiller hat bei Porsche einen Vierzylinder aus der letzten Saison gekauft. Auch Joakim Bonnier fährt einen Vierzylinder, allerdings in ungewohnter Lackierung: Da die Nennung über die italienische Scuderia SSS Repubblica di Venezia erfolgt war, rollt für ihn ein roter Porsche aus dem Transporter.

Der Belgier Willy Mairesse, als Nachfolger von Richie Ginther Neuling in der Scuderia Ferrari, geht mit seinem Sechszylinder, dem mehr als 190 PS nachgesagt werden, als Favorit ins Rennen. Seine härtesten Konkurrenten sind Stirling Moss (Lotus), Jim Clark (Lotus), John Surtees (Lola) und Graham Hill (B.R.M.).

Aufregung schon in der ersten Runde: Der Trainingsschnellste, Jim Clark auf Lotus, muss mit Ventilschaden aufgeben, und Moss kommt als Letzter bei Start und Ziel vorbei, weil er in einer Kurve den Notausgang nehmen muss. Er kämpft sich durch das gesamte Feld und beendet den Lauf als Zweiter hinter Graham Hill. Mairesse wird Dritter, Bonnier Sechster, Schiller kommt auf den 12. und Seidel auf den 14. Platz.

Weil Hills B.R.M. vor dem zweiten Lauf angeschoben wird – vorgeschrieben ist der Start per Anlasser – legt Ferrari-Rennleiter Dragoni Protest ein, der zum Ausschluss des Briten führt. Als Mairesse im zweiten Lauf einen Dreher produziert und Moss mit Zündungsschaden aufgeben muss, führt Bonnier plötzlich das Feld an. Aber die Aufholjagd von Mairesse ist erfolgreich, er geht in der 17. Runde an dem Schweden vorbei. Auch der dritte Lauf sieht Mairesse vor Bonnier. Beide belegen diese Plätze auch in der Gesamtwertung.

Auch bei den folgenden fünf Rennen ist Porsche werksseitig nicht vertreten. Bei der Lombank Trophy fährt Stirling Moss sowohl im Training als auch im Rennen die schnellste Runde, kommt beim Rennen in Snetterton jedoch nur auf den siebten Rang. Vergaserprobleme zwingen den Engländer in der zweiten Rennhälfte mehrfach an die Boxen. Es gewinnt Jim Clark (Lotus) vor Graham Hill (B.R.M.) und Joakim Bonnier (Porsche). Der dritte Rang des Schweden ist ein Erfolg der Zuverlässigkeit. Vom achten Startplatz gestartet, profitiert er von den Ausfällen seiner Konkurrenten und wird Dritter, ohne einen Gegner überholt zu haben. Wolfgang Seidel kommt auf einem guten sechsten Rang ins Ziel.

Neben Bonnier und Heinz Schiller ist Ludwig Heimrath am 23. April 1962 dritter Porsche-Pilot beim Grand Prix von Pau in Südfrankreich. Der Kanadier hat sich einen Vorjahreswagen im Werk ausgeliehen und lässt sich dessen Einsatz von der Players Tobacco Company finanzieren.

Erneut ist der Schotte Jim Clark auf Lotus Trainingsschnellster, mit fast zwei Sekunden Rückstand komplettieren Ricardo

Swiss driver, Heinz Schiller, a four-cylinder from the previous year. Jo Bonnier drove another four-cylinder, which was painted in an unusual colour scheme for a Porsche. As it was entered by the Italian team Scuderia Serenissima Repubblica di Venezia, it wore a paint scheme in glaring red.

Belgian Willy Mairesse had displaced Richie Ginther in the Scuderia Ferrari line-up. He was provided with a six-cylinder that was said to deliver more than 190 horsepower and thus was considered as the odds-on favourite. His strongest competitors were Stirling Moss (Lotus), Jim Clark (Lotus), and Graham Hill (BRM) all of whom were now powered by V8 1.5-litre engines while John Surtees's Lola still had the 4-cylinder Climax.

The race, run in three heats, started with Jim Clark taking the lead in the first heat from pole position but then retiring with a dropped valve in his engine. Moss went up an escape road and finished the first lap in last place. He caught up and finished second behind Graham Hill with Mairesse third while Bonnier came in sixth, Schiller was twelfth and Seidel fourteenth.

Both the BRMs of Hill and his team mate, Tony Marsh, were push-started before the second heat. As an onboard starter was mandatory, Ferrari's racing director Dragoni lodged a protest and both cars were disqualified. Bonnier found himself in the lead after Mairesse got into a slide, hit a wall and reversed onto the track hitting Trevor Taylor's Lotus as he did so. However, Mairesse managed to catch up and passed the Swede on lap seventeen while Moss retired with total ignition failure. In the third heat too Mairesse finished ahead of Bonnier and that corresponded to the overall finishing positions.

There were no Porsche works cars entered for the following five races. Stirling Moss (UDT Lotus) drove the fastest lap in practice for the Lombank Trophy race at Snetterton on April 16th but he finished only seventh in the race thanks to a carburettor problem. Jim Clark (Lotus) won ahead of Graham Hill (BRM) and Jo Bonnier (Porsche). The Swede benefitted from the reliability of his car as he had started from eighth on the grid, but other competitors were forced to retire and thus Bonnier finished third without having passed anybody. Wolfgang Seidel finished sixth.

Ludwig Heimrath was the third Porsche driver at the Grand Prix held at Pau on April 23rd. For this race in southern France, the Canadian had borrowed one of the previous year's cars from Porsche and was sponsored by Players Tobacco Company. Jim Clark was fastest in practice with the Lotus with Mexican Ricardo Rodriguez (Ferrari) and Bonnier (Porsche) two seconds behind him. In the race, the Swede took the lead after Clark retired but then sadly he too had to retire with gearbox failure a couple of laps later. Surprisingly Maurice Trintignant won the race in his Lotus entered by the Rob Walker team nearly lapping Rodriguez in the process. Heimrath retired after an accident while Schiller finished ninth

Wolfgang Seidel was the only Porsche driver entered for the Glover Trophy and Lavant Cup races at Goodwood on Easter Monday, April 23rd. In the Glover Trophy he finished tenth but in the Lavant Cup held just for four-cylinder Formula One cars he finished seventh. This particular weekend of racing at Goodwood is most remembered as the point in time when Stirling

Rodriguez (Mexiko) im Ferrari und Bonnier die erste Startreihe. Der Schwede liegt nach Clarks Ausfall sogar einige Runden in Führung, muss dann aber, wie der Lotus-Pilot zuvor auch, mit Getriebeschaden aufgeben. Der Sieg geht überraschend an Maurice Trintignant, der auf einem Lotus des Rob Walker Teams Rodriguez im Ferrari fast eine Runde abnimmt. Heimrath scheidet im Porsche nach einem Unfall aus, Schiller kommt als Neunter ins Ziel.

Als einziger Porsche-Fahrer startet Wolfgang Seidel im Lavant Cup und der Glover Trophy in Goodwood. Er wird im Hauptlauf Zehnter, in einem eigens für Vierzylinder-Fahrzeuge des Vorjahres angesetzten Rennen kommt er auf den siebten Rang. Aber dieses Rennwochenende in Goodwood wird nicht aufgrund seiner Ergebnisse in Erinnerung bleiben, sondern als das Rennen, das den Schlusspunkt in der Karriere von Stirling Moss setzt. Der Engländer kommt in einer schnellen Rechtskurve von der Strecke ab und prallt gegen einen Erdwall. Es dauert fast dreißig Minuten, bis die Helfer ihn aus dem deformierten Wrack befreien können. Zwar wird sich der Ausnahmepilot von Kopf- und Rückenverletzungen sowie Rippenbrüchen erholen, seine sportliche Laufbahn aber hat der Unfall beendet. Unter diesen Umständen treten die Siege von Graham Hill und Bruce McLaren in den beiden F1-Rennen in den Hintergrund.

Waren die Ferrari im Vorjahr noch das Maß aller Dinge, können Phil Hill und Giancarlo Baghetti beim B.A.R.C. 200 in Aintree mit dem Lotus-Piloten Jim Clark nicht mithalten. Der Schotte siegt vor Bruce McLaren, die beiden Ferrari liegen bei der Zieldurchfahrt eineinhalb Minuten zurück. Wolfgang Seidel scheidet mit Antriebsschaden aus.

Das Formel-1-Rennen um die International Trophy machen Fahrer von den britischen Inseln in diesem Jahr unter sich aus. Jim Clark hat bereits einen Vorsprung von 20 Sekunden herausgefahren, als der Trainingsschnellste, Graham Hill im B.R.M., zur Aufholjagd startet. Er kämpft sich Meter um Meter an seinen schottischen Rivalen heran, bis beide nebeneinander in die letzte Kurve des Rennens einbiegen. Hill setzt sich in diesem Duell knapp durch, Clark wird vor John Surtees Zweiter. Bonnier belegt im Porsche der Scuderia Serenissima Repubblica di Venezia Rang Zwölf.

Derweil versucht Huschke von Hanstein, die Erwartungen der Fachpresse an den neuen F1-Porsche im Zaum zu halten. In einem Brief an einen Journalisten heißt es:

„Sehr geehrter, lieber Herr Kollege,

vor ca. einem Jahr trat die neue Formel 1 in Kraft. Soweit es die Beteiligung der Firma Porsche anging, wurde – insbesondere das Rennen in Zandvoort – für Sie und die Öffentlichkeit zu einer Enttäuschung.

Weitgehend ohne unser Zutun war während des Winters der erste Start von Porsche in einem echten Grand Prix publizistisch hochgespielt worden und die Öffentlichkeit erwartete ein veni, vidi, vici und war bitter enttäuscht als dies nicht so war. Obwohl sich im weiteren Verlauf des Jahres die ‚alten' Porsche-4-Zylinder hervorragend schlugen und Dan Gurney im offiziellen Klassement der Fahrerweltmeisterschaft den 3. Platz belegte, blieb trotz eines erneuten Sieges in der Europa-Berg-Meisterschaft und der Europa-Rallye-Meisterschaft weitgehend der Eindruck bestehen, Porsche habe ein schlechtes Sportjahr hinter sich, während in

Moss's racing career came to a sudden end. The UDT-Lotus of Moss left the track in a fast right bend and crashed into a bank. It took nearly thirty minutes for officials and helpers to extricate him from the distorted wreck. Though Moss later recovered from his severe injuries, effectively his driving career was ended. For the record, Graham Hill (BRM) and Bruce McLaren (Cooper) respectively won the two Formula One races.

In the previous year, the Ferraris had had the measure of the other cars but in the 1962 BARC Aintree 200 on April 30th, Phil Hill and Giancarlo Baghetti were simply outclassed by Jim Clark in the Lotus. He finished first ahead of Bruce McLaren in a four-cylinder 1961 Cooper and the two Ferraris were one and a half minutes down in third and fourth place respectively. Seidel retired with engine failure.

It was mainly drivers from the United Kingdom who fought out the Formula One race for the International Trophy at Silverstone on May 14th. In the cold, wet weather, Jim Clark was soon out in front with a twenty-second lead, but then Graham Hill, who had been fastest in practice with his BRM, started a serious attempt to catch up with the leader. Hill approached him gradually until the two of them raced neck-and-neck into the last bend of the race. Hill finally came out a whisker in front leaving Clark second in front of John Surtees. Bonnier in the Scuderia Serenissima Repubblica di Venezia Porsche finished twelfth.

Meanwhile Huschke von Hanstein was peppered with questions concerning the new Formula One Porsche. He wrote a letter to a journalist:

"My dearest colleague,

About a year ago, the new Formula One came into effect. The participation of Porsche under the new regulations, especially the race at Zandvoort, turned out to be a disappointment for you and the general public.

Through no fault of our own, during the winter prior to the first entry of Porsche in a real Grand Prix race, the press exaggerated our chances of success. Thence the public expected us, like Caesar, to "Veni, Vidi, Vici" and were bitterly disappointed when it did not turn out like that. The fact is that during that year, the 'old' Porsche four-cylinder cars were doing pretty well with Dan Gurney coming second in the World Drivers Championship. And despite a new victory in the European hill climb championship plus one in the European rally championship, the impression given in the press was that Porsche had suffered a bad year. The truth it is that it just was not able to match their high expectations of our performance in Grand Prix racing."

"Now it is that time again! We took advantage of the few winter months – do not forget that our small team had also been racing in South Africa for two months – and developed a new chassis plus a new gear box and new brakes while we carried on working on the eight-cylinder engine."

"It was Mr Porsche's wish to not enter the new car until it could have been tested on a Grand Prix track and not until it had proved that it was equal to the performance of its rivals."

"Due to circumstances beyond our control, such as the crash some days ago at Hockenheim of the first car to be built, such as permanently wet test circuits, and such as the influenza suffered by our driver Jo Bonnier, we still lack that proof."

Wirklichkeit nur den wohl allzu hoch gesteckten Erwartungen im Grand-Prix-Sport nicht entsprochen wurde. Jetzt ist es wieder soweit! Die wenigen Wintermonate – unser Team war ja in der Zwischenzeit 2 Monate in Südafrika – haben wir benutzt, um ein neues Chassis mit einem neuen Getriebe und neuen Bremsen zu entwickeln, während auf der Motorenseite am 8-Zylinder weiter gearbeitet wurde.

Der Wunsch von Herrn Porsche war es, dieses Fahrzeug erst zum Einsatz zu bringen, wenn es wirklich bei Versuchsfahrten auf einer Grand-Prix-Rennstrecke gezeigt hätte, daß es den besten Konkurrenzfabrikaten ebenbürtig ist.

Durch eine Reihe von äußeren Umständen, auf die wir ohne Einfluß waren, wie Zerstörung des ersten fertigen Wagens vor wenigen Tagen in Hockenheim, ständig nasse oder feuchte Renn-pisten, eine fiebrige Grippeerkrankung unseres Fahrers Joakim Bonnier und andere, ist es zu diesem Beweis bisher nicht gekom-men.

Trotzdem hat sich Herr Porsche aus sportlichen Gründen entschlossen, den Versuch zu wagen, bis zum 1. Trainingstag in Zandvoort in Tag- und Nachtarbeit zwei Wagen versuchsweise fertigzustellen. Beim alten preußischen Kommiß gab es eine Me-thode, den Rekruten das Schwimmen beizubringen, nämlich sie

"Anyway Mr Porsche has, for sporting reasons, decided to complete two more cars by way of experiment. They had to be ready for the first practice day and they were completed in day and night shifts. In the old Prussian army, they had a way to teach the recruits swimming, namely to throw them into deep water hoping they would pick up the skill quickly and live. We were in a similar situation to those recruits on the first day of practice at Zandvoort where the cars had to take their first steps in public because there was no time left for further testing. It is not until the results from those sessions are in hand that Mr Porsche and his co-directors will decide whether the cars will be entered for the race or whether it turns out to be too soon to do that."

"I kindly ask for your understanding, dear colleague, why it has been that during the last weeks and months it was impossi-ble for us to say much about the development of the car. Today, I merely want to advise you of the fact that we will use the prac-tice sessions at Zandvoort for this first test drive and I wanted to avoid that you should have learnt this only by the words and pictures coming from your colleagues at Zandvoort."

"At the same time I am asking for your understanding as we had a rough time with the well-proven cars of the English and

Kleiderordnung: Es war einmal eine Zeit, das hier ist das Jahr 1962, da ließen sich die Fahrer, hier ist das Jo Bonnier, modisch nur an der Kopf-bedeckung von den übrigen Menschen, beispielsweise von Rennleiter Huschke von Hanstein, unterscheiden.

Dress code: back in 1962, drivers like Jo Bonnier could be recognized by their head-gear which allowed them to stand out from the the rest of the people, in this case Huschke von Hanstein in his usual outfit.

Foto: Porsche

ins kalte Wasser zu werfen in der Hoffnung, sie würden es dann schon lernen. In einer ähnlichen Situation befinden wir uns am 1. Trainingstag in Zandvoort, wo die Wagen dann praktisch ihren ersten Gehversuch machen, da es zeitlich einfach nicht mehr möglich ist, sie erneut zu erproben. Erst auf Grund der Trainingsergebnisse wird von Herrn Porsche und dem Unterzeichneten entschieden werden können, ob die Autos im Rennen eingesetzt werden oder ob es eben einfach noch zu früh ist.

Ich bitte Sie daher, lieber Herr Kollege, nochmals nachträglich um Ihr Verständnis, daß es uns nicht möglich war, in den zurückliegenden Wochen und Monaten viel über den Werdegang dieses Autos zu berichten und möchte Ihnen heute nur mitteilen, daß wir das Training in Zandvoort für diesen ersten Probegalopp benutzen werden, da ich nicht möchte, daß Sie dies in Wort und Bild erst durch in Zandvoort anwesende Kollegen erfahren müssen.

Gleichzeitig bitte ich um Ihr Verständnis dafür, daß wir einen sehr schweren Gang gegen die bereits in einem halben Dutzend Rennen erprobten Fahrzeuge der Engländer und gegen Ferrari gehen und, daß wir daher – um es einmal im Galopp-Sport-Jargon zu sagen – nach der ‚Papierform‘ kaum eine Chance haben.

Daher eine Bitte: Nehmen Sie von diesem ersten Startversuch nicht allzu viel Notiz, sondern – wenn Sie überhaupt dazu Stellung nehmen wollen – helfen Sie uns ein wenig, indem Sie darauf hinweisen, daß es bei Porsche darum geht, erste Erfahrungen mit völlig neuen Dingen zu gewinnen und, daß das Phänomen der Vorkriegs-Silberpfeile, die ‚kamen, sahen und siegten‘, sich wie so viele schöne Dinge der Vorkriegszeit heute nicht unbedingt wiederholen läßt.

Last not least, darf man nicht vergessen, daß wohl noch nie in der Geschichte des Automobilrennsports sich eine so gleichwertig starke Konkurrenz verschiedener Fabrikate gegenüber gestanden hat wie in der Saison 1962.

Ihr ergebener Huschke von Hanstein, 16. Mai 1962"

Zugleich versucht Porsche, für die 1,5-Liter-Formel-1 zu werben. In einer weiteren Pressemitteilung heißt es: „Wie Sie wissen, hat der Streit um die Richtigkeit und Nützlichkeit, die Formel 1 1962 auf 1,5 Liter zu begrenzen, hohe Wogen geschlagen. Insbesondere die Engländer, an ihrer Spitze Stirling Moss, und so hervorragende Kenner der Rennsportmaterie wie der rennfahrende Journalist Paul Frère, haben die 1,5 Liter Formel in Grund und Boden verdammt. Es mag daher für Sie von Interesse sein zu hören, was Dan Gurney, Dritter in der Fahrerweltmeisterschaft 1961, in einem Artikel in der ‚Competition Press‘, (California) gesagt hat:

‚Es sind jetzt nur noch wenige Tage bis zum Beginn der GP Saison 1962 und es scheint mir, daß es noch nie ein solches Aufgebot an guten Wagen und talentierten Fahrern im Automobilsport gab, wie in diesem Jahr.

Ich wurde gefragt, was ich von der 1,5-Liter Formel halte. Ich bin sicher, daß sie eine wesentliche Verbesserung gegenüber der vorherigen Formel ist.

Das heutige Leistungsgewicht hat fast das der 2,5-Liter-Wagen erreicht, die Straßenlage ist besser als es bei den 2,5-Liter-Wagen der Fall war und ich glaube, daß in diesem Jahr auf allen Rennstrecken neue Streckenrekorde aufgestellt werden.

Darüberhinaus werden die Leistungen von Fahrzeug und Fahrer immer gleichwertiger und ich bin der Ansicht, daß es von

the Ferraris in half a dozen races. On top of that – to say it in the argot of the Sport of Kings – to judge by our "form book", we do not stand much of a chance."

"So would you please watch our first steps with no great expectations, but rather – if you want to comment at all – help us a little bit by pointing out that Porsche is trying to collect its first experiences with completely new things, and that the phenomenon of the pre-war Silver Arrows that "Came, Saw and Conquered", is nowadays maybe not so easy to repeat. Last but not least, one should perhaps remember that there has never been such a strong level of competition in the history of automobile racing as exists in the 1962 season."

"Yours respectfully Huschke von Hanstein, May 16th 1962"

In the meantime Porsche tried to push the 1.5-litre Formula One. A press release from that time read like this:-

"As you all know, the argument over the wisdom and utility of limiting the Formula One to 1.5 litres has caused quite a stir. Especially with the English, the most outspoken of whom is Stirling Moss, and even great connoisseurs of racing like the experienced driver and journalist, Paul Frère, have condemned the 1.5-litre Formula. Thence it may be of interest for you to hear what Dan Gurney, who finished second in the 1961 drivers championship, said in an article in 'Competition Press' of California: 'Now there are only few days until the beginning of the GP season of 1962 and it seems to me that never before has there been such an array of fine cars and talented drivers in a motor sport competition. I was asked my opinion about the 1.5-litre formula. I am sure that it is a remarkable improvement compared to the former formula. Today's power-to-weight ratios have nearly reached the level of the 2.5-litre cars while their road holding is even better than that of the 2.5-litre cars. I believe that this year new records will be established on every track. Furthermore the performances of both drivers and cars become more and more comparable and in my opinion that means from year to year it becomes more and more demanding to win, as happens, incidentally, in all other sports. In terms of the spectators, I think they will see more exciting races with every year that passes.'"

The new eight-cylinder 804s made their first appearance at the Dutch Grand Prix at Zandvoort on May 20th. Porsche's statements about the car were conservative and, for instance, they claimed that the power output was only a bit more than 180 horsepower. In first practice, Gurney lapped in 1:34.7 minutes. That was two seconds slower than Graham Hill in the BRM but at least Gurney had left the Ferrari behind and was fifth on the grid at that point. During the next practice session, Gurney failed to improve on that result and slipped down to eighth. Bonnier started from thirteenth place with the second 804 while de Beaufort and his countryman Ben Pon (both in 718/2s) from fourteenth and eighteenth positions respectively.

Gurney hurried away from the start and found himself in third position even by the start of the Tarzan bend. Unfortunately, by lap ten the Porsche was out of the race with gear box failure. Bonnier's car did not run properly and for some time even de Beaufort in the old four cylinder was faster than the Swede. Bonnier nevertheless finished seventh, thanks admittedly to some retirements. De Beaufort finished sixth thus scoring

Foto: Porsche

Ausgebremst: Joakim Bonniers Auto läuft in Zandvoort nicht so gut wie es soll, zeitweise ist er langsamer als de Beaufort im 718/2.

Outbraked: Jo Bonnier's car failed to run properly at Zandvoort, so much so that sometimes he was actually slower than de Beaufort with his 718/2.

Jahr zu Jahr schwieriger wird zu gewinnen, wie übrigens auch in allen anderen Sportarten.

Und was die Zuschauer anbetrifft, glaube ich, daß sie jedes Jahr spannendere Rennen zu sehen bekommen.'"

Auf dem Dünenkurs von Zandvoort kommen die neuen Achtzylinder-Formel-1-Porsche beim Grand Prix von Holland tatsächlich zu ihrem ersten Einsatz. Die Techniker aus Zuffenhausen geben sich zurückhaltend und schätzten die Leistung der neuen Motoren auf etwas mehr als 180 PS. Gurneys Bestzeit im Training liegt bei 1:34,7 Minuten. Damit ist er im ersten Training zwei Sekunden langsamer als Graham Hill auf seinem B.R.M., hat aber immerhin die Ferrari hinter sich gelassen und liegt auf dem

a championship point in his home Grand Prix. Ben Pon retired after an accident. Graham Hill (BRM) won the Grand Prix ahead of Trevor Taylor (Lotus) and Phil Hill (Ferrari).

The same weekend, the Naples Grand Prix was held at Posillipo with twenty-one cars entered of which just ten were admitted to the start. The only works team was Ferrari's and their drivers, Willy Mairesse and Lorenzo Bandini, fought it out between them for the win. Heinz Schiller failed to qualify and Carlo Abate finished fifth in a 718/2 entered by the Scuderia Serenissima Repubblica di Venezia.

These circumstances meant that Porsche's press office had quite a bit of work to do. Here is another letter that von Hanstein sent to a journalist at that time:-

"Dear colleague,

Let me first express my gratitude that you reacted so kindly to my letter of May 16th 1962 and that you correctly interpreted the somewhat difficult situation of the Porsche company concerning the debut of its new eight-cylinder Formula One car at Zandvoort. Because of the results realised at Zandvoort, Mr

Foto: Porsche

fünften Rang. In den weiteren Trainingsläufen kann sich Gurney nicht mehr verbessern und rutscht in der Startaufstellung auf Platz acht ab. Bonnier wird 13., de Beaufort und sein Landsmann Ben Pon stehen mit ihren 718/2 auf den Startplätzen 14 und 18.

Gurney kommt blendend vom Start weg und liegt eingangs der Tarzan-Kurve schon auf dem dritten Platz. In der zehnten Runde ist der bestplatzierte Porsche aus dem Rennen, Gurney muss den 804 mit Getriebeschaden abstellen. Bonniers Wagen läuft nicht einwandfrei, phasenweise ist sogar de Beaufort im 718 schneller. Zu Beginn des Rennens auf Platz zwölf gelegen, kommt Bonnier, begünstigt durch zahlreiche Ausfälle, noch auf den siebten Platz. De Beaufort ist der bestplatzierte Porsche-Pilot und sichert sich mit dem sechsten Rang einen WM-Punkt in seinem Heim-Grand-Prix. Ben Pon scheidet nach einem Unfall aus. Das Rennen gewinnt Graham Hill (B.R.M.) vor Trevor Taylor (Lotus).

Zeitgleich mit dem Rennen in Zandvoort wird in Posillipo der Große Preis von Neapel ausgetragen. Immerhin sind 21 Wagen gemeldet, von denen zehn zum Start zugelassen werden. Nur Ferrari ist werksseitig vertreten, dessen Fahrer Willy Mairesse und Lorenzo Bandini das Rennen unter sich ausmachen. Heinz Schiller scheitert an der Qualifikationshürde, Carlo Abate belegt in einem 718/2 der Scuderia SSS Repubblica di Venezia einen guten fünften Rang.

Unter diesen Umständen ist in der Öffentlichkeitsarbeit des Hauses Porsche weiterhin Erklärungsbedarf vorhanden:

Logenplatz Strandkorb: Das Publikum bleibt steif im offenbar kühlen Mai 1962, als zum ersten Mal die 804 in Zandvoort starten, – es hat auch wenig Grund zur Begeisterung.

Chairs from the beach: the crowds kept cool in May 1962 despite he fact that Porsche entered the first 804s at Zandvoort. In fact there was little reason to be enthusiastic.

Porsche took the decision to first evaluate the information from that race before the cars were entered again."

"This was impossible until Monte Carlo as the 1,000 kilometre race on the Nürburgring was held in between that kept our small racing department very busy with the new two-litre eight-cylinder sports cars. So there was actually no time left to work on our Formula One car, even more so as we were not allowed by the municipal authorities at Stuttgart to work more than one overtime hour each day per man."

"Following the news coverage about the Nürburgring race, I thank you for rectifying an often-heard opinion that was evidently based upon the pre-race propaganda of the ADAC, the race organiser, that Porsche's new eight cylinder was certain to win overall immediately. After all, a car with a four-litre engine is hundred per cent more powerful than a car with a two-litre engine regardless of the number of cylinders."

"In fact, we were quite satisfied with third and fourth place but we feel it was a shame that the experts, just like the public,

Aus einem Brief Huschke von Hansteins an einen Journalisten:
„Lieber Herr Kollege,

ich möchte zunächst meinen Dank dafür zum Ausdruck bringen, daß Sie auf mein Schreiben vom 16. Mai 1962 so freundlich reagiert und die etwas prekäre Situation des Hauses Porsche beim ersten Start der neuen 8-Zylinder Formel 1 Wagen in Zandvoort richtig interpretiert haben. Auf Grund der Zandvoort-Ergebnisse kam Herr Porsche zwangsläufig zu der Überlegung, die dortigen Erkenntnisse zunächst einmal auszuwerten, ehe die Wagen selbst erneut in ein Rennen geschickt werden sollten.

Dies war aber bis Monte Carlo nicht möglich, da ja dazwischen das 1000-km-Rennen auf dem Nürburgring lag, das an unsere kleine Rennabteilung durch den Einsatz der beiden neuen 2-Liter-8-Zylinder ebenfalls enorme Anforderungen stellte, so daß praktisch für Arbeiten am Formel 1 überhaupt keine Zeit blieb, zumal das Gewerbeaufsichtsamt trotz der Notlage nur eine

were confused by the mess of different classes, even more so as the ADAC did not issue an overall classification for the race."

"Concerning the upcoming Grand Prix at Monte Carlo, Mr Porsche has, despite these several problems, reached the decision to enter the car driven by Dan Gurney at Zandvoort once again for Monte Carlo. First the gear lever trouble will be fixed. Meanwhile, the Bonnier car that was not performing to our expectation at Zandvoort will be checked over."

Angerempelt: Dan Gurney fährt den einzigen 804 in Monaco. Er wird in eine Karambolage verwickelt und muss das Auto stehen lassen.

Dodgem cars: Dan Gurney drove the only 804 entered at Monaco. He was caught up in someone else's first lap accident and instantly retired.

Foto: Porsche

Überstunde pro Tag und Mann genehmigt. Ich darf auch im Anschluß an die Berichterstattung vom Nürburgring dafür danken, daß Sie die oft zu hörende und wohl zum Teil auf der Zweckpropaganda des ADAC basierende Publikumsmeinung, Porsches neuer 8-Zylinder müsse nun gleich das Gesamtklassement gewinnen, weitgehend dahin richtig gestellt haben, daß ja nun einmal ein 4-Liter-Wagen von Hause aus hundertprozentig stärker ist als ein 2 Liter-Wagen, gleichgültig wieviel Zylinder er hat.

Wir jedenfalls waren mit dem 3. und 4. Platz im Gesamtklassement recht zufrieden, bedauern allerdings, daß es nicht nur für das Publikum, sondern auch für Fachleute oft schwer gewesen ist, in dem Durcheinander der verschiedenen Klassen sich zurecht zu finden, zumal der ADAC leider kein Gesamtklassement der Veranstaltung aufstellte.

Was nun das bevorstehende Rennen von Monte Carlo angeht, so hat sich Herr Porsche trotz der oben angedeuteten technischen Bedenken entschlossen, das von Dan Gurney in Zandvoort gefahrene Auto nach Behebung des Schalthebeldefektes, im übrigen aber so wie es von Zandvoort zurückkam, nochmals für Monte Carlo zur Verfügung zu stellen, während der Wagen Bonnier, der ja in Zandvoort noch nicht voll befriedigte, inzwischen überprüft wird.

Herrn Porsche ist dieser Entschluß um so leichter gefallen als die betont faire Berichterstattung durch die deutsche und ausländische Presse über das Rennen in Zandvoort ihm die Hoffnung gibt, daß auch eine Niederlage im augenblicklichen Entwicklungsstadium von der deutschen Öffentlichkeit verstanden wird. Darüber hinaus hat sich die SSS Republica di Venezia bereit erklärt, den bereits mehrfach mit Bonnier in diesem Jahr erfolgreich eingesetzten Porsche-4-Zylinder-Vergaser-Formel-1 aus dem vorigen Jahr, Bonnier für den „Großen Preis von Monaco" zur Verfügung zu stellen.

Ihr ergebener Huschke von Hanstein, 30. Mai 1962."

In Monte Carlo geht Porsche am 3. Juni 1962 nur mit einem 804 ins Rennen, der Dan Gurney anvertraut wird. Während de Beaufort an der Qualifikationshürde scheitert, kann sich Bonnier im zweiten Vierzylinder-718 wenigstens als Fünfzehnter für das Rennen qualifizieren. Gurney fährt die drittschnellste Zeit, steht damit aber „nur" auf dem fünften Startplatz. Bruce McLaren und Willy Mairesse haben exakt die gleiche Zeit erzielt, allerdings früher als der Amerikaner und platzieren sich somit vor ihm. Hart an der Grenze zu einem Frühstart schießt Mairesse aus der zweiten Reihe zwischen den vor ihm stehenden Clark und Hill hindurch, dabei den Lotus und den B.R.M. zur Seite schiebend. Das daraus entstehende Durcheinander führt zu zahlreichen Kollisionen, in deren Folge Trevor Taylor und Innes Ireland die Box aufsuchen und Gurney, Trintignant und Ginther das Rennen sogar aufgeben müssen. Der 804 ist am Heck von Taylors Lotus gerammt worden, was zu mehreren Rissen im Rahmen führt.

Graham Hill liegt bei dem über 100 Runden führenden Rennen bis zur 93. Runde an der Spitze, dann muss er seinen B.R.M. mit Motorproblemen abstellen und Bruce McLaren den Sieg überlassen. Bonnier kommt nach zuverlässiger Fahrt als Fünfter ins Ziel und sichert Porsche nach einem eher enttäuschenden Wochenende noch zwei WM-Punkte.

Obwohl Gurneys Ausfall auf äußere Einflüsse zurückzuführen ist, wünscht er umfangreiche Veränderungen am 804. Am 6. Juni

"Mr Porsche's decision was made much easier thanks to the remarkably fair reporting by both the German and foreign press about the Zandvoort race. It gave him hope that the German public will understand that occasionally a defeat will be suffered during a development period. Moreover, the SSS Republica di Venezia have agreed to let Bonnier drive their Porsche 4-cylinder carburettor Formula One car for the Monaco Grand Prix, a car which he has driven in the past with success."

"Yours respectfully Huschke von Hanstein, May 30th 1962"

So for the Monte Carlo Grand Prix on June 3rd 1962, Porsche entered only one 804 driven by Dan Gurney. In practice, De Beaufort failed to qualify and Bonnier put his four-cylinder 718/2 in fifteenth position on the grid. Gurney actually drove the third fastest lap in practice but started fifth since Bruce McLaren and Willy Mairesse drove an identical time to the American but were placed ahead as they recorded their time before Gurney had done so. In the race, Mairesse dashed from the second row, narrowly missing a penalty for a jump start, and shot between the cars of Clark and Hill, pushing them aside and causing a veritable havoc behind him with a multiplicity of collisions. Trevor Taylor and Innes Ireland had to return to the pits for repairs, but for Gurney, Trintignant and Ginther the race was over. Taylor's Lotus had rammed the 804 so hard in the rear that it had caused some cracks in the chassis frame.

For ninety-three of a hundred laps Graham Hill held the lead until he had to retire with engine trouble thus leaving the victory to Bruce McLaren. Bonnier finished fifth and secured two championship points for Porsche after what had been an otherwise disappointing weekend.

Though someone else had caused Gurney's early retirement, he had driven enough laps in the car to be able to note some alterations that were needed for the 804. On June 6th, Herbert Linge brought this list to the workshop.

"On the occasion of the race at Monte Carlo, Herr Gurney asked me to have the following things altered or looked into before the next race:

1. The brake pedal should be bigger and its surface made non-slip.
2. The brake pedal's free travel should be limited.
3. Fit a locked gear-shift gate and make sure that the lever is in the vertical position when third and fourth gear respectively are engaged. If the gate could not be fitted before the next race, then remove the stop to the side of first and second gear.
4. The fuel tank under the legs is too high and takes up too much room.
5. Provide the steering wheel with a quick-release fastener.
6. Incline the back rest about 20 mm more to the rear.
7. The headrest is annoying and should be mounted further aft.
8. Alter carburettor linkage in order to make proper adjustment possible.
9. Oil tank ventilation must be improved.
10. Fit a windscreen with new shape but with the same height as at Monaco.
11. Prepare panel for oil cooler.
12. Lower the car.

leitet Herbert Linge die Änderungswünsche des Amerikaners an die Techniker weiter:

„Anläßlich des Rennens in Monte Carlo bat mich Herr Gurney, daß folgende Punkte möglichst bis zum nächsten Rennen geändert bzw. berücksichtigt werden:

1. Bremspedal sollte größer und griffiger sein
2. Der Bremsen-Leerweg sollte kleiner gehalten werden
3. Gesperrte Kulisse für Schaltung vorne anbringen und darauf achten, daß bei eingelegtem 3. und 4. Gang der Schalthebel senkrecht steht. Wenn Kulisse bis zum nächsten Rennen nicht gemacht werden kann, soll der Anschlag auf die Seite des 1. und 2. Ganges verlegt werden.
4. Kraftstofftank unter den Beinen ist vorne zu hoch und ragt zu weit vor.
5. Lenkrad mit Schnellverschluß versehen.
6. Sitz-Rücklehne am oberen Ende ungefähr 20 mm weiter zurücklegen.
7. Kopfstütze stört, sollte weiter nach hinten.
8. Vergasergestänge in Ordnung bringen, so daß eine saubere Einstellung möglich ist.
9. Öltankentlüftung muß verbessert werden.
10. Windschutzscheibe in neuer Form, aber in gleicher Höhe wie Monte Carlo.
11. Blende für Ölkühler vorbereiten.
12. Wagen insgesamt tiefer stellen.
13. Im Fahrerraum ist es zu heiß. Trennwand zwischen Öltank und Pedalen vorsehen."

Bei den „2000 Guineas" in Mallory Park kann sich John Surtees im Lola 4 des Reg-Parnell-Teams über einen Start-Ziel-Sieg freuen. Jack Brabham und Graham Hill, beide am Steuer eines Lotus 18, folgen auf den Plätzen zwei und drei. In der Startaufstellung stehen Bonnier und de Beaufort noch auf den Plätzen fünf und sechs, aus der ersten Runde kommen sie aber auf den Rängen acht und elf zurück. Beide können noch Tony Shelly auf Lotus überholen, profitieren zudem von Clarks Ausfall und beendeten das Rennen auf den Plätzen sechs und neun.

Beim Grand Prix von Belgien am 17. Juni 1962 warten die

13. It is too hot in the cockpit. Provide for a bulkhead between oil tank and pedals."

A winning start was the result for John Surtees at Mallory Park on June 10th where the "2,000 Guineas" were held. The winner drove a Lola V8 entered by the Reg Parnell team. Lotus drivers Jack Brabham (V8) and Graham Hill (4-cylinder) finished second and third respectively. At the start Bonnier and de Beaufort had been placed fifth and sixth, but by the end of the first lap they had fallen back to eighth and eleventh places. However, both of them managed to pass Tony Shelly (Lotus) and, profiting from Jim Clark's retirement, they eventually finished sixth and ninth.

The German fans waited in vain for the Porsche truck and the appearance of Bonnier and Gurney at the Belgian Grand Prix on June 17th. As one 804 had been badly damaged in Monaco, Porsche would once again have been entering only one of the new cars. Thus they withdrew the entry for Spa and used the time that this gave them to work on the cars. As Heinz Schiller and Lucien Bianchi also withdrew their 718s, Godin de Beaufort remained the only Porsche driver once again. He started from thirteenth place and finished seventh. Winner was Jim Clark in the new Lotus 25.

While the Porsche team did their homework by testing the 804/01 over fifteen laps on the Nordschleife (average lap time 8:58.0; fastest lap 8:44.4) their competitors met at the Reims Grand Prix on July 1st. Sadly, de Beaufort and Bonnier had no chance at all in their outclassed 718/2s. Bruce McLaren

Unermüdlich: In Spa steht nach dem Unfall von Monaco nur ein Porsche am Start. Carel de Beaufort steuert seinen 718/2 gekonnt auf den siebten Platz.

Indefatigable: after the Monaco accident, there was only one Porsche entered at the Spa GP. Carel Godin de Beaufort finished seventh driving with his usual determination.

aus Deutschland angereisten Fans vergeblich auf den Porsche-Transporter und den Auftritt von Bonnier und Gurney. Weil in Monaco ein 804 zerstört worden war, hätte Porsche wieder nur mit einem neuen Wagen an den Start gehen können. Um nicht erneut einen Fahrer benachteiligen zu müssen und zugleich den Technikern mehr Zeit zur Vorbereitung zu geben, ziehen die Zuffenhausener ihre Nennung für Spa zurück. Dies tun auch Heinz Schiller und Lucien Bianchi, die beide mit einem 718 an den Start gehen wollten. So ist wieder einmal de Beaufort der einzige Porsche-Fahrer im Feld. Als 13. qualifiziert, fährt er ein fehlerfreies Rennen und wird Siebter. Als Sieger fährt der Schotte Jim Clark in seinem neuen Lotus 25 über die Ziellinie.

Während die Porsche-Mannschaft „Hausaufgaben" erledigt und dabei den 804/01 einem 15-Runden-Test auf der Nürburgring-Nordschleife unterzieht (Rundendurchschnitt 8:58,0, schnellste Runde 8:44,4), trifft sich die Konkurrenz am 1. Juli 1962 zum Grand Prix von Reims. Mit ihren Vorjahres-718/2 sind Carel de Beaufort und Joakim Bonnier chancenlos. Bruce McLaren gewinnt das Rennen auf einem Cooper vor Graham Hill im B.R.M., der Holländer wird mit zwei Runden Rückstand Siebter vor Bonnier.

Nach der selbst verordneten Zwangspause von vier Wochen erscheint Porsche beim Großen Preis von Frankreich in Rouen wieder mit zwei 804, deren Hinterradaufhängung modifiziert worden ist. Außerdem haben die Techniker die Einstellung der Weber-Vergaser eingehend erprobt. Schnellster im Training ist Jim Clark, neben ihm qualifizieren sich Graham Hill und Bruce McLaren für die erste Startreihe. Gurney steht als Sechster in Reihe drei, Bonnier in Startreihe vier. Metallarbeiterstreiks in Italien haben das Werk von Enzo Ferrari lahmgelegt, dessen

(Cooper) won the race ahead of Graham Hill (BRM) with the Dutch driver finishing seventh one place ahead of Bonnier.

After a four week break Porsche entered two 804s with improved rear suspension and carefully tuned Weber carburettors for the French Grand Prix at Rouen on July 8th. Jim Clark, Graham Hill and Bruce McLaren put their cars on the first row with Clark on pole position. Gurney was sixth in row three, Bonnier in row four. Ferrari did not turn up at Rouen as the metalworkers were on strike in Italy and had paralysed the factory at Modena.

After the start Hill took the lead ahead of Surtees and Clark. At first the Porsche drivers maintained their positions and then made up two places after Brabham and McLaren slid off the track. Surtees was slowed down by having to make a pit stop and Innes Ireland retired. Suddenly the two Porsches were running third and fourth overall. Bonnier fell back after a pit stop on lap twenty-one and then retired on the forty-first lap. For Clark the race was over after thirty-three laps so now Gurney was second behind Hill who had a lead of thirty seconds. Then with twelve laps to go, Hill's car developed a problem with the throttle linkage and slowed allowing Gurney to take the lead. His closest pursuers were one lap behind. Thus Gurney reached the finishing line unchallenged and gained Porsche their first Grand Prix victory.

Back in Zuffenhausen, the technicians carried on working, seeking all the time to understand and improve the car. Measured on the local municipal scales, the dry weight of the 804 was 480 kilograms. With the tanks filled up and a driver in the car it went up to 652 kilograms, with the driver estimated to weigh 80 kilograms.

Durchbruch: In Rouen gelingt Gurney der erste GP-Sieg für Porsche. Hier fährt gerade de Beaufort zur Arbeit.

Breakthrough: Dan Gurney gained the first GP victory for Porsche at Rouen. Here de Beaufort drives his car to the circuit.

Pechvogel: Während Gurney dem Sieg entgegeneilt, wird Bonnier (32) durch einen Boxenstopp aufgehalten und fällt schließlich ganz aus.

Jinxed: while Gurney raced on to victory, Bonnier (32) was slowed by having to make a pit stop and finally had to retire.

Scuderia aus diesem Grund nicht in Rouen vertreten ist. Nach dem Start übernimmt Graham Hill die Führung vor Surtees und Clark. Die Porsche-Piloten haben zunächst ihre Startpositionen verteidigen können, gewinnen dann zwei Plätze, als Brabham und McLaren unabhängig voneinander von der Strecke fliegen. Nach einem Boxenstopp von Surtees und dem Ausfall von Innes Ireland liegen die 804 schon auf den Plätzen drei und vier. Bonnier fällt durch einen Boxenstopp in der 21. Runde zurück und muss im 42. Umlauf ganz aufgeben, Gurney hingegen profitiert von Jim Clarks Ausfall in der 33. Runde. Der Amerikaner liegt nun mit knapp einer halben Minute Rückstand auf Hill auf Platz zwei. Zwölf Runden vor dem Fallen der Zielflagge wirft ein Defekt am Gasgestänge auch den Engländer zurück und Gurney führt mit seinem Porsche 804 plötzlich das Rennen an. Seine Verfolger in dem stark dezimierten Feld haben eine Runde Rückstand, so dass der Amerikaner die letzten Runden unbedrängt zu Ende fahren und damit den ersten Grand-Prix-Sieg für Porsche sichern kann.

Die Techniker tüfteln weiter. Messungen auf der Stadtwaage von Zuffenhausen ergeben für den 804 ein Leergewicht von 480

The only works teams that entered for the Solitude Grand Prix just outside Stuttgart were Porsche (two cars again) and Lotus. Jim Clark and Trevor Taylor drove Lotus 25s and, in practice, Clark had been two seconds faster than Gurney but the American dominated the race. He had a good start, took the lead and was always able to control Clark. When Clark had to retire after a spin six laps before the finish, the way was open for a double for the 804s with Gurney finishing first ahead of Bonnier while de Beaufort came in fifth with a 718/2.

Hopes for a repeat of this success at the British Grand Prix at Aintree on July 21st were not fulfilled. Jim Clark was unbeatable that weekend. He started from pole position, drove the fastest lap and crossed the finishing line nearly fifty seconds ahead of Surtees and McLaren. Gurney started from third place on the grid but had to let McLaren pass him on the twelfth lap and later fell back further and further. A clutch problem was slowing him down and finally he finished ninth. Even worse was that Bonnier had retired on the twenty-seventh lap with a mechanical problem. Godin de Beaufort in the old four-cylin-

Fotos: Porsche

Extrablatt: Nach Gurneys Sieg in Rouen erscheinen eine Pressemitteilung und eins von Porsches legendären Triumph-Plakaten.

Extra, extra ! After Gurney's victory at Rouen, Porsche published a press release and one of its legendary posters to celebrate the triumph.

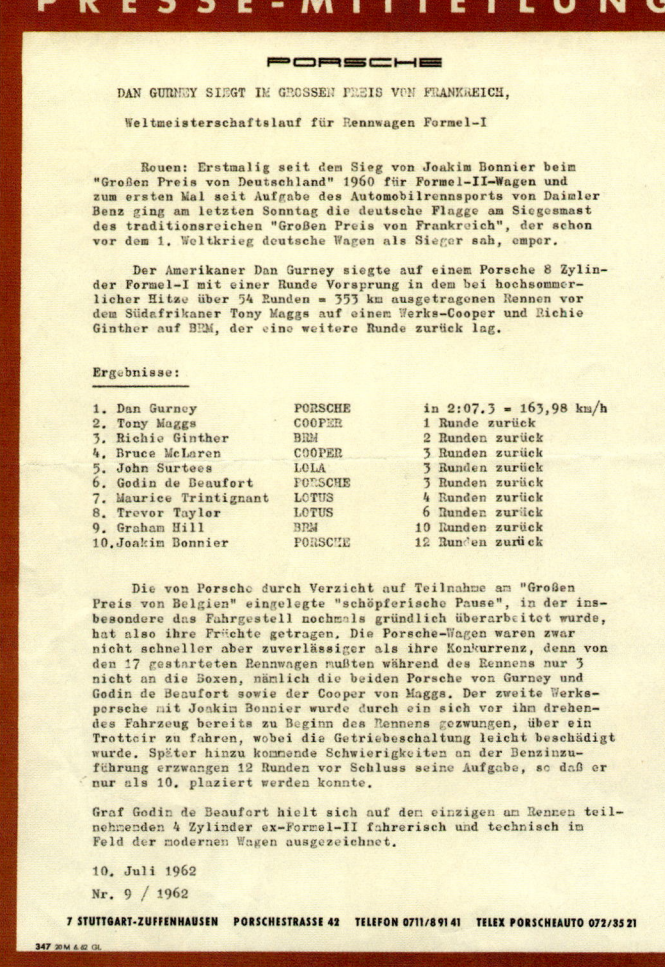

Fotos: Porsche

Start-Ziel-Sieg: Das Solitude-Rennen gewinnt Gurney (10) unangefochten. Zweiter wird Bonnier (11), und de Beaufort (18) macht die Sache mit dem fünften Platz rund.

Winning start: Gurney (10) won the Solitude race in style. Bonnier (11) finished second and de Beaufort (10) made the weekend complete with fifth place.

Fotos: Porsche

Heimvorteil: Nach dem bravourösen Rennen im Ländle vor den Toren Stuttgarts stehen die Porsche-Piloten Gurney und Bonnier auf dem Siegertreppchen.

Home advantage: after the great race in the „Ländle", which is how the Swabians refer to their home country, Porsche drivers Gurney and Bonnier climbed the victory rostrum.

Kilogramm, betankt mit Fahrer sind es 652 (Fahrer 80 Kilogramm).

Beim Großen Preis der Solitude vor den Toren Stuttgarts sind neben den beiden Porsche die Lotus 25 von Jim Clark und Trevor Taylor die einzigen Werkswagen am Start. Clark hat im Training eine um zwei Sekunden schnellere Zeit als Gurney hingelegt, aber das Rennen wird eine klare Angelegenheit für den Amerikaner. Er feiert einen Start-Ziel-Sieg und hat Clark zu jeder Zeit im Griff. Als der Schotte nach einem Dreher sechs Runden vor Schluss aufgeben muss, ist der Weg frei für einen Porsche-Doppelsieg durch Gurney und Bonnier. Mit einem fünften Platz rundet de Beaufort das tolle Ergebnis für die Zuffenhausener ab.

Die Hoffnungen auf eine Fortsetzung der in Rouen und auf der Solitude begonnen Porsche-Erfolgsserie werden beim großen

der car managed to cross the finishing line in fourteenth place. Once back at Stuttgart, 804/01 was put into the wind tunnel. Different windscreen designs, bodywork with spats for the front wheels and smaller rear wheels were all tested.

During practice on the Nordschleife before the German Grand Prix at the beginning of August, there was a momentous accident. In the section of the circuit called the Fuchsröhre, de Beaufort lost a 16-millimetre camera that had been mounted on the rear of his Porsche. Graham Hill in his brand new BRM ran over the debris and skidded off the track. In doing so, his car shed oil on to the track and this caused Tony Maggs' Cooper to go off the road as well. None of the cars could be repaired in time to take part in the race. On Sunday the legendary Eifel weather lived up to its reputation and it rained cats and dogs.

Enttäuschung in Aintree: Gegen Jim Clark war am 21. Juli 1962 nichts zu machen. Gurney wird nur Neunter, Bonnier fällt aus, und de Beaufort landet auf dem vierzehnten Platz.

Disappointment at Aintree: on July 21st 1962, Jim Clark showed himself to be unbeatable. Gurney finished ninth, Bonnier retired and de Beaufort came in fourteenth.

Foto: Porsche

Preis von England in Aintree enttäuscht. Jim Clark ist an diesem Wochenende nicht zu schlagen. Er geht von der Pole Position ins Rennen, fährt die schnellste Rennrunde und gewinnt mit fast 50 Sekunden Vorsprung vor Surtees und McLaren. Gurney liegt zu Beginn des Rennens auf einem guten dritten Platz, muss aber in der 12. Runde McLaren passieren lassen und fällt immer weiter zurück. Eine schleifende Kupplung verhindert eine schnellere Fahrt des Amerikaners, der auf einem enttäuschenden neunten Platz ins Ziel kommt. Bonnier hat das Rennen schon in der 27. Runde wegen schadhaften Kegel- und Tellerrads aufgeben müssen. De Beaufort hingegen sieht erneut die Zielflagge, dieses Mal als Vierzehnter.

Zurück in Stuttgart stehen Windkanalmessungen für den 804/01 auf dem Programm. Erprobt werden unterschiedliche Windschutzscheiben, Heckformen, Radabdeckungen, Verkleidungen hinter den Vorderrädern und kleinere Hinterräder

Während des Trainings zum Großen Preis von Deutschland auf der Nordschleife des Rings ereignet sich ein besonderer Zwischenfall: Im Streckenabschnitt „Fuchsröhre" verliert de Beaufort

Anyway the fans were not bothered as Graham Hill, now driving a 1961 specification BRM, Dan Gurney on a Porsche 804 and John Surtees in his Lola V8 provided an extraordinarily exciting race at the end of which all three of them crossed the finishing line within 4.4 seconds of one another. Jim Clark provided an extra dose of adrenalin for the spectators by stalling the engine of his Lotus at the start and then driving flat-out to catch up. It was only because his engine refused to deliver full performance in the final stage of the race, that Clark had to settle for fourth place.

After the start, Gurney managed to defend his pole position until Graham Hill passed him on the third of the fifteen-lap race and Surtees soon also passed Gurney. It is possible that they were simply faster than the American but in fact, Gurney was fully occupied in the cockpit of the Porsche. The battery, mounted in front in the cockpit near the pedals, had become loose. Thus the driver had to do what he was hired for – racing a Formula One car in the rain round the Nürburgring – while at the same time holding the loose battery with his left foot as

Fotos: Porsche (2/sw)

In der Boxengasse: Zum Rennen um den Großen Preis von Deutschland gehen auf dem Nürburgring an den Start Bonnier (oben), de Beaufort und Gurney (links).

In the pits: Bonnier, de Beaufort and Gurney were entered for the German GP on the Nürburgring.

Sauwetter I: Auf dem Nürburgring haben es die Fahrer 1962 mit unangenehm großen Wassermassen zu tun.

Filthy weather one: at the Nürburgring, the drivers had to cope with large amounts of water on the track.

Sauwetter II: In der Mitte Joakim Bonnier im 804, dahinter Beauforts und Vaccarellas Autos.

Filthy weather two: in the centre, Joakim Bonnier in an 804 while behind him can be seen the cars of de Beaufort and Vacarella.

Leider nur schwarzweiß: Der rote 718/2 der Scuderia Serenissima, den Nino Vaccarella 1962 auf dem Ring fuhr.

Unfortunately only black and white: the red Scuderia Serenissima 718/2 driven by Nino Vacarella at the 'Ring in 1962.

Wurde Vierzehnter: Heini Walter im 718/2 der Ecurie Filipinetti.

Finished fourteenth: Heini Walter in the Ecurie Filipinetti 718/2.

Foto: Porsche

Balanceakt: Dan Gurney schafft bravourös noch den dritten Platz auf dem Ring, nachdem sich seine Batterie gelöst hatte und er sie ständig mit dem Fuß festhalten muss.

Balancing act: Dan Gurney managed to finish third though he had to fight with a loose battery, holding it in place with his foot while trying to beat Hill and Surtees.

eine auf dem Heck seines Porsche montierte 16-mm-Filmkamera. Mit seinem brandneuen B.R.M. fährt der dichtauf folgende Graham Hill über die Trümmer und kommt von der Piste ab. Auf dem Motoröl des aufgeschlitzten B.R.M. kreiselt auch Tony Maggs´ Cooper von der Strecke. Beide Wagen können nicht mehr rechtzeitig für das Rennen repariert werden.

Sonntags wird das Eifelwetter allen Vorurteilen gerecht, es gießt in Strömen. Aber die Fans bereuen ihr Kommen nicht, denn Graham Hill, jetzt am Steuer eines Vorjahres-B.R.M., Dan Gurney im Porsche 804 und John Surtees auf Lola liefern sich einen sensationellen Dreikampf. Nur 4,4 Sekunden trennt das Trio im Ziel. Zusätzliche Würze erhält der GP durch Jim Clark. Nachdem er seinen Lotus beim Start abgewürgt hat, zeigt der Schotte eine grandiose Aufholjagd. Nur weil der Motor seines Autos in der Schlussphase nicht mehr die volle Leistung abgibt, muss Clark alle Hoffnungen auf den Sieg begraben und sich mit Rang vier begnügen.

Die Pole Position verteidigt Gurney zunächst erfolgreich, bis es Graham Hill im B.R.M. in der dritten von 15 Runden schafft, vorbeizuziehen. Dass dieses Manöver anschließend auch Lola-Fahrer Surtees gelingt, hat einen Grund, den der außer Gurney bis zum Ende niemand kennt – der ihn aber scheußlich in Atem hält: Die Batterie, die vorn im Cockpit untergebracht ist, hat sich aus ihrer Befestigung gelöst. Nun muss der Porsche-Pilot nicht bloß auf dem höllisch anspruchsvollen Eifelkurs seinen dritte Position hinter Klassefahrern verteidigen. Nein, mit dem linken Fuß muss er obendrein die Batterie daran hindern, ihm zwischen die Füße zu kippen oder sich gar von den Polkabeln zu lösen. Es ist kaum zu glauben, aber der Parforceritt plus Balanceakt gelingt. Er gelingt derart gut, dass Gurney, Surtees und Hill die restlichen zwei Drittel des Rennens in pfeilschneller geschmeidiger Formation absolvieren. Der dritte Platz ist mehr als respektabel und das Rennen längst legendär. Bonnier verliert alle Chancen auf eine gute Platzierung durch eine falsche Reifenwahl, er wird Siebter.

Vor dem nächsten großen Rennen in Monza fährt der Schwede den 804-01 noch zwei Mal. Auf der Rennstrecke von Karlskoga feiert der Amerikaner Masten Gregory beim Kannonloppet den ersten Sieg in einem Formel-1-Rennen. Mit seinem UDT-Lotus verweist er Roy Salvadori im Cooper auf Rang zwei. Nach einem langem Rad-an-Rad-Zweikampf mit dem Cooper-Piloten muss sich Bonnier im 804 um zwei Zehntelsekunden geschlagen geben. Der Schwede wird Dritter, de Beaufort Sechster. Beim Bergrennen Ollon-Villars in der Schweiz stellt Bonnier dagegen mit einem Schnitt von 107,5 Stundenkilometern einen neuen Rekord auf.

Ferrari entsendet als einziges Werks-Team zwei Wagen zum Großen Preis des Mittelmeeres nach Pergusa, die Lorenzo Bandini und Giancarlo Baghetti anvertraut werden. Die beiden Italiener machen das Rennen auch unter sich aus und siegen mit einer Runde Vorsprung. Hinter Bandini und Baghetti wird Carlo Abate im Porsche 718/2 Dritter. Ein zweiter 718/2 im Feld wird von Heinz Schiller pilotiert, der das Rennen aber wegen einer defekten Ölpumpe in der 13. Runde aufgeben muss.

Jack Brabham dominiert mit seinem privaten Lotus 24-Climax den Großen Preis von Dänemark auf dem Roskildering. Er entscheidet alle drei Läufe für sich und verweist Masten Gregory (Lotus 24-Climax) und Innes Ireland (Lotus 24-Climax) auf die Plätze. De Beaufort wird Siebter.

it threatened to tumble between his feet. It is hard to believe but Gurney managed to drive at full speed and at the same time handle the balancing act with the battery. He did it so well that he, Hill and Surtees completed the race in almost perfect formation. Thus his third place was more than just respectable and the race is still legendary. Unfortunately Bonnier finished only seventh due to the fact that he chose unsuitable tyres.

Before the next great race, the Italian Grand Prix, Jo Bonnier drove 804/01 twice. On the Karlskoga track, American UDT-Lotus driver, Masten Gregory, gained his first Formula One victory in the Kannonloppet. He relegated Roy Salvadori (Cooper) to second while behind them, by just two-tenths of a second after a race-long struggle with Salvadori, came Bonnier. The Swede finished third and de Beaufort sixth. Then at the hill climb at Ollon-Villars, Bonnier flew up the hill and set a new record with an average speed of 107.5 kph.

The Grand Prix of the Mediterranean at Pergusa saw only one works team present. Ferrari entered two cars for Lorenzo Bandini and Giancarlo Baghetti who fought it out between them and crossed the finishing line with a lap lead over the rest of the field. Behind Bandini and Baghetti came Carlo Abate in a Porsche 718/2 in third place. Heinz Schiller drove another 718/2 but retired on lap thirteen with oil pump failure.

Jack Brabham entered his own Lotus 24 Climax for the Danish Grand Prix. On the Roskildering he won all three heats ahead of Masten Gregory and Innes Ireland, both also in Lotus 24 Climax. Godin de Beaufort finished seventh.

Neither Ferrari nor Porsche turned up with works cars at the Gold Cup at Oulton Park. But all of the British teams had entered for this, the most lucrative race in England. Clark in his Lotus and Graham Hill in his BRM fought it out and again the Scot finished first. The only Porsche driver was de Beaufort who finished seventh.

Meanwhile back in Germany, Herbert Linge did some testing at Hockenheim on September 11th the result of which was a fastest lap of 2:11.42.

Five days later on September 16th, the Italian Grand Prix was held at Monza and once again Jim Clark was fastest in practice with his Lotus. From pole position, he took the lead but had to visit the pits after three laps with gearbox trouble. One lap before that Graham Hill had passed him for the lead followed by team mate Richie Ginther and the two BRM drivers finally made it a 1-2 for the British marque.

On this high speed Italian track, the open-wheelers from Zuffenhausen got the short end of the stick. Though Dan Gurney moved up from seventh to fourth place, he had to defend it hard against Bruce McLaren (Cooper), Tony Maggs (Cooper) and Giancarlo Baghetti (Ferrari). Following on the heels of this squabbling group was Bonnier who managed to stay with them. Gurney retired on lap sixty-seven with gearbox failure and, with the disappearance of Surtees (Lola) from third place, Mairesse inherited the position but had to cede it to McLaren twelve laps later. Bonnier finished sixth nursing a gear-change problem and de Beaufort came tenth.

At Watkins Glen on October 7th, Jim Clark and Graham Hill again showed themselves to be in a class of their own. They finished first and second respectively and left the rest of

Am 1. September fehlen Ferrari und Porsche beim Gold Cup in Oulton Park, aber die britischen Teams sind im höchstdotierten Rennen in England vollzählig vertreten. Das Rennen ist geprägt vom Duell zwischen Jim Clark im Lotus und Graham Hill im B.R.M., das der Schotte wieder einmal für sich entscheidet. Mit dem einzigen Porsche im Feld fährt de Beaufort erneut auf einen guten siebten Rang.

Am 11. September dreht Herbert Linge im 804-01 zahlreiche Runden auf dem Kurs von Hockenheim, seine schnellste Runde wird mit 2:11,42 Minuten protokolliert.

Fünf Tage später findet der Grand Prix von Italien statt. Auch in Monza dominiert Jim Clark im Lotus das Training und sichert sich die Pole Position. Er schießt beim Start auch gleich in Führung, kommt aber schon in der dritten Runde mit Getriebeproblemen an die Box. Bereits in der Runde zuvor hat Graham Hill die Führung übernommen und soll sie bis ins Ziel nicht mehr abgeben. Auf Rang zwei etabliert sich sein Teamkollege Richie Ginther, der so für einen B.R.M.-Doppelsieg sorgt. Auf dem

In den Schweizer Bergen: Auch 1962 steht Bonnier wieder in Ollon-Villars am Start, diesmal im 804.

In the Swiss mountains: again in 1962, Bonnier took part at Ollon-Villars, this time with an 804.

the competition at least one lap behind. In the race, Gurney, McLaren and Brabham followed them in third, fourth and fifth until a misfiring engine caused by a broken valve spring slowed the American so that he finally finished fifth. Neither Bonnier nor de Beaufort managed to cross the finishing line after both of them had unintentionally left the track. Bonnier's Porsche appeared to have sustained only minor damage at the rear and to the exhaust pipes. He returned to the track but the engine output was severely reduced. It turned out that the gear-shift gate was also damaged. So Bonnier again returned to the pits to try to have it fixed. He was eventually classified thirteenth. Beaufort's car suffered a broken chassis frame and was not able to continue

italienischen Hochgeschwindigkeitskurs sind die Zuffenhausener Monoposti wieder etwas weiter von der Spitze entfernt. Dan Gurney kann zwar, von Startplatz sieben aus ins Rennen gehend, bis zur 43. Runde auf den dritten Rang vorstoßen, muss um diese Position aber immer wieder hart mit Bruce McLaren (Cooper), Tony Maggs (Cooper) und Giancarlo Baghetti (Ferrari) kämpfen. In dieser Gruppe hält sich auch Bonnier, der im 56. Umlauf selbst einmal an der Spitze dieses Pulks liegt. In der 67. Runde ist das Rennen für Gurney wegen eines Getriebeschadens zu Ende. Seinen dritten Rang erbt zunächst Mairesse, der sich aber zwölf Runden später McLaren beugen muss. Bonnier beendet das Rennen schließlich als Sechster, de Beaufort wird Zehnter.

Auch beim Grand Prix der USA in Watkins Glen sind Jim Clark und Graham Hill eine Klasse für sich. Die beiden Briten kommen in dieser Reihenfolge ins Ziel und lassen den Rest des Feldes eine Runde hinter sich. Auf den weiteren Plätzen folgen zunächst Gurney, McLaren und Brabham, bis der Amerikaner wegen nachlassender Motorleistung auf den fünften Platz zurückfällt. Ursache dafür ist eine gebrochene Ventilfeder. Sowohl Bonnier als auch Beaufort kommen von der Strecke ab und müssen das Rennen vorzeitig beenden. Am Porsche des Schweden scheint nur

the race. Nobody knew it at the time, but in many ways it was a foregone conclusion that Watkins Glen was to be the last race for the Porsche 804 even though the 1962 season had not yet ended.

Just before the start of the non-championship race at Mexico City the Lotus mechanics realized, that the battery of Clark's car was broken. The organizer agreed to postpone the start but then Clark's car was push-started which led to a black flag for him on lap five. Lotus called in Trevor Taylor who was at that time lying third behind Brabham and McLaren and made him hand his car over to Clark. Then began a remarkable drive through the field and the Scot managed to win ahead of Jack Brabham while behind them for Porsche, De Beaufort finished seventh.

The whole Mexican weekend was overshadowed by a fatal accident in practice. After a full season with Ferrari, Ricardo Rodriguez was driving the Rob Walker Lotus 24 to try and win his home Grand Prix. He went off the track, crashed into a guardrail and was thrown out of his car. The twenty year-old Mexican suffered severe injuries to his head and neck and died while being taken to hospital

Fotos: Porsche

das Heck und der Auspuff zu Schaden gekommen zu sein, er kann nach einer Reparatur mit verminderter Motorleistung weiterfahren. Aber auch die Schaltkulisse ist beschädigt, Bonnier hält nochmals an und lässt sie ersetzen. De Beauforts 718 ist bei dem Crash am Rahmen beschädigt worden, er kann sein Rennen nicht mehr fortsetzen. Was zu diesem Zeitpunkt noch keiner weiß: Das Rennen in Watkins Glen ist der letzte Renneinsatz des Porsche 804, obwohl die Saison noch nicht zu Ende ist.

Vor dem Start des nicht zur Weltmeisterschaft zählenden Grand-Prix-Rennens in Mexiko-City stellen die Lotus-Mechaniker fest, dass Clarks Batterie defekt ist. Der Veranstalter verschiebt deswegen den Start, zu dem Clarks Wagen später angeschoben wird. Wegen dieses Regelverstoßes erhält der Schotte in der fünften Runde die schwarze Flagge. Der zu diesem Zeitpunkt hinter Brabham und McLaren liegende Trevor Taylor wird an die Box geholt und muss seinen Wagen an Clark abtreten.

Ausfall in Watkins Glen: Bonnier (11) kommt von der Strecke ab und muss aufgeben. Gurney schafft es nur auf Platz 5.

Non-finish at Watkins Glen: Bonnier (11) left the road and had to retire from the race while Gurney could only make fifth place.

In the South African Grand Prix held on December 29th at East London, Clark put his Lotus on pole and, in the lead for sixty-two of the eighty-two laps, it looked as if he was on his way to win the World Championship. However, an oil leak stopped him with just twenty laps to go. Thus Graham Hill gained both the victory in this race and the title. The only Porsche driver entered after the factory had withdrawn its entries was Godin de Beaufort who retired near the end of the race.

A magazine: "Does Porsche give up? Porsche's racing director, Huschke von Hanstein, had been at Puerto Rico and gave

Der Schotte startet nun eine beeindruckende Aufholjagd und gewinnt tatsächlich noch vor Brabham, der damit das bis zu diesem Zeitpunkt beste Ergebnis mit seiner Eigenkonstruktion erzielt. De Beaufort glänzt erneut mit einem siebten Rang. Das Rennwochenende aber wird von einem tödlichen Unfall im Training überschattet. Auf der Jagd nach der Trainingsbestzeit kommt Ricardo Rodriguez mit seinem Lotus von der Strecke ab, prallt gegen eine Leitplanke und wird aus dem Wagen geschleudert. Dabei zieht sich der zwanzig Jahre alte Mexikaner so schwere Verletzungen zu, dass er noch auf dem Transport ins Krankenhaus verstirbt.

62 Runden lang ist Jim Clark auf dem besten Weg, Weltmeister des Jahres 1962 zu werden. Er führt den Großen Preis von Südafrika an und scheint seine letzte Chance zu nutzen, kann er den Titel doch nur mit einem Sieg gewinnen. Ein Ölleck im Climax-Motor seines Lotus stoppt den Schotten 20 Runden vor Schluss, der damit den Sieg in Südafrika und den WM-Titel Graham Hill überlassen muss. Wegen einer defekten Benzinpumpe scheidet auch de Beaufort aus, der nach dem Startverzicht des Werks einziger Porsche-Pilot im Feld war.

Eine führende Fachzeitschrift titelt: „Gibt Porsche auf? Porsche-Rennleiter Huschke von Hanstein, der in Puerto Rico drüben war, gab dort einem AP-Korrespondenten ein Interview, das die Sportbeteiligung und die Produktion des Hauses Porsche betraf, und das in vielen Zeitungen falsch wiedergegeben wurde, nämlich so, als ob sich Porsche nunmehr vom Rennsport zurückziehen würde. Wir geben in dieser Sache am besten Huschke von Hanstein selbst das Wort:

‚In den letzten Tagen ist in großen Teilen der deutschen Presse ein angebliches ‚Interview‘ mit mir in Puerto Rico zitiert worden. Je nach Auslegung hat man aus dem Inhalt Schlüsse gezogen, die sich in Überschriften wie ‚Hört Porsche auf?‘, ‚Porsche kündigt Rückzug an‘ und ‚Auch Porsche macht Schluß‘ niedergeschlagen haben. Tatsache ist, daß ich im Trubel der Preisverteilung des Großen Preis von Puerto Rico von einem AP-Korrespondenten angesprochen und über die Rennsituation in Europa im allgemeinen und bei Porsche im speziellen befragt wurde.

Ich habe dabei erklärt, daß wir für das kommende Jahr keine neuen Sportwagen zum Verkauf bauen, einmal, weil die Neukonstruktion eines solchen Wagens Kosten verursacht, die nicht viel geringer wären als die eines Grand-Prix-Autos, und zum anderen, weil durch den Wegfall der bisherigen Sportwagenwertung und Ausweitung der ‚Prototypen-Rennen‘ auf unlimitierten Zylinderinhalt (theoretisch können also 10 Liter-Wagen starten) unsere 1,5- oder 2-Liter-Waogen, d. h. also Wagen mit kleinem Zylinderinhalt, noch weniger eine ehrliche Chance haben, als das bisher der Fall war.

Im Originaltext der AP-Meldung heißt es dann richtigerweise auch wörtlich: ‚Hanstein declares that his company may discontinue producing racing cars.‘ Was die ‚Racing cars‘, d. h. also die Formel-1-Wagen anbetrifft, so kann ich die vor einer Woche an dpa gegebene Auskunft, daß über unsere Teilnahme an der kommenden Grand-Prix-Saison noch nicht entschieden ist, nur wiederholen.

Es wäre ja auch mehr als merkwürdig, wenn ich so kurze Zeit nach Bekanntgabe des offiziellen Werksstandpunkts gegenüber einer deutschen Agentur plötzlich in Puerto Rico das Gegenteil gesagt hätte. Was immer aber auf dem Grand-Prix-Feld gesche-

an interview there to an AP correspondent. The interview concerned both the sports ambitions and the commercial production of Porsche. Sadly, it was misquoted by many newspapers that interpreted it as giving the impression that Porsche would retire from racing. Here we can pass over to Huschke von Hanstein himself: 'During the last days, in many parts of the German press, a so-called 'interview' with me at Puerto Rico was cited. Its content was variously interpreted and led to headlines like 'Is Porsche retiring?', 'Porsche announces retreat' and 'Also Porsche packs up'. The fact is that in the confusion of the awards ceremony, I was tackled by an AP correspondent who asked generally about the motor sport situation in Europe and especially how it was at Porsche. I told him that we would not build any sports car for sale in the coming year. The design of such a car would cost nearly as much money as a Grand Prix car. Furthermore our 1.5 and two-litre cars are robbed off any prospect of success thanks to the unfair sports car scoring and the expansion of the 'prototype races' to engines of unlimited displacement (thus theoretically allowing ten-litre cars).'"

"Then the original AP text says correctly: 'Hanstein declares that his company may discontinue producing racing cars.' Concerning the 'racing cars', which means the Formula One cars, I would like to repeat the information I gave DPA (Deutsche Presseagentur – German News agency) last week that our entry for the next Grand Prix season is not yet decided. Anyway it would be more than curious if I had told a German news agency that the official works might be proceeding just to say the reverse a few days later at Puerto Rico. Whatever may happen with the Grand Prix scene, Porsche will not only never fully retreat from racing but will next year defend the title that we gained this year in the GT Championship.'"

"That was von Hanstein. Meanwhile the President of the AvD, Prince Metternich, had called on Ferry Porsche to do everything he could to keep a German car in Grand Prix arena."

However, as soon as von Hanstein released his drivers from their duties in December 1962, it became abundantly clear that the 1963 Formula One season would be held without a Porsche factory presence. Günther Molter described Porsche's situation at that time in "Motor Revue" 3/62:

"The year of the eight-cylinder cars.

Porsche today is the only make in Grand Prix sport representing Germany, a country with a Grand Prix tradition no less than those of Italy, France and Great Britain. Regrettably Ferry Porsche lacks the help of the German automotive industry unlike his British rivals who receive help from the petroleum and the tyre industry in the UK. Hence Porsche races with petrol from British Petroleum and with tyres from the British manufacturer, Dunlop. That is sad considering how the German oil and tyre business has developed in recent years. Considering also that Daimler-Benz, a car manufacturer possessing much larger resources than Porsche, found German firms like Esso and Continental willing to help them to go racing, the actual lack of interest of relevant German companies is doubly deplorable. The spirit of enterprise of Ferry Porsche and his men should thus win a special recognition."

"For the new 1.5-litre Formula One, Porsche came with a completely new racing car powered by an air-cooled flat eight-

hen mag, Porsche wird sich in keinem Fall ganz vom Rennsport zurückziehen, sondern beabsichtigt, den in diesem Jahr auf dem GT-Sektor gewonnenen Weltmeistertitel im nächsten Jahr zu verteidigen.'

Soweit Hanstein. Inzwischen hat AvD-Präsident Fürst Metternich einen Appell an Ferry Porsche gerichtet, er möge alles tun, damit eine deutsche Marke im Grand-Prix-Sport bleibe."

Als von Hanstein im Dezember 1962 die Porsche-Werksfahrer freigibt, wird jedoch klar, dass die F1-Saison 1963 ohne die Schwaben stattfinden wird.

Die Situation, in der sich Porsche zu diesem Zeitpunkt befindet, hatte schon Günther Molter in der Motor Revue 3/62 treffend beschrieben:

„Das Jahr der Achtzylinder"

Porsche repräsentiert heute als einzige Firma Deutschland im Grand Prix-Sport, also ein Land, das über eine nicht minder reiche Grand-Prix-Tradition verfügt wie Italien, Frankreich und England. Bedauerlicherweise findet Ferry Porsche bei seinem Grand Prix-Einsatz von der dem Automobil verwandten deutschen Industrie nicht die Unterstützung, wie sie zum Beispiel England allein von der Mineralöl- und Reifenindustrie zuteil wird. So fährt Porsche Benzin der British Petrol und Reifen der englischen Dunlop. Das ist ein sehr trauriges Zeichen, wenn man überlegt, wie sich das Geschäft der deutschen Mineralöl- und Reifenindustrie entwickelt hat. Bedenkt man außerdem, daß die über weitaus größere Geldmittel verfügende Firma Daimler-Benz deutsche Unternehmen wie die Esso und die Continental sehr unterstützungswillig bei ihrem Grand Prix-Einsatz fand, dann ist das derzeitige Desinteresse einschlägiger Firmen der Branche doppelt bedauernswert. Der Unternehmungsgeist von Ferry Porsche und seinen Männern sollte deshalb besondere Anerkennung finden.

Porsche hatte für die neue Formel 1 den Einsatz eines völlig neu konstruierten Rennwagens geplant, der als Triebwerk einen luftgekühlten Achtzylinder-Boxermotor erhalten sollte, das einzige Antriebsaggregat dieser Bauart der neuen Formel.

Dieser Motor hat eine Bohrung von 66 mm und einen Hub von 54,6 mm und besitzt eine neunfach gelagerte Kurbelwelle. Die vier obenliegenden Nockenwellen werden über Kegelräder und Königswellen angetrieben. Die Kühlung erfolgt über ein Gebläse mit horizontal angeordnetem Gebläserad aus Kunststoff. Die Gemischaufbereitung übernehmen vier 38 mm-Weber-Doppelkörper-Vergaser.

Die Zündanlage ist konventioneller Bauart System Bosch mit vier Zündspulen und zwei Verteilern. Das Fahrwerk hat einen Rohrrahmen mit einzeln an je zwei ungleichen Querlenkern aufgehängten Vorder- und Hinterrädern. Der hintere Arm des unteren Dreiecklenkers der Vorderradaufhängung ist als Längsschubstrebe ausgebildet. Nach Zandvoort erhielt die Vorderradaufhängung eine zusätzliche obere Längsschubstrebe. Die Abfederung bewirken vorne und hinten Torsionsstabfedern und im Rahmen angeordnete Stoßdämpfer. Der Porsche hat ein Sechsganggetriebe eigener Konstruktion, eine verbesserte Ausführung des 1961er Getriebes und Scheibenbremsen in den Rädern, ebenfalls eigener Konstruktion. Radstand 2300 mm, Spur vorne 1300 mm, hinten 1290 mm. Reifen vorne 5,00X15, hinten 6,50X15.

cylinder, the only engine of that kind in the new formula. The engine has a bore of 66 millimetres and stroke of 54.6 millimetres and a crankshaft supported by nine bearings. It has four overhead camshafts driven by bevel gears and crown wheels. The engine is cooled by air via a horizontally mounted plastic fan. There are four 38-millimetre Weber twin carburettors. Its ignition comes from Bosch and features four coils and two distributors.'

"The car's tubular frame chassis features independent suspension and wishbones of different length. The rear arm of the lower wishbone on the front suspension works as longitudinal connecting rod. After Zandvoort the front suspension received an additional upper rod. At the front as in the rear, torsion bars are used as springs and the telescopic dampers are mounted inside the frame. The Porsche has a six-speed transmission designed by them in-house. It is the improved version of the 1961 gearbox. There are disc brakes at all four wheels, also specially designed by Porsche. The wheelbase is 2,300 millimetres, the track at the front 1,300 millimetres and at the rear 1,290 millimetres. Front tyres are 5.00x15, rear tyres 6.50x15."

"Development of the eight-cylinder caused a lot of difficulties since an air-cooled eight-cylinder engine is necessarily much more sophisticated than a water-cooled V8 as used by their rivals. Since by the summer of 1961, it was not quite clear whether the eight-cylinder would be competitive, for 1962 the staff decided to build an interim solution thanks to the commitment of Swiss fuel-injection specialist, Michael May."

"May was asked to convert the four-cylinder, four-cam racing engine once designed by Dr. Fuhrmann, that had been for years the basic engine for Porsche's sports and racing cars, from carburettors to direct fuel injection. The development was successful and, at the beginning of the 1962 season, the four-cylinder unit with a Bosch direct fuel injection system delivered 189 horsepower on the test bench. However, this was taken when May already had left the Stuttgart factory. The causes of May's departure are of no interest here. It is certain however that the eight-cylinder in 1962 never managed to reach the output level of the injected four-cylinder. For the first race at Zandvoort, the eight-cylinder was giving slightly over 180 horsepower and fell back during the season to about 176 horsepower. Before the Monza Grand Prix, it had risen again to about 180 hp. Meanwhile, May has gone to Ferrari and is working on an injected version of the Dino 156."

There was no officially announcement concerning Porsche's withdrawal from its Formula One adventure. For some while the team continued to work on the design but the internal decision to cease this expensive foray into the top rank of motor sports soon took effect and Porsche confined themselves to sports cars and sports car races.

Ferry Porsche explained the reasons in his autobiography "Mein Leben" ("My Life"): "Regarding all our efforts, one should not overlook the fact that Formula One is a pretty expensive affair. In 1962 we took over the Reutter firm [the company in Zuffenhausen that had been assembling cars for Porsche]. To us it was a very important investment. So in the autumn of 1962, I once again checked the costs of our Formula One participation. After I had analysed the situation thoroughly

Foto: Porsche

Mit May-Motor: 1962 fährt Ben Pon in Zandvoort den modifizierten Wagen mit dem von May präparierten Motor.

Die Entwicklung des Achtzylindermotors bereitete enorme Schwierigkeiten, wie ja ein luftgekühltes Achtzylinder-Aggregat weitaus schwieriger zu beherrschen ist als ein wassergekühlter V 8-Motor. Da es im Sommer des Jahres 1961 durchaus noch nicht sicher war, ob der Achtzylindermotor 1962 mit einer der Konkurrenz entsprechenden Leistung eingesetzt werden konnte, entschloß sich die Werksleitung zu einer Übergangslösung, die sich mit der Verpflichtung des Schweizer Einspritz-Spezialisten Michael May anbot.

May sollte den einst von Dr. Fuhrmann entworfenen Vierzylinder-Viernockenwellen-Rennmotor, der jahrelang das Haupttriebwerk der Porsche-Rennsport- und Rennwagen war, auf direkte Benzineinspritzung umstellen. Die Arbeiten wurden mit Erfolg durchgeführt, und zu Beginn der Saison gab das Vierzylinder-Aggregat mit Direkteinspritzung, System Bosch, auf der Bremse 187 PS ab. Mit einem zweiten Motor, bei dem die Teile alle neu waren, wurden sogar auf dem Prüfstand 189 PS erreicht. Allerdings wurde diese Messung vorgenommen, als May das Stuttgarter Werk bereits wieder verlassen hatte. Die Art und Weise, wie es zum Ausscheiden von May aus der Firma Porsche kam, soll hier nicht weiter erörtert werden – fest steht nur, daß der Achtzylindermotor 1962 nie an die Leistung des Vierzylinder-Einspritzmotors herankam. Beim ersten Wertungslauf in Zandvoort gab der Achtzylinder etwas über 180 PS ab, um im weiteren Verlauf der Saison wieder auf eine Leistung von 176 PS abzufallen. Für den Grand Prix von Italien in Monza wurde dann wieder ein Wert erreicht, der um 180 PS lag.

May ist inzwischen zu Ferrari gegangen und arbeitet dort an einer Einspritzversion des Dino 156."

Es gibt kein offiziell verkündetes Ende des Abenteuers Formel 1. Zwar wird noch eine Zeitlang weiter an der Technik gearbeitet, die Entscheidung gegen den sündhaft teuren Einsatz in der

May power: in 1962 at Zandvoort, Ben Pon drove a modified car powered by a four-cylinder engine prepared by Michael May.

and after due consideration, I concluded that we could barely afford to go Grand Prix racing. Thus I finally decided that we would stop. After the American Grand Prix at Watkins Glen, we retired. There was no doubt for me that sports car races were more important to us and to our customers. They are much more closely related to our commercial product than a pure bred open-wheel racing car. But at least the experiences we made with the Grand Prix cars were ultimately of benefit in our sports car engagement."

Finally, the Porsche technicians managed to squeeze out the elusive 200 hp from the 1.5- litre that they had initially expected. The 753/1 was a derivative of the eight-cylinder with an even shorter stroke. The usual 753 revved to nearly 10,000 rpm, but the new engine went well beyond that mark. Thanks to the valve drive, 12,000 rpm would have been possible. But ultimately, the engine was never raced.

However, 753's big brother had an impressive career. The technicians had developed the 771 simultaneously with the 753. It displaced half a litre more (1,982 cubic centimetres – later it was taken out to 2.2 litres) and had from the beginning a power output of about 240 horsepower. It was mounted into the sports cars such as the 718, 904, 906, 910, 907 and 909. Victories at the Targa Florio and numerous hill-climb titles were the triumphs of this highly capable eight cylinder that had profited so much from the Formula One development. It was not displaced until the arrival of the incredible successful flat six of the 911

Königsklasse aber ist gefallen. Porsche zieht sich wieder auf den Sportwagenbau und auf die Sportwagenrennen zurück.

Die Gründe dafür hat Ferry Porsche in seiner Autobiografie „Mein Leben" noch einmal erläutert: „Man sollte aber bei unseren Anstrengungen nicht übersehen, daß der Formel-1-Sport eine sehr kostspielige Angelegenheit ist. Wir übernahmen im Jahre 1962 die Firma Reutter, für uns war das eine sehr wichtige Investition, und so schaute ich mir im Herbst 1962 einmal die Kosten für den Renneinsatz in der Formel 1 an. Nach gründlichem Studium der Situation und reiflichen Überlegungen kam ich dann zu dem Schluß, daß wir uns den Grand-Prix-Sport finanziell eigentlich gar nicht leisten konnten, so daß ich schließlich entscheiden mußte: ‚Wir hören damit auf!' Nach dem Grand Prix von Amerika in Watkins Glen zogen wir uns von der Formel 1 zurück. Für mich gab es auch keinen Zweifel daran, daß die Sportwagen-Rennen für uns und unsere Kunden wichtiger waren. Sie sind nun einmal dem Produkt, das wir herstellen, enger verwandt als der reine Rennwagen. Die Erfahrungen, die wir mit dem Grand-Prix-Wagen gesammelt hatten, konnten wir aller-

and of the brand new three-litre destined for the 908 that in fact had 350 horsepower.

All further entries of Porsche open-wheelers in Formula One were privateers. Here is the complete list:

April 15th 1963, Pau Grand Prix

The Lotus Team was the only works team entered for the race in Southern France. Thus Jim Clark and Trevor Taylor never had to fear for their 1-2 victory. Private entries Heinz Schiller and Carel de Beaufort took their chance and finished third and fourth respectively. Both drove Porsche 718/2.

April 21st 1963, Imola Grand Prix

Even in Italy, Lotus driver Jim Clark had no strong competitors and finished first at Imola. Second was a young Swiss privateer at the onset of his career who was later to have a distinguished career for Porsche. His name was Jo Siffert. Porsche drivers Carlo Abate, Carel de Beaufort and Jack Fairman came in fifth, sixth and seventh.

Zuffenhausener Express: Der 804 im Porsche-Werkshof.

High performance racing car made in Zuffenhausen: the 804 in the factory yard.

dings auch bei unserem Sportwagen-Engagement anwenden." Und so holen die Porsche-Techniker am Ende doch noch die angestrebten 200 Pferdestärken aus dem Anderthalbliter heraus. Der 753/1 ist eine noch kürzerhubige Version des Achtzylinders. Drehen die normalen 753 an die 10.000er Marke heran, schafft der extreme Kurzhuber weit mehr als 10.000 Touren. Technisch wären 12.000 möglich gewesen, soviel gibt der Ventiltrieb her. Der Motor wird allerdings nicht eingesetzt.

Eine beeindruckende Karriere erlebt hingegen der große Bruder des 753. Den 771 haben die Techniker parallel entwickelt. Er ist einen halben Liter größer (1982 Kubikzentimeter) – später hat er 2,2 Liter – und leistet von vornherein um die 240 PS. Eingebaut wird er in die Sportwagen 718 RS 61, 904, 906, 910, 907 und 909. Targa-Florio-Siege und Bergtitel sind die Triumphe des potenten Achtzylinders. Ihn verdrängen erst die unglaublich erfolgreiche Sechser aus dem 911 und – nach dem Paradesieg in

April 25th 1963, Syracuse Grand Prix

As the Lotus team had returned home to England to compete in the BARC 200 that was to be held two days later at Aintree, no works team turned up at Syracuse. Jo Siffert took his chance and gained his first Formula One victory at the wheel of the Ecurie Filipinetti Lotus-BRM. De Beaufort was the only other driver who remained un-lapped in the race and finished second.

May 11th 1963, International Trophy

At Silverstone the créme de la créme of the Grand Prix drivers met two weeks before the first championship race of the season.

Daytona – der nagelneue Dreiliter-Achtzylinder des 908. Der hat dann aber auch gleich 350 PS.

Alle weiteren Einsätze der Porsche-Monoposti in der Formel 1 werden von Privatfahrern vorgenommen. Verlauf und Ausgang dieser Rennen sind nachstehend protokolliert:

15. April 1963 Grand Prix von Pau

Zum Rennen in Südfrankreich ist außer der Lotus-Mannschaft kein Werksteam erschienen. Jim Clark und Trevor Taylor fahren so einen ungefährdeten Doppelsieg nach Hause. Die Privatiers Heinz Schiller und de Beaufort nutzen diese Chance und belegen in ihren Porsche 718/2 die Plätze drei und vier.

21. April 1963 Grand Prix von Imola

Auch in Italien ist Jim Clark im Lotus ohne ernsthafte Gegner und entscheidet das Rennen in Imola klar für sich. Auf Rang zwei kommt ein junger Schweizer Privatfahrer, der noch ganz am Anfang seiner Karriere steht: Jo Siffert. Mit Carlo Abate, Carel de Beaufort und Jack Fairman sind gleich drei Porsche-Piloten am Start, die in dieser Reihenfolge die Plätze fünf bis sieben belegen.

25. April 1963 Grand Prix von Syrakus

Da das Lotus-Team wegen eines nur zwei Tage später stattfindenden Rennens in Aintree (B.A.R.C. 200) die Heimreise angetreten hat, gehen in Syrakus keine Werksteams an den Start. Jo Siffert lässt sich diese Chance nicht entgehen und sichert sich im Lotus-B.R.M. seinen ersten Formel-1-Sieg. Als einziger nicht überrundeter Fahrer kommt de Beaufort in seinem 718/2 auf einen hervorragenden zweiten Platz.

11. Mai 1963 International Trophy

In Silverstone ist die gesamte Grand-Prix-Elite am Start, um zwei Wochen vor dem WM-Auftakt in Monaco eine letzte Standortbestimmung vornehmen zu können. In den ersten drei Runden führt Bruce McLaren im Cooper, dann übernimmt der aus der zweiten Reihe gestartete Jim Clark auf Lotus die Führung und gibt sie bis ins Ziel nicht mehr ab. Die sechs Runden Rückstand von de Beaufort, der als Neunter und Letzter ins Ziel kommt, verdeutlichen, dass der nun fünf Jahre alte Porsche 718 technisch nicht mehr auf dem aktuellen Stand ist.

19. Mai 1963 Grand Prix von Rom

Die Werksteams gehen eine Woche vor dem Grand Prix von Monaco kein Risiko mehr ein, hingegen haben sich sechs Privatiers, die in Silverstone dabei waren, auf den Weg nach Vallelunga gemacht. 19 Fahrer stehen in der Startaufstellung. Der unermüdliche Einsatz von de Beaufort wird hier mit der Pole Position belohnt. Er ist im Training eine Sekunde schneller als Bob Anderson im Lola. Beim Start geht Anderson in Führung, weil der holländische Porsche-Pilot die Vorteile seines Startplatzes nicht nutzen kann. De Beaufort kommt erst als Sechster aus der Startrunde zurück. Während Anderson sich mit Franco Bernabel im de Tomaso um die Spitze duelliert, kämpft sich de Beaufort in die Spitzengruppe zurück. Als Bernabel in der 27. von 40 Runden aufgeben muss, ist das Rennen zugunsten von Anderson entschieden. De Beaufort belegt mit knapp 21 Sekunden Rückstand Platz zwei.

Over the first three laps, Bruce McLaren in a Cooper led the race until Jim Clark, who had started from the second row, passed him to finish first. Six laps down, de Beaufort came in ninth and last. It was fast becoming obvious, that a five-year old Porsche 718 was not up-to-date any more.

May 19th 1963, Rome Grand Prix

With one week to go before Monaco, the works teams avoided any risks, but six privateers who had raced at Silverstone came to Vallelunga. There were nineteen drivers entered for the race. De Beaufort put his car on pole just one second faster than Bob Anderson. Anyway the Lola driver took the lead after the start while at the end of the first lap, de Beaufort was only on sixth position but caught up while Anderson and Franco Bernabel (de Tomaso) struggled for the lead. Bernabel retired on the twenty-seventh of forty laps with engine failure and Anderson finished first with de Beaufort second, twenty-one seconds behind him.

June 9th 1963, Belgian Grand Prix

A shower of rain just before the start gave the drivers a taste of the race to come on the Ardennes track. While Jim Clark made another winning start, Graham Hill had to retire due to transmission trouble. At the end of lap two, de Beaufort was lucky. Braking coming into the hairpin at La Source, he collided with Lucien Bianchi but managed to finish the race without stopping. In contrast, the Belgian had to enter into the pits and later retired. In the second half of the race a thunderstorm caused the track to be flooded and this led to some further retirements. After Hill had parked his car, de Beaufort who had started from eighteenth place had caught up to eighth. Finally, he even managed to score a point for being sixth thanks to the retirements of John Surtees and Tony Maggs.

June 23rd 193, Dutch Grand Prix

For his home GP, de Beaufort entered two 718/2s. They were the only four-cylinder open-wheelers on the track. Gerhard Mitter drove half of a second faster in practice than de Beaufort but that only gave him sixteenth position on the grid. Once again Jim Clark and his Lotus showed themselves to be unbeatable. Dan Gurney in a Brabham-Climax finished second. Mitter retired on lap three with clutch failure while de Beaufort profited from further retirements and finished ninth.

July 20th 1963, British Grand Prix

The race at Silverstone seemed to be a welcome change when Clark fell back to fourth during the first lap. But of course he managed to catch up quickly, took over the lead in lap four and finished first. Nearly half a minute further back, Graham Hill and John Surtees finished second and third respectively. De Beaufort came in seven laps down and was classified tenth.

July 28th 1963 Großer Preis der Solitude

At Stuttgart, the two Porsche drivers were de Beaufort and Mitter. Twenty-seven cars took the start and among the drivers were many famous names. Again Clark put his car in pole position. However a drive shaft broke in practice and the Scot failed to

9. Juni 1963 Grand Prix von Belgien

Ein kurz vor dem Start niedergehender Schauer stimmt die
Fahrer richtig auf das Rennen in den Ardennen ein. Während Jim
Clark einem weiteren Start-Ziel-Sieg entgegenfährt, muss Graham Hill mit Getriebeproblemen vorzeitig aufgeben. Am Ende
der zweiten Runde hat de Beaufort Glück. Beim Anbremsen der
La Source kollidiert er mit Lucien Bianchi, kann das Rennen
aber ohne Unterbrechung fortsetzen. Der Belgier hingegen muss
die Box aufsuchen und fällt später aus. In der zweiten Rennhälfte
lässt ein Gewitter sintflutartige Regenfälle auf die Strecke nie-
dergehen, was zu zahlreichen Ausfällen führt. Nach Hills Ausfall
liegt de Beaufort, als 18. gestartet, schon auf dem achten Rang.
Die weiteren Ausfälle von John Surtees und Tony Maggs lassen
den Holländer gar in die Punkteränge vorstoßen. Ein WM-Punkt
ist der Lohn für seine konstante Fahrt unter widrigen Bedingungen.

23. Juni 1963 Grand Prix von Holland

Bei seinem Heim-Grand-Prix setzt de Beaufort zwei 718/2 ein,
es sind die einzigen Vierzylinder-Monoposti im Feld. Gerhard
Mitter ist mit dem Porsche eine halbe Sekunde schneller als der
Holländer, steht aber trotzdem nur auf dem sechzehnten Startplatz. Schnellster ist wieder einmal Jim Clark, der in seinem
Lotus auch an diesem Tag nicht zu schlagen ist. Er erringt einen
weiteren Start-Ziel-Sieg, dieses Mal vor Dan Gurney im Brabham-Climax. Mitter scheidet bereits in der dritten Runde wegen
eines Kupplungsschadens aus. De Beaufort profitiert wieder durch
die Ausfälle anderer Fahrer und wird Neunter.

20. Juli 1963 Grand Prix von England

Das Rennen in Silverstone macht Jim Clark wenigstens am
Anfang etwas spannend, als er in der Startrunde auf Rang vier
zurückfällt. Dann aber verbessert er sich in jeder Runde um eine
Position, geht im vierten Umlauf in Führung und gibt sie bis
ins Ziel nicht mehr ab. Mit fast einer halben Minute Rückstand
kommen Graham Hill und John Surtees auf die nächsten Plätze.
De Beaufort belegt mit sieben Runden Rückstand Rang zehn.

Die letzten Porsche-Monoposti: 1963 bringt de Beaufort in den Niederlanden zwei 718/2 an den Start. Der vielversprechende Gerhard Mitter scheidet mit defekter Kupplung aus, sein Teamchef wird Neunter.

The last Porsche open-wheelers: in 1963, Godin de Beaufort entered two 718/2 in the Dutch GP. The up-and-coming driver, Gerhard Mitter, retired with clutch failure while his team leader finished ninth.

Fotos: Porsche

28. Juli 1963 Großer Preis der Solitude

In Stuttgart stehen, wie beim holländischen Grand Prix, mit de Beaufort und Mitter wieder zwei Porsche-Piloten am Start. 27 Wagen umfasst das gesamte Feld, in dem zahlreiche Spitzenpiloten vertreten sind. Trainingsschnellster ist Jim Clark, der seine Pole Position jedoch nicht nutzen kann. Beim Start bricht eine Halbwelle am Lotus, der Schotte bleibt an der Spitze des Feldes stehen. Um noch in den Genuss des Startgelds zu kommen, wird der Schaden repariert und Clark geht mit 16 Runden Rückstand ins Rennen. Der Schotte glänzt noch durch die schnellste Runde des Rennens. Während Brabham auf seinem Eigenbau das Rennen anführt und schließlich auch gewinnt, gelingt es Mitter, den vor ihm fahrenden Beaufort zu überholen und den fünften Platz nach Hause zu fahren. Der Holländer hat ab der Hälfte des Rennens keine funktionierende Kupplung mehr und darf froh sein, noch als Siebter ins Ziel zu kommen.

Dauerläufer: De Beaufort wird 1963 im Solitude-Rennen Siebter.

Long-term performance: in 1963 de Beaufort finished seventh in the Solitude race.

start as the car was not ready in time. But in order to qualify for start money, the car was fixed and Clark rejoined the race the race sixteen laps down. At least he drove the fastest lap. Brabham finished first in a car of his own design, while Mitter passed de Beaufort and finished fifth. The Dutch driver suffered clutch problems during the second half of the race and was lucky to finish seventh.

August 4th 1963, German Grand Prix

In contrast to the previous year in the Eifel, the weather was fine and the track was dry. At the front, John Surtees, who was now driving for Ferrari, and Jim Clark fought for the lead. From the fifth lap of fifteen, Surtees was alone in the lead as Clark's engine refused to run properly. So just a couple of weeks after his victory in the 1,000-kilometre race on the 'Ring, Surtees gained the victory in the GP race as well. The race was overshadowed by some

4. August 1963 Großer Preis von Deutschland

Im Gegensatz zum Vorjahr präsentiert die Eifel zu diesem Grand Prix warmes und trockenes Wetter. An der Spitze des Feldes liefern sich der nun für Ferrari fahrende John Surtees und der Schotte Jim Clark im Lotus ein spannendes Duell. Ab der fünften der fünfzehn Runden liegt Surtees allein an der Spitze, weil Clarks Motor nicht mehr rund läuft. So siegt Surtees wenige Wochen nach seinem Triumph beim 1000-Kilometer-Rennen auf dem Nürburgring nun auch im Grand Prix. Leider ereignen sich einige Unfälle. So muss Bruce McLaren nach einem Sturz eingangs der Fuchsröhre mit einer Gehirnschütterung ins Krankenhaus gebracht werden. Willy Mairesse kommt am Flugplatz von der Strecke ab. Der Belgier wird aus dem Wagen herausgeschleu-

bad accidents. A Red Cross paramedic was killed when Belgian Ferrari driver, Willy Mairesse, went off the track and his car hit the man. Mairesse was thrown out of the car and broke both of his arms. Bruce McLaren went off the track just before the Fuchsröhre and suffered a concussion. De Beaufort lost a wheel after a rim broke but luckily was not injured. Gerhard Mitter finished fourth in the second Porsche.

August 11th 1963, Kannonloppet

Jim Clark and Trevor Taylor fought it out at Karlskoga. Jack Brabham finished third two minutes behind them. Denis Hulme came in fourth with the second Brabham and de Beaufort finished seventh.

Campingatmosphäre: Traumhaft leger scheint die Szene – immerhin handelt es sich um die Vorbereitungen zum Grand Prix auf dem Nürburgring. Gerhard Mitter (26) und Carel de Beaufort (17) zeigen im Rennen noch einmal, was im alten Vierzylinder-Formel-Renner steckt.

Just like camping: the scene appears wonderfully laid-back. However, it is the preparation immediately before the German GP at the Nürburgring where Gerhard Mitter (26) and Carel de Beaufort (17) showed what the old four-cylinder Formula One car could do.

Talentprobe: Gerhard Mitter fährt ein paar Mal für Carel de Beaufort und wird – im Vierzylinder – 1963 Vierter auf dem Nürburgring.

A new talent: Gerhard Mitter started a couple of times for Carel Godin de Beaufort and, with a four-cylinder car, finished fourth at the Nürburgring in 1963.

dert und bricht sich beide Arme, Wrackteile seines Ferrari aber erfassen einen Sanitäter des Roten Kreuzes, der tödlich verletzt wird. De Beaufort verliert nach einem Felgenbruch ein Rad, kann seinem Porsche aber unverletzt entsteigen. Begünstigt durch die zahlreichen Ausfälle steuert Gerhard Mitter den zweiten Porsche nach hervorragender Fahrt auf den vierten Rang.

11. August 1963 Kannonloppet

Das Rennen in Karlskoga wird eine sichere Beute der Lotus-Piloten Jim Clark und Trevor Taylor, die Jack Brabham mit zwei Minuten Rückstand auf Platz drei verweisen. Während der spätere Weltmeister Denis Hulme den zweiten Brabham in seinem ersten Formel-1-Rennen auf Rang vier fährt, belegt de Beaufort nach zuverlässiger Fahrt den siebten Platz.

18. August 1963 Großer Preis des Mittelmeers

Weil de Beaufort nach einem Achsschenkelbruch im Training auf die Teilnahme am Rennen in Enna verzichten muss, stellen sich nur noch 15 Wagen zum Start. Surtees geht sogleich in Führung und fährt das Rennen, trotz des stets nur geringen Vorsprungs, sicher nach Hause.

Dahinter entbrennt ein heftiger Kampf um die Plätze. Dabei berühren sich Lorenzo Bandini und Trevor Taylor, dessen Lotus ins Schleudern kommt und gegen die Absperrungen prallt. Der Engländer zieht sich einige Prellungen und Quetschungen zu. Bandini aber kann seine Fahrt fortsetzen und wird hinter Surtees und Arundell Dritter. Auf Platz sieben kommt der Italiener Carlo Abate auf einem Porsche 718/2 ins Ziel.

1. September 1963 Großer Preis von Österreich

Weil seine härtesten Widersacher, die Lotus-Piloten Jim Clark und Innes Ireland, vorzeitig aufgeben müssen, kann Jack Brabham auf seiner Eigenkonstruktion das Rennen in Zeltweg klar für sich entscheiden. Hinter Tony Settember auf einem Scirocco kommt de Beaufort auf den dritten Platz. Kurt Bardi-Barry, der mit dem zweiten 718/2 von de Beaufort ins Rennen gegangen ist, gibt nach drei Runden auf, weil ihm der Wagen nicht konkurrenzfähig erscheint.

8. September 1963 Grand Prix von Italien

Mit einem Sieg sichert sich Jim Clark vorzeitig den WM-Titel 1963, de Beaufort dagegen scheitert an der Qualifikationshürde. Auf dem Hochgeschwindigkeitskurs von Monza liegt die Zeit des Holländers mehr als neun Sekunden über der Trainingsbestzeit von John Surtees auf Ferrari.

21. September 1963 Gold Cup

Auch beim Gold Cup in Oulton Park ist Jim Clark nicht zu schlagen. Der Lotus-Pilot gewinnt mit mehr als 20 Sekunden Vorsprung vor den B.R.M.-Teamgefährten Richie Ginther und Graham Hill. De Beaufort kommt mit sechs Runden Rückstand auf den zehnten Rang.

6. Oktober 1963 Grand Prix der USA

In Watkins Glen profitiert Graham Hill vom Pech seiner Landsleute Jim Clark und John Surtees. Während der Motor

August 18th 1963, Grand Prix of the Mediterranean

Because an axle bearing broke on his car in practice, Carel de Beaufort did not start at Enna and thus only fifteen cars took the start. John Surtees went into the lead and finished first while, in the battle behind him, Lorenzo Bandini and Trevor Taylor collided, the Lotus went into a skid and crashed into the barriers with Taylor suffering multiple bruises. Bandini carried on and finished third behind Surtees and Arundell. Italian Porsche driver Carlo Abate finished seventh.

September 1st 1963, Austrian Grand Prix

Since his strongest opponents, the Lotus drivers Jim Clark and Innes Ireland, both retired, Jack Brabham in a Brabham finished first at Zeltweg. Behind him was Tony Settember (Scirocco) and de Beaufort finished third. Kurt Bardi-Barry in de Beaufort's second 718/2 gave up after three laps as he considered that his car was not competitive.

September 8th 1963, Italian Grand Prix

With his victory here in Italy, Jim Clark had the champion's title in his pocket. De Beaufort failed to qualify. On the high-speed track at Monza he lapped nine seconds slower than Ferrari driver John Surtees.

September 21st 1963, Gold Cup

This was another victory for Jim Clark, the new World Champion. The Lotus driver won the Gold Cup at Oulton Park in style with a twenty second lead ahead of BRM drivers Richie Ginther and Graham Hill. De Beaufort finished tenth.

October 6th 1963, American Grand Prix

At Watkins Glen, Jim Clark and John Surtees were unlucky. The Lotus driver's engine stalled at the start and it was not until it was running two minutes later that he re-started his race. Surtees led the race up to lap eighty-one when his engine failed thus opening the way for a BRM double with Graham Hill and Richie Ginther. De Beaufort finished sixth and scored one point.

November 3rd 1963, Mexican Grand Prix

It was a winning start for World Champion, Jim Clark, in the Mexican Grand Prix. Carel de Beaufort finished tenth thanks to his reliable old car.

December 28th 1963, South African Grand Prix

The race in South Africa was the tenth and last race of the 1963 season. Jim Clark gained his seventh GP victory of that year. Since Juan Manuel Fangio, there had not been a driver who had dominated a season so completely. De Beaufort, finishing tenth in South Africa, wound up with two points for the year and thus was classified fourteenth. It was his best score in the Formula One championship.

May 2nd 1964, BRDC International Trophy at Silverstone

Though the International Trophy of the British Racing Drivers Club was a non-championship race, all the best drivers were at

des Lotus-Piloten beim Start ausgeht und der Schotte erst nach einer fast zwei Minuten dauernden Reparatur dem Feld hinterherhetzen kann, führt Surtees das Rennen bis zur 81. Runde an. Ein Motordefekt beendet dessen Fahrt und macht den Weg frei für einen B.R.M.-Doppelsieg durch Graham Hill und Richie Ginther.

Die konstante Fahrt von de Beaufort wird mit einem WM-Punkt für den sechsten Rang belohnt.

3. November 1963 Grand Prix von Mexiko

Mit einem Start-Ziel-Sieg des neuen Weltmeisters Jim Clark endet der Grand Prix von Mexiko. De Beaufort sieht mit dem sehr zuverlässigen Porsche auf Rang zehn erneut die Zielflagge.

the start in Silverstone. Even Ferrari gave Surtees a car. The race turned into a great success for the young team of Australian Jack Brabham. Dan Gurney in his Brabham-Climax BT7 started from pole position but retired after the first half of the race. Jack Brabham drove the fastest lap and finished first just ahead of BRM driver Graham Hill and Lotus-Climax driver Peter Arundell. Carel de Beaufort finished eleventh and was five laps down on the leaders.

May 24th 1964, Dutch Grand Prix

Carel de Beaufort definitely did not want to miss out on his home GP. Of course it was something one could better define as the Olympic Spirit, rather like "participating is everything". In order

28. Dezember 1963 Grand Prix von Südafrika

Das Rennen in Südafrika ist der zehnte und letzte WM-Lauf des Jahres 1963. Jim Clark holt sich den siebten Grand-Prix-Sieg der laufenden Saison. Seit Juan Manuel Fangio hat kein Fahrer eine Saison so eindeutig dominiert. De Beaufort, der auch in Südafrika als Zehnter in Ziel kommt, beendet die Saison 1963 mit zwei WM-Punkten auf Platz 14, seine bis dahin beste Platzierung in einer Formel-1-Weltmeisterschaft.

2. Mai 1964 BRDC International Trophy in Silverstone

Die Internationale Trophäe des British Racing Drivers Club ist zwar kein Weltmeisterschaftslauf, aber dennoch steht fast die gesamte Weltelite am Start. Sogar Ferrari stellt John Surtees einen Wagen zur Verfügung. Das Rennen wird ein großer Erfolg für das noch junge Team des Australiers Jack Brabham. Dan Gurney startet mit seinem Brabham-Climax BT7 von der Pole Position, fällt aber zur Hälfte des Rennens aus. Brabham kann das Rennen knapp vor Graham Hill im B.R.M. und Peter Arundell auf Lotus-Climax für sich entscheiden und fährt außerdem die schnellste Runde des Tages. Carel de Beaufort wird mit fünf Runden Rückstand Elfter.

24. Mai 1964 Grand Prix von Holland in Zandvoort

Bei seinem Heim-Grand-Prix darf der holländische Graf natürlich nicht fehlen. Dabei steht der olympische Gedanke im Vorder-

Niederlande – ein Punkt: Für seinen sechsten Platz in Watkins Glen kassiert de Beaufort am 6. Oktober 1963 einen WM-Zähler.

To the Netherlands – één punt: his sixth place at Watkins Glen on October 6th 1963 earned de Beaufort a championship point.

to go easy on his aged racing car, the Dutch driver only took part in one practice session. But eventually it was all for nothing as already in lap eight he was brought to a halt by engine failure. World Champion Clark finished first.

July 19th 1964, Großer Preis der Solitude

The race near Stuttgart was held under extreme weather conditions. In heavy rain, the race was started after a warm-up lap, a procedure that was unusual for that time. Jim Clark took the lead but was pressured by Ferrari driver, John Surtees. On lap ten, the Ferrari was in the lead but Clark countered on lap sixteen and finally finished first. De Beaufort came in eighth.

August 2nd 1964, German Grand Prix

Once again Dutch Count de Beaufort was the only Porsche driver entering for the German Grand Prix on August 1st. While trying to qualify for the race at the 'Ring, he went off the track in the notorious right-hand bend called Bergwerk and the car fell down

grund, und so nimmt de Beaufort nur an einer Trainingssitzung teil, um den betagten Porsche zu schonen. Diese Vorsichtsmaßnahme hat leider nicht den gewünschten Effekt, schon in der achten Runde stoppt ein Motorschaden seine Fahrt. Das Rennen wird eine sichere Beute des amtierenden Weltmeisters Jim Clark.

19. Juli 1964 Großer Preis der Solitude

Das Rennen vor den Toren Stuttgarts wird unter extremen Wetterbedingungen ausgetragen. Das Feld geht bei starkem Regen erst nach einer zu dieser Zeit noch nicht üblichen Einführungsrunde ins Rennen. Jim Clark übernimmt die Führung, wird aber hart von John Surtees im Ferrari bedrängt. In der zehnten Runde liegt der Ferrari vorn, aber Clark kontert in der 16. Runde, übernimmt die Spitzenposition und gibt sie bis ins Ziel nicht mehr ab. De Beaufort ist mit seinem Vierzylinder-Porsche ins Rennen gegangen. Er fährt ein besonnenes Rennen und kommt als Achter ins Ziel.

Großer Preis von Deutschland 1964: Carel de Beaufort vor dem Abschlusstraining.

German Grand Prix 1964: during practice for the German Grand Prix, Carel Godin de Beaufort suffered fatal injuries in a severe accident.

a slope. Beaufort was taken to hospital but all help was in vain. That evening, Carel Godin de Beaufort died of the severe skull and back injuries he has sustained in the accident.

With this tragic incident, the history of Porsche in Formula One racing came to an end. The least that could be said was that the aged open wheelers from Zuffenhausen still cut a pretty fine figure racing against competitors with much better and much more up-to-date cars. Thus Porsches' legendary reliability impressed even more. And by the way, right up to the present moment, de Beaufort is still the driver with the most racing hours in a Porsche Formula One car. (mb) ■

2. August 1964 Großer Preis von Deutschland auf dem Nürburgring

Wieder ist es der holländische Graf de Beaufort, der die Porsche-Fahnen im deutschen Grand Prix hochhalten will. Er kämpft im Abschlusstraining am 1. August um seine Qualifikation, als er im Abschnitt Bergwerk von der Strecke abkommt. Der Porsche 718 stürzt einen Abhang hinab und Beaufort muss ins Krankenhaus gebracht werden. Am Abend des Renntages, der John Surtees als Sieger sieht, erliegt der sympathische Holländer seinen schweren Schädel- und Rückenverletzungen.

Mit dem tragischen Unfall des holländischen Grafen endet die Geschichte der Formel-1-Rennen mit Porsche-Beteiligung. Zwar war der technische Vorsprung der Konkurrenz gegenüber den betagten Porsche-Monoposti der Privatiers augenfällig, aber neben einzelnen WM-Punkten ist die stets erneut unter Beweis gestellte, ja schon sprichwörtliche Zuverlässigkeit der Zuffenhausener Konstruktionen auch in diesem letzten Kapitel besonders beeindruckend. Carel Godin de Beaufort ist bis heute der Fahrer mit den meisten Einsätzen in einem Porsche-Formel-1-Rennwagen. (mb) ∎

Letzte Dokumente: Vor dem Großen Preis von Deutschland kommt de Beaufort im Training ums Leben.

"Last document: the practice times show de Beaufort's name but, by the time of the race, he was fighting for his life in hospital."

Foto: Porsche

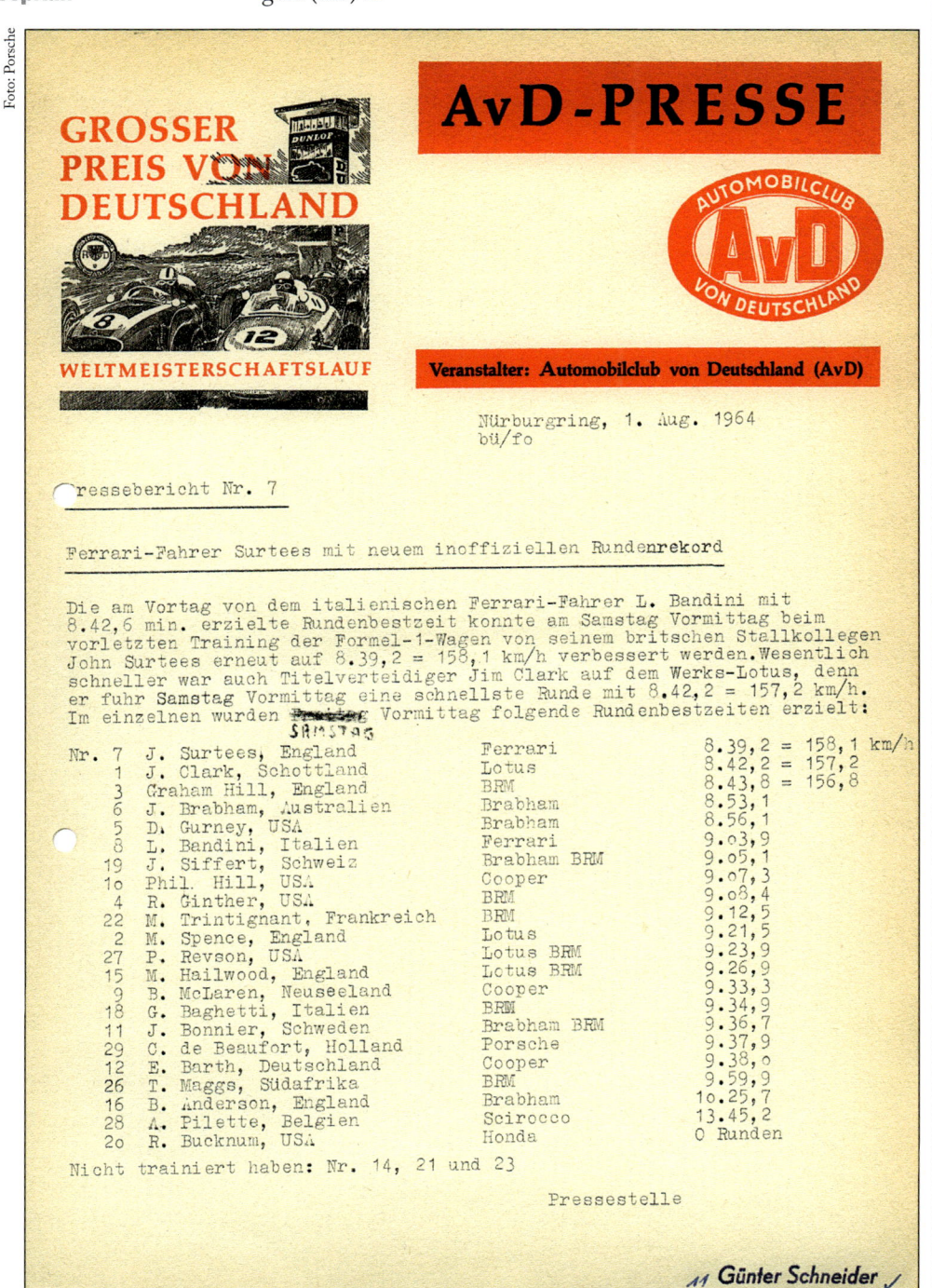

Fahrerlager
Eine Frau und 38 Männer haben die Formelrenner 718 und 804 im Rennen gefahren oder waren zumindest gemeldet.

Paddock
A total of one woman and thirty-eight men raced Porsche's Formula One cars, the 718 and 804, or at least were entered to race.

Carel Godin de Beaufort	57
Joakim Bonnier	45
Dan Gurney	22
Edgar Barth	13
Hans Herrmann	13
Wolfgang Seidel	10
Stirling Moss	9
Heinz Schiller	7
Jean Behra	5
Masten Gregory	5
Carlo Abate	4
Christian Goethals	4
Gerhard Mitter	4
Graham Hill	4
Wolfgang Graf Berghe von Trips	4
Christian Heinz	2
Umberto Maglioli	2
Anton von Dory	1
Auguste Veuillet	1
Ben Pon	1
Claude Storez	1
Colin Davis	1
Dawie Gous	1
Ernst Vogel	1
Fred Gamble	1
Gerard Laureau	1
Giancarlo Baghetti	1
Harry Blanchard	1
Harry Schell	1
Heini Walter	1
Jack Fairman	1
Jean Kerguen	1
John Surtees	1
Kurt Bardi-Barry	1
Lloyd Casner	1
Lucien Bianchi	1
Ludwig Heimrath	1
Marie-Therese de Filippis	1
Nino Vaccarella	1

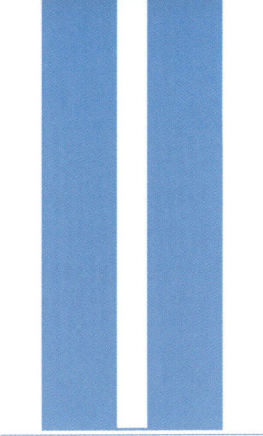

„Ich hab so viel gelernt bei diesem Projekt: Wie man's machen soll, und vor allem auch, wie man es nicht machen soll."

Hans Mezger berichtet von Erfolgen und Rückschlägen, vcn Zwangssteuerungs-Experimenten und innenumgriffenen Bremsscheiben

Vielversprechend, enttäuschend, eine Episode, ein Abenteuer – kommt die Sprache auf das erste Formel-1-Experiment von Porsche, ist viel von gemischten Gefühlen die Rede. Die Geschichte des 804 ist zu gleichen Teilen von Erfolgen wie von Rückschlägen geprägt. Die dabei waren, sind denn auch immer noch hin- und hergerissen zwischen einer gewissen Zufriedenheit und dann doch wieder Enttäuschung. „Ich will mal so sagen: Es war so schlecht nicht, aber es gab auch Leute in der Firma Porsche und in der Familie selbst – also, es waren schon noch ein paar Leute enttäuscht." Das sagt Hans Mezger, lange Jahre der Kopf der Motorenentwicklung in Zuffenhausen und an den meisten wichtigen Projekten aus dem Hause Porsche beteiligt.

Ganz so schlecht sei der Formelrenner freilich nicht gewesen. „Wir sind dann ja auch ein paar Mal unter Wert geschlagen worden, weil irgendwelche Kleinigkeiten nicht gestimmt haben. Da kann ich mich erinnern: Am Nürburgring gab es eine Art Vortraining, und da ist man Superzeiten gefahren." Das war vor dem Großen Preis von Deutschland 1962, in dem dann alles bestens lief, wenn es nicht ein Malheur gegeben hätte. „Da ist jede Runde über die volle Distanz schneller als die vorige gewesen. Und dann ist dem Gurney im Rennen die Sache mit der verrutschten Batterie passiert." Der Rennfahrer schlug sich bravourös, obwohl er mit dem Fuß immer wieder den aus der Fassung geratenen Stromspeicher stabilisieren musste. Nun kann so etwas schon mal passieren,

"I learned a lot: what to do and what not to do"

Hans Mezger recalls successes and setbacks, valve gear experiments and a special kind of disc brake

Promising and disappointing, both an episode and an adventure – whenever the subject of Porsche's first Formula One project comes up, one quickly discovers a lot of mixed emotions. The 804's biography is a story of success as well as being a story of setbacks and anti-climaxes. Those who took part in that project are still torn between satisfaction and disappointment. "Let me put it like this. It wasn't that bad but there were certain people within the firm and in the family who were really disappointed." So says Hans Mezger, the long-standing head of the engine development department at Zuffenhausen and who was involved in most of Porsche's major projects.

The Formula One racing car had not been too bad. "Anyway we were beaten some times when we shouldn't have been only because some minor thing didn't work properly. I remember a training session at the Nürburgring where the drivers lapped in really quick times." This was before the 1962 German Grand Prix. "Every lap was faster than the previous one and then, in the race, Gurney had that mishap with the loose battery." The driver made an excellent job though he had to hold the battery in place with his foot.

One might just say that things like that can happen to everybody but not in Mezger's view of how things should be: "At Porsche we always set high standards and made big demands on everybody to get things right."

Foto: Porsche

Handarbeit: 1961 entstehen in der Werkstatt in Zuffenhausen die Achtzylinder-Renner.

Handiwork: in 1961, the eight-cylinder racing cars were built in the Zuffenhausen workshop.

Foto: Porsche

irgendeine Kleinigkeit ist immer. Nichts da: „Beim Porsche hat man natürlich auch damals schon Ansprüche gestellt."

Hat also das Werk den Formelrenner sterben lassen, weil er nicht vom Fleck weg ordentlichen Erfolg gebracht hat? Ganz so einfach sei es nicht, sagt Mezger. „Man hat mit Sicherheit nicht mit bloß einem Jahr gerechnet. Kein Mensch hätte das getan." Eine Rolle spielen aber ganz klar die Kosten des Projekts. Porsche stemmt das Formel-Engagement komplett mit den eigenen Schultern. „Wenn man einen Vertrag macht, wie mit McLaren oder mit TAG, dann legt man natürlich einen finanziellen Rahmen fest mit der Option, dass man weitermacht, wenn alles gut läuft. Wenn man alles allein macht, muss man schon schauen, wie es weitergeht, wie sich zum Beispiel das Reglement ändert." Dass Porsche nicht gleich Weltmeister wird, „war mit Sicherheit nicht der einzige Grund, warum man gesagt hat: Dann machen wir es nicht mehr".

Zunächst läuft alles ziemlich vielversprechend an. Startschuss ist die Reglementänderung, die praktisch aus der Formel 2 die Formel 1 mit den kleinen 1,5-Liter-Motoren macht. „Da hat man nicht schlecht ausgesehen", sagt Mezger. Das ist noch geschmeichelt. Porsche ist seit Jahren der ewige Underdog, der bei jeder Gelegenheit mit motorisch eigentlich unterlegenen Wagen die Konkurrenz alt aussehen lässt. Beste Voraussetzung also, in der neuen „kleinen" Formel mit der großen Erfahrung in solchen Hubraumklassen zu reüssieren. Es kommt noch etwas dazu, das Mezger gleich spürt, als er damals „beim Porsche" anfängt: „Ende der 50er Jahre gab es so eine Art Aufbruchstimmung. Da war man dann schon, ich sag es mal so: gut etabliert." Zu jener Zeit hat die Entwicklung eines Sechszylinders für die Serie begonnen. „Der hatte zwar noch nicht viel mit dem späteren Elfer zu tun", aber die bis dato so erfolgreichen Vierzylindermotoren sind – da ist nicht dran zu rütteln – mittlerweile ausgereizt. Der Sechszylinder soll also kommen, „für das Auto gab es aber noch keine konkreten Pläne". Gleichzeitig tüfteln die Techniker an einem Achtzylinder, der im Rennen die dort ebenfalls in die Jahre gekommenen Vierzylinder („die waren auch am Ende") ersetzen soll. Die offenbar schier unschlagbaren britischen Renner sind allesamt mit potenten Achtzylindern erfolgreich.

Seit 1956 ist Mezger dabei. Zunächst arbeitet er in einer Abteilung, deren Mitarbeiter vor allem für die technischen Berechnungen zuständig sind. „Das war schon gut. Ich habe ja nicht nur gerechnet, sondern so auch alle Konstruktionen kennengelernt." Mezgers Spezialgebiet ist die Ventilsteuerung, „da hab ich natürlich von Anfang an mit dem Vierzylinder zu tun gehabt". Da geht es unter anderem darum, den Spyder schneller zu machen, doch „da sind uns dann ständig die Ventilfedern gebrochen". Das Problem: Mangelhaftes Material mit Schlackeeinschlüssen, Besseres ist aber nicht verfügbar. So bleiben höheren Drehzahlen – eins der Mittel, kleinen Motoren größere Leistung abzuringen – natürliche Grenzen gesetzt.

1960 stößt Mezger zu dem Team, dass den 804 entwickelt. Noch ist er natürlich nicht der Chef, sein Vorgesetzter ist Hans Hönick. Zunächst ist auch ein Vierzylindermotor für den Formelrenner im Gespräch. „Da war der Michael May da, der hat sich mit der Vierzylinder-Einspritzung beschäftigt." Der will enorme Leistung herausgeholt haben, „die man dann aber später, ich sag mal so: bestritten hat". Bis heute wird kolportiert, dass der Vier- so stark wie dann der Achtzylinder gewesen sei. Mezger hat auch später

Was it that Porsche let the formula racer die because it hadn't been immediately successful? It had not been that simple. Mezger again: "For sure they did not plan for just one year. Nobody would have done that." One reason for the cessation of the programme was obviously the enormous cost. Porsche started the project working entirely on its own. "If you make a supply contract for example with McLaren or with TAG, you will fix the financial limit of your involvement including the option to carry on in the case of success. If you're doing it all by yourself, you have to plan very carefully. For example, there is always the possibility that the regulations will be changed." The fact that Porsche did not become champion at its first attempt had surely not been the reason for their withdrawal.

At first things went pretty well. The starting signal for Porsche's involvement in Grand Prix racing was the introduction of a new Formula Two with small 1.5-litre engines. "Back then, to us it didn't look bad at all" Mezger says. That's a big understatement. Porsche had for a long time been making its competitors look silly with what were seemingly underdog cars. Thus conditions were very favourable for an entry in the new "small" formula. But Porsche was also well positioned to do something like that thanks to a certain mood prevalent in the company that Mezger felt the instant he started working at Zuffenhausen. "Everybody seemed to be getting ready to go for it at the end of the fifties. We were, as you might say, well set up at that time." At that time, the development of a six-cylinder engine for normal production had already begun. "It didn't have too much in common with the later 911 engine though." Although the four-cylinder engines were still successful, a six-cylinder was intended to replace the flat four in Porsche's road cars to keep up with the performance increases of their rivals. But at the same time, the engineers were mulling over the idea of an eight-cylinder as a replacement for the "Fuhrmann" engine then being used in the racing cars "which were also getting near the limit of their performance". And by the beginning of the 1960s, the British formula racing cars all had strong eight-cylinder engines.

Mezger joined Porsche in 1956 and at first he became part of a team responsible for technical calculations. "That was fine with me as I did not just have to calculate, but also learned to know every element of the design." Mezger's special area was valve gear and "thus I dealt with the four-cylinder right from the beginning". The team tried to make the Spyder faster "but the valve springs tended to break". The problem was traced to faulty material that had inclusions of slag in the steel alloy that was being used. Unfortunately better steel was not available at that time and thus higher revolutions, the proven means of wringing more performance from small engines, were off the menu.

In 1960, Mezger joined the team that was responsible for the 804 and to start with he worked under Hans Hönick. At first a four-cylinder had been considered for the new formula racing car. "Michael May was there and he had worked on an injection system for the four-cylinder which he said had made the engine perform sensationally well, though later that assertion was at least partly withdrawn." It is still commonly accepted that the injected flat four tweaked by May was at least as strong as the eight-cylinder. Mezger doubts this although he later worked on the four-cylinder himself, particularly with the two-litre version destined for the 904. His reckoning is that the quoted 190 horsepower from that 1.5-litre four-cylinder is highly improbable.

noch mit dem Vierzylinder zu tun, etwa in der Zweiliter-Version für den 904, an Werte von um die 190 PS mag er aber nicht glauben. „Das war fast nicht möglich."

Erste Entwürfe für den Achtzylinder entstehen 1959, im September des nächsten Jahres läuft er erstmals auf dem Prüfstand. Wie das mit der Formel 1 werden soll, steht noch in den Sternen. „Das war ja nicht so unser Hauptfeld. Auch der Ferry Porsche war ja immer für einen Motorsporteinsatz, der in gewisser Weise so ein bisschen seriennah war." Der Porsche-Chef hat stets die Sportwagenproduktion im Auge, mit der das Werk sein Geld verdient. Der Verkauf aber profitiert natürlich direkt von den Erfolgen im Motorsport. „Der Ferry Porsche hat immer gefragt: Was bringt uns das für die Serie? Und da war halt die Formel 1 weit entfernt – damals allerdings vielleicht nicht so sehr wie heute."

Immerhin: Für das Projekt soll ein Achtzylinder her, weil von vornherein eine Leistung von 200 PS gefordert ist. Die ist auch vonnöten, um gegen die englische Konkurrenz bestehen zu können. Den Ingenieuren ist klar, dass sie es da auch mit horrend hohen Drehzahlen von um die 10.000 Touren zu tun bekommen. Ein weiterer Punkt im Lastenheft: Mehr Hubraum soll sich im neuen Motor ebenfalls realisieren lassen, der Achtzylinder soll auch die Langstreckenrenner befeuern. „Zuerst hat man gesagt: Wir machen einen Zweiliter. Und dann kam ja auch relativ schnell der 2,2-Liter, mit dem man dann später die Langstreckenrennen gefahren ist." Der entsteht übrigens zunächst ohne das Wissen der Porsche-Oberen. „Wir haben den mehr oder weniger heimlich gemacht, einfach im Versuch die Teile bestellt." Die luftgekühlten Motoren lassen sich mittels größerer Zylinder und Köpfe verhältnismäßig leicht vergrößern. „Mit den Einzelzylinderköpfen war das eigentlich eine Kleinigkeit."

Eine Zeitlang experimentiert der Versuch mit einer Ventilzwangssteuerung für den hochdrehenden Motor. Im herkömmlich aufgebauten Zylinderkopf halten starke Federn die Ventile geschlossen, bis der Nocken sich zum richtigen Zeitpunkt dagegenstemmt und dem Gemisch den Weg freimacht respektive den Abgasen den Ausgang in den Auspuff gestattet. Die Feder macht, sobald der Nocken vom Ventilschaft wieder abgerutscht ist, den Ausgang dann gleich wieder dicht. Das dauert zwar nicht lange, im sinnverwirrend schnellen Hin und Her der Rennmechanik aber kann schon das Zurückschnellen der Feder derart träge sein, dass der Nocken seine nächste Umdrehung hinter sich hat, wenn das Ventil noch auf dem Weg zurück in seinen Sitz ist. Dann herrscht Unordnung, es gibt massive Rhythmusstörungen, und am Ende ist dann der Motor kaputt. Die Idee der Zwangssteuerung ist nun die: Wenn ich das Ventil präzise durch die Nockenkraft aufstemmen kann, ließe sich das gleiche Verfahren doch für den Schließmechanismus anwenden. Ein Hebel drückt das Ventil nieder, ein zweiter zieht es gleich darauf wieder in Position. Nun, das geht ohne weiteres, und Ducati-Renn- wie Serienmaschinen sind bis heute fix mit ihrer Desmodromik unterwegs. Es ist aber ein herzlich aufwendiges Unterfangen, und für den neuen Rennmotor Anfang der 60er Jahre soll es sich als wenig zweckmäßig erweisen. Nach etlichen Versuchen und viel Feinarbeit – und vor allem, nachdem es endlich bessere Ventilfedern gibt – wandert das Projekt Zwangssteuerung wieder in die Schublade.

Keine Experimente gibt's beim Grundkonzept. Der neue Motor wird ein Boxer, und die Kühlung besorgt die Luft. So

The first blueprints of the eight-cylinder were made in 1959 and, in September 1960, the engine was tested for the first time on the dynamometer. Its Formula One debut was still in the stars. "The Formula One was not the main business of the company. Ferry Porsche preferred a kind of racing that ideally had as much as possible in common with serial production." The Porsche boss always kept an eye on the everyday sports car production as that was what earned the money to pay for everything else. Any racing success was of course good advertising but: "Ferry Porsche always asked: What's the point of the racing? Of course the Formula One was very far away – maybe at that time not as far as it is today."

Nevertheless an eight-cylinder was necessary since 200 bhp was needed to compete with the British racers. The engineers knew that they would have to design it to cope with about 10,000 rpm. And at the same time there was another requirement as the new engine had to be designed with the option of having a bigger displacement. In the future, the eight-cylinder was intended to power Porsche's long distance racers as well. "At first they said: Let's make a two-litre. Relatively soon came the 2.2-litre which was used later for long distance racing." The top echelons of Porsche at first knew nothing about the 2.2-litre. "We designed it more or less secretly and just ordered the necessary parts in the testing department." Enlarging the displacement was comparatively simple since it was only necessary to replace the cylinders and the heads by bigger ones. "Thanks to the single head configuration, this was a relatively small thing."

For a while the "Versuchsabteilung" (Research and Development Department) experimented with a desmodromic valve gear for the high-revving eight-cylinder engine. In a conventionally designed cylinder head, the valves are kept closed by strong springs until the cam or cam follower thrusts on the stem of the valve and thus opens it. If it is an inlet valve, this allows the mixture to surge into the combustion chamber or, in the case of an exhaust valve, to allow the exhaust gases to escape. The spring slams shut as soon as the pressure from the cam is removed. All this happens in a fraction of a second and the velocities and accelerations of the valve and its springs are such that at very high revs the valve can be a little sluggish to the extent that it is still on its way back into its seat when the cam pressure has already been removed. The consequence can be that power is lost through leakage and also that the valve gear may break. To avoid this, it is possible to design a valve gear with one lever to push the valve open and another to lift it back into its seat. This is without doubt an elegant solution. Ducati for instance still makes very fast motorcycles with desmodromic valve gear. But it is a very complicated mechanism and after quite a few experiments, and of course after better quality springs finally became available, Porsche put the project aside.

There were no daring innovations attempted for the basic design. The new engine was a horizontally opposed engine and of course it was air-cooled. Every Porsche all over the world had the same basic engine layout. It was also the case that winning races with air-cooled, boxer engines would be good public relations for all the company's products. Anyway there were sensible technical reasons for using a boxer engine since it guaranteed smooth running allied to a low centre of gravity.

In Germany, Volkswagen used the advertising slogan "air doesn't boil and air doesn't freeze" for promoting air-cooled

Endausbau: Bosch-Einspritzung, überarbeitete Ansaugkanäle mit langen Tüten und ein liegendes Lüfterrad hauchen dem 547 noch ein paar PS mehr ein.

Going to the limit: Bosch fuel injection, refined inlet ports plus long intake tracts and a horizontally mounted cooling fan extracted some additional bhp from the 547 engine.

Foto: Porsche

Foto: Porsche

Werkssport: Die Porsche-Spe-zialität Leichtbau demons-triert am 804-Rahmen der freundliche Porsche-Mann, der dafür noch nicht einmal besonders gut gefrühstückt haben muss.

Lightweight construction: your friendly Porsche employee did not need to be a professional weightlifter to pick up the 804 frame.

rollen sämtliche Seriensportwagen mit Motoren dieser Bauart gut klingend und gut gehend auf den Straßen dieser Welt, und ein paar gebläsegekühlt und im Boxertakt eingefahrene Erfolge sind bestimmt nicht schlecht für die Werbung. Dann aber bleiben auch ganz handfeste Vorteile. Mehrzylinder mit entgegengesetzt ange-ordneten Töpfen bringen guten Massenausgleich von Haus aus mit – das bedeutet runden Lauf – und der Schwerpunkt lässt sich tief halten, weil der Boxer in die Breite baut und nicht in die Höhe.

Der alte VW-Werbespruch „Luft kocht nicht – Luft gefriert nicht" spielt im Rennen eher eine untergeordnete Rolle. Die Luft-kühlung aber bringt einen entscheidenden Vorteil: Das Kühlmedi-um muss der Wagen im Gegensatz zu Konkurrenten mit Wasser-kühler nicht mit sich herumschleppen, er saugt es einfach aus der Umgebung ab und pustet es postwendend wieder in die Umwelt hinaus. Das Gebläse schluckt zudem nur einen kleinen Teil der Leistung, und mit diesem Prinzip hat Porsche von Beginn an reich-lich Erfahrung. Noch im Übersportwagen 917 zehn Jahre später hält ein Lüfterrad den Motor kühl, und die schrittweise Einfüh-rung von Kühlwasser in Technik made in Zuffenhausen sorgt bis heute immer wieder für Diskussionsstoff im Unternehmen wie im Kundenkreis. Vor dem Rennen in Monza 1962 probieren die Tech-

engines. Maybe boiling over was not the biggest concern in rac-ing but air-cooling brought another advantage since the Porsche did not have to carry dead weight in the form of gallons of water. Also the fan drive did not take very much performance from the engine and, to cap it all, air-cooling was a Porsche specialty. Even ten years later, the giant 917 sports car used air as its coolant and the introduction of water-cooling for Porsches is a continuing subject for discussion until today. Before the 1962 GP at Monza, the technicians experimented with a cooling fan that could be disengaged. By doing so, they tried to increase the performance by the nine horsepower that the fan drive consumed. A thermo-statically regulated disengagement device was tested but when none of the drivers could sense the extra power, the device was abandoned.

Periodically Porsche technicians experimented with water-cooling. But as long as the fan cooling worked well, the traditional method was not abandoned. It was only much later when the cyl-inder heads ran with four valves for each cylinder that there was insufficient space left for the cooling air. Anyway it was not until 1977 when Jürgen Barth managed to finish first in his 936 despite a burned-out cylinder that the problem became acute. Mezger:

niker am 804 übrigens ein auskuppelbares Lüfterrad aus. So soll kurzfristig der Motor um jene neun PS stärker gemacht werden, die der Gebläseantrieb schluckt. Sogar mit einer thermostatgeregelten automatischen Trennung wird experimentiert. Die Zusatzleistung erweist sich dann aber nicht als derart spürbar, dass der Aufwand gerechtfertigt wäre.

Experimente mit Wasserkühlung machen die Porsche-Leute immer mal wieder – solange die Luftkühlung bestens ihren Dienst verrichtet, wird am Althergebrachten aber nicht gerüttelt. Schwierig wird es erst, als die Köpfe vier Ventile pro Zylinder erhalten. Der Ventiltrieb wird dadurch größer und erfordert voluminösere Gehäuse. Irgendwann ist zwischen den Zylindern und den Köpfen schlicht nicht mehr genügend Platz für einen ausreichend kühlen Luftstrom. Es soll aber noch bis 1977 dauern, als Jürgen Barth den 936 in Le Mans trotz eines ausgeglühten Zylinders noch zum Sieg fährt. „Das war das Alarmzeichen. Jetzt wussten wir, wir müssen im Motorsport auf Wasserkühlung und Vierventiler umsteigen."

Ende der 1950er, Anfang der 60er Jahre ist das Konzept jedenfalls absolut auf der Höhe der Zeit. Schade, dass es in der kurzen Ära der ersten Formel-1-Beteiligung Porsches mit der Leistung noch nicht so ganz klappen will. Ein bisschen mehr Zeit, und der Motor wäre wohl vollkommen konkurrenzfähig gewesen. Am Ende holen die Techniker echte 200 PS – freilich bei Drehzahlen

"That was an alarm signal. We knew then that in racing we had to switch to water cooling with a four-valve layout."

Anyway at the time of the 804, its design was state-of-the-art. It was just a shame that during the short era of Porsche's first Formula One entry, the 804 failed to achieve its expected performance. With a bit more time available, the engine might well have been fully competitive as eventually the technicians managed to squeeze 200 bhp out of it using a fraction under 10,000 rpm. At least the larger capacity derivatives of the eight-cylinder would prove their worth in the years to come.

While he was working on the Formula One project, Mezger shared a small office with seven colleagues. "We worked solely on the 804." They had to start from scratch as it was not just the engine that was new but also the chassis and bodywork. The engine was the starting point for the design since the chassis and finally the body were subsequently tailored around it. The body shape followed the contours of the mechanical parts more than it helped to improve the aerodynamic qualities of the car. "That was not seen as being so important then as it is today" Mezger says. "One did not know much about things like lift or down force." Anyway the cigar-shaped bodies did not produce as much lift as the enclosed design of the sports car's bodies. The 917, for example, only became driveable when the "Kurzheck" (short tail) was introduced

Formgestaltung: Hölzerne Rippen deuten an, wie der elegante 804 einmal aussehen wird.

Design: wooden templates give a hint of how the elegant 804 will look when clothed in its bodywork.

Foto: Porsche

Gelenkig: Auf dem Bild aus dem Werk sind die Vorderradaufhängung samt Drehstab – der schwarze Stab, der längs zur Fahrtrichtung unterm oberen Rahmenrohr verläuft – sowie die Bremssättel der sogenannten innenumgriffenen Scheibenbremse zu sehen.

Supple: this picture was taken in the Zuffenhausen workshop and it shows the front suspension including the torsion bar – the longitudinal mounted black rod underneath the upper tube of the chassis frame – and the assembly comprising the unique disc brake.

von knapp unter 10.000 – heraus, und die hubraumstärkeren Weiterentwicklungen des Motors werden sich ja auch bewähren.

Mit sieben weiteren Kollegen sitzt damals Hans Mezger „in einem relativ kleinen Raum zusammen. Da hat man sich nur mit dem 804 beschäftigt". Es muss ja alles neu gemacht werden, neben dem Motor auch das Chassis – und die Karosserie. Für die ist ein Mann zuständig, der allerdings nicht direkt zu dem kleinen Team gehört. Auch am Getriebe arbeitet ein Konstrukteur aus der entsprechenden Abteilung des Werks. Das Auto entsteht gleichsam um den Motor herum, der zunächst in ein taugliches Fahrgestell eingepasst wird, um das dann die Karosserie geschneidert wird. Die folgt eher den Konturen der Technik, die sie kleiden soll, als den Gesetzen der Aerodynamik. „Die haben da noch nicht die Rolle gespielt wie das heute der Fall ist. Man wusste ja noch nicht ganz so viel über Auftrieb und Abtrieb." Allerdings produzieren die zigarrenförmigen Körper der Formelrenner auch nicht so viel unerwünschten Auftrieb wie die Vollverkleidungen der Sportwagen – den 917 etwa bekommt Porsche erst in den Griff, nachdem der Wagen mittels Abrissheck ausreichend Abtrieb erfährt. Obendrein hat der 804 fast zehn Zentimeter Bodenfreiheit, für heutige Ver-

with much increased down force. It is also interesting to note that the 804 had a ground clearance of nearly ten centimetres, which is a pretty good benchmark today for an off-road machine.

"The only thing to which we attached great importance was air resistance and drag", Mezger remembers. If you compare the old 718 with the 804, the progress being made in that area becomes obvious. "You can't do anything much wrong when you make the body so long as you just make it as sleek and as narrow as possible." An even more important role in all this was by played the stature of the driver since the car had to be adapted to his build. Mezger remembers the tall Dan Gurney trying the seat in the prototype. The department did not have a special seat designer. "The first designs for the seat were made by a man from the chassis department."

As soon as the first chassis was ready to move under its own steam, the test drivers appeared on the scene and started driving it. Very soon one thing became clear: "It was not without some faults." The suspension caused most trouble. The new double wishbone axle vibrated severely when the driver braked really hard. It turned out that money had been unwisely saved. In an attempt to keep the un-sprung weight down, the suspension was a little

Fotos: Porsche

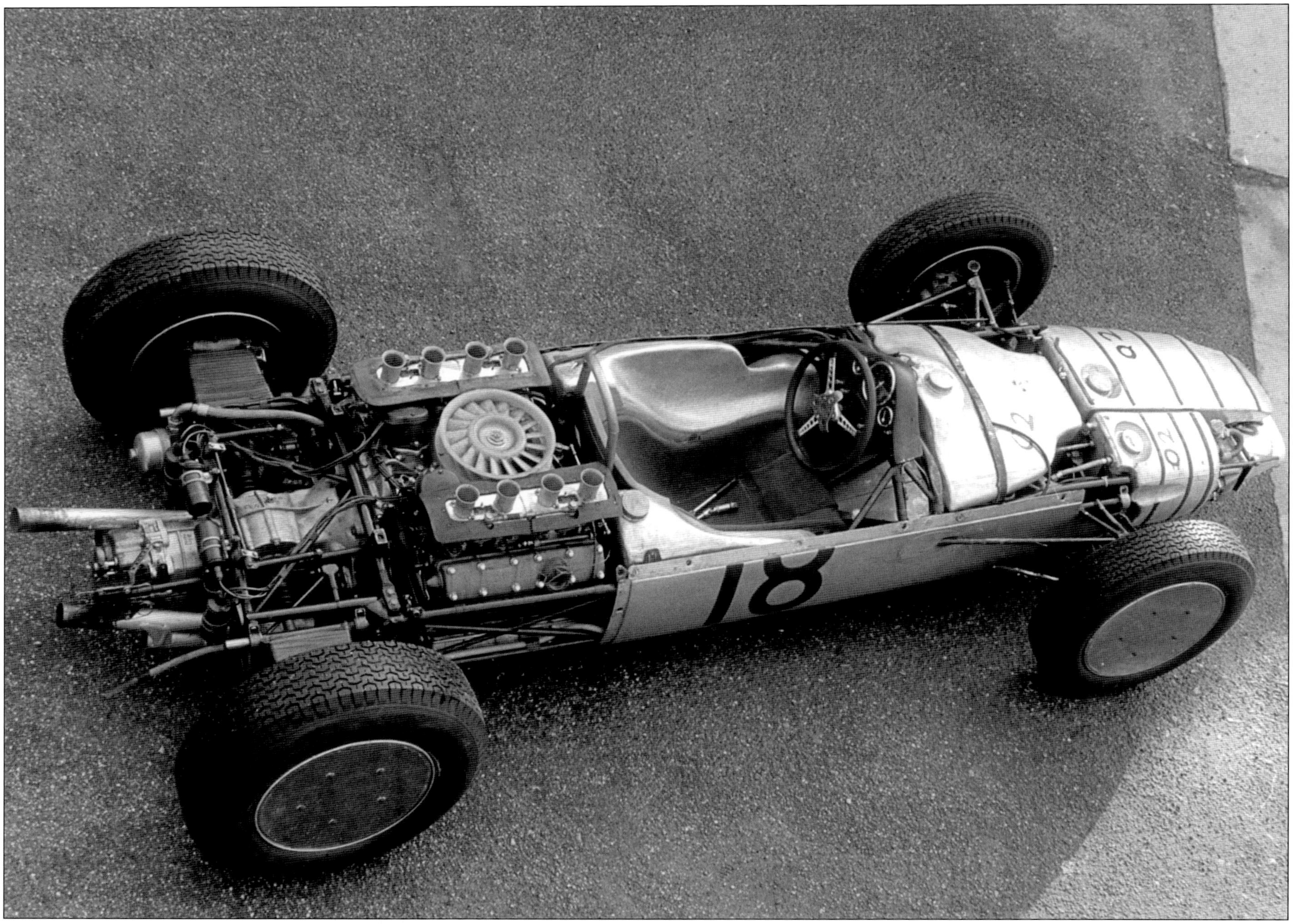

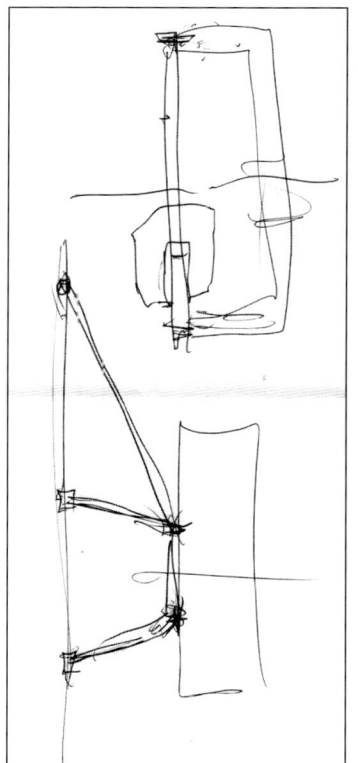

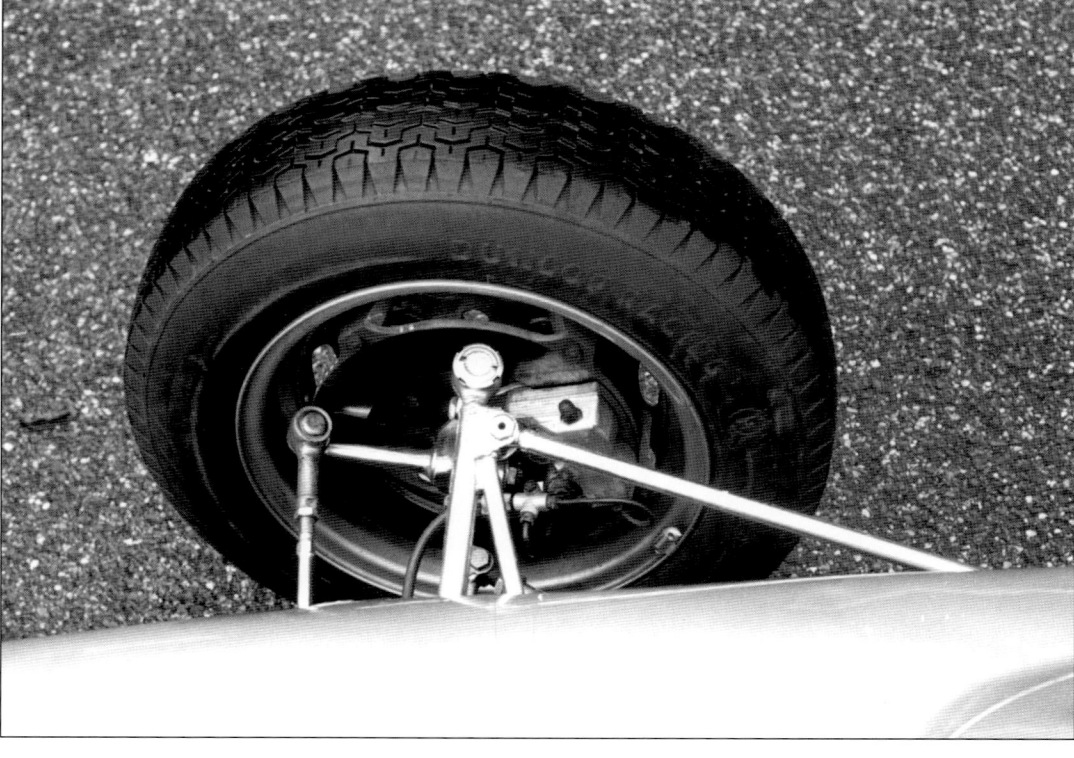

Monza-Trimm: Mit Radkappen geht Bonnier 1962 in Norditalien an den Start. Gut zu erkennen ist die Unterbringung der Tanks. Das Prinzip der innenumgriffenen Scheibenbremse hat Hans Mezger in einer Skizze festgehalten, die er während des Interviews für dieses Buch anfertigte.

Made for Monza: Bonnier's car for the race in Italy sported hubcaps. This picture also shows the location of the fuel tanks. The drawing was made by Hans Mezger who sketched it while being interviewed by the authors during the research for this book.

Foto: Porsche

hältnisse ist das beinahe ein Geländewagen-Wert.

„Das Einzige, worauf man wirklich Wert gelegt hat, war ein möglichst geringer Luftwiderstand. Der Luftwiderstandsbeiwert war immer das Maß aller Dinge." Der Fortschritt lässt sich sehen, wenn der alte Formel 2 neben dem neuen Formel-1-804 steht. „Beim Aufbau der Karosserie können Sie dann nicht viel falsch machen. Man baut sie halt so schlank wie möglich und so niedrig wie möglich." Eine Rolle spielt dann schon eher die Statur des Fahrers, dem das Auto angepasst werden soll. Mezger erinnert sich, dass Dan Gurney einige Male Probe saß im Prototypen. Einen eigens bestellten Designer habe es jedoch nicht gegeben. „Die ersten Striche hat mit Sicherheit einer aus der Chassis-Abteilung gemacht."

Sobald das erste Fahrgestell sich auch aus eigener Kraft bewegen kann, kommen die Testfahrer ins Spiel. Schnell stellt sich heraus: „Das Auto hatte schon einige Mucken." So geht beim Anbremsen vor der Kurve leicht die Haftung verloren, weil die Radaufhängung – neu im 804 ist die Doppelquerlenkerachse, die anstelle der alten Kurbellenker-Konstruktion eingesetzt wird, und die das Team früher schon einmal getestet hat – ins Vibrieren gerät. Es stellt sich heraus, dass man am falschen Ende gespart hat. Im Bestreben, alles möglichst leicht zu halten, sind auch die Radauf-

too weak and flexed easily. The addition of some stiffening struts helped to improve the car's comportment on the road. It seemed as if every time drivers like Herbert Linge tested the car, the engineers had to devise some new solution to get round a problem. "In the beginning the car was somewhat un-drivable. Certainly it was not ready to go racing."

Another feature was that the brakes were entirely new. Porsche had made something really special. It was called the "innenumgriffene Scheibenbremse" which literally translates as "interior embraced disc brake". Porsche had tried conventional disc brakes on one of their sports cars in 1959 and discovered that they wore out their brake pads very quickly. They were also dissatisfied with the weight of the disc / caliper assembly when compared to the drum brakes that they had been using. Rejecting convention, they designed their own disc brake system that took advantage of the VW/Porsche type wheels that possessed an open centre. With a conventional disc brake that was mounted to the car at its centre, wheels were needed that possessed a substantial centre boss. What Porsche came up with was a disc brake in the form of an annulus that was attached through its outer edge to the aluminium wheel carrier by five substantial arms. The calipers were mounted to the

hängungen zu klein dimensioniert worden. Verstärkungsstreben helfen dem ab. Immer wieder testen Fahrer wie Herbert Linge das Fahrverhalten, und immer wieder müssen die Ingenieure nachbessern. „Das Auto war am Anfang unfahrbar, oder doch zumindest nicht reif für ein Rennen."

Ganz neu ist auch die Bremse. Da hat sich Porsche etwas ganz Besonderes ausgedacht. Das Ding nennt sich innenumgriffene Bremsscheibe. Mezger erläutert das Prinzip und zeichnet es sicherheitshalber gleich noch mit auf. Für diese Art Außenläuferscheibenbremse nehmen die Techniker eine der ziemlich großen Bremstrommeln, die bis dato auch im Rennsport für Verzögerung sorgen. In die Reibfläche hinein fügen sie einen Ring, den eine Zange packt, die an der Nabe befestigt ist. Für den Versuch bearbeiten die Techniker die alten Aluminiumtrommeln, später gibt es dann eigens angefertigte sternförmige Teile. Es ist beeindruckend, was die Männer damals alles im eigenen Haus selbst entwickeln, ausprobieren und anfertigen, statt einfach Lösungen von außen zu übernehmen oder ganze Komponenten schlicht einzukaufen. Porsche greift nicht auf die Hilfe etwa von „Garagisten", also Chassis-Herstellern zurück, um den eigenen Renner auf die Räder zu stellen. Fazit Mezger: „Ich hab so viel gelernt bei diesem Projekt: Wie man's machen soll, und vor allem auch, wie man es nicht machen soll."

Fest steht, dass die Arbeit am 804 und die vielen Erfahrungen, die er damals gemacht hat, ihn sein gesamtes berufliches Leben begleitet haben. So fließt einiges in weitere Projekte mit ein. Als Beispiel nennt Mezger die Erkenntnisse, die er bei der Entwicklung der Brennräume gewinnt. „Da hat dann auch der 911er profitiert. Als wir Ende 1962 mit dem 804 aufhörten, machten wir an dem weiter. Der Brennraum im 911-er Motor war ja am Anfang falsch. Den haben wir noch 1962 laufend verändert." Das Problem war der Winkel, in dem Einlass- und Auslassventil zueinander standen. „Mit jedem Schritt, mit dem man den Winkel – anfangs waren es 90 Grad – kleiner gemacht hat, sind Leistung und Verbrauch besser geworden."

Genauso läuft es auch am Achtzylinder. Von 90 Grad schrumpft der Ventilwinkel über 84 auf schließlich 72 Grad. Dazu eine Kurbelwelle, die leichter durch den Ölsumpf flutscht und extraleichte Titanpleuel – und irgendwann bringt der Rennmotor endlich auch die standfesten 200 PS, die er von Anfang an hätte leisten sollen.

Das Triebwerk ist eine gute, aber auch eine komplexe Konstruktion – nicht zuletzt wegen des aufwendigen Ventiltriebs. Königswellen treiben die vier obenliegenden Nockenwellen an. Einmal montiert und fein justiert, funktioniert das einwandfrei. Es will aber auch zusammengesetzt sein. Mezger erinnert sich an das 917-Projekt, als ihm die Mechaniker warmen Dank sagen, weil der Zwölfzylinder so herrlich einfach aufgebaut ist. „Die Montage dauerte nur etwa ein Drittel so lange wie die des Achtzylinders."

Das Königswellenprinzip ist eine edle Sache: Anstelle von Ketten oder Zahnriemen übernehmen Wellen den Antrieb der Nockenwellen. Die Kraft holen sie sich an der Kurbelwelle über Kegelräder, und über weitere Kegelräder geben sie sie oben im Kopf (oder beim Boxer: an den Seiten des Motors) an die Nockenwellen weiter. Die Königswelle sichert stets die richtige Geschwindigkeit, weil sie ein stabiles Bauteil ist. Ketten und Riemen können sich längen oder schlimmstenfalls reißen.

suspension upright inside the disc and faced outwards. The calipers were also made of aluminium and Porsche were very proud that their disc brake assembly weighed only slightly more than their drum brakes. The benefit of being able to use a very large diameter disc of 30 cm (11.8 inches) meant that the performance of the brakes was considerably enhanced largely due to the very much greater swept area of the disc.

During an interview in 2008, Mezger described the design and sketched it on a piece of paper. The callipers were fixed to the hub and grasped the disc from the inside. It is still very impressive how much the men at Zuffenhausen made on their own instead of purchasing designs or parts from outside suppliers. Mezger: "I learned so much with the project. On the one hand how to do things right, and on the other how to avoid making mistakes."

One thing is for certain. The work on the 804 and the many experiences he gained along with it accompanied Mezger throughout his working life. Thus a lot of it influenced future projects, for instance, the knowledge he gained by the development of the combustion cambers on the type 753 engine. "So the 911 profited from that. When we stopped working on the 804 at the end of 1962, we picked up with the 911. The combustion cambers of the six-cylinder had at first been wrongly designed. In 1962 we altered them over and over again to find the right solution."

The angle between inlet and exhaust valves was what was causing the problems. "At first they were at right angles to each other, but with every decrease we made in that angle, both performance improved and fuel consumption decreased."

The eight-cylinder was redesigned in the same way. At first the angle between the valves also measured 90 degrees, then it went to 84 and at last to 72 degrees. This plus a smoother running crankshaft and titanium connecting rods helped to make the engine turn into the reliable 200-bhp power plant that it should have been right from the word go.

It was a fine though very complex design not least because of the sophisticated valve gear. Shafts that took their power from the crankshaft drove the four overhead camshafts. Once assembled and precisely adjusted it worked extremely well. But it had to be assembled first and Mezger remembers the gratitude of the mechanics in the era of the 917. They thanked Mezger for the refreshingly simple design of the twelve-cylinder. "It took three times longer to assemble the eight- cylinder engine."

The camshaft drive system was a very interesting development from the type 547. Instead of just one half-speed shaft running parallel to and driven by the crankshaft, there were two half-speed shafts, one above the crankshaft and one below it. The upper one drove the inlet camshafts via two further shafts at right angles to it that were turned by bevel gears while the lower one drove the exhaust camshafts in the same manner. The use of two half-speed shafts enabled the shafts driving the camshafts to be shorter than in the 547 thus enabling the 753 to pull higher revs. The whole concept was to reduce the inertia of rotating parts wherever possible and thus allow the 753 to turn even faster than the 547. And following this strategy even further, the upper half-speed shaft also drove the horizontal cooling fan through a shaft by means of another set of bevel gears thus eliminating the V-drive of the earlier engines.

Foto: Porsche

Anderthalbliter-Kunstwerk und Mechaniker-Alptraum

Erst will er gar nicht anspringen, dann startet der fürchterlich komplizierte Achtzylinder durch – aber leider nicht mehr im 804

Es klingt immer so leicht und einleuchtend, wenn Porsches Einstieg in die neue kleine Formel 1 des Jahrgangs 1961 als eigentlich ganz mühelos beschrieben wird. Immerhin sind Rennwagen aus Zuffenhausen mit dem bewährten und ausgereiften Vierzylinder-Boxer, Typ 547, in der Formel 2 recht flott unterwegs. Und auf den ersten Blick wird ja aus der Formel 2, zumindest was die Motoren angeht, nun die Formel 1 – also mit anderthalb Liter großen Motoren. Kein Problem für Porsche, so scheint's, haben die Schwaben doch mit dieser Größe allerbeste Erfahrung. Das stimmt selbstverständlich auch. Sie haben diese Erfahrung aber in den vergangenen Jahren vor allem mit jenem Motor eingefahren, der als „Fuhrmann-Motor" berühmt geworden ist. Die exzellente Boxer-technik mit oberfeinen Königswellen hat nur leider einen Nachteil. Es kommt langsam in die Jahre. Irgendwann ist auch beim besten Motor Schluss mit Frisieren, wenn er denn eine nennenswerte Zeit lang durchhalten soll.

Nun erweist sich selbst das betagte Rennerherz als immer noch ziemlich gesund gegen die viel jüngere Konkurrenz, doch wer Anfang der 1960er Jahre in der immer schnelleren Formel 1 mithalten will, muss mehr bieten als den „Old Faithful" made in Zuffenhausen. Den Porscheleuten ist das natürlich klar. Und sie wissen auch, wie man einem kleinen Motor noch mehr Leistung abzuringen vermag: Man lässt ihn vor allem schneller laufen.

A 1.5 litre work of art but a mechanic's nightmare

At first the eight-cylinder refused to give of its best, then it revved up fast – though unfortunately not in the 804

Porsche's foray into Formula One racing always sounds simple and untroubled as it is usually described as being nearly effortless. In fact it was not. The Zuffenhausen racers with their well-proven flat four engines were reasonably fast in Formula Two racing. At first sight the new Formula One of 1961 simply looked as if it was a barely altered Formula Two using engines limited to 1.5-litre displacement. Porsche was very familiar with this engine size and thus switching to Formula One seemed from the outside to be no problem at all for the Swabian manufacturer. But Porsche's experience was founded first of all on the famous „Fuhrmann" engine. The excellent flat four with its unique shaft driven valve train unfortunately had a disadvantage. It was getting on a bit.

Anyway the aged racer's heart still showed itself to be pretty lively in competing with much younger designs. Yet at the beginning of the 1960s with the introduction of several manufacturer's multi-cylinder engines, Formula One racing became faster and faster and anyone who tried to survive on the tracks had to offer more than the "Old Faithful" from Zuffenhausen could muster. Of course the Porsche people knew that. And they knew how to make small engines into big performers. The critical thing was to be able to push the rotational speed as high as possible.

Normally any calculation of horsepower is pretty simple and is based on capacity. A big engine with big bore cylinders is capab-

Es ist ja eigentlich ganz einfach: Ein großer Motor mit großen Zylindern bringt gleichsam von Haus aus ordentlich Leistung mit und muss sich nicht allzusehr hetzen. Zu gewaltig sind die Feuerwerke in den Brennräumen, deren Druck unwiderstehlich die Kolben hinabpresst. Allzu schnell drehen sollte der Hubraumriese ohnehin nicht. Die bewegten Massen wollen im Zaum gehalten sein, zu hohe Kolbengeschwindigkeiten machen es schwer, den Kolben im Zylinder möglichst reibungslos auf- und abfahren zu lassen. Das ist auch einer der Gründe, warum die Kandidaten für die neue Formel 1 sehr schnell auf mehr Zylinder setzen.

Natürlich lässt sich auch ein Vier- oder ein Sechszylinder – 1,5 Liter sind ja scheinbar nicht die Welt – per Drehzahlbeschleunigung mehr Leistung abringen. Nur: Die Kolben rasen dann bald derart schnell durch die Laufbuchsen, dass auch die beste Schmierung nicht mehr mitkommt und alles viel zu heiß wird. Verteilt der Ingenieur die Last jedoch auf mehr Töpfe, lässt er zwar doppelt so viele Teile arbeiten, die aber haben es viel leichter.

Ein Achtzylinder also. Schön. Im Jahr vor der ersten Saison mit der neuen Formel 1 beginnt die Entwicklung. Im Sommer macht sich Hans Hönick ans Werk. Abgesehen von der Zylinderzahl ähnelt der neue Motor konstruktiv durchaus dem Fuhrmann-Triebwerk. Königswellen treiben zwei Paar obenliegende Nockenwellen

le of delivering a certain amount of horsepower. It relies on the sheer strength of its combustion in those big cylinders to produce the power. And it does not have to turn over very fast to do so. In any case, big bore engines are not keen on revving too high since a heavy piston whizzing up and down at high speeds does not spell reliability. That is one of the reasons why most of the designers preferred engines with eight or more cylinders in order to keep the reciprocating masses as small as possible. Of course, Porsche could have made a four cylinder that turned over faster to produce more horsepower. Yet this would have caused enormously high friction between the relatively large pistons and the cylinder walls due to the higher speed of the piston. Adequate lubrication would be impossible and overheating almost a certainty. More cylinders meant more moving parts but less stress for each individual part.

So an eight-cylinder was chosen. One year before the new Formula One was introduced, the development of the Porsche racer got under way. In summer 1960, Hans Hönick set to work. Apart from the fact that it had double the number of cylinders, the new engine had quite a lot in common with the „Fuhrmann" flat four. Shafts drove two pairs of overhead camshafts. The engine was cooled by a fan (the horizontally mounted device pumped up to 84.000 litres of cooling air into a sophisticated port system

Feinabstimmung: Ein Jammer, dass es nur ein stummes Bild ist.

Fine tuning: it is a pity that this picture has no sound track.

an, der Motor hat Gebläsekühlung (das liegende Schaufelrad bläst bis zu 84.000 Liter in der Minute in ein raffiniertes Luftkanalsystem und schluckt nur neun PS Leistung) und ist ein Boxer – und zwar wiederum ein echter. Das bedeutet, dass sich je zwei Pleuel einen Kurbelzapfen teilen. Zum Vergleich: Der Zwölfzylinder des 917 ist trotz gegenläufiger Zylinderreihen streng genommen kein Boxer, sondern ein V-Motor mit 180 Grad Zylinderwinkel, weil jedes Pleuel einen eigenen Zapfen auf der Kurbelwelle hat.

Die geschmiedete Welle hat neun Hauptlager. Sie treibt zwei weitere parallele Wellen an, die im Rücken respektive im Bauch des Motorgehäuses rotieren. Jeweils in deren Mitte reichen Kegelräder die Drehkraft an Hohlwellen weiter – die eigentlichen Königswel-

and absorbed only nine horsepower) and had opposed cylinders. It was a genuine Boxer engine with two connecting rods each mounted on one crank pin. By comparison, the twelve-cylinder engine of the 917 also had opposed cylinders but was in fact a V-engine with a cylinder angle of 180 degrees and each connecting rod was mounted on its own crank pin.

The forged crankshaft had nine main bearings. It drove two additional shafts rotating parallel to it, one above and one underneath. Each of them bore a bevel gear in the middle driving a hollow shaft – the "Königswellen" – and these shafts drove the camshafts, again via bevel gears. Ball bearings were used for the entire valve train, but shell bearings were retained on the

Foto: Porsche

Antriebseinheit: Aus der Vogelschau lassen sich alle für Vortrieb und Verzögerung wichtigen Elemente gut erkennen.

Drive train: this bird's-eye view shows every important part of the rear suspension and power train.

Foto: Porsche

Eingespannt: Der Motor 753 ist ein echter Boxer. Gut zu sehen sind die beiden oberen Königswellenrohre, die zu den Nockenwellen der Einlassseite führen. Das runde Ding dazwischen ist der Antrieb des Lüfterrads, links davon sitzen die beiden Verteiler. Vorn ist übrigens rechts.

Clamped to the bench: the 753 is a genuine horizontally opposed engine. Here you can see the two tubes containing the drive shafts to the camshafts on the inlet side. The round thing between them is the drive for the cooling fan and to the left of that are the two distributors. The front of the engine is to the right of the photo.

len. Sie münden – oben für die Einlass-, unten für die Auslassseite – im Zylinderkopf, wo sie wiederum über Kegelräder die Nockenwellen antreiben. Alles ist komplett kugelgelagert, die Kurbelwelle hat Gleitlager, obwohl auch mit Rollenlagern experimentiert wird. Die Auslassventile, hohl wie die Pendants auf der Einlassseite, sind zur Kühlung mit Natrium gefüllt. Dank des liegenden Gebläses und der ultrakompakten Bauweise fällt der Achtzylinder in fast allen Maßen kleiner aus als der alte Vierzylindermotor – nur in der Länge sind es zehn Zentimeter mehr.

Wie dem 547 wird auch dem 753 (respektive dem 2,2 Liter großen 771) ein erstaunlich langes Leben beschieden. Von 1962 bis 1968 wird er eingesetzt, zuletzt mit strammen 270 Pferdestärken. Den glorreichsten Sieg erringen Porsche-Renner im Februar 1968 in Daytona. Bis dahin hat Hans Mezger das Triebwerk komplett überarbeitet. Der junge Ingenieur leistet ganze Arbeit. Das Langstreckentriebwerk ist große Klasse. Einer der Motoren hat im Vortraining eine derart gute Figur gemacht, dass er zum Rennen

crankshaft, though experiments were made initially with roller bearings. The hollow valves were filled with sodium on the exhaust side to give better cooling. Thanks to the horizontally mounted cooling fan and the ultra compact construction, the eight-cylinder was – despite being ten centimetres longer, a mere hand's breadth – considered overall it was smaller than the old four-cylinder.

Like the 547 the 753 engine was destined to have an astoundingly long life thanks to its 2.2-litre derivative 771. This was used from 1962 up to 1968 and at the end of its life was developing some 270 horsepower. The most famous victory for that engine was the one-two-three at Daytona in 1968. By that time, Hans Mezger had totally revised the engine. The young engineer made an excellent job. One of the long distance engines performed so well in testing and practice for Daytona that it was kept in the chassis and used in the race. The finish became legendary. Three 907s passed the finishing line in perfect formation. Working on the eight-cylinder was a real headache for the mecha-

gleich so im Auto bleibt. Das Bild ist legendär: Drei 907 passieren in Formation die Ziellinie.

Für die Mechaniker ist der raffinierte Achtzylinder kein reiner Quell der Freude. Dafür ist er einfach zu komplex. Es dauert mindestens 100 Stunden, bis einer der Boxer zusammengebaut ist. Das liegt vor allem am Ventiltrieb. Passen die vielen Kegelräder des Königswellenantriebs endlich tipptopp zusammen, haben die Mechaniker mitunter eine veritable Geduldsprobe bestanden. Kämmen da die Zähne zweier Räder nicht absolut präzise ineinander, ist irgendwo ein Spiel um ein Geringes zu klein oder zu groß, muss alles wieder auseinandergenommen werden.

Das ist noch längst nicht alles: Ende 1960 soll der neue Motor auf den Prüfstand. Die Montage hätten sich die Leute beinahe sparen können. Das Ding will nicht einmal anspringen. Erst nach langem Zureden und unter Aufbietung aller Tricks erwacht der Achtzylinder endlich zum Leben. Jetzt geht es bloß noch um die Frage: Was bringt der Neue? Eins ist klar: Es sollten mindestens 175 PS sein, weil zu denen auch der alte Fuhrmann-Boxer imstande ist. Darüber sollte die Zahl dann der magischen 200 möglichst nahe kommen. So viel Leistung wünschen sich die Porsche-Leute, weil sie nur dann reelle Chancen auf gute Platzierungen haben.

Immerhin: Das Ergebnis ist dreistellig. Das war's dann aber auch schon. Ansonsten ist es ein Schock: Mühsam quält sich der Zeiger über die 100-PS-Marke, um gleich dahinter zu verharren. 105 PS sind zweifellos ganz nett für einen Anderthalbliter, Baujahr

nics thanks to its the highly sophisticated design. It took at least one hundred hours to assembly one engine. The largest part of that was thanks to the valve gear. Assembling the many bevel gears correctly was a supreme test of a mechanic's patience. If just two gears failed to mesh with absolute precision, the whole thing had to be taken apart again.

But there had been even worse times at the beginning of the type 753 programme. At the end of 1960, the new engine was put on the test bench. The mechanics could have probably have saved themselves the trouble of assembling it as the thing refused point blank to run. It simply refused to start up. It took a great deal of taking apart and then a lot of coaxing and the mobilisation of all kinds of legal and illegal tricks to get this eight-cylinder to reluctantly come to life.

Once it was running, the question became one of how much horsepower was it producing. It should have been at least the same 175 bhp that the old „Fuhrmann" flat four was able to deliver. Beyond that, anything on the way up to 200 bhp would be very welcome since that was the magic mark at which performance level Porsche would have a chance of winning races.

At least that initial result was a three-digit figure but that was about it and the actual figure was a shock. Only with great reluctance did the needle of the gauge stagger past the 100 bhp mark. And it did not reach much higher. Perhaps 105 bhp was not too bad for a run-of-the-mill 1.5-litre engine in 1960 but with

Foto: Porsche

Warmgelaufen: 1961 wird es langsam mit dem 804. Zum Einsatz kommt er aber erst im darauffolgenden Jahr.

Warming up: in 1961, the 804 was beginning to show some performance but it was not before 1962 that it was raced.

Vor dem Rennen in Monza 1962: Zusätzlich zu den Radblenden hat der Wagen an den oberen Querlenkern der Hinterräder Verkleidungen erhalten.

Before the 1962 race at Monza: in addition to its hubcaps, the car was fitted with strengthening fillets in the upper wishbones.

1960. Porscheschriftzug auf den Ventildeckeln und stolze Formel-Ambitionen aber machen das Ergebnis zu einem für die Schublade mit dem Etikett „nicht mehr drüber reden".

Die Porsche-Leute geben aber nicht klein bei. Sie sind ja schließlich keine Anfänger. Alles können sie gar nicht falsch gemacht haben. Es stellt sich dann auch bald heraus, dass allein mit der Verkleinerung des Ventilwinkels allerhand rauszuholen ist. Außerdem werden Titanpleuel eingebaut und die Pleuelzapfen verkleinert. Das verringert die bewegten Massen erheblich. Der 753 leistet schließlich im Formel-1-Renner 185 PS. Das hört sich schon viel besser an, das bleiben aber nur schlappe zehn PS mehr als die des bewährten Vierzylinders und 15 weniger als erhofft.

Also muss der Motor nochmal in die Box – mitten in der Saison. Grund für die Zwangspause sind allerdings auch schwerwiegende Probleme mit dem bockigen Fahrwerk. Am 8. Juli gelingt Dan Gurney dann im mittlerweile besser abgestimmten 804 der erste – und bis heute einzige – Formel-1-Sieg mit einem komplett von Porsche auf die Räder gestellten Auto. Gurney fährt großartig, allerdings scheiden auch die vor ihm liegenden Jim Clark (Lotus) und Graham Hill (BRM) aus.

Übrigens holen die Porsche-Techniker doch noch die angestrebten 200 Pferdestärken aus dem Anderthalbliter heraus. Der 753/1 ist eine noch kürzerhubige Version des Achtzylinders. Drehen die normalen 753 an die 10.000er Marke heran, schafft der Kurzhuber weit mehr als 10.000 Touren. Technisch wären 12.000 möglich gewesen, soviel gibt der Ventiltrieb her. Der Motor wird allerdings nicht eingesetzt. (jn) ■

Porsche's name on its cylinder heads and its high-flown ambition of winning Formula One races, this was really a disastrous result.

Anyway the Porsche people did not despair. They knew that they were not beginners in the engine business and thus they could not have done everything wrong. And indeed it turned out that by simply altering the inclination of the valves and thus reducing the angle between, there was a significant increase in performance. Also titanium connecting rods were adopted and the gudgeon pins reduced in diameter. That significantly reduced the inertia of the reciprocating parts and at last the type 753 delivered 185 hp. Of course, that sounds much better but it was only ten bhp more than the flat four's performance – and fifteen less than the target that had been set for it. Thus the programme suffered since engines were being worked on between races to try to improve on their performance. At the same time, the results might have been better had the chassis also not required a lot of sorting to make the whole package competitive. Finally on July 8, Dan Gurney gained the first and to this day only victory with a Formula One racer entirely designed and built by Porsche. Gurney drove extremely well at Rouen, but it is as well to recall that both Jim Clark (Lotus) and Graham Hill (BRM) retired.

Eventually the Porsche technicians managed to extract 200 bhp out of a 1.5-litre but only after changing many things. The 753/1 engine had a much shorter stroke and a further narrowing of the angle between the valves in the cylinder head. The conventional 753 could run up to about 10,000 rpm while the new engine went far beyond that with 12,000 rpm theoretically possible from the improved valve train, but this engine never was used in a race. (jn) ■

„Es war nicht Porsche-like, weil wir eigentlich kaum eine Chance hatten"

Peter Falk erinnert sich an das Experiment 804 –
und daran, warum es nicht klappte, obwohl er noch das
Fahrwerk verstärkt hat

Was tun, wenn bei voller Fahrt die Motorhaube aufspringt? Klare Sache: sofort anhalten und die wackelnde Sichtbehinderung schleunigst wieder verriegeln. Sie tun das nicht, sondern fahren fröhlich weiter und genießen den Blick auf Luftfilterdeckel und Kühlerverschluss? Dann sind Sie vielleicht ein Ingenieur. Von einem Menschen ist bekannt, das er sich gelegentlich so verhält, denn er hat es selbst verraten. Ende der 1960er Jahre war's, da sitzt Peter Falk, bei Porsche vor allem für die Fahrwerke zuständig, mit seinem Chef Helmuth Bott in einem NSU Ro 80. Die beiden sind auf dem Weg nach Le Mans, als das Malheur mit der Motorhaube passiert, die bei der Wankelsänfte aus Neckarsulm glücklicherweise vorn angeschlagen ist. So springt das große Blech nicht gleich in die Vertikale, sondern lässt sich noch gerade so eben überblicken. Falk und Bott lassen sich nicht weiter irritieren, sondern ihre Augen nicht mehr vom – zumindest für den Fahrwerksingenieur – spannendsten Bauteil: Der Federung. „Wir haben lange zugeschaut", erinnert sich Falk.

Kein Wunder – da vorn links und rechts des mutmaßlich für die allermeisten Menschen viel interessanteren Kreiskolbenmotors arbeiteten gut sichtbar die Aufhängungen der beiden Federbeine, für die sich die Neckarsulmer Ingenieure einiges haben einfallen lassen müssen. Für Falk eine eminent interessante Geschichte. „Das war ja ein sehr weiches, sehr komfortables Auto." Zu verdanken ist das dem langen Radstand des eleganten und

"It was very un-Porsche like – because we didn't really stand a chance"

Peter Falk recalls the 804 Formula One project
and why it failed despite him managing to improve the chassis

What should you do if the bonnet of the car you are driving pops open while you are driving full speed? Of course, the answer is obvious. You pull over and close it. What is that you say, you do not do that? You would prefer to carry on and enjoy a wonderful view of the air cleaner and the engine? Then it is possible that you are an engineer. One person is known for behaving in such a fashion and he revealed it himself. It was at the end of the 1960s when Peter Falk, at that time working on chassis development at Zuffenhausen, was sitting side by side with his boss, Helmuth Bott, in an NSU Ro 80. The two Porsche men were travelling to Le Mans when the mishap with the bonnet occurred. Luckily the front lid of the Wankel driven rickshaw from Neckarsulm is hinged at its front edge. Because of that, the bonnet did not smash back over the windscreen and the driver and his passenger could still look over it to see the road. But they could also see what was, for them, the most exciting part in the engine compartment, the suspension. "We kept watching it at work for a pretty long time" Falk recalled.

And no wonder. While most people's attention would have been grabbed by the legendary rotary engine, either side of it were the two front suspension struts. The Neckarsulm engineers had had to tax their brains to make them work properly. Falk looks back on it as an interesting story: "It was a very soft and comfortable car and it was interesting to witness how they had

topmodernen Viertürers, vor allem aber auch dem respektablen Federweg – der große NSU soll so komfortabel wie die legendären Citroën ID/DS mit hydropneumatischem Fahrwerk werden. Keine schlechte Leistung, immerhin müssen die NSU-Leute gewaltig tricksen. So bekommen sie die rekordverdächtig kleine Stirnfläche des Ro 80 und seine flache Wagenfront überhaupt erst hin, weil sie den kleinen Wankelmotor auch noch extrem tief einbauen. In einer derartigen Flunder aber bleibt kaum Platz für die langen Federbeine – damals noch keineswegs Usus im Autobau –, die dem großen Auto das Gleiten beibringen sollen. Falk nötigt das Ergebnis Respekt ab – und lässt ihn genussvoll zuschauen, als die holprige Landstraße die Haube aufstößt.

Was das alles mit dem 804 zu tun hat? Nun, seit 1959 ist

achieved that." The elegant and up-to-date Ro 80 sedan had an exceptionally long wheelbase combined with a long spring travel and was thought by some to rival the legendary Citroën ID/DS with its hydro-pneumatic suspension. The NSU engineers had made a pretty good job of it. They had to make the big car streamlined and thus they placed the engine as low as possible to keep the frontal area small. Consequently there was not much space left for the long suspension struts that gave the sedan its luxurious comportment on the road. The NSU suspension commanded Falk's admiration and, after the bumpy road forced the bonnet to flip open, he watched it working with pleasure.

And what has all this to do with the 804? Peter Falk was a Porsche employee since 1959 then and, as within Zuffenhausen

Radfüllend: Gewaltig sind die Trommelbremsen im 718/2. Längst haben Federbeine und Querlenker die Torsionsstäbe und Kurbellenker ersetzt.

Big drums: the 718/2's brake drums filled the wheel rims while suspension struts and wishbones had replaced torsion bars and arms..

Peter Falk schon Ingenieur bei Porsche, und weil in Zuffenhausen eigentlich nie so ganz klar zwischen Serienproduktion und Rennabteilung zu unterscheiden ist, hilft auch der schlaksige junge Mann mit der großen Leidenschaft für Federungen bald mit beim großen Formel-Experiment. Schlank und hochaufgeschossen ist der Ingenieur noch heute, und ganz bescheiden nennt er seine Rolle im Stück namens 804 eine ganz kleine. Immerhin, und er zeigt lächelnd auf ein Bild des Rennwagens, „das da ist von mir". „Das da" sind jene beiden Längsstreben, mittels derer sich die Vorderachse nach hinten am Fahrgestell abstützt. Dieses filigrane Stück Metall hilft eine der Kinderkrankheiten des neuen Formelrenners zu beseitigen. „Der Wagen war beim Bremsen äußerst unruhig, wie die alten Autos mit Starrachsen." Trotz neuentwickelter Drehstabfederung und Einzelradaufhängung an Querlenkern tanzen die Vorderräder beim scharfen Bremsen jenen gefürchteten Tanz, der als Shimmy zumindest im Automobilbau einen ganz schlechten Ruf genießt. Im normalen Straßenverkehr ist der Effekt von mehr oder weniger alten Straßenkreuzern made in USA bekannt, wenn deren Fahrer mehr oder weniger erfolgreich versuchen, den Wagen flott und sauber um die Kurve zu bekommen.

Auf der Rennstrecke geht so etwas natürlich gar nicht – und an der Vorderachse erst recht nicht. Darum kümmern soll sich also Peter Falk, der junge Mann aus dem Fahrversuch. „Das Auto kam dann erst einmal auf den Spannrost." Das muss man sich so vorstellen: Erst werden die Räder abgenommen. Dann nehmen starke stählerne Halter ihren Platz ein, an denen sich nach Herzenslust in allen Richtungen ziehen und zerren lässt – ganz so, als sei das Auto höllisch flott auf der Piste unterwegs. Nun ist Ende der 1950er, Anfang der 60er Jahre die Messtechnik noch

no one was able to say where the serial production ended and the racing department began, the lanky young man with his passion for suspension was involved in the Formula One project. Nowadays, he tends to be modest about his contribution and calls his role in the development of the 804 a pretty small one. "At least" and he grins „this one is something I can claim to have made." "This one" is actually two longitudinal bars that support the front axle. It was this solution that helped to cure some of the teething troubles with the chassis. "Initially the car felt like older models with rigid axles – especially in braking." In spite of new torsion springs and independent suspension with double wishbones, the front wheels had the tendency to dance a quite dangerous shimmy. Anyone who has driven an old US road cruiser will be familiar with that kind of behaviour from the front end of a car.

In racing, such a characteristic is less than undesirable and it can be positively dangerous. Peter Falk was asked to solve the problem. At first the car was clamped to rigid bed. The wheels were removed and strong steel brackets fixed to the car at the ends of its axles. On this torsional torture rack, the car's suspension and chassis could be loaded up with the kind of forces that it would encounter on a racetrack. Of course, at the end of the 1950s, measuring instruments were not as sophisticated as they are today with all the resources of electronics that are now available. One could not turn a car into a rolling laboratory. But the improvised rack was pretty effective. The test results when added to the reports from the test drivers and their "popometers" (see Page 179) added up to something quite useful – even without computers and micro sensors.

There was a lot of testing to do. At first there was the little eight-cylinder engine that had so shocked the engineers by making its first disappointing dynamometer tests. Falk remembers: "This

Abgestützt: Peter Falk kümmert sich um das Fahrwerk des 804, namentlich um die Längsstreben.

Framework: Peter Falk took care of the 804 chassis, especially its longitudinal support bars.

Foto: Porsche

Auf Herz und Nieren: Immer wieder geht Herbert Linge mit dem Testwagen auf die Strecke, hier auf die Südschleife des Nürburgrings.

Acid test: again and again Herbert Linge took the car out for thorough testing as here on the Südschleife.

nicht soweit, dass sich ein Auto gleichsam zum rollenden Labor machen lässt, das während der Fahrt alle wichtigen Ergebnisse gleichsam dem Bordcomputer ins Berichtheft diktiert. Die Streck- und Stauchbank aber ist ein recht brauchbarer Ersatz, weil ja die Techniker messen können, wie stark sie das arme Auto auf dem Foltertisch malträtieren. Die Ergebnisse zusammen mit denen per „Popometer" der Testfahrer ermittelten ergeben dann am Ende schon etwas ziemlich Brauchbares – auch ohne Computer und Mikrosensoren.

Zu testen gibt es allemal genug am ehrgeizigen Formel-1-Projekt. Das betrifft den gebläsegekühlten kleinen Achtzylinder, der seine ersten Umdrehungen zum Entsetzen der Entwickler mit erschütternd geringem Einsatzwillen leistet – Falk: „Das war ja schon ein Drama für sich" –, das betrifft auch das Fahrwerk. So erinnert sich Falk an „eine ganze Menge Stoßdämpferversuche auf der guten alten Südschleife". Dort, auf jenem heute nurmehr rudimentär vorhandenen Streckenabschnitt, der sich so hervorragend zum Testen eignet, drehen unter anderem Herbert Linge und Dan Gurney Runde um Runde, um die beste Abstimmung zu finden. Eingebaut werden neuerdings auch Dämpfer von Bilstein. „Mit uns haben die mit der Formel 1 überhaupt begonnen", sagt Falk. An den Testfahrten beteiligt sich auch der Ingenieur

was in fact a major drama and not at all what was expected." Then there was the chassis. The test team made several runs with different dampers on the Südschleife of the Nürburgring. This part of the 'Ring was particularly suited for such testing. Herbert Linge and Dan Gurney drove there in order to find out the best setup. At that time, they were trying new dampers supplied by the German manufacturer, Bilstein. „It was through this Porsche programme that they got their first involvement in Formula One" Falk says. Despite being an engineer, Falk took his turn behind the wheel from time to time and has particularly fond memories of the laps that he did later in models such as the 906 and 908.

All the track testing plus the results of braking, acceleration and cornering forces applied on the infamous torture rack lead to Falk's special longitudinal bars that were intended to strengthen the weak front end of the 804. The chassis and suspension components had been optimistically designed with the intention of being as light as possible. Now in order to keep them rigid enough to handle the forces being generated by the braking, accelerating and cornering of a Formula One car, the engineers were compelled to compose what was a real artwork of braces and struts. This strengthening of chassis and components was necessary as there were some alarmingly large forces at work on the chassis, especially under braking.

Foto: Porsche

immer wieder, besonders gern erinnert er sich an die Runden in den Modellen 906 und 908.

Testfahrten und die Ergebnisse der Brems-, Beschleunigungs- und Kurvensimulation im Spannrost führen schließlich dazu, dass Falk die schwammige Vorderachse mittels der Längsstreben abstützt. Angesichts der immer filigraneren Fahrwerksteile lässt sich Stabilität schließlich nurmehr durch statisch geschickt komponiertes Strebwerk herstellen – immerhin wirken namentlich beim brutalen Bremsen im Rennen gewaltige Kräfte. Nun sind allerdings auch die Bremsen am 804 anders als bei anderen Autos. Porsche leistet wieder einmal eine Portion Pionierarbeit. Nicht durchgesetzt

In terms of brake development, the Porsche engineers carried out some pioneering work in this field. Their new variant of a disc brake assembly with "inside" calipers worked well but in the long term was not adopted as a commercial proposition. It was in complete contrast to the customary arrangement where the disc is mounted to the hub by its centre and rotates like a potter's wheel inside the wheel rim. In the Porsche system, the disc was fixed to the inner rim of the wheel carrier that was driven by the drive shaft emerging from the hub/suspension upright. The ca- lipers thus faced outwards from the centre line of the drive shaft and acted on the disc from the inside. Despite some difficulties

Klassisch Fünfloch: Modifizierte Trommeln halten die Bremsscheiben. Die gewöhnlichen Stahlfelgen werden dann einfach auf die Bolzen aufgeschraubt.

Classic five-hole wheel rim: cut- away drums carried the brake discs and the customary steel wheels were simply bolted on to the former drums..

hat sich die Variante, die sich „Außenläufer-Scheibe" taufen ließe und die bei Porsche innenumgriffene Scheibenbremse heißt. Im Gegensatz zur herkömmlichen Konstruktion – die Scheibe ist mit dem Radträger verbunden und dreht sich wie eine Töpferscheibe geschützt im Schüsselinnern der Felge – ist die Bremsscheibe im 804 als stählerner Ring auf den inneren Rand einer der großen Trommelbremsen aufgeschraubt. Auf die wird in bekannter Manier die Felge mit dem Fünflochkranz geschraubt. Der Vorteil liegt auf der Hand: Je weiter außen die Bremse zugreift, desto weniger Kraft bedarf es, das Rad zu verzögern. Wer schon einmal den Reifen seines Fahrrads geflickt und zur Kontrolle des Mantels noch einmal lustvoll das Rad des auf Sattel und Lenker kopfüber stehenden Gefährts gedreht hat, weiß: Greift er in Nabennähe in die Speichen, wird er sich die Finger brechen, packt er das rotierende Rad weit außen an der Felge, wird's schlimmstenfalls ein bisschen warm. Der Nachteil der außenliegenden Bremsscheibe: „Das ist fürchterlich kompliziert zu bauen und zu warten", sagt Falk.

Gegenstand von Experimenten und bald Erfolgslösung sind simple Löcher: Als die Porsche-Leute Bremsscheiben zu perforieren beginnen, gelingt die wohl einzige gewünschte Verzögerung im Rennbetrieb immer besser. Gute Gründe für die Lochung gibt es vier: Der erste erschließt sich schon beim ganz groben Nachdenken: Scheiben mit Löchern wiegen weniger als massive. Weiter: Luftlöcher halten die Scheibe kühler. Und: Löcher beugen Aquaplaning vor, das es nicht nur zwischen Reifen und Asphalt gibt. Bei Regen schwimmt auch auf der schnell rotierenden Bremsscheibe ein feiner Wasserfilm, auf dem der Bremsbelag zunächst kaum Halt findet. Erst wenn das Wasser verdampft und verdrängt ist, gelingt die erwünschte Reibung. Wir reden da zwar von extrem kurzen Zeiten, vor allem im Rennbetrieb können das aber lebensrettende Sekundenbruchteile sein. Und schließlich, so erklärt Peter Falk, erhöhen Löcher – obwohl da ja eigentlich nichts mehr ist, auf ihre Art die Bremswirkung. Weil der Belag um einiges elastischer ist als die stahlharte Scheibe, drückt sich selbst bei den atemberaubenden Geschwindigkeiten der durch die Bremszange sausenden Scheibe immer ein wenig Material in die Öffnung hinein – es entsteht eine winzige Delle, die dann wieder aus dem Scheibenloch herausmuss. Dieser kaum sichtbare Kanteneffekt macht eine ganze Menge aus, weiß Falk.

Nun, es nutzt alles nichts, auch nicht die Falksche Längsstrebe – Ferry Porsche zieht irgendwann den Schlussstrich unter das teure und aufwendige Kapitel 804, „ein bisschen musste er schon an seine Firma denken". Immerhin gilt der Sohn des Unternehmensgründers eher als Skeptiker in Bezug auf das gewagte Projekt. Das ist nach Einschätzung Falks allerdings vielleicht auch deshalb zustandegekommen, weil „der Professor" – Ferdinand Porsche – ja einst mit der Auto Union schon im Grand-Prix-Geschehen mitgemischt hat. Und dann hat es da ja auch das hochinteressante Projekt Cisitalia gegeben.

Wie auch immer: 1963 fällt die Entscheidung gegen die Fortsetzung des 804-Projekts. Doch auch Peter Falk sagt noch heute: Es hätte noch etwas werden können aus dem Zuffenhausener Formelrenner. „Hätte man weitergemacht, hätte man mit Sicherheit noch einen oder zwei Grand Prix' gewonnen." Nach den modifizierten Formel-2-Autos sei der 804 „schon ein Mordssprung" gewesen. Selbstverständlich sei vor allem die britische Konkurrenz mit ihren V8-Motoren schwer zu schlagen gewesen, und an

with the caliper's pistons, the brake was quite efficient but: "It was awfully complicated and maintenance was a real menace."

The next object for experimentation were simple holes – and they turned out to be a real recipe for success. There is probably only one welcome kind of retardation in racing and that is truly efficient braking when the pedal is activated. They discovered that holes drilled though the disc in the area swept by the pads helped to make the brakes markedly more effective. There are four arguments for perforating the discs. The first one is obvious since discs with holes weigh less then solid ones. Also holes help to keep the disc cool. Holes are also giving a positive advantage in wet weather as, when racing in the rain, a wafer-thin film of water covers the disc. As soon as the brake pad touches the disc the water will be wiped away or fades in the friction heat. This takes time and the holes give somewhere for the excess water to hide thus shortening the time elapsing before the brakes bite. Perhaps this is only a fraction of a second but maybe it is also the critical moment that could make all the difference in a race. And finally, holes improve the retardation achieved despite the fact that they consist simply of nothing. Falk describes the reason for this: "The brake pad material is much more elastic than the metal disc. Thus when they are applied, some of that material is pressed into the holes of the perforated disc – no matter how fast it is rotating. A little bump is created and has to be brought out of the hole again thus increasing the friction considerably. That matters a lot."

But finally, all this work was to go almost for nothing. Once Ferry Porsche had made up his mind to stop the Formula One, he then considered the matter closed. Falk: "At least he had the future of his company in mind." The son of Porsche's founder was considered to be a sceptic concerning the rather risky Formula One project. It is just possible that he thought like this thanks to Ferdinand Porsche's involvement in Grand Prix racing years ago with that exiting project called the Cisitalia.

It is of little consequence what might have been behind the decision for in 1963 the 804 project was abandoned. Peter Falk is still sure that it would eventually have been successful. "If they had kept going, I am sure that we would have won one or two Grand Prix races." There may be truth in that for the 804 had been a big step forward from Porsche's modified Formula 2 cars. Of course the British teams with their V8 engines and the V6 from Italy were going to be strong opponents but the 804 was not that far away from being fully competitive. Even its air-cooling system had never actually been a handicap. Porsche had tried to find out whether the cooling fan absorbed too much power from the engine. Falk: "We made an experiment with a clutch that allowed us to decouple the fan from the power train." But the fan cost only few horsepower and none of the drivers could detect any difference.

It was all a great shame but the job of encouraging the eight-cylinder engine to deliver more power during that first year proved to be an uphill task. In fact, it was very unlike Porsche to race a car like the 804 before that job had been properly achieved. It was very different from their normal style of operation. Falk thinks that "we actually hadn't a chance." It was a shame as everything else was coming together including having the best drivers. Falk says that perhaps Jo Bonnier was not fully at ease

der Luftkühlung habe es übrigens keineswegs gelegen, wenn dem Schwaben-Boxer nur schwer angemessene Leistung beizubringen war. „Wir haben einmal das Experiment mit einer Trennkupplung zwischen Antrieb und Lüfterrad gemacht", berichtet Falk. So will Porsche herausfinden, ob der – wenige PS kostende – Leistungsverlust durch den Gebläseantrieb spürbar ist. Keiner der Fahrer, die jeweils mit und kurzfristig ohne bremsendes Schaufelrad unterwegs sind, habe einen großen Unterschied verspürt.

Dennoch bringen die Porsche-Leute dem Achtzylinder nur mühsam Leistung bei. Dass der 804 dann trotz allem recht schnell zum Einsatz kommt, nennt Falk „eigentlich nicht Porsche-like, weil wir eigentlich kaum eine Chance hatten". Trotz brauchbarer Fahrer. Zwar sei Joakim Bonnier „nicht so richtig mit dem Auto klargekommen, aber der Gurney hatte es schon raus".

Schwerer für den Abschied vom Formel-1-Zirkus habe vielmehr der riesige finanzielle Aufwand gewogen – und der personelle. Die Ingenieure und Techniker seien dringend in den zahlreichen weiteren Motorsport-Projekten benötigt worden, in der Serienherstellung und in der Entwicklung von Produkten unter anderem Markenamen – „etwa für die vielen VW-Sachen, die wir immer nebenher gemacht haben". Oder eben Sachen von NSU, wie den Ro 80, dessen Federbeine Peter Falk damals so gefangen nahmen. (jn) ■

with the 804 "but for sure Gurney was able to get the maximum out of it".

But, ignoring the dearth of major results, the main reasons for Porsche's farewell to Formula One were the enormous costs in materials, travel and particularly personnel. Porsche needed the engineers and the technicians for all the other motor sport projects that were going on in the company and, of course, for engineering their normal sports cars that they were manufacturing. In addition, there was the development of products for other manufacturers, for example the many things they designed and made for Volkswagen or for NSU. (jn) ■

Eingepackt: Nicht besonders groß muss der Transporter sein, mit dem die Porsche-Leute den 804 zum Testen auf die Südschleife bringen.

Light cargo: a small truck was big enough to carry the comparitively tiny 804 racers to the 'Ring for testing.

Foto: Porsche

Ein Leben mit Federern

Wenn Peter Falk von seinem langen Leben mit der Technik erzählt, fällt immer wieder vor allem ein Wort: Federn. Gut, das ist jetzt in der Geschichte eines professionellen Fahrwerk-Entwicklers nicht wirklich verwunderlich. Die möglichst stoßschluckende Führung von Rädern aber hat den Mann wirklich von Kindesbeinen an beschäftigt. Angefangen hat alles mit Spielzeugautos, „diesen schönen alten – noch aus Blech". Ganz wichtig aber: „Es mussten welche mit drei Achsen sein." Nur an einer Doppelachse lässt sich beim Rollen über die Teppichkante so schön sehen, wie die beiden Räder einer jeden Achse sich unabhängig voneinander auf- und abbewegen. Jungingenieur Peter schreitet zum ersten Tuning seines Lebens: Er verlängert die „Federwege", indem er die Führungen der einfachen Drahtachsen vergrößert. Nun schwingen die Räder auf unwegsamem Kinderzimmerterrain umso dramatischer auf und nieder. Von nun an gibt es kein Zurück mehr. Der in Athen als Sohn eines Archäologen geborene Falk hat bloß noch Technik im Kopf. Es geht schnell voran. Als Halbwüchsiger stattet er bereits ein altes Damenrad mit Vollfederung aus, vorn à la NSU Fox gar mit Schwinge. Dass einer wie Peter Falk irgendwann Maschinenbau studieren wird, ist wohl dann auch klar, und die Einschreibung an der Hochschule in Stuttgart beinahe zwangsläufig. Dass er einen eigenen Kopf hat, beweist der Kandidat Falk, als es um die Wahl des Themas für die Diplomarbeit geht. Wie es Brauch ist, bekommt er eins gestellt. „Der Professor sagte: ‚Schreiben Sie doch mal alles zusammen, was es so über Federung und Stoßdämpfung gibt.' Das wäre aber fürchterlich langweilig geworden." Falk hat sich längst umgetan und weiß: Gleich in der Nachbarschaft bei NSU suchen sie die Lösung eines Federungsproblems beim Prinzen. Er wird bei den Neckarsulmern vorstellig und gleich danach beim Professor. Der stimmt zähneknirschend zu. Alles klappt, der Prinz rollt mit Falkscher Problemlösung ab, und der Student ist Ingenieur. Porsche nimmt den jungen Mann – und behandelt ihn wie jeden anderen Anfänger. So darf Peter Falk zwar entwickeln, fahren aber keineswegs. Sein erster Auftrag: Probeweiser Einbau einer Klimaanlage in einen 356. Als der Apparat passt, will er noch mit Freon gefüllt sein. Dafür muss Falk zur Firma Behr nach Stuttgart-Feuerbach. „Ich durfte halt im ersten Vierteljahr nicht ans Steuer von Testwagen, da hat man dann den Edgar Barth abgestellt, und der ist dann mit mir hingefahren." Da hilft es auch gar nichts, dass der Nachwuchsingenieur bereits Rennerfahrung gesammelt hat, erst auf Motorrädern, dann auf Rallies im 356. Bei der Wintersternfahrt nach Garmisch-Partenkirchen 1956 hat er gar Wolfgang Graf Berghe von Trips den Klassensieg abgenommen. Irgendwann ist er dann auch fest „beim Porsche" und immer wieder in der Rennentwicklung mit dabei, schließlich ab 1982 als Rennleiter in der Ära des 956/962. Ab 1964 hat er mit einer Ausnahme 30 Jahre lang jedes 24-Stunden-Rennen in Le Mans besucht. Treu geblieben ist er übrigens stets seiner Vorliebe für lange Federwege. Dass Rennwagenfederungen im Lauf der Jahrzehnte immer härter geworden sind, findet er fürchterlich. Spaß gemacht hat ihm deshalb das 911er-Derivat für die Rallye Paris-Dakar. Da durfte ein Rennsportauto endlich mal wieder herrlich lange Federwege haben. „Aber wissen Sie, welches Auto als allerletztes noch lange Federwege hatte", fragt Falk und gibt die Antwort gleich selbst: „Der 908/3 musste ja auch auf dem Nürburgring fahren und durfte da schließlich nicht ständig springen."

Experimentalklasse: Peter Falks gefedertes Fahrrad.

A life with springs

Talking to Peter Falk about his long career in mechanical engineering means talking about springs. That might be not very surprising as Falk was someone who specialized in suspension systems. But in fact he was a man whose life right from childhood was involved with all kinds of suspension components.

It all began with model cars that he refers to as "those old tin toys". But they were not just cars: "They had to be vehicles with three axles." Little Peter loved the sight of a twin axle moving up and down when he pushed a tiny truck over the rim of the carpet in his parent's living room. At one point, he took his first step towards design modification to improve performance. He took a file to the truck and increased the suspension movement of the simple wire axles. There was no turning back now. Falk was the son of an archaeologist working in Athens. All he ever thought about was engineering and as a teenager, he converted an old ladies bicycle into a fully sprung luxury vehicle along with a fork copied from an NSU Fox. It was obvious to all that someone like Peter Falk should go to an engineering school and so it was that he enrolled at the University of Stuttgart. He always had a mind of his own and thus he chose a special topic for his dissertation despite it being the custom that the students were told their topic. His professor had said to Falk: "Well, why don't you write out everything that you can find about suspension and damping?" Falk thought that this on its own could have been pretty boring, but he had an idea to enliven it. Close at hand in Neckarsulm, engineers were brooding over a problem concerning the suspension of the NSU Prinz. Falk applied to NSU and, soon after to his professor, to be allowed to work on the problem as part of his studies. With great reluctance, his teacher consented and he got to work. Everything went well and finally the Prinz rolled out with a working solution à la Falk. The young student had metamorphosed into an engineer. When he graduated, Porsche picked him up immediately – and treated him like every other rookie. Thus Falk was allowed to work in their development department, but for sure he was not allowed to drive anything. As an example, his first job was an air conditioning device for the Porsche 356. Once the apparatus was installed in the tiny sports car, it needed to be filled up with Freon. The Behr Company at Stuttgart-Feuerbach had the stuff. "Well, in the first quarter of my year at Porsche, I was not allowed to drive a test car, so they gave me Edgar Barth as a chauffeur and the two of us went with the car to Feuerbach." It did not make any difference to Porsche's attitude that by that time Falk was already an experienced competition driver, first on motorcycles, then later in rallies with a 356. In a winter car rally to Garmisch-Partenkirchen, he even won his class in front of Wolfgang Graf Berghe von Trips. Finally, the day arrived when Peter Falk became a full member of the Porsche team. He was regularly involved with the work of the racing department that he has now headed since 1982 and guided it through the glorious era of the 956/962. Furthermore, since 1964 and for the subsequent thirty years he has visited every 24 Hour race at Le Mans with just one exception. Also through all this time he has remained true to his liking for long suspension movements. Over the years, racing car suspensions have become stiffer and stiffer and Falk thinks this is simply dreadful. Thus he very much liked the 911 derivatives made for the Paris-Dakar Rally as they had a wonderfully long movement for their struts. "But do you know which was the last racing car to have a really long spring travel?" Peter Falk asks the question and delivers the answer almost in one breath: "The 908/3 was made to race at the Nürburgring and Targa Florio and it would have been embarrassing if it had bounced and hopped around the track."

Experimental: Peter Falk's bicycle with springs.

„Die Bremswirkung war toll – du musstest den Bremsen vor der Kurve aber erstmal Bescheid sagen"

Herbert Linge ist Testfahrer beim Formel-1-Projekt – „Das Auto war nur zu 60 Prozent ausgereizt"

„Zack!" Und noch einmal: „Zack". Und ein weiteres Mal und immer so weiter. Mehr ist nicht drauf auf dem Tonband, das sich Helmuth Bott ganz genau anhört. Die Stimme auf dem Band gehört Herbert Linge. Der Testfahrer hat offenbar nicht viel zu sagen, aber sein stereotypes „Zack" ist für Bott ausgesprochen aufschlussreich. Der Porsche-Versuchsmann hat Linge das einsilbige Tondokument aufnehmen lassen, weil er wissen will, wo der mit seinem Formelrenner wie schnell auf dem Nürburgring unterwegs ist. Vor der Testfahrt hat er ein Tonbandgerät im Auto verstaut und ein Mikrofon am Lenkrad montiert. Jedesmal, wenn Linge eine der Kilometertafeln am Rand des Eifelkurses passiert, ruft er „Zack!" Bott sitzt nun nach dem Ende einer Testfahrt am Bandgerät, sammelt Zacks und stoppt die Zeiten zwischen den Rufen seines Fahrers. „So wusste der Bott, wo der Linge schnell und wo er langsam war."

Derart archaischer, aber durchaus effektiver Methoden wissen sich die Porscheleute zu bedienen, als es noch keine Computer und keine hochsensiblen Sensoren im Westentaschenformat gibt. Es ist der Beginn der 1960er Jahre, und die kleine feine Zuffenhausener Sportwagenschmiede hat Großes vor. Die erfolgreiche Formel-2-Technik aus dem Hause Porsche ist mit einem Mal ge-

"The brakes were great – However you had to let them know when the next bend was coming"

Herbert Linge was the test driver for the Porsche single seater project – "The car's potential was never fully realised"

"Zack!" And once again: "Zack!" And once again and again and yet again. That was all anyone could hear on the tape recorder that Helmuth Bott listened to so intently. The voice was that of Herbert Linge. The test driver did not sound as if he had much to tell, but the repeated "Zack" was in fact very revealing to Bott. Porsche's testing expert had deliberately told Linge to record just that one sound. He wanted to know how fast his driver and the new Porsche single seater were on the Nürburgring. Before the test itself, he had mounted a tape recorder in the car with a microphone on the steering wheel. Every time Linge passed one of the kilometre markers at the side of the track, he was to shout "Zack". Then when the car returned to the pits, Bott could listen to the tape with his stopwatch in his hand, count the "Zacks" and create an analysis of the lap timing. Thus Bott could know where the car was fast and where it was not.

This was an archaic but quite effective method in an era before the arrival of computers and sensitive pocket size electronic devices. This was the beginning of the 1960s and the diminutive giant-killer, Porsche, had taken on a big task. More or less overnight their successful Formula Two cars were being prepared so as to pave the way for the Zuffenhausen firm to enter the pinnacle of motor sport, Formula One. Herbert Linge, who had worked as a Porsche em-

Foto: Porsche

eignet, dem Werk auch Motorsportehren in der Königsklasse, der Formel 1, zu verleihen. Mit dabei ist Herbert Linge, schwäbisches Urgestein und seit 1943 Porsche-Werksangehöriger – und wohl der einzige in dieser Funktion, der Testfahrer war und Rennen im Namen des Hauses gefahren ist. In seinem Büro in Weissach hängt ein Foto vom 804. „Mit dem haben wir die Kreisbahn im neuen Versuchszentrum eingeweiht." Das war damals nagelneu, Linge hat maßgeblich daran mitgearbeitet und es lange geleitet. Der Versuch bei Porsche ist ohne den heute immer noch beeindruckend fitten 80-Jährigen nicht denkbar. So ist es auch kein Wunder, dass er allerhand über die kurze, aber spannende Ära des ersten Formel-1-Engagements der Zuffenhausener zu berichten weiß.

Die endet bekanntlich vor der Zeit – nach einer Saison ist Schluss. „Da war das Auto natürlich erst zu 60 Prozent ausgereizt", sagt Linge. „Da war noch mehr drin." Doch Ferry Porsche zieht den Schlussstrich, nachdem der Wagen zwar nicht versagt, sich aber auch nicht gerade als Meistermacher erweist. „Der Ferry Porsche war ja immer ein bisschen skeptisch. Das sei ein Formelauto, wir bauen aber lieber Sportwagen, weil: Die wollen wir verkaufen." Die Spyder-Entwicklung sei wichtiger für den

ployee since 1943, had a key role. He was probably the only Porsche employee who worked as both a test and a race driver. In his office at Weissach, he still has a picture showing the 804. "With this one, we christened the new skid pad in our test centre." Linge had played a decisive role in establishing the Weissach centre and was its head for many years. Still amazingly fit even now at eighty-years of age, back in the 1960s Linge was indispensable to the Porsche test department. So it comes as no surprise that he knows a lot about that exciting era when Porsche was first involved in Formula One.

As everybody now knows, it was an involvement that ended before its time. After only one season of racing, it was shutters down for the 804. "The car's potential of course was never fully realised" Linge says. "Quite a lot was still possible in the way of development." But once the decision was taken to stop the programme, Ferry Porsche considered the matter closed. The car had not really failed, but it was not as successful as had been expected. "Ferry Porsche always was a little bit sceptical. ,This is a formula racer' he said, ,but we always prefer to build sports cars. After all, that is what we sell.'" The head of Porsche gave priority to the simultaneous development of the Spyder. "About the Formula One car, he said: ,Here we spend a lot of money for something we won't sell'."

Lässig: Pullover und Polohemd reichen als Renndress, wenn Herbert Linge sich zur Testfahrt im 718 begibt. Immerhin haben sich schon Helme durchgesetzt.

Casual wear: a jumper and polo shirt make a contemporary racing uniform for 718 test driver Herbert Linge. At least they used helmets.

Foto: Porsche

Porsche-Chef gewesen. „Der hat gesagt: Wie geben hier viel Geld aus für etwas, was wir nicht verkaufen können."

Immerhin: Die Leistung war laut Linge „schon in Ordnung". Porsche sei auf dem besten Weg gewesen, zur Konkurrenz aufzuschließen. Ganz anders habe es vor allem anfangs mit dem Fahrgestell ausgesehen. Zunächst hat der Wagen immer noch stolze 15 Zoll große Räder, wie sie sich auch am Käfer und am 356 drehen. „Das waren ja Bleiräder, denken Sie an die ungefederten Massen." Die Konkurrenz fährt da schon kleine 13-Zöller.

Fahrwerk und Motor lernt Linge gut kennen. Allein 4000 Kilometer ist er auf der Nordschleife des Nürburgrings unterwegs, „mit einem Auto und mit dem gleichen Motor". Einen ganzen Tag lang absolviert er Runde um Runde auf der anspruchsvollen Strecke, auf der sich schnell erweist, was ein Auto kann. Der Motor macht alles mit, „wir haben nie was dran machen müssen". Auch auf den Hockenheimring geht es mit dem 804. Dort testet Linge aber vor allem Dinge, bei denen es auf „reproduzierbare Ergebnisse" ankommt. Soll heißen: Die Kühlung etwa lässt sich besser auf der Strecke unweit von Stuttgart auf Herz und Nieren prüfen, weil die Testfahrer stetige Runden unter vergleichbaren Bedingungen drehen. Die Nordschleife dagegen taugt vor allem für den Härtetest von Fahrgestell und Motor. „Am Ring fuhr man auch zu sehr nach Gefühl, machte Fehler." Und die Testfahrer

Nevertheless, the 804's performance was "all right" Linge says. Porsche had been on the right track way to catch up with the competitors. However, especially in the early days of the project, there was a lot of fuss with the chassis. Initially the racer had fifteen-inch diameter wheels – the same size as on the Beetle and the Porsche 356. "They were steel wheels, so just think of the un-sprung weight in such a light car!" Other Formula One manufacturers had long since moved to using smaller, lighter thirteen-inch wheels.

Linge got to know the chassis and engine of the new car extremely well. He drove more than 4,000 kilometres just on the Nordschleife of the Nürburgring "in the same car and with the same engine". He would drive through a complete day to add more laps on the demanding track. The engine proved to be adequately tough and up to the task. "We never had to fix anything." Then they moved to the Hockenheimring. On the faster, less twisty track near Mannheim it was easier to test, for example, the cooling system because the test drivers could turn in almost identical laps thus giving comparable results. In contrast, he Nordschleife was ideal for endurance tests. "On the 'Ring you drove more instinctively and thus you tended to make mistakes." It was difficult for the drivers to report each time exactly where they had made a little mistake, which was why Bott had invented his analytic device based on a tape recorder and the kilometre markers.

Rustikal: Sehr viel Platz haben die Mechaniker nicht in den Boxen des Fahrerlagers am Nürburgrings, wo Linge 1959 Testfahrten mit dem 718 unternimmt.

Rustic: the old paddock at the Nürburgring did not offer the mechanics very much space. This was 1959 when Linge tested the 718.

Foto: Porsche

Foto: Porsche

Gelassen: Noch scheint es ganz geruhsam zuzugehen auf dem Ring im Jahre 1959. Gleich gibt Herbert Linge aber wieder richtig Gas.

Easygoing: everyone seems to be relaxed at the ‚Ring in 1959. But you can be certain that it was not long before Herbert Linge put the pedal to the metal again.

können auch nicht immer gleich sagen, dass sie da und dort einen Fahrfehler gemacht haben. Deshalb ersinnt ja auch Helmuth Bott seine Band-Registriermaschine mit Ansage.

Die Grand-Prix-Piloten müssen sich dem Zack-Test nicht unterziehen. Aber es gilt: „Nur der hat ein gutes Auto gekriegt, der ein guter Versuchsfahrer gewesen ist." Linge erinnert sich, wer gut war in dieser Funktion und wer nicht. „Der Bonnier kam manchmal und sagte schon nach zwei Runden auf der Südschleife sein Urteil übers Auto." Der Hinweis darauf, er solle vielleicht auch noch zwei, drei Runden auf der Nordschleife absolvieren, sei da mitunter folgenlos verhallt. „Das war also an und für sich keine Aussage. Für so was konnte man eigentlich nur den Hans Herrmann gebrauchen, weil er konstant und gleichmäßig fuhr. Da ließ sich alles immer gut vergleichen." Dann fällt Linge noch Dan Gurney ein. „Wenn man mit dem über die Technik geredet hat, wusste der auch, worum es ging."

Woran der neue Formelrenner krankt, ist gleich klar. „Das Hauptproblem waren die Radaufhängungen." Das liegt zum Teil daran, dass die Messmethoden damals noch nicht so ausgereift sind. In vielen Fällen entscheiden immer noch das „Popometer" sensibler Fahrer und die Qualität von deren Aussagen darüber, wie ein Auto abgestimmt wird. Linges körpereigene Sensoren melden Folgendes: „Je schneller das Auto gefahren wird, je

The race drivers did not have to take part in the "Zack" test. But one thing was common to all of them: "The drivers who were best at testing got the best cars." The reason for that was a good race driver was not necessarily a good test driver. "Bonnier, for example, sometimes came back into the pit after only two laps on the Südschleife and was ready to give his judgement on the car." The Swedish driver regularly refused to go out for two or three additional laps on the Nordschleife to do some further testing. "So we didn't have a complete information about the car. The best test driver was without doubt Hans Herrmann who drove constantly and steadily." Then there was Dan Gurney. "If you discussed a technical matter, you could be sure he knew what you were talking about."

It soon became obvious what the problem was with the car. "The suspension caused most of the trouble." Back then testing methods were not as sophisticated as they are today. Much of the testing results in the 1960s were based on what was known in engineer's jargon as the "popometer" – a device perhaps better known as the lower end of the backbone. It was that sensitive spot where the driver could best ascertain what the road was doing to his car and vice versa. The drawback to this system was that it depended entirely on the ability of the driver to tell the engineers what his "popometer" was telling him. Linge's built-in sensors told him that "The further you put the pedal to the metal and harder the suspension was pushed

Fotos: Porsche

Angeschoben: Immer wieder werden die Autos zum Testen auf den Nürburgring gebracht. Mit dabei sind auch John Surtess (rechte Seite, unten links) sowie Edgar Barth (2.v.l.), Joakim Bonnier (2.v.r.) und Hans Herrmann (r.).

Testing times: again and again the cars were sent to the Nürburgring for further testing. Drivers were John Surtees (right page, bottom left), Edgar Barth (2nd from left), Joakim Bonnier (2nd from right) and Hans Herrmann (right).

härter also die Belastungen, desto härter wird das Auto auch. An bestimmten Stellen wird es buckelhart." Der Wagen fühlt sich an, als habe er keinerlei Federung. „Es hat tagelang gedauert, bis wir drauf gekommen sind, was da passiert." Unter dem Druck der Stöße verhärten und verklemmen sich jene Gummipuffer, die eigentlich der Dämpfung dienen sollen, derart, dass die Federwirkung praktisch aufgehoben wird. Sobald die Radaufhängung wieder entlastet wird, erhalten auch die Gummis ihre alte Elastizität zurück. Das ist natürlich schwer zu ermitteln. In der Box per Hand ein- und ausgefedert, fühlt sich alles geschmeidig und elastisch an. Erst der enorme Druck bei der Fahrt im Renntempo lässt die Puffer zäh und schließlich hart werden. Es ist ein bisschen so wie beim Kaugummikauen: Gemütlich vor sich hingeschmatzt bleibt der Gummi sämig, hektisch hart gemalmt, erweist er sich als erstaunlich kompaktes Kaugut.

Doch vom Erfühlen des Problems bis zur Erkenntnis der Ursache ist es ein mühevoller Weg – und ein gefährlicher obendrein. „Das Auto ist beim Anbremsen vor den Kurven ja wie wild gesprungen. An jeder Bodenwelle hat der Wagen einen Satz gemacht wie ein wilder Reiter." Nur mit Mühe behält Linge Kurs. Er lässt Schweißdrahtstücke an den Fahrwerksteilen befestigen, die als Messlatten dienen sollen. Er will sehen, ob er recht hat mit seiner Vermutung, dass der Federweg unter Druck gegen Null geht.

Weil die Gummis, kaum dass Linge wieder an die Boxen fährt, sich vorbildlich benehmen, schenkt ihm zunächst niemand Glauben. Im Gegenteil, der Testfahrer bekommt zu hören, das Auto sei eher zu weich als zu hart abgestimmt. Erst als Dan Gurney ebenfalls Testfahrten unternimmt und die gleichen

to its limits, the stiffer the car became. In some certain places it was almost like torture." The car felt as if it had no suspension at all. "This lasted for days until we found out what was going on." Under severe pressure, the rubber bushes for the dampers hardened and finally jammed. They should have functioned as flexible mounts but in fact they seized and the suspension was rendered completely ineffectual. As soon as the car was back in the pit and the suspension had the opportunity to relax a little and cool down, the rubber bushes returned to their normal behaviour and were smooth and elastic. So this irritation was well hidden and took a bit of finding. With the car stationary, it was easy to press the body down and feel the suspension working perfectly. But in real life out on the track, the rubber soon went stiff and finally as hard as steel. It was a little bit like chewing gum. Chew it slowly and relaxed and it will stay soft and smooth. Chomp vigorously and it will turn out to be really tough.

It's a long way from just feeling that something is going wrong to the point where you recognize what the problem is – and in the meantime, it can be dangerous. "The car jumped like a wild horse when you braked into a corner. On every bump, you felt a bit like a rodeo rider." Linge took a lot of trouble to sort out the problem. He got the mechanics to weld thin rods to the wishbones so he could see how the suspension worked out on the track. In that way, he tried to find out whether his feeling was right that the suspension was virtually inoperative at high speed.

Top start with, it was all for nothing. As soon as Linge returned to the Porsche pit, the suspension worked perfectly well. No one believed him. In fact he was told that everyone else said: It's not too stiff, it's too soft. It was not until Dan Gurney had the same experience that the engineers got to work to locate the source of the

Foto: Porsche

Vor der Haustür: Natürlich unternehmen die Porsche-Leute auch in Hockenheim regelmäßig Testfahrten mit den Formel-Rennern.

Right in their backyard: of course the cars were also tested at Hockenheim as it was the home track for the Zuffenhausen crew.

Foto: Porsche

Mit „Öhrchen": Auch der 787 mit seinen Hutzen über den Ansaugstutzen wird ausgiebig auf dem Hockenheimring getestet.

With „ears": the 787 with its characteristic scoops over the air intakes was tested at Hockenheim.

Horrormeldungen liefert, machen sich die Konstrukteure noch einmal ans Werk. Schwenklager „statt der Gummiknödel" sorgen für Abhilfe. Motor und Getriebe machen weniger Probleme, aber, und Linge grinst: „Die Engländer waren trotzdem besser."

Die Testerei zieht sich hin, namentlich auf dem Nürburgring. „Da musstest du immer auf schönes Wetter warten." Weil es immer wieder Niederschläge gibt, muss die Truppe einmal auch kurz vor Weihnachten in die Eifel. Da ist ausnahmsweise mal die Piste trocken. „Dafür sind wir im April nicht aus der Box gekommen, weil soviel Schnee lag." Dennoch bleibt der Ring als Teststrecke das Maß der Dinge: „Was dort net geht, kannsch vergesse."

Trotz aller Schwierigkeiten ist Linge immer noch überzeugt: „Das Auto wär' schon was geworden, wenn man das durchgezogen hätte." So sei der Motor bestimmt nicht schlecht gewesen. „Mit dem haben wir auf den langsameren Strecken später ja noch ganz schön abgesahnt."

1959, da ist der Monoposto noch ganz Formel 2, macht „Count Crash" seinem Namen alle Ehre. Wolfgang Graf Berghe von Trips zerlegt seinen Wagen gleich zu Anfang des Rennens in Monaco. Das ist mehr als schade, denn auf dem Renner ruhen große Hoffnungen. Nicht zu unrecht, weiß Linge: „Das Auto war

problem. New bearings instead of the rubber bushes proved to be the solution. By contrast, the engine and gear box were absolutely trouble free. Linge can laugh about it now and say: "The British teams were better all the way at those things."

Testing always took a lot of time – especially at the Nürburgring. "You always had to wait for good weather." Because there was shower after shower, rain and even snow, all of which interrupted their work, the team once went back to the 'Ring just before Christmas. For once the track was dry. "That was just amazing and then in April we couldn't leave the pit because there was too much snow." The Nürburgring nevertheless stayed first choice for the test team. They used to say that "If something doesn't work there, it won't work anywhere."

In spite of all the trouble in the initial stages, Linge is still sure it would have been good: "The car should have been something. If they had carried it through to the finish of development." The engine for example was certainly not so bad. "With the eight-cylinder, we were able to be very quick on the slower tracks."

In 1959, the Porsche's open wheel Formula Two car was still just a sports car with the wheels exposed. "Count Crash", as Wolfgang Graf Berghe von Trips was known in the team, once again showed

Fotos: Porsche

Wetterfest: Wenig verwöhnt sind Mechaniker und Testfahrer wie Herbert Linge (rechts), die unter den widrigsten Bedingungen immer wieder auf die Strecke gehen.

Weather proof: mechanics and test drivers (Linge on the right) were not mollycoddled when they went out for winter testing.

Zugelassen: Der 718/2 trägt zwar eine rote Nummer, er dürfte aber kaum je auf eigener Achse nach Hockenheim gerollt sein.

Registered: though the 718/2 bore a licence plate, it was certainly not driven to Hockenheim on the road.

Foto: Porsche

Und wieder ist es Linge: Erst im 718, später dann im 804 spult Herbert Linge Kilometer um Kilometer auf dem Nürburgring ab.

And Linge again: first in the 718/2 and later with the 804, Herbert Linge reeled off hundreds of miles at the Nürburgring.

Fotos: Porsche

Südschleife in Farbe: Klassisch in silber und auch mal in schottisch-blau brausen die 718 durch die Eifel.

In colour: normally in classic silver grey but occasionally painted blue, the 718s were frequently rushing through the Eifel.

gut.“ Er hat den Wagen wenige Tage zuvor auf dem Nürburgring gefahren. „Wir waren ganz zuversichtlich, dass der Trips mit dem Auto da was vorführen könnte.“ Der populäre Rennfahrer aus der Voreifel hat zwar nicht allzu viel Zeit für Testfahrten, aber: „Der war begeistert von dem Auto.“

Dann kommt die Reglementänderung hin zur kleineren Hubraumklasse. „Da gab's dann schon schnell Stimmen, die gesagt haben: ‚Das hatten wir ja schon im Sportwagen.‘ Und der Formel 2 war ja kein schlechtes Auto. Der Motor war gut, mit dem Getriebe hatten wir keine Schwierigkeiten, die Achsen hatten wir ja schon in den Spydern.“ Bleibt immerhin dennoch ein wenig der Verdacht, Porsche schicke ohne Not einen Lückenbüßer ins Rennen. Immerhin hat die Konkurrenz reichlich Formel-1-Erfahrung und muss nur im Hubraum eins runtergehen. „Na ja“, sagt Linge, „man hat damals einige Sachen nicht mit der Power angegangen, mit denen man solche Projekte eigentlich angehen sollte. Das lief alles so ein bisschen nach dem Motto: Na, probieren wir's halt mal“.

Bei Porsche habe es zwei Fraktionen gegeben. „Die einen waren dafür, die andern haben gesagt: Finger weg, das gibt eh nix.“ Ein Einwand: „Wir haben ja nicht einmal eine richtige Rennabteilung.“ Zwar gibt es den Versuch, aber da arbeiten die gleichen Leute an Rennwagen, die sonst auch für die Serienproduktion verantwortlich sind. „In dem Sinne hatten wir tatsächlich keine Rennabteilung.“ Ganz anders bei der Konkurrenz: „Die haben richtige Rennabteilungen mit 20, 30 Leuten, bei uns machen zwei, drei nebenher die Rennmotoren. Der Mezger hat sicher mal zu einem gesagt: Zeichne mal was uff.“ So sei es schon mit dem Mittellenker gelaufen. Wieder frei nach dem Motto: „Probieren wir's mal.“

Die spezielle Bremsanlage des Formelrenners mag Linge nicht so recht goutieren. An der Bremswirkung habe es nicht viel auszusetzen gegeben, der Weg zur Verzögerung jedoch sei steinig gewesen. „Das Problem mit dem Pedal, das haben wir bei der Porschebremse ewig nicht weggekriegt.“ Die spezielle Konstruktion der innenumgreifenden Scheibenbremse birgt unangenehme Eigenschaften. „Jede Bewegung in der Lenkung, im Radlager oder von der Felge her ist auf die Scheibe gegangen.“ Soll heißen: Die Bremsbeläge, die in Lauerstellung auf den nächsten Pedaldruck harren, werden bei jeder sich bietenden Gelegenheit tiefer in die Bremszange zurückgeschoben. Das wäre nicht weiter schlimm, wenn der Fahrer nicht vor jeder Kurve daran denken muss, ausreichend Bremsdruck wiederherzustellen, indem er mit

why he earned that nickname when he wrecked the car right at the beginning of its debut at the Monaco GP. That was nothing less than sad. The car was the great hope for that race and rightly so as Linge himself knows: "The car was good." It had only been a couple of days prior to Monaco that he had driven it at the Nürburgring. "We had been quite optimistic that von Trips would turn in a good performance." The popular driver did not have much time for practising but as Linge recalls: "He was enthusiastic about the car."

Then came the change in regulations for the 1961 season and the smaller engines arrived and with them the chance for Porsche to be a contender for outright wins, not just in the F2 category of a F1 race. "The first guys came and said ‚that's exactly what we had in the sports cars. At least our Formula Two was not at all a bad car. The engine was pretty fine, we didn't have any difficulties with the gear box and the axles came straight out of the Spyder." But still there were rumours that Porsche had sent a stopgap car to the races. Their rivals were old hands at Formula One racing and simply had to downsize their engines. Linge: "Well, perhaps we didn't do things as thoroughly as we should have. Sometimes it went a little bit too much according to the principle of ‚Let's just try it and find out.'"

At Zuffenhausen there were two groups in opposition to each other. "One was in favour for it, the others said ‚don't touch, this won't work at all'." One argument even went: "We don't even have a racing department." There was the test department, but the people there who worked on the racing cars were the same people who were also responsible for the series production cars. "Looked at from that point of view, it was true in fact that we had no racing department as such." And their Formula One competitors? "They had real racing departments with twenty or thirty people. At our place two or three mechanics made the racing engines on the side, so to speak. I am sure Hans Mezger occasionally told one of them: ‚Would you please make this piece for me?'" That would have been the way it worked ever since the early days of the RSK with central steering. Everything would just go along according to the principle of ‚Let's try it out'.

The new brakes on the car were not to Linge's liking. They did their job well enough but the way they worked was, to put it rather mildly, somewhat hairy. "For an awfully long time we had problems with the brake pedal." It was a sophisticated solution to have the disc and calipers mounted inside the wheels but it caused its own problems with what is known as pad knock-off. "With every movement of the steering, the cornering forces acting on the disc and the rim together pushed the pistons back into the calipers." That meant

Pumpbewegungen die Beläge wieder in Position schiebt. „Da hab ich bei Start und Ziel schon angefangen, die Beläge hochzupumpen, damit ich in der Südkehre eine Bremswirkung hatte. Wir mussten der Bremse erstmal Bescheid sagen: ‚Du, ich brauch Dich demnächst.'"

Nun genießt Porsche durchaus den Ruf, in Sachen Bremsen oft genug die Nase vorn zu haben. „Stimmt auch", sagt Linge. „In der Wirkung war die Bremse überlegen. Wir konnten die anderen einwandfrei ausbremsen." Aber: Die Fahrer müssen sich auskennen. „Der Abflug vom Barth aus der Südkehre war symptomatisch: Freilich hatte der neue Beläge, aber der hatte vergessen zu pumpen."

Porsches eigentümliche Konstruktion mit der außen angeschlagenen Bremsscheibe hat einen entscheidenden Vorteil: Dank günstigeren Angriffspunkts und größerer Fläche ist Überhitzung kaum ein Thema. „Wir sind sogar mit den kleinen Felgendurchbrüchen hingekommen." Weil das Fading-Risiko so klein ist, darf gar etwas mehr gebremst werden als üblich. „Auf der Nordschleife hab ich oft genug den linken Fuß auf dem Bremspedal liegen lassen." Da bleiben die Bremsen sogar in besserer Bereitschaft, weil die Scheiben stets auf Temperatur sind. Zu danken ist das ständige Auseinandersetzen mit der Bremsanlage auch der Firmenpolitik: „Bei uns hat's immer einen Ingenieur gegeben, der sich nur mit Bremsen beschäftigt hat." Andere hätten Bremsen nur eingebaut, „wir haben sie immer selbst entwickelt. Das ist meiner Meinung nach ein ganz großer Vorteil." Die immer wieder zitierten kurzen Wege im Werk bewähren sich bei jeder Gelegenheit. „Der Mezger etwa konnte jederzeit auf jede Entwicklung zurückgreifen und hat die Leute alle gekannt. Die sind zusammengekommen

that the driver always had to be alert to pump up enough pressure to get the pads back next to the disc before the following bend. This meant that he had to press the pedal at least a couple of times. "For instance, I had to pump right from the start line, just to have a firm brake pedal by the time I reached the South Curve of the Nürburgring. You had to say to the brakes in good time: ‚Hey, wake up. I will need you soon!'"

Naturally, Porsche never had a reputation for fitting bad brakes. "That's right", Linge says. "In terms of sheer efficiency, these brakes were superior to almost anything." But still the driver had to know the track like the back of his hand. "Barth's accident at the South Curve was a good example. He had brand new brake pads, but he forgot to pump up the pressure before he got there."

Porsche's special brake configuration with the calipers inside the discs had a decisive advantage. Thanks to their location and their bigger surface area, overheating was seldom a problem. "We even managed with just small cooling holes in the wheel rims." Because the risk of brake fade was small, the drivers were allowed to brake longer and more often. "At the Nordschleife, I even used to leave my foot on the brake pedal." As well as keeping the discs warm, it meant that the pads never got the chance to move far away from the disc and thus were always ready for action.

The long struggle with the brakes was partly due to a policy that was adhered to throughout the company. "At Porsche, we always had one engineer who devoted his whole time to the development of the brakes." Other Formula One teams just used ready-made brake systems and built them into their design. "We always made them by ourselves. That in my opinion is a great advantage." Such close connection within the factory often turned out to be very effective."

Ende einer Dienstfahrt: Herbert Linge steigt an der Südschleife aus dem 804.

The end of a business trip: at the Südschleife, Linge has parked his car.

Foto: Porsche

Fotos: Porsche

Ungeduldig: „Der Bonnier kam manchmal und sagte schon nach zwei Runden sein Urteil übers Auto", erinnert sich Herbert Linge. Hier erprobt der Schwede den 804 mit May-Motor in Hockenheim.

Impatient: „Bonnier, for example, sometimes came back into the pit after only two laps on the Südschleife and was ready to give his judgement on the car" is Linge's recollection today. Here the Swede tries the 804 at Hockenheim with the four-cylinder engine modified by May.

Die langen Tüten verraten: Das ist ein 804 mit Vierzylinder, der da 1962 in Hockenheim getestet wird.

Inlet tract give-away: the long protruding inlets of the four-cylinder engine from Michael May reveal the 804 testing with the small engine at Hockenheim in 1962.

Hausstrecke: In Hockenheim testen die Porscheleute den 804 auf Herz und Nieren.

Home track: At Hockenheim the Porsche team put the 804 through its paces.

und zusammengehockt und haben gesagt: ‚Wie machen wir das?'" Jeder habe sich alles holen können, jederzeit und überall.

Es ist dennoch nicht immer leicht. Die Leute müssen Ende der 1950er, Anfang der 60er Jahre viel Enthusiasmus mitbringen. Auch einer wie Herbert Linge, der mit Porsche verwachsen ist wie kaum ein zweiter, verdient sich trotz einiger bedeutender Erfolge kaum etwas von dem hinzu, was man heute von derartigen Leistungen erwarten würde. Da fallen vom Ausrüster Dunlop mal ein Satz Reifen für seinen Simca und einer für den 750er Fiat seiner Frau ab, da ist das Preisgeld für eine grandiose Wertung in Le Mans schon nach dem Abendessen, das er für die Mechaniker ausgibt, auf den letzten Pfennig ausgegeben. Da werden brillante Fahrer in den USA nicht eingesetzt, weil sich das eiskalte PR-Genie Huschke von Hanstein mehr Zeitungsartikel von US-amerikanischen Namen auf der Starterliste erhofft – und erhält. Und da machen dennoch alle, alle mit. „Wir haben praktisch keine Fluktuation gehabt", erinnert sich Linge. „Da ist keiner gegangen." In der Werkstatt haben 16 von 20 Leuten den Meistertitel, „da ist keiner gegangen, und die haben als Mechaniker gearbeitet". Das geht noch weiter: „Ingenieure wie der Mezger oder der Singer oder der Falk, die sind von der Schule gekommen und haben gearbeitet, bis sie in Rente gingen – alle." Das Wort ist noch nicht im Umlauf, aber Helmuth Bott ist Talentscout par excellence. Er geht in die Hochschule und greift sich die Talente heraus. Und die jungen Männer kommen gern. Es lockt der Ruf des Rennsportruhms, die Namen der Grand-Prix-Kurse und die

Hans Mezger for example could always get every new development that came along and knew everyone in the firm. They simply got together and said: ‚How can we do this?'" It was the case that everyone had had access to everything, every time and everywhere.

In spite of that it was not all easy. In this period at the end of the 1950s and beginning of 1960s, it was necessary to posses a lot of enthusiasm to work with the team. Even a man like Herbert Linge who was deeply rooted in the Porsche business did not earn what would be normal nowadays for his efforts. Once he received a set of tyres for his Simca and some for his wife's Fiat 750. Buying a dinner for his mechanics after the race used up all the prize money that he won for a good result at Le Mans. Top class German drivers were not sent to the races in the USA because the cold-as-ice PR genius, Huschke von Hanstein, hoped to get bigger headlines in US newspapers when Porsche's winners bore US names – and he got them of course. Believe it or not, the Porsche people – all of them – went along with all this. "There was no turnover at all", Linge remembers. "No one quit." Sixteen of the twenty men in the workshop were master craftsmen, they bore the German title of "Meister". "But no one left the team even though they were employed as just simple mechanics." And even more amazing was that "Engineers like Mezger or Singer or Falk came straight from college and worked in the company until they retired – all of them." Helmuth Bott was a talent scout par excellence. He used to go to the engineering colleges and picked up the young talents as they qualified. And they were keen to follow him. The fame and excitement of motor racing

Foto: Porsche

der berühmten Fahrer können sie im Schlaf herbeten. Und Porsche ist bestimmt keine schlechte Adresse.

Vor dem Einsatz des Formel-1-Renners ist Linge dauernd auf Achse und prüft den Monoposto auf Herz und Nieren. Dass der Formelwagen Wurzeln im Sportwagen hat, ist zu spüren. „Ich war eine Dreiviertelminute schneller als im Sportwagen, aber gespürt hab ich das nicht unbedingt." Zumindest, was die schiere Motorleistung angeht. Besser ist vor allem das Handling, das liegt aber eher daran, dass der Fahrer in der kleinen Zelle fast im Schwerpunkt sitzt und hervorragende Sicht aus dem Cockpit genießt. Und dann sind da eben auch die Bremsen. „Wenn ich ein paar Tage lang im Formelwagen rumgefahren bin, musste ich mich schon schwer auf Sportwagen und auch auf Spyder umstellen. Das hat ein Paar Runden gedauert. Da hatte ich dann die ganzen Bremspunkte und alles noch von dem leichten Auto im Kopf. Umgekehrt war's natürlich leicht."

Auch der Wechsel von der ursprünglichen Formel-2-Technik auf den 804 bedeutet eine Umstellung. „Der Formel 2 war vom Fahrverhalten her eher der Spyder. Das eine war ein Rennauto, das andere eher ein Sportwagen, der keine Kotflügel hatte." Der 804 sei schon ein Schritt nach vorn gewesen. Umso mehr enttäuscht es ihn, dass es nicht mehr weitergehen soll mit dem Formel-1-Projekt. „Man hätte noch zwei Jahre weiterfahren sollen." Das Aus kommt zur Unzeit. „Wir waren an einem Punkt, wo man sagen konnte: Wenn wir jetzt alle Erkenntnisse, die wir bis dahin gewonnen haben, umsetzen würden, also 13-Zoll-Räder, andere Radaufhängung, die ganzen Anlenkpunkte und das alles, dann wären wir richtig bei der Musik." Aber es ist eine politische Entscheidung. Privater Einsatz wie der von de Beaufort

plus the chance to go the racetracks and work with the well-known drivers was what drew them in. And of course, Porsche was not the worst company to work for in order to earn one's living.

Before the first entry of the single-seater, Linge was rushing around from one place to another in order to put the car through its paces. There were a lot of the RSK sports car's genes in this open-wheeler. "I didn't really realize that I was lapping the 'Ring three quarters of a minute faster than in the sports car." Such improvement did not result from a major increase in engine power over the sports car from which it was derived. However the handling was much better thanks to the driver's position which was nearly at the centre of gravity. In addition the driver had an unrivalled view of the track. And of course there were those new brakes. Linge: "When I had driven around for a couple of days in the Formula-Two car, it was a bit of rude awakening to climb back into the sports car or the Spyder. I needed some laps to cope again because in my head I had all the braking points for the lighter car. Vice versa it was much easier of course."

In a similar fashion, the changeover from the Formula Two to the Formula One 804 was similarly disconcerting. "Concerning its comportment on the road, the Formula Two was much more like the Spyder. The 804 was a pure racing car while the Formula Two was more of a sports car without bumpers." The 804 had been a big step forward for the 1962 season. That is why Linge was so disappointed when the project was cancelled. "They should have carried on for two further years." The end came at an inopportune time. "We had reached a point where we could say with confidence, if we put all our latest findings together now, that is thirteen inch wheels, new suspension and all the other things, we would be out in front."

im alten 718/2 beweist, dass Musik drin ist. Linge hat die Autos in der Werksreparatur gesehen. „Die waren absolut gleichwertig." Jedenfalls bleibt eine gewisse Wehmut. „Überhaupt der Achtzylinder: Der hat mir gefallen. Das war einfach was Besonderes. Und das war es auch."

Vielleicht ist schon beim Formel 2 zuviel falsch gemacht worden. „Damals hat sich alles viel zu sehr auf den Motor konzentriert. Was ich nie verstanden hab'." Linge diskutiert auch mit Michael May, „weil der immer geglaubt hat, es ist nur der Motor". Das Fahrwerk hält May für eine zu vernachlässigende Größe. „Da hätte man viel, viel mehr draus machen können." Die Leistung des Vierzylinders nennt Linge „nicht schlecht". An der Radaufhängung aber habe sich noch einiges machen lassen. „Die Aufhängung vom Spyder war einfach altbacken, ein alter Hut."

Wie stark die Konkurrenz von den britischen Inseln ist, erfährt Linge schon, als er Elva-Sportwagen testet, für die Porsche Motoren liefert. „Da hast Du natürlich damals schon gemerkt, was diese englischen Leichtgewichte für ein Spielzeug sind gegen unsere Autos. Das waren ja richtige Straßenbahnen dagegen."

Wer sich eine Weile umsieht in Herbert Linges Büro in der beschaulichen Wohnsiedlung in Weissach, findet den 804 als einen unter vielen fürchterlich berühmten Rennsportwagen. Es ist kaum zu glauben: Der gemütlich schwäbelnde Mann, der da im Stuhl vor seinem Schreibtisch sitzt, hat sie alle gefahren – schneller als die allermeisten. Und dann gibt es da noch ein Foto in dem kleinen Raum, in dem auch der alte Werksausweis aus dem Jahr 1943 hängt, der die Nummer 745 trägt und Linge als Mechani-

But it was a question of company policy. Private entries like the one for Godin de Beaufort who raced on in 1963 proved that it would have been possible. Linge saw the racing cars just sitting in the firm's workshop. "They were absolutely competitive." Then came a note of melancholy. "Just take the eight-cylinder. I really liked it. It was simply something special. And that's what it was."

Perhaps too much went wrong in the period when the Formula Two was racing. "At that time, there was too much effort concentrated on the engine. I never understood that." Linge also talked to Michael May, the Swiss racing driver and engine specialist brought in to work on the 1961 4-cylinder. "He also thought that it was all a question of engines and engine power." May did not think that the chassis was really very important. "But there were so many possibilities that existed to improve it." The four-cylinder's power output had not been bad. "But the suspension was old hat."

Porsche's rivals from Great Britain were very good with chassis and suspensions. Linge realised that while he was testing an Elva sports car fitted with a Porsche engine. "These lightweight cars were like toys compared to ours. Ours were a bit more like trams."

If one looks around Herbert Linge's office in his house at Weissach, you will find photographs and models of the 804 as just one amongst many famous racing cars. It is hard to believe that the easy-going man sitting there in front of his desk once drove them all – and that there were not many other drivers that were quicker. Then there is the old employee's card, issued in 1943. It has the number 745 and Linge is registered as "mechanic's apprentice". Amongst all the racing cars, there is a photo among them

Hartgesotten: Unter abenteuerlichen Bedingungen haben die Porsche-Tester im Wald bei Hockenheim ihr Lager aufgeschlagen.

Hard-boiled: The test crew has made themselves comfortable under odd circumstances in the forest at Hockenheim.

Foto: Porsche

Was für ein zierliches Auto: Der 804 bei Testfahrten in Hockenheim 1962. Hinten links steht Herbert Linge.

What a tiny car!: the 804 during trials at Hockenheim in 1962. Behind on the left is Herbert Linge.

Fertig für Frankreich: Die beiden 804, die Gurney (30) und Bonnier (32) in Rouen fahren.

Ready for France: these two 804s will be driven by Gurney (30) and Bonnier (32) at Rouen.

ker-Lehrling nennt. Es zeigt – natürlich – einen Porsche, freilich einen Trecker mit dem magischen Namen. In Weissach ist Linge nach wie vor eine Größe, auch als Porsche-Pensionär. Jahr für Jahr gibt es in der schwäbischen Kleinstadt ein namhaftes Old-timer-Stelldichein, Ausrichter ist der örtliche Club, in dem sich Linge engagiert. „Was in den letzten Jahren unheimlich stark geworden ist, das ist die Schlepper-Fraktion." Zuerst waren es zwei Unentwegte, die mit den eher rustikalen Porsches auftauchten. „Was wollen denn die da mit ihren Schleppern, hat es geheißen." Mittlerweile ist die 15 Köpfe starke Traktorgruppe eine feste Größe und macht Ausfahrten auch gern mal über 300 Kilometer. Linge hat natürlich auch einen, „der ist morgen dabei beim Pferdemarkt in Leonberg." Der Trecker zieht den Planwagen einer Jugendgruppe. „Der sieht aus wie im Wilde Weschte." Schnell ist er nicht, aber er läuft und läuft und läuft. Und das Schönste: „Zackzack" geht es da bestimmt nicht zu.

Linge ist den Nürburgring übrigens zuletzt vor einem Jahr gefahren. In einem modernen 11er und in beeindruckend schneller Zeit. Vor 40 Jahren wäre er praktisch automatisch qualifiziert gewesen. Die Zeit ruft anerkennende Pfiffe hervor. Linge grinst breit und muss das gar nicht – der kleine bullige Schwabe mit seiner auf den ersten Blick so behäbigen Art kann allein mit den Augen kommunizieren. Die blitzen schelmisch, als er ganz bescheiden sagt: „No jo, für mei Alter." Der Mann ist Jahrgang 1928 – der Ring ist nur ein Jahr älter. (jn) ■

that is very different. Of course it shows a Porsche, but a very special one - a tractor. In Weissach, Linge is renowned for his past achievements. Every year a famous old timer meeting is arranged in the small Swabian village and Linge is member of the organisation team. "Over the last few years, the tractor section has become more important." In the beginning, there had been only two devotees who brought their farming Porsches. "To start with, everyone said what the hell do they want with those tractors." Nowadays there are fifteen Porsche tractor owners who are an institution and they make journeys of up to three hundred kilometres and more to be there. Linge of course has his own tractor. "Tomorrow, it will pull the youth group's covered wagon to the horse market at Leonberg. It will look a bit like the Wild West." The rural Porsche is not very fast but it goes on reliably. And the best of it? You will not hear any "Zack", "Zack" as he drives it.

Linge drove for the last time at the Nürburgring about a year ago. He sat at the wheel of an up-to-date 911 and he was impressively fast. Forty years ago with that lap time he would have qualified easily for a Formula One race. At the end of his drive, Linge wore a big grin on his face. Not that he has to smile to communicate what he is thinking. The stocky Swabia with his ostensibly sedate behaviour is quite capable of communicating simply using his eyes. And his eyes at that moment sparkled with roguish humour as he said quite modestly: "Well, perhaps not too bad for a man of my age." Linge was born in 1928 – the 'Ring is just one year older. (jn) ■

Die Fahrer

Die Schnellsten am Steuer der Formel-2- und der
Formel-1-Porsches

Foto: Porsche

**Porsche-Piloten: Dan Gurney
(im Cockpit) und Joakim Bonnier 1962 in Watkins Glen.**

**Porsche drivers: Dan Gurney
(at the wheel) and Jo Bonnier
at Watkins Glen, 1962.**

The Drivers

The Fastest Men behind the Wheels of he Formula-Two
and Formula-One Porsches

Edgar Barth

Edgar Barth wurde am 26. Januar 1917 in Herold im Erzgebirge geboren. Er begann seine Karriere im Motorsport 1934 auf DKW-Motorrädern, da er in Zschopau, damals Heimat des zur Auto Union zählenden DKW-Werkes, seine Ausbildung absolvierte. Schnell wurde er Mitglied der Werksmannschaft für Geländewettbewerbe.

Nach dem Krieg waren die Möglichkeiten motorsportlicher Betätigung in der sowjetisch besetzten Zone und später in der Deutschen Demokratischen Republik sehr begrenzt. Erst die Rennwagen der Marke EMW (Eisenacher Motorenwerke), hergestellt in Eisenach und abgeleitet von den dort vor 1940 produzierten BMW-Sportwagen, ermöglichten es Barth und mit ihm Fahrern wie Arthur Rosenhammer

Edgar Barth.

und Paul Thiel, an internationalen Wettbewerben teilzunehmen. Während diese Mannschaft in der Deutschen Meisterschaft durchaus erfolgreich war, blieb der Start von Edgar Barth beim Grand Prix von Deutschland 1953 ohne zählbares Resultat, er fiel mit einem defekten Auspuff aus. Nach der Auflösung des Rennkollektivs 1956 siedelte Barth in die Bundesrepublik über und bekam einen Porsche-Werksvertrag. Von nun an feierte er bei Langstreckenrennen und vor allem bei den seinerzeit sehr beliebten Bergrennen große Erfolge. 1959, 1963 und 1964 errang er für Porsche den Meistertitel in der Europa-Bergmeisterschaft. 1963 gewann er sechs von sieben Rennen, im Jahr darauf wiederholte er dieses Kunststück. Daneben holte er zahlreiche Klassensiege in den Rennen zur Markenweltmeisterschaft und errang 1959 zusammen mit Wolfgang Seidel gar den Gesamtsieg bei der Targa Florio.

Auch im Formel-Rennsport war Barth erfolgreich. So gewann er auf Porsche 1957 das Formel-2-Rennen beim GP auf dem Nürburgring, im folgenden Jahr wurde er in der Formel-2-Wertung des deutschen Grand Prix Zweiter. Sein letztes Formel-1-Rennen bestritt er 1964 auf einem Cooper für das Team von Rob Walker. Eine defekte Kupplung zwang ihn zur Aufgabe. Zu diesem Zeitpunkt litt er bereits an einem Krebsleiden, dem der sympathische Mann aus dem Erzgebirge, der auf allen Rennpisten der Welt geschätzt wurde, am 20. Mai 1965 erlag. (mb) ■

Edgar Barth

Edgar Barth was born on January 26th 1917 at Herold in the Erz Mountains of Saxony. He started his motor sport career in 1934 riding DKW motorbikes. He had taken up an apprenticeship with the DKW factory in Zschopau, and managed to become a member of their official factory off-road team.

After the Second World War, opportunities to take part in motor sport events in the Soviet sector and later in the German Democratic Republic were rather limited. Nevertheless Barth found a way and entered for his first international competitions with racing cars based on pre-war BMW sports cars and manufactured by EMW (Eisenacher Motorenwerke) at Eisenach in the GDR. Racing at the same time with him in EMWs were drivers like Arthur Rosenhammer and Paul Thiel.

While the team was pretty successful in the German Championship, Barth did not finish in the German Grand Prix of 1953 when he retired with a broken exhaust on his Rennkollektiv EMW Straight-6. In 1956, the racing collective was disbanded and Barth relocated to the Federal Republic of Germany where he got a contract to drive for Porsche. He was very successful in endurance races and also in many of the equally popular hill climbs of that era. In the years 1959, 1963 and 1964, he won the European Hill Climb Championship for Porsche dominating to such an extent that in both the last two of his championship years, he won six out of the seven events. In addition, he collected several class victories in the endurance races that counted for the World Sports Car Championship while in 1959, he and Wolfgang Seidel took the overall victory at the Targa Florio with a 718 RSK.

Barth was also successful in GP racing, winning a Formula Two race in 1957 at the Nürburgring with a Porsche while in 1960 he finished second in the Formula Two division at the German Grand Prix. In his last Formula One race, the German GP in 1964, he drove a Cooper T66 for the Rob Walker team but retired thanks to a broken clutch. At that time, he was already suffering from cancer to which he finally succumbed on May 20th, 1965. (mb) ■

Edgar Barth, Großer Preis von Deutschland 1957.

Edgar Barth, German GP 1957.

Carel de Beaufort

Carel Godin de Beaufort wurde am 10. April 1934 in Maasbergen (Holland) geboren. Als Privatfahrer bestritt der Niederländer zwischen 1957 und 1964 insgesamt 28 Grand-Prix-Rennen, 26 davon auf Porsche. Mit seinen finanziellen Möglichkeiten hätte de Beaufort die Möglichkeit gehabt, in kleineren Rennserien Erfolge zu feiern. Er zog jedoch die große Bühne vor und stellte sich mit seinem betagten Porsche ans Ende der Formel-1-Startaufstellungen. Vier WM-Punkte stehen für einen der letzten Privatfahrer der Formel 1 zu Buche, die auch in den Statistiken die Erinnerung an den sympathischen Holländer wach halten. Auch in Sportwagenrennen war er im Porsche unterwegs und erreichte einige gute Platzierungen, so 1958 mit einem fünften Rang im 24-Stunden-Rennen von Le Mans zusammen mit Herbert Linge auf einem Porsche 550RS.

Carel Godin de Beaufort.

Für seine Rennleidenschaft zahlte er den höchsten Preis, als sein Porsche im Training zum Grand Prix von Deutschland 1964 am Bergwerk von der Strecke abkam. Carel Godin de Beaufort starb am 2. August 1964 an den Folgen der Verletzungen, die er sich bei diesem Unfall zugezogen hatte. (mb) ∎

Carel de Beaufort

Carel Godin de Beaufort was born on April 10th, 1934 at Maarsbergen Castle in the Netherlands. As a privateer he took part in twenty-eight Grand Prix races between 1957 and 1964. As he was a well-off aristocrat, he could have been pretty successful in minor racing divisions. However he preferred the style of the top echelon and repeatedly put his aged Porsche – painted in the national colours of Holland, orange – at or near the back of the Formula One grid. He scored four championship points from twenty-eight starts and is renowned for being one of the last privateers in Formula One. He also gained some good results in sports car races, for example, in the 24-hour race at Le Mans, where he finished fifth in 1958 sharing a Porsche 550RS with Herbert Linge. His passion for Formula One eventually cost him his life when, on August 1st, he crashed his Porsche 718 in practice for the 1964 German Grand Prix at the bend of the Nürburgring called Bergwerk. Two days later he died from the severe injuries that he had incurred. (mb) ∎

Carel de Beaufort, GP von Holland 1960.

Carel Godin de Beaufort, Dutch GP 1960.

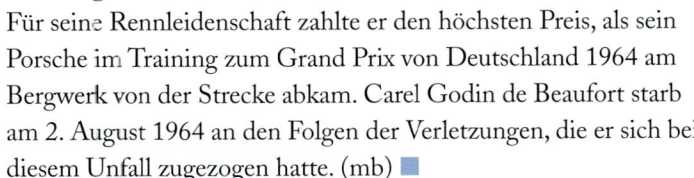

Jean Behra

Jean Behra wurde am 16. Februar 1921 in Nizza geboren und begann seine sportliche Laufbahn, wie viele Rennfahrer seiner Zeit, auf dem Motorrad. Mit einer Moto Guzzi gewann er zwischen 1949 und 1951 jeweils die französische Meisterschaft in der Klasse bis 500 ccm. Nach dem Wechsel zum Automobilsport führte sein Weg rasch in die Formel 1, in der er oftmals mit unterlegenem Material an den Start gehen musste. Seine beste Saison erlebte er 1956, in der er auf einem Maserati 250F einen zweiten und vier dritte Plätze herausfuhr. Rang vier in der Weltmeisterschaft war der verdiente Lohn. 1958 erhielt er einen Vertrag bei dem noch jungen B.R.M.-Team aus England. Sieben Ausfälle in zehn Grand-Prix-Rennen zeigten, dass das Team erst am Anfang stand. Mit einem dritten Rang beim Großen Preis von Deutschland hatte der Franzose aber erneut unter Beweis gestellt, dass er nichts von seinen fahrerischen Qualitäten eingebüßt hatte. 1959 folgte ein Gastspiel bei Ferrari, das nach kurzer Zeit wegen heftiger Differenzen mit Rennleiter Tavoni vorzeitig beendet wurde. Seine Vielseitigkeit stellte der Franzose auch in Sportwagen-Rennen unter Beweis. So gewann er 1956 das 1000-Kilometer-Rennen auf dem Nürburgring und 1957 die „12 Stunden von Sebring". Auch am Steuer von Rennwagen aus dem Hause Porsche feierte er zahlreiche Erfolge und sorgte zudem für Aufsehen durch die Entwicklung seines Behra-Porsche-Formel-2. Diesen Wagen wollte er auch beim deutschen Grand Prix am 1. August 1959 auf der Avus pilotieren. Aber in einem vorhergehenden Rahmenrennen für Sportwagen kam der Franzose in der Avus-Steilkurve ins Schleudern. Sein Porsche prallte gegen einen Betonsockel, Behra wurde aus dem Fahrzeug geschleudert und überlebte den Aufprall auf einen Fahnenmast nicht. (mb) ■

Jean Behra.

Jean Behra

Jean Behra was born on February 16th, 1921 at Nice in France. Like so many other drivers of this era, he began his racing career on motorbikes. From 1949 and 1951 he was French champion in the 500cc class with a Moto Guzzi. He made the change to sports cars in 1952 and that same year entered his first Formula One races in a Gordini Type 16. The Gordini was not the fastest or most reliable car on the grid and in 1955 he moved to the Maserati team. His best season was in 1956 when his Maserati 250F finished second once and third four times placing him fourth in the World Championship. In 1958, he signed on with BRM but the British team was just starting out and he suffered seven retirements in ten Grand Prix races. By finishing third in the German Grand Prix with the unsorted BRM, he showed that he was still a skilled driver. Then in 1959 he joined Ferrari alongside Tony Brooks but, after he retired in the French GP with a broken engine, he had an argument with team manager, Romolo Tavoni, which ended with the Frenchman punching the Italian and promptly being sacked from the team.

Behra had showed his ability in sports car races for in 1956 he had won the 1,000-kilometre race at the Nürburgring and in 1957 the 12-hours of Sebring. He was pretty successful driving Porsches and did some stirring drives with his own Behra-Porsche Formula Two car. He should have driven it just one month after the French GP in the German Grand Prix on August 1st, 1959 at the Avus circuit in Berlin but, unfortunately, he took part in the sports car race that preceded it. In the pouring rain, he lost control of his Porsche RSK on the famous banked Nord Kehre of the Avus and the car went over the top and crashed into a concrete structure. Behra was thrown completely out of the car and against a flagpole. He was killed instantly. (mb) ■

Fotos: Porsche

Jean Behra, Reims 1958.

Jean Behra, Reims 1958.

Joakim Bonnier

Joakim Bonnier wurde am 31. Januar 1931 in Stockholm geboren. Der Sohn eines Universitätsprofessors war der erste Schwede, der in der Formel 1 erfolgreich war. Sein Renndebüt gab er 1953 bei einem Eisrennen, bei dem er jedoch auf dem letzten Platz landete. Auf einem Alfa GT errang Jo Bonnier in der Saison 1956 internationale Erfolge. 1957 stieg er in die Formel-1-Weltmeisterschaft ein und holte ein Jahr später seine ersten WM-Punkte. 1959 fuhr er für das noch junge B.R.M.-Team und sicherte sich beim Großen Preis von Holland seinen ersten und einzigen Grand-Prix-Sieg. 1960 zeigte er sein Können im 1,5 Liter-Formel-2-Porsche, als er in Modena und am Nürburgring gewann. Bei der Targa Florio siegte er zusammen mit Hans Herrmann, ebenfalls auf Porsche. Nach dem Ende seines Formel-1-

Joakim Bonnier.

Engagements für Porsche nahm der Schwede noch bis 1971 an Grand-Prix-Rennen teil, fuhr aber mit den zumeist unterlegenen Wagen nur noch selten in Punkteränge. Erfolge feierte er dagegen weiterhin im Sportwagen. So gewann er 1963 erneut die Targa Florio und die „12 Stunden von Reims 1963" sowie 1966 das 1000-Kilometer-Rennen auf dem Nürburgring. Sein großes Ziel, ein Sieg im 24-Stunden-Rennen von Le Mans, verfolgte er bis 1972. Mit seinem Lola-Cosworth lag er zeitweise auch in Führung, aber das Rennen endete tragisch. Nach einer Kollision mit einem Ferrari wurde Bonniers Lola in die Bäume neben der Strecke geschleudert. Der Schwede starb an diesem 11. Juni 1972 noch am Unfallort. (mb) ■

Joakim Bonnier

Joakim "Jo" Bonnier was born on January 31st, 1931 at Stockholm. Son of a university professor, he was the first Swede to be successful in Formula One racing. His debut on a track was in 1953 at an ice race in which he finished last. In 1956, he gained international success with an Alfa GT. Finally, in 1957 he entered Formula One and took his first finish in a Maserati 250F in Argentina. Towards the end of 1958 he got a drive with BRM and he gained his first and only Grand Prix victory with them in the 1959 Dutch Grand Prix. In 1960 Bonnier drove a 1.5-litre Formula Two Porsche and won at Modena and at the 'Ring. Together with Hans Herrmann he also won the Targa Florio in a Porsche 718 RS60.

When Porsche terminated their Formula One programme, he entered for Grand Prix races right up until 1971 though he only scored few championship points.

In sports car racing he was more successful. In 1963 he won again the Targa Florio plus the 12-hour race at Reims. He finished first in the 1,000-kilometre race at the Nürburgring in 1966 and in 1970 he won the Group 6 category of the European 2-litre Sports Car Championship with a Lola T210.

His dream was a victory at Le Mans after finishing second there in a Ferrari 330P in 1964. In 1972, he was even in the lead at times with his Lola T280 but then collided with a slower Ferrari Daytona. He crashed into a tree and died from his injuries on June 11th. (mb) ■

Joakim Bonnier, GP von Deutschland 1962.

Joakim Bonnier, German GP 1962.

Dan Gurney

Der am 13. April 1931 in Port Jefferson geborene Dan Gurney hat sich nicht nur als Rennfahrer, sondern auch als Hersteller seiner eigenen „Eagle"-Rennwagen einen Namen gemacht. Die Rennkarriere des Kaliforniers begann 1955 auf Triumph und Porsche. Er erzielte bei amerikanischen Veranstaltungen zahlreiche Erfolge, dass der Schritt nach Europa die logische Konsequenz war. 1959 wurde Gurney Werks-Fahrer bei Ferrari und erlangte bei nur vier Grand-Prix-Starts in Frankreich, Deutschland, Portugal und Italien 13 WM-Punkte. 1960 fuhr er für das britische B.R.M.-Team, wo er jedoch eine niederschmetternde Saison erlebte. Erfolge stellten sich dagegen im Sportwagen ein, an der Seite von Stirling Moss gewann Gurney das 1000-Kilometer-Rennen auf dem Nürburgring. 1961 und 1962 startete Gurney für Porsche. Nach einem dritten Rang in der Formel-1-Weltmeisterschaft 1961etablierte sich der Kalifornier mit dem Sieg beim Grand Prix von Frankreich in Rouen 1962 endgültig in der Weltelite. Von 1963 bis 1965 er für Jack Brabham und dessen neu aufgebautes Team, für das er 1964 bei den Großen Preisen von Frankreich und Mexiko die ersten WM-Läufe gewann.

Zusammen mit Carroll Shelby gründete Dan Gurney 1966 das Anglo American Racers-Team. Mit seinem Eagle-Weslake gewann er im März 1967 das „Race of Champions" in Brands Hatch und im Juni den Grand Prix von Belgien in Spa-Francorchamps. Auf einem Ford triumphierte Gurney zusammen mit A.J. Foyt in diesem Jahr auch beim 24-Stunden-Rennen von Le Mans. Parallel nahm er stets auch an Rennen in Amerika teil und erzielte gute Resultate in der Canadian-American-Challenge-Cup und beim 500-Meilen-Rennen von Indianapolis. Nach dem Tod von Bruce McLaren 1970 startete er noch dreimal für dessen Rennteam, beendete dann aber seine Formel-1- Karriere, um sich als Konstrukteur und Manager nur noch seinem eigenen Rennstall zu widmen.

Dan Gurney, der mit der früheren Porsche-Mitarbeiterin Evi Butz verheiratet ist, zählt längst zu den amerikanischen Renn-Legenden. (mb) ■

Dan Gurney.

Dan Gurney

Born on April 13th, 1931 at Port Jefferson in the state of New York, Dan Gurney was renowned as a driver and then later as the constructor of his own Eagle racing cars. His motor sport career began in 1955 driving Triumphs and Porsches. He was sufficiently successful in the USA with these sports cars that a changeover to Europe seemed to be an obvious next step. In 1959 Gurney became a Ferrari works driver and scored thirteen World Championship points in just four GP races in France, Germany, Portugal and Italy. In 1960 he was member of the BRM team but it was a poor season for the British marque. In sports car racing however, he found success winning, for instance, the 1,000-kilometre race at the Nürburgring with Stirling Moss in a Maserati. For the 1961 and 1962 seasons, Gurney drove for Porsche and in his first year of the Formula One championship he finished third. In 1962 he won the French Grand Prix at Rouen. Between 1963 and 1965 he drove for Jack Brabham and his newly established team and it was in 1964 that he won the first two GPs for the team in France and Mexico.

Together with Carroll Shelby, in 1966 he established a Formula One team called Anglo-American Racers with bases in California and England. With his Eagle-Weslake, he won the 1967 Race of Champions at Brands Hatch and the Belgian Grand Prix at Spa-Francorchamps. In the same year, he and A.J. Foyt won the 24-hours race at Le Mans in a Ford GT40 Mk4. In North America, he had some success in the Canadian-American Challenge Cup and in the Indianapolis 500 where Bobby Unser won with an Eagle in 1968. After a poor season in Formula One during 1968 including doing some races in the McLaren team, Gurney's own driving career took a back seat though he did return to substitute temporarily for Bruce McLaren for three races following his friend's death testing at Goodwood in early June of 1970. He subsequently concentrated on working as designer and manager of his own team in the USA. Dan Gurney, who is married to the former Porsche employee Evi Butz, has long ago passed into the status of an American racing legend. (mb) ■

Dan Gurney, Nürburgring 1962.

Dan Gurney, Nürburgring 1962.

Hans Herrmann

Hans Herrmann wurde am 23. Februar 1928 in Stuttgart geboren. Schon 1953 holte der Schwabe Klassensiege bei der Mille Miglia und beim 24-Stunden-Rennen von Le Mans. 1955 hatte er, mittlerweile Werkspilot bei Mercedes-Benz, mehrfach Pech. Bei der Mille Miglia startete er auf einem Mercedes 300 SLR. Er hätte das Rennen quer durch Italien wohl auch gewonnen, wenn nicht ein defekter Tankdeckel die rasante Fahrt vorzeitig beendet hätte. Im Training zum Großen Preis von Monaco kam es noch schlimmer, Herrmann prallte dort mit seinem Mercedes W196 in eine Mauer und wurde schwer verletzt. Der Bruch eines Lenden- und eines Brustwirbels sowie die Knochensplitterung der Hüftgelenkpfanne setzten ihn für Monate außer Gefecht. Nach dem Rückzug von Mercedes wurde Herrmann 1957 Werkspilot bei Borgward,

Hans Herrmann.

aber auch das Bremer Werk beendete 1958 sein motorsportliches Engagement. Gelegentliche Grand-Prix-Starts auf zweitklassigen Formel-1-Rennwagen brachten keine zählbaren Ergebnisse, aber auf der Avus 1959 einen der berühmtesten Unfälle der Geschichte. Die Fotos von diesem Unfall gingen um die ganze Welt und brachten ihm den Spitznamen „Hans im Glück" ein.

Ab 1960 gehörte Herrmann wieder zum Porsche-Werksteam. Mit seinen Triumphen bei den 12-Stunden von Sebring und der Targa Florio 1960 und zahlreichen Klassensiegen wusste er durchaus zu überzeugen, dennoch endete das Porsche-Engagement aufgrund von Differenzen mit Rennleiter Huschke von Hanstein. Von Juli 1962 bis 1965 ging Herrmann für den Turiner Rennstall von Carlo Abarth an den Start und bestritt zahlreiche Berg- und Langstreckenrennen. Zu den größten Erfolgen dieser Jahre zählen seine Siege in den 500-Kilometer-Rennen auf dem Nürburgring 1963 und 1964. Auf Betreiben von Ferdinand Piëch, seinerzeit Versuchsleiter in Zuffenhausen, kehrte Herrmann 1966 zu Porsche und damit auf die Siegerpodien der großen Rennen zurück. So gewann er zusammen mit dem Schweizer Jo Siffert das 24-Stunden-Rennen von Daytona, die 12 Stunden von Sebring, mit Rolf Stommelen das 1000-Kilometer-Rennen von Paris. Er hatte wesentlichen Anteil an der Entwicklung des legendären Porsche 917, den der Stuttgarter nicht nur zur Rennreife, sondern auch zum ersten Sieg beim 24-Stunden-Rennen von Le Mans steuerte. Noch heute führt Herrmann seine eigene Firma und ist gern gesehener Gast bei historischen Motorsport-Veranstaltungen. (mb) ■

Hans Herrmann

Hans Herrmann was born on February 23rd, 1928 at Stuttgart. Already in 1953, he won class victories at the Mille Miglia and the 24-hour race at Le Mans. In 1955, while he was a works driver for Mercedes-Benz, he seemed to attract bad luck. He was entered in the Mille Miglia with a 300 SLR. He should have won the race had not a broken filler cap stopped him. Even worse happened in practice before the Monaco Grand Prix. Herrmann crashed his Mercedes W196 into a wall and was badly hurt. He broke two vertebrae, one a lumbar vertebra and the other thoracic. This plus a splinter fracture in his hip joint put him out of action for months. After Mercedes had stopped racing, Herrmann became a works driver for Borgward but they also retired from motor sport in 1958. Occasionally he obtained drives in Grand Prix races but not only did he not score any significant results but was involved in one of the most remarkable accidents at the Avus circuit in Berlin. The pictures of the event with the car above him in the air went around the world and earned him his nickname "Hans im Glück" (Lucky Hans) after the title of a fairy tale.

In 1960 Herrmann came into the Porsche works team. He was pretty successful and won the twelve-hour race at Sebring as well as the Targa Florio and gained numerous class victories. However differences between him and Porsche's racing director, Huschke von Hanstein, lead to a parting of the ways. Between July 1962 and 1965, Herrmann drove for the Italian team of Carlo Abarth, mainly in hill climbs and endurance races. Among the greatest successes of these years were victories in the 1963 and 1964 500-kilometre races on the Nürburgring. It was at the instigation of Ferdinand Piëch, at that time the director of the research and development department at Zuffenhausen, that Herrmann returned to Porsche in 1966. In the years that followed, he was often on the victory rostrums of the great motor racing events. He drove both 907s that finished first and second at the 24-hour race at Daytona of 1968 and went on to win the 12-hour race at Sebring with Jo Siffert and the Paris 1,000-kilometre race with Rolf Stommelen. He also played an important role in the development of the legendary Porsche 917 which he did not only help making race-ready but drove to victory in the 24-hour race at Le Mans in 1970 with Richard Attwood. Herrmann nowadays still manages his own firm and appears at many historic motor sport events. (mb) ■

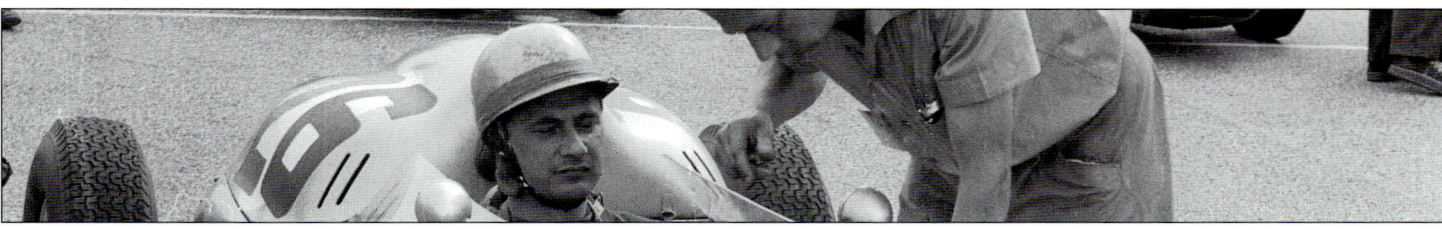

Hans Herrmann, Monza 1960.

Hans Herrmann, Monza 1960.

Graham Hill

Der am 15. Februar 1929 in Hampstead (England) geborene Graham Hill kam erst spät und auf Umwegen zum Rennsport. Nach dem Besuch einer Rennfahrerschule in Brands hatte er nur ein Ziel: Rennfahrer zu werden. Um diesen Ziel näher zu kommen, arbeitete er zunächst in eben dieser Rennfahrerschule als Mechaniker. Im April 1953 startete er bei seinem ersten Formel-3-Rennen aus der ersten Reihe und kam als Vierter ins Ziel. Wenig später bot ihm Colin Chapman einen Job als Mechaniker an. In der Saison 1956 gewann Hill vier Rennen und erhielt 1957 endlich einen Vertrag von Lotus-Chef Chapman, doch es war noch ein weiter Weg bis zu seinen wirklich großen Erfolgen. Immer wieder gab es Schwierigkeiten mit dem Lotus, doch Hill nahm Niederlagen mit dem für ihn typischen Humor hin. 1960 wechselte er zu B.R.M. und errang seine ersten WM-Punkte beim Grand Prix von Holland. In der Saison 1961 dominierten die Ferrari-Rennwagen nicht an, doch 1962 wurde Graham Hill mit dem neuen 1,5-Liter-V8-BRM nach vier Siegen und weiteren guten Platzierungen zum ersten Mal Formel-1-Weltmeister. In den folgenden drei Jahren gewann Hill – ebenfalls auf B.R.M. - jeweils die Vize-Weltmeisterschaft. 1966 siegte er im 500-Meilen-Rennen von Indianapolis und wurde nach seiner Rückkehr zu Lotus 1968 ein zweites Mal F1-Weltmeister. 1969 überlebte der inzwischen 40-jährige Hill einen schweren Unfall in Watkins Glen mit mehrfachen Beinbrüchen. Nach der Genesung setzte er seine Karriere fort und siegte 1972 auf Matra-Simca im 24-Stunden-Rennen von Le Mans. Bis heute ist er der einzige Fahrer, der sowohl die F1-WM als auch die „Indy-500" und die „24-Stunden von Le Mans" gewinnen konnte. Nach Engagements bei Rob Walker und im Brabham-Team gründete Hill Ende 1973 einen eigenen Rennstall. Am 29. November 1975 starb Graham Hill zusammen mit seinem Fahrer Tony Brise und vier weiteren Mitgliedern seines Teams beim Absturz seines Privat-Flugzeuges in der Nähe von London. (mb) ∎

Graham Hill.

Graham Hill

Born on February 15th, 1929 at Hampstead in Great Britain, Graham Hill found his way into racing in a roundabout way. After having visited a drivers' school at Brands he had only one goal, which was to be a racing driver himself. He got a job as a mechanic in racing school and In April 1953 he entered in his first Formula 3 race using one of the school's Cooper 500s and, starting from the first row, he finished fourth. Soon after that he was offered a job as a mechanic with the Lotus team by Colin Chapman and quickly managed to get himself a drive. By 1956, Hill had won four races and finally got a Lotus driving contract. But there was still a long way to go. Again and again he had troubles with the Lotus racing cars but he took the defeats in good humour. In 1960, he changed over to BRM and scored his first World Championship points at the Dutch Grand Prix.

In 1962 he became Formula One World Champion for BRM after four outright victories. In the following three years, he was runner-up in the championship, still with BRM. In 1966 driving a Lola T90, he won the Indianapolis 500 and in 1968, after having returned to Lotus, became World Champion for the second time. In 1969 at the age of forty, Hill survived a severe accident at Watkins Glen but suffered multiple leg fractures. After recovering, he returned to GP racing with Rob Walker in a Lotus for 1970 and then drove for Brabham in 1971 and 1972. Also in 1972 he won the 24-hours race at Le Mans in a Matra-Simca. To this day, he is the only driver to have won the Formula One Championship as well as the Indy 500 and Le Mans. Hill established his own Embassy-Hill team for the 1973 season with first Shadow and then Lola chassis.

On November 21st 1975, he and five of his team members died when his airplane crashed just north of London in foggy conditions. (mb) ∎

Foto: Porsche

Graham Hill, Solitude 1960.

Graham Hill, Solitude 1960.

Umberto Maglioli

Umberto Maglioli wurde am 5. Juni 1928 im norditalienischen Bioglio geboren. Er begann seine Motorsportkarriere bei Lancia und feierte schon zu Beginn seiner Laufbahn die größten Erfolge im Sportwagen. Einem zweiten Rang bei der Mille Miglia 1951 folgte 1953 ein Sieg bei der Targa Florio und 1954 der bei der Carrera Panamericana. Zwischen 1953 und 1957 bestritt der Italiener zehn Formel-1-Rennen ohne nachhaltigen Erfolg. Zwei dritte Plätze erreichte er insgesamt, allerdings jeweils zusammen mit anderen Fahrern, weil zu dieser Zeit die Übergabe eines Rennwagens an Teamgefährten noch möglich war.

Bei Sportwagenrennen, besonders bei jenen zur Markenweltmeisterschaft, triumphierte er aber weiterhin. Dort blieb er eine feste Größe und stand immer wieder bei Ferrari, Ford und Porsche unter Vertrag. 1956 und 1968 gewann er für Porsche erneut die Targa Florio, 1964 zudem auf Ferrari die „12 Stunden von Sebring". In Le Mans hatte er dagegen häufig Pech, der dritte Rang im Rennen 1963, erzielt auf Ferrari an der Seite von Mike Parkes, blieb sein bestes Ergebnis. Am Ende der Saison 1968 zog sich der sympathische Italiener vom Motorsport zurück. Umberto Maglioli starb am 6. Februar 1999 in Monza. (mb) ■

Umberto Maglioli.

Umberto Maglioli

Umberto Maglioli was born on June 5th, 1928 in Bioglio in northern Italy. His motor sport career started with Lancia and, already in the beginning, he was most successful in sports car races. A second place in the 1951 Mille Miglia was followed by a victory in the 1953 Targa Florio and another one in the 1954 Carrera Panamericana. Between 1953 and 1957, he entered ten Formula One races mainly with Ferrari and Maserati but was not very successful. Twice he finished third but had to split the points as at that time it was still possible to share a car with teammates.

However he was a very good sports car driver and gained several victories driving Ferraris, Fords and Porsches. For Porsche he won the Targa Florio in 1956 and in 1968, for Ferrari the 1964 12-hour race at Sebring. At Le Mans he was often unlucky so that finishing third in the 1963 race with a Ferrari 250P shared with co-driver Mike Parkes was his best result at the Sarthe.

At the end of the 1968 season the likeable Italian retired from racing. Umberto Maglioli died on February 6th, 1999 at Monza. (mb) ■

Umberto Maglioli, GP von Deutschland 1957.

Umberto Maglioli, German GP 1957.

Foto: Porsche

Gerhard Mitter

Gerhard Mitter wurde am 30. August 1935 in Krásná Lípa/Schönlinde in der Tschechoslowakei geboren. Nach dem Krieg wuchs er in Leonberg auf und absolvierte im elterlichen Betrieb eine Lehre zum Kfz-Mechaniker. Ab 1953 nahm er mit einer 125er NSU an Straßenrennen teil und wurde 1954 Deutscher Vizemeister, 1955 gewann er die Deutsche Junioren-Meisterschaft. 1959 konstruierte er seinen ersten Rennwagen, einen Formel Junior, mit dem er im selben Jahr mehrere Siege errang. 1960 wurde Mitter Deutscher Meister in der Formel Junior und gab 1962 sein Formel-1-Debüt. In diesem Jahr ging Mitter für das Team des Holländers Carel Godin de Beaufort mit einem Porsche 718/2 beim Grand Prix der Niederlande, beim Großen Preis der Solitude und beim GP von Deutschland an den Start. Auf dem Nürburgring belegte er mit dem betagten Formel-1-Porsche einen sensationellen vierten Platz.

Gerhard Mitter.

Ab 1965 zählte Mitter zur Porsche-Werksmannschaft für die Langstrecken-WM und für die Berg-Europameisterschaft. 1966, 1967 und 1968 gewann er die Berg-Europameisterschaft und triumphierte 1969 zusammen mit Udo Schütz auf einem Porsche 908 Spyder bei der Targa Florio.

Neben seinem Porsche-Engagement strebte Mitter immer sein großes Ziel an, den Platz in einem Formel-1-Team. So ging er 1969 auf einem BMW auch in der Formel 2 an den Start. Für den Großen Preis von Deutschland, der 1969 auf dem Nürburgring ausgetragen wurde, hatte BMW drei F-2-Werkswagen gemeldet. Am 1. August 1969 verunglückte Gerhard Mitter im Training zu diesem Rennen tödlich. Im Streckenabschnitt „Schwedenkreuz" war sein BMW nach einem technischen Defekt von der Strecke abgekommen. (mb) ■

Gerhard Mitter

Gerhard Mitter was born on August 30th, 1935 in Krásná Lípa in Czecho-slovakia, then known as Schönlinde. After the Second World War, his family were forced to move and settled in Leonberg in West Germany where the young Mitter was an apprentice mechanic in his father's business. Beginning in 1953, he raced a 125 cc NSU motorbike on circuits and was runner-up in the German championship of 1954 going on to be Junior Champion the following year. In 1959 he built his own racing car for Formula Junior with which he gained several victories in that same year. By 1960, Mitter had become German Formula Junior Champion and in 1963 he won the Formula Junior Eifelrennen at the 'Ring as well as taking his first steps in Formula One when he drove Godin de Beaufort's second 718/2 at the Dutch, the Solitude and the German Grands Prix. At the latter race on the Nürburgring, he finished fourth in his aged four-cylinder Porsche thus creating quite a sensation.

From 1965 Mitter was a member of the Porsche works team and took part in events of the World Sports Car Championship and the European Hill Climb Championship. He was Hill Climb Champion from 1966 until 1968 and won the Targa Florio in 1969 together with Udo Schütz in a Porsche 908.

Despite his involvement with Porsche, Mitter never lost sight of his aim to succeed with a Formula One team. He drove the German GP twice for Team Lotus, in 1964 and 1965, while in 1969 he drove a BMW 269 in Formula Two races. For the 1969 German Grand Prix, held at the Nürburgring, BMW entered three Formula Two works cars. In practice on August 1st, Mitter's car went off the track at Schwedenkreuz due to mechanical failure and he died from his injuries. (mb) ■

Gerhard Mitter, GP von Deutschland 1963.

Gerhard Mitter, German GP 1963.

Stirling Moss

Der am 17. September 1929 in West Kensington/London (England) geborene Stirling Moss zählt zu den herausragenden Fahrer-Persönlichkeiten des letzten Jahrhunderts. Er begann seine Karriere 1948 und bestritt 1951 auf einem HMW bereits sein erstes Formel-1-Rennen. Die große Chance kam, als ihn Alfred Neubauer 1955 ins Mercedes-Werks-Team holte. Der athletisch gebaute Engländer schrieb Renngeschichte. Vor Fangio gewann er den britischen Grand Prix, bei der Mille Miglia siegte er auf einem Mercedes-Benz 300 SLR. 1958 winkte der Weltmeistertitel, doch Mike Hawthorn auf Ferrari hatte mit einem Punkt Vorsprung die Nase vorn. In seiner gesamten Formel-1-Karriere sorgte Moss immer wieder für positive Schlagzeilen. Es ist fast unmöglich, alle Erfolge seiner Karriere aufzuzählen, in der er auch Tourenwagenrennen und Rallyes bestritt. Bis 1962 fuhr er insgesamt 466 Rennen, von denen er 194 gewinnen konnte. Er gewann 16 Formel-1-Grand-Prix, wurde jedoch Weltmeister. Bei zahlreichen Langstreckenrennen bewies Moss seine absolute Weltklasse, so gewann er allein vier Mal die „1000 Kilometer" auf dem Nürburgring. Immer wieder triumphierte Moss mit unterlegenem Material, so auch in der Saison 1961. Ferrari hatte mit dem Dino 156 das stärkere Auto, doch der Engländer konnte mit seinen fahrerischen Qualitäten die schnellen Ferrari-Piloten Richie Ginther, Phil Hill und Graf Berghe von Trips auf den fahrerisch anspruchsvollen Kursen in Monaco und am Nürburgring auf die Plätze verweisen. Mehrfach kehrte Moss nach Unfällen auf die Rennpisten zurück, aber sein schwerer Sturz Osterrennen in Goodwood 1962 beendet seien Karriere. Nach dem Ausheilen seiner schweren Verletzungen unternahm der Engländer noch einmal Testfahrten, erklärte dann aber im Alter von 34 Jahren seine Karriere für beendet. Stirling Moss verlor jedoch nie den Kontakt zum Rennsport. Er begann Oldtimer-Rennen zu fahren und ist noch heute einer der besten Botschafter des Motorsports in aller Welt. (mb) ∎

Stirling Moss.

Stirling Moss

One of the most remarkable drivers of the Twentieth Century was Stirling Moss. Born on September 17th at West Kensington, London, Moss started his racing career in 1948 and soon made a name for himself with a Cooper 500 F3. He first drove in Formula One in 1951 in an HWM and then a variety of other cars between 1952 and 1954. His break came when he was invited by Alfred Neubauer to join the Mercedes works team in 1955. The athletic Briton wrote racing history when he won the British Grand Prix ahead of Juan-Manuel Fangio while his victory at the Mille Miglia in a Mercedes-Benz 300 SLR has become the stuff of legend. In 1958 when he was driving for Vanwall, the World Champion's title was in reach but Ferrari driver, Mike Hawthorn, finally took it by one point. It is nearly impossible to count Moss' successes in motor sport since he tried his hand at many disciplines, including touring cars and rallying. Up until 1962, he had entered 466 races of which he had won 194. Though he won sixteen Formula One Grands Prix he never became World Champion.

As an endurance driver he was also world-class. He won the 1,000-kilometre race at the Nürburgring four times. His outstanding characteristic was that he frequently gained victories with inferior cars as for example in 1961 in the Lotus 18. Though Ferrari had built a more powerful car, Moss, thanks to his driver's skills, was faster than Richie Ginther, Phil Hill and Wolfgang Graf Berghe von Trips on the demanding tracks at Monaco and the 'Ring. He was involved in several accidents but each time returned on the track. But finally, a bad accident in the Easter race at Goodwood in 1962 ended his career. Though he recovered from his severe injuries, a test session convinced him that he should abandon his racing career at the age of just thirty-four. Stirling Moss never lost contact with motor sport and in the 1980s he began to enter classic races and rallies and is still one of the most popular ambassadors for motor sport in the world today. (mb) ∎

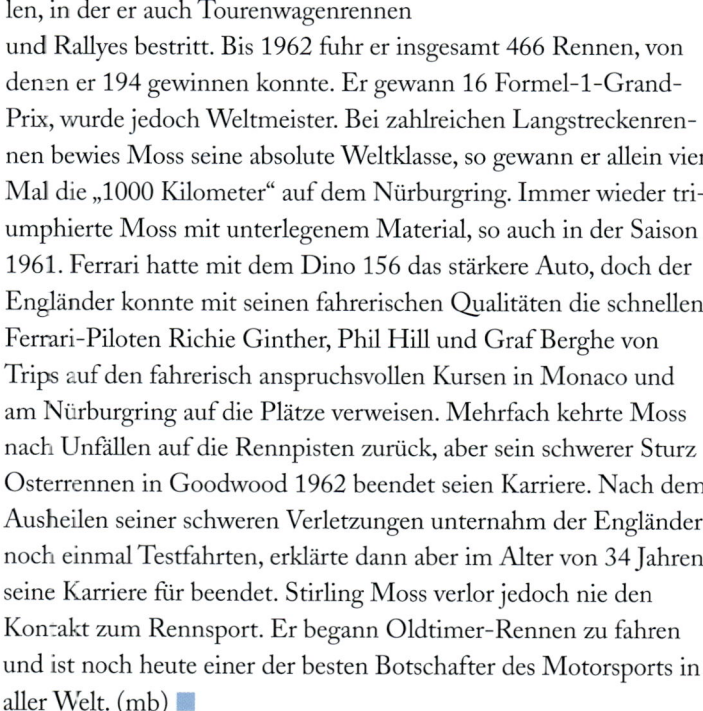

Foto: Porsche

Stirling Moss, Aintree 1960.

Stirling Moss, Aintree 1960.

John Surtees

John Surtees, geboren am 11. Februar 1934 in Tatsfield (England), gelang als bisher einzigem Fahrer das Bravourstück, auf zwei und auf vier Rädern Weltmeister zu werden. Im Alter von 17 Jahren startete er 1951 zum ersten Mal bei einem Grasbahnrennen. 1953 holte er bei 40 Motorradrennen 27 Siege und schlug 1955 mit einer Werks-Norton den Größten von damals, Geoff Duke. Auf MV-Agusta holte Surtees sieben Weltmeisterschaftstitel. 1960 fuhr er neben Motorradrennen bereits einem Lotus-Formel-1-Rennwagen, der ihm von Colin Chapman zur Verfügung gestellt wurde. Der „Neuling" John Surtees belegte hinter Jack Brabham den zweiten Platz beim Großen Preis von England in Silverstone. 1961 fuhr er einen Cooper-Climax für das Yeoman-Credit-Team, 1962 pilotierte Surtees einen Lola. Zwischen 1963 bis 1966 stand er bei Enzo Ferrari unter Vertrag. Dem Sieg beim Großen Preis von Deutschland 1963 folgte ein Jahr später der Gewinn der Formel-1-Weltmeisterschaft. Auch im Sportwagen feierte der Engländer Erfolge, so siegte er 1963 und 1965 beim 1000-Kilometer-Rennen auf dem Nürburgring und holte 1966 den Titel in der CanAm-Serie. 1966 gewann er für die Scuderia noch den Grand Prix von Belgien, aber dann endete sein Engagement bei Ferrari abrupt nach einem Streit mit dem damaligen Rennleiter Eugenio Dragoni. Surtees fuhr den Rest der Saison für Cooper, gewann noch den Großen Preis von Mexiko und stand ab 1967 bei Honda unter Vertrag. Für die Japaner holte er deren einzigen Grand-Prix-Sieg, der zugleich Surtees' letzter war. Mit einer Eigenkonstruktion debütierte er 1970 beim britischen Grand Prix und beendete seine aktive Karriere 1972 mit Formel-2-Siegen in Japan und Imola. Bis 1978 koordinierte er die Einsätze seines eigenen Rennstalles und war in den vergangenen Jahren gern gesehener Gast bei zahlreichen historischen Automobilveranstaltungen. (mb) ■

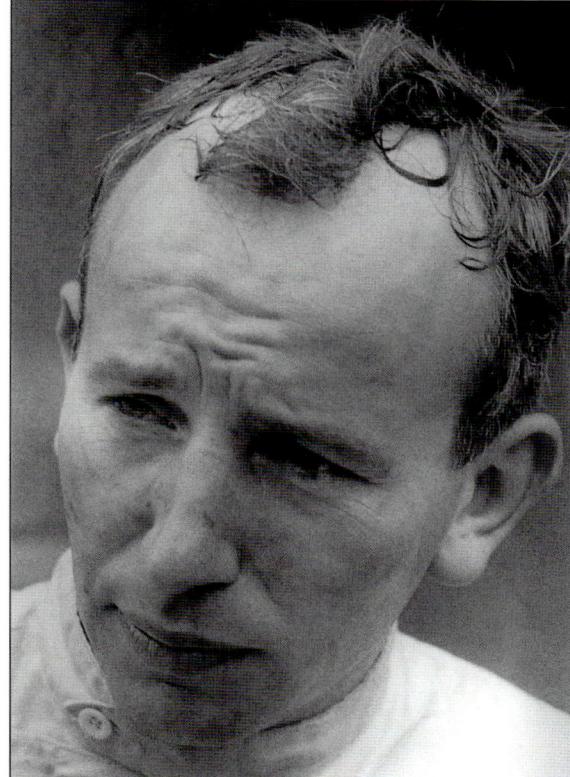

John Surtees.

John Surtees

John Surtees is the only driver to have gained the World Champion's title on two wheels as well as on four. He was born on February 11th 1934 at Tatsfield in England. At the age of seventeen in 1951 he entered his first grass track race. In 1953 he won twenty-seven of forty motorcycle races and even beat the greatest rider of his time, Geoff Duke, who was on a works Norton. Seven times he won the World Championship while riding for MV Agusta. In 1960, while still racing motorcycles, he was invited by Colin Chapman to drive a Lotus Formula One car. The "rookie" Surtees finished second behind Jack Brabham in the British Grand Prix at Silverstone. In 1961 he drove a Cooper Climax for the Yeoman Credit team and in 1962 a Lola. From 1963 until 1966 he was a works driver for Ferrari and after winning the German Grand Prix in 1963 he became World Champion in 1964.

He was also successful in sports car races. In 1963 and 1965, he won the 1,000 kilometre race at the Nürburgring for Ferrari while in 1966, driving a Lola T70, he won the Can Am series. In Formula One, his contract with Ferrari ended following his victory in the 1966 Belgian GP after a quarrel with racing director, Eugenio Dragoni. Surtees promptly got a drive with Cooper in which he won the Mexican GP. In 1967, he signed a contract with Honda and gave the Honda RA300 its only Grand Prix victory at the Italian GP of that year. It was to be his last win. For the 1970 season, he ran his own team and drove the TS7 on its debut at the British GP. He finished his career behind the wheel in 1972, winning the F2 race at Imola in a Surtees TS-10, and until 1978 he managed his own team and since then has been a welcome guest at classic motorsport events. (mb) ■

John Surtees, Tests auf dem Nürburgring 1960.

John Surtees, test session at the Nürburgring 1960.

Foto: Porsche

Wolfgang Graf Berghe von Trips

Wolfgang von Trips wurde am 4. Mai 1928 in Köln geboren. Nach ersten Rennerfahrungen auf dem Motorrad stieg er 1954 auf vier Räder um und startete Anfang Mai bei der Mille Miglia, bei der er sich zusammen mit Hampel den Klassensieg sicherte. Danach startete er für Mercedes bei Sportwagenrennen, nahm an Formel-2-Läufen und an Bergrennen teil. 1956 wurde er als erster deutscher Rennfahrer in den Ferrari-Rennstall aufgenommen. Neben Formel-1-WM-Läufen bestritt Trips in den folgenden Jahren für Ferrari zahlreiche GT-, Sportwagen- und Langstreckenrennen. Die Mille Miglia 1957 beendete er auf dem zweiten Platz. Beim 1000-Kilometer-Rennen auf dem Nürburgring verunglückte er mit einem Ferrari 250 GT LWB, die Verletzungen setzten ihn für Monate außer Gefecht.

Wolfgang Graf Berghe von Trips.

1958 startete Trips mit einem Porsche bei der Berg-Europameisterschaft und gewann dieses Championat. Auf der Erfolgsliste des Grafen standen weiterhin Siege bei den „12 Stunden in Sebring" zusammen mit Joakim Bonnier, im Formel-Junior-Lauf auf dem Nürburgring, beim Großen Preis von Berlin, beim Grand Prix von Syrakus und bei den Formel-2-Läufen auf der Solitude und in Monza. In der Fahrer-Weltmeisterschaft 1960 wurde er Sechster. 1961 errang er die wichtigsten Erfolge seiner Karriere. Graf Trips siegte in Zandvoort beim GP von Holland und stellte im englischen Aintree seine fahrerischen Qualitäten bei Regen unter Beweis: Mit rund 45 Sekunden Vorsprung gewann er seinen zweiten Grand Prix und führte in der WM mit 27 Punkten. Auch bei den Läufen zur Sportwagen-Weltmeisterschaft unterstrich Trips seine Klasse: zweiter Platz in Sebring, Sieger der Targa Florio, dritter Platz beim 1000-Kilometer-Rennen auf dem Nürburgring.

Nach dem Großen Preis von Europa und Deutschland auf dem Nürburgring, Trips wurde Zweiter hinter Stirling Moss, lag der Deutsche klar auf Titelkurs – nur noch ein Punkt trennte ihn vom Weltmeistertitel. Am 10. September 1961 kollidierte Graf Trips in der zweiten Runde des Großen Preises von Italien mit dem Schotten Jim Clark. Der Ferrari von Trips überschlug sich mehrfach und schleuderte den Fahrer heraus. Trips war sofort tot, mit ihm starben 15 Zuschauer. Das Rennen in Monza gewann der Amerikaner Phil Hill, der dadurch auch Weltmeister 1961 wurde. (mb) ∎

Wolfgang Graf Berghe von Trips

Wolfgang Graf Berghe von Trips was born on May 4th 1928, at Cologne. After gaining some initial experiences in motorbike races, he switched to four wheels in 1954. In May of that year, he entered the Mille Miglia with a Porsche 356 1300 and finished second in class. Then he entered sports car races for Mercedes, as well as Formula Two races and hill climbs in various cars. In 1959, he became the first German to drive for the Ferrari team. In cars from Maranello, he entered Formula One, sports car and endurance races. In May 1957, he finished second overall in the Mille Miglia driving a Ferrari 315 Sport but later that month suffered severe injuries as the result of an accident in a Ferrari 250 GT LWB on the Nürburgring and was put out of action for months.

In 1958, von Trips was back behind the wheel for Ferrari driving six Formula One races in the Dino 246 with a best result of third at the French GP. He drove a Porsche in the European Hill Climb Championship and won the title. Then there were victories in a Formula Junior heat at the Nürburgring, in the Berlin Grand Prix, the Syracuse Grand Prix and the Formula Two races at Solitude and Monza. With Ferrari he finished seventh in the 1960 World Drivers Championship and in 1961 he was going even better. First he won the Dutch Grand Prix at Zandvoort while at the British GP at Aintree he demonstrated his talent in the rain, finished first with a forty-five second lead. He thus put himself at the head of the title race with twenty-seven championship points. At the same time, he was also making his mark with Ferraris in the World Sports Car Championship finishing second at Sebring, winning the Targa Florio and taking third place in the 1000-kilometre race at the Nürburgring.

The situation after the German GP at the Nürburgring where he finished second behind Moss was that he only needed to finish third or higher at the Italian GP to clinch the title. On September 10th during the second lap at Monza, von Trips touched wheels with Jim Clark's Lotus. The Ferrari spun several times, hit the guardrail and cannoned back into the Lotus. The impact shot the Ferrari over the rail and into the crowd. Trips and fifteen spectators were killed. He still finished second in that year's championship and was posthumously named German Sportsman of the Year for 1961. (mb) ∎

Foto: Porsche

Wolfgang von Trips, Monaco 1959.

Wolfgang von Trips, Monaco 1959.

Heini Walter

Heini Walter wurde am 28. Juli 1927 in Alpthal in der Schweiz geboren. Nach seiner Ausbildung zum Kfz-Mechaniker nahm er von 1947 bis 1952 sporadisch an Bergrennen teil. Das Jahr 1955 brachte erste Erfolge, aber auch die größte Enttäuschung seiner Karriere. Walter kaufte sich einen 1100er Porsche und gewann damit fast alle Läufe zur Schweizer Meisterschaft. Kurz vor Ende der Saison wurde das Fahrzeug durch die Rennleitung des Kandersteg-Rennens überprüft und dabei ein Hubraum von 1300 ccm festgestellt. Alle Saisonsiege und der Titel waren verloren.

Erst 1957 ging es aufwärts. Walter kaufte sich einen Porsche 550, wurde damit erstmals Schweizer Sportwagenmeister und verteidigte diesen Titel bis 1961 erfolgreich. Auf einem Porsche RSK holte er sich 1959 auch den Titel des Internationalen Deutschen Rennsportmeisters und gewann 1960 und 1961 die Europa-Bergmeisterschaft. 1964 wiederholte er diesen Triumph auf einem Porsche 904 GTS in der Klasse der GT-Fahrzeuge.

Das Highlight seiner sportlichen Laufbahn aber kam 1962. Walter: „Die Teilnahme beim Großen Preis von Deutschland 1962 auf dem Nürburgring mit dem Porsche 718 F1, gemeldet von der Scuderia Filipinetti, war sicher einer der Höhepunkte meiner Karriere." Der Schweizer qualifizierte sich für die vierte Startreihe und kam bei sehr schlechten Witterungsbedingungen auf Rang 14 ins Ziel. Seine letzte Saison absolvierte er 1967 auf einem Porsche 910. Danach widmete er sich dem elterlichen Betrieb. Heini Walter starb am 12. Mai 2009. (mb) ∎

Heini Walter.

Heini Walter

Heini Walter was born on July 28th 1927 at Alphtal in Switzerland. After an apprenticeship as a mechanic in the Hess Company in Basel, he started work in his parent's garage. He occasionally entered for hill climbs between 1947 and 1952 but it was in 1955 that he gained his first successes – and the biggest disappointment of his career. Walter had bought himself a Porsche 1100 and had won nearly all the races in the Swiss hill-climb championship. Then, just before the end of the season, the officials at the Kandersteg meeting had his car scrutineered. It turned out that the engine had a displacement of 1,300 cc. His season's victories were denied and the title was lost. It was not before 1957 that Walter's career was resurrected. He bought a Porsche 550, became Swiss Sportscar champion and kept the title until 1961. With a Porsche RSK, he won the title of German International Racing Champion in 1959 ahead of drivers like Bonnier and von Trips and was second in the European Hill-climb Championship. In 1960 and in 1961 he won that championship outright and was later to win it again in 1964 with a Porsche 904 GTS. Then came 1962 when he was able to state that: „Driving in the German GP on the Nürburgring in a Porsche 718 Formula One, entered by Scuderia Filipinetti, was surely the peak of my career." He qualified on the fourth row of the grid and finished fourteenth in extremely bad weather. After his last season, in 1967 with a Porsche 910, he retired from racing and, following the death of his father in 1968, concentrated on running the family business. Heini Walter died on May 12th, 2009. (mb) ∎

Heini Walter, Fahrerlager am Nürburgring 1962.

Heini Walter, Nürburgring paddock, 1963.

Statistik

Die Rennen von 1957 bis 1964

Foto: Porsche

Start zum Solitude-Rennen 1962: Dan Gurney siegt vor seinem Teamkollegen Joakim Bonnier.

Statistics

The Races from 1957 to 1964

Start of the 1962 Solitude race where Dan Gurney took victory ahead of his team-mate, Jo Bonnier.

1957

Datum	Wettbewerb	Veranstaltung /Ort	Fahrer	Nr.	Bewerber	Typ	Training	Ergebnis	Bemerkungen
28. April	Formel 1 und Formel 2	Grand Prix von Neapel/ Posillipo	Umberto Maglioli	21	Umberto Maglioli	1500 RS	8.	8.	Zweiter der Formel-2-Wertung
14. Juli	Formel 2	Coupe International de Vitesse/Reims	Christian Goethals	50	Christian Goethals	550 RS	k. A.	5.	
4. August	Formel-1-WM	Großer Preis von Deutschland/Nürburgring	Umberto Maglioli Edgar Barth Carel Godin de Beaufort	20 21 27	Dr. Ing. hc F. Porsche KG Dr. Ing. hc F. Porsche KG Ecurie Maarsbergen	550 RS 550 RS 550 RS	15. 12. 20.	Ausfall 12. 14.	Motor Sieger der Formel-2-Wertung Dritter der Formel-2-Wertung

Auf dem Ring: Edgar Barth auf Porsche 550.

At the Ring: Edgar Barth in the Porsche 550.

Date	Competition	Race	Driver	No.	Entrant	Type	Qualification	Result	Remarks
April 28	Formula 1 and Formula 2	Grand Prix of Naples/ Posillipo	Umberto Maglioli	21	Umberto Maglioli	1500 RS	8th	8th	2nd in Formula-2 category
July 14	Formula 2	Coupe International de Vitesse/Reims	Christian Goethals	50	Christian Goethals	550 RS	–	5th	
August 4	Formula-1-World-Championship	German Grand Prix/ Nürburgring	Umberto Maglioli Edgar Barth Carel Godin de Beaufort	20 21 27	Dr. Ing. hc F. Porsche KG Dr. Ing. hc F. Porsche KG Ecurie Maarsbergen	550 RS 550 RS 550 RS	15th 12th 20th	did not finish 12th 14th	engine winner Formula-2 category 3rd in Formula-2 category

1958

Datum	Wettbewerb	Veranstaltung /Ort	Fahrer	Nr.	Bewerber	Typ	Training	Ergebnis	Bemerkungen
7. April	Formel 2	Grand Prix von Pau/Pau	Heinz Schiller	4	Heinz Schiller	1500 RS	8.	6.	
			Auguste Veuillet	8	Auguste Veuillet	1500 RS	7.	5.	
25. Mai	Formel-1-WM	Grand Prix von Holland/Zandvoort	Carel Godin de Beaufort	18	Ecurie Maarsbergen	RSK	17.	11.	
6. Juli	Formel 2	Coupe International de Vitesse/Reims	Jean Behra	14	Dr. Ing. hc F. Porsche KG	RSK	1.	1.	
			Anton von Dory	42	Anton von Dory	1500 RS	21.	12.	
27. Juli	Formel 2	Trophee D'Auvergne/Charade	Claude Storez	23	Auguste Veuillet	1500 RS	k. A.	5.	
			Robert Buchet	24	Auguste Veuillet	550 RS	k. A.		nicht gewertet
3. August	Formel-1-WM mit Formel-2-Wertung	Großer Preis von Deutschland/Nürburgring	Carel Godin de Beaufort	18	Ecurie Maarsbergen	RSK	15.	Ausfall	Motor; als Ersatzfahrer war Stuart Lewis-Evans gemeldet, kam aber nicht zum Einsatz
			Edgar Barth	21	Dr. Ing. hc F. Porsche KG	550 RS	13.	6.	Zweiter Formel-2-Wertung; als Ersatzfahrer war Stuart Lewis-Evans gemeldet, kam aber nicht zum Einsatz
21. September	Sportwagen und Formel 2	Großer Preis von Berlin/Avus	Masten Gregory	9	Dr. Ing. hc F. Porsche KG	RSK	k. A.	3.	Sieger Formel-2-Wertung
			Christian Heinz	26	Christian Heinz	1500 RS	k. A.	Ausfall	gemeldet in der Sportwagenklasse bis 2000 ccm
			Jean Behra	34	Dr. Ing. hc F. Porsche KG	RSK	k. A.	1.	startete in der Sportwagenklasse bis 1500 ccm
			Edgar Barth	35	Dr. Ing. hc F. Porsche KG	RSK	k. A.	4.	startete in der Sportwagenklasse bis 1500 ccm
			Carel Godin de Beaufort	39	Ecurie Maarsbergen	RSK	k. A.	disqualifiziert	startete in der Sportwagenklasse bis 2000 ccm
19. Oktober	Formel 1	Grand Prix von Marokko/Casablanca	Jean Kerguen	46	Jean Kerguen	550 RS			gemeldet, aber nicht am Rennen teilgenommen

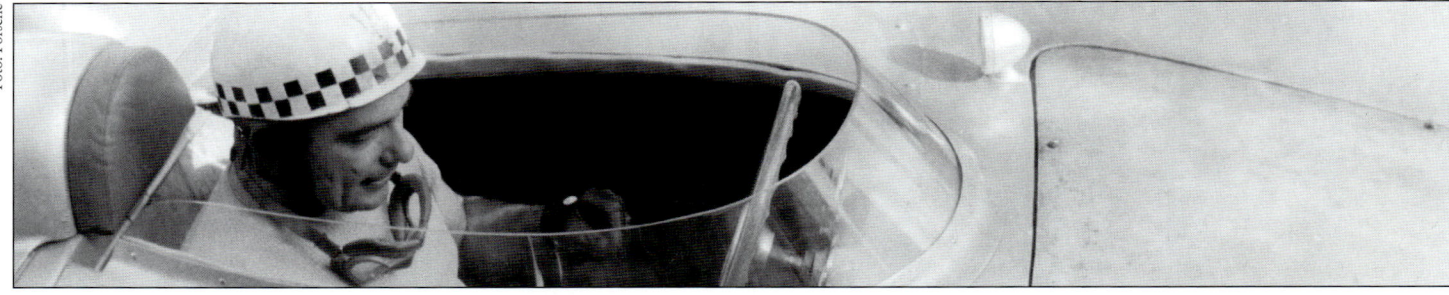

Jean Behra, Reims 1958.

Jean Behra, Reims 1958.

Date	Competition	Race	Driver	No.	Entrant	Type	Qualification	Result	Remarks
April 7	Formula 2	Pau Grand Prix/Pau	Heinz Schiller	4	Heinz Schiller	1500 RS	8th	6th	
			Auguste Veuillet	8	Auguste Veuillet	1500 RS	7th	5th	
May 25	Formula-1 WC	Dutch Grand Prix/Zandvoort	Carel Godin de Beaufort	18	Ecurie Maarsbergen	RSK	17th	11th	
July 6	Formula 2	Coupe International de Vitesse/Reims	Jean Behra	14	Dr. Ing. hc F. Porsche KG	RSK	1st	1st	
			Anton von Dory	42	Anton von Dory	1500 RS	21th	12th	
July 27	Formula 2	Trophee D'Auvergne/Charade	Claude Storez	23	Auguste Veuillet	1500 RS	–	5th	
			Robert Buchet	24	Auguste Veuillet	550 RS	–		not scored
August 3	Formula-1 WC plus Formula-2 category	German Grand Prix/Nürburgring	Carel Godin de Beaufort	18	Ecurie Maarsbergen	RSK	15th	retired	engine; substitute driver was Stuart Lewis-Evans, but he did not drive
			Edgar Barth	21	Dr. Ing. hc F. Porsche KG	550 RS	13th	6th	second Formula-2 category substitute driver was Stuart Lewis-Evans, but he did not drive
September 21	sports cars and Formula 2	Großer Preis von Berlin/Avus	Masten Gregory	9	Dr. Ing. hc F. Porsche KG	RSK	–	3rd	1st Formula-2 category
			Christian Heinz	26	Christian Heinz	1500 RS	–	retired	entered for sports-car category up to 2000 cc
			Jean Behra	34	Dr. Ing. hc F. Porsche KG	RSK	–	1st	started sports-car category up to 1500 cc
			Edgar Barth	35	Dr. Ing. hc F. Porsche KG	RSK	–	4th	started sports-car category up to 1500 cc
			Carel Godin de Beaufort	39	Ecurie Maarsbergen	RSK	–	disqualified	started sports-car category up to 2000 cc
October 19	Formula 1	Morocco Grand Prix/Casablanca	Jean Kerguen	46	Jean Kerguen	550 RS			entered, but did not participate

1959

Datum	Wettbewerb	Veranstaltung /Ort	Fahrer	Nr.	Bewerber	Typ	Training	Ergebnis	Bemerkungen
25. April	Formel 2	Grand Prix von Syrakus/Syrakus	Wolfgang Seidel	22	Wolfgang Seidel	RSK	15.		wegen technischer Probleme nicht gestartet
			Christian Heinz	24	Christian Heinz	RSK	7.	6.	
10. Mai	Formel-1-WM	Grand Prix von Monaco/ Monte Carlo	Wolfgang Seidel	2	Dr. Ing. hc F. Porsche KG	RSK			gemeldet, aber nicht am Rennen teilgenommen
			Marie-Therese de Filippis	4	Dr. Ing. hc F. Porsche KG	Behra-Porsche			nicht qualifiziert
			Wolfgang Graf Berghe von Trips	6	Dr. Ing. hc F. Porsche KG	718/2-01	12.	Ausfall	Unfall
18. Mai	Formel 2	Grand Prix von Pau/Pau	Harry Schell	10	Porsche Paris	RSK	11.	8.	
			Wolfgang Seidel	12	Scuderia Colonia	RSK	19.	Ausfall	Ventilteller
			Jean Behra	28	Jean Behra	Behra-Porsche	2.	5.	
			Carel Godin de Beaufort	30	Ecurie Maarsbergen	RSK	15.	Ausfall	Nockenwelle
			Christian Goethals	36	Christian Goethals	RSK	13.	Ausfall	
31. Mai	Formel-1-WM	Grand Prix von Holland/ Zandvoort	Carel Godin de Beaufort	15	Ecurie Maarsbergen	RSK	14.	10.	
5. Juli	Formel 2	Coupe Internationale de Vitesse/Reims	Wolfgang Graf Berghe von Trips	42	Dr. Ing. hc F. Porsche KG	RSK	k. A.	5.	
			Joakim Bonnier	44	Dr. Ing. hc F. Porsche KG	718/2-01	k. A.	3.	
			Colin Davis	46	Jean Behra	RSK	k. A.	9.	
			Hans Herrmann	48	Jean Behra	Behra-Porsche	3.	2.	
12. Juli	Formel 2	Grand Prix von Rouen-Les-Essarts/ Rouen-Les-Essarts	Hans Herrmann	8	Jean Behra	Behra-Porsche	1.	Ausfall	Getriebe
			Gerard Laureau	36	Jean Behra	RSK	21	9.	
26. Juli	Formel 2	Grand Prix der Auvergne/ Clermond-Ferrand	Jean Behra	12	Jean Behra	Behra-Porsche	k. A.	12.	
			Carel Godin de Beaufort	13	Ecurie Maarsbergen	RSK	k. A.		nicht gewertet
2. August	Formel-1-WM	Großer Preis von Deutschland/Avus/Berlin	Jean Behra	12	Jean Behra	Behra-Porsche			nicht gestartet, tödlicher Unfall in einem Rahmen-rennen
			Wolfgang Graf Berghe von Trips	14	Dr. Ing. hc F. Porsche KG	718/2-01			nicht gestartet, Nennung nach Behras Unfall zurück gezogen
29. August	Formel 2	Kentish 100/ Brands Hatch	Joakim Bonnier		Dr. Ing. hc F. Porsche KG	718/2-01	k. A.	4.	
23. September	Formel 2	Flugplatzrennen Zeltweg/ Zeltweg	Ernst Vogel	17	Porsche Österreich	RSK	4.	3.	
			Carel Godin de Beaufort	18	Ecurie Maarsbergen	RSK	6.	6.	
			Wolfgang Seidel	19	Wolfgang Seidel	RSK	k. A.	Ausfall	
12. Dezember	Formel-1-WM	Grand Prix der USA/ Sebring	Harry Blanchard	17	Harry Blanchard	RSK	16.	7.	

Date	Competition	Race	Driver	No.	Entrant	Type	Qualification	Result	Remarks
April 25	Formula 2	Syracuse Grand Prix/ Syracuse	Wolfgang Seidel	22	Wolfgang Seidel	RSK	15th		did not start due to technical problems
			Christian Heinz	24	Christian Heinz	RSK	7th	6th	
May 10	Formula-1 WC	Monaco Grand Prix/ Monte Carlo	Wolfgang Seidel	2	Dr. Ing. hc F. Porsche KG	RSK			entered, did not paticipate
			Marie-Therese de Filippis	4	Dr. Ing. hc F. Porsche KG	Behra-Porsche			did not qualify
			Wolfgang Graf Berghe von Trips	6	Dr. Ing. hc F. Porsche KG	718/2-01	12th	retired	accident
May 18	Formula 2	Pau Grand Prix/Pau	Harry Schell	10	Porsche Paris	RSK	11th	8th	
			Wolfgang Seidel	12	Scuderia Colonia	RSK	19th	retired	valve
			Jean Behra	28	Jean Behra	Behra-Porsche	2nd	5th	
			Carel Godin de Beaufort	30	Ecurie Maarsbergen	RSK	15th	retired	camshaft
			Christian Goethals	36	Christian Goethals	RSK	13th	retired	
May 31	Formula-1 WC	Dutch Grand Prix/ Zandvoort	Carel Godin de Beaufort	15	Ecurie Maarsbergen	RSK	14th	10th	
July 5	Formula 2	Coupe Internationale de Vitesse/Reims	Wolfgang Graf Berghe von Trips	42	Dr. Ing. hc F. Porsche KG	RSK	–	5th	
			Joakim Bonnier	44	Dr. Ing. hc F. Porsche KG	718/2-01	–	3rd	
			Colin Davis	46	Jean Behra	RSK	–	9th	
			Hans Herrmann	48	Jean Behra	Behra-Porsche	3rd	2nd	
July 12	Formula 2	Rouen-Les-Essarts Grand Prix/ Rouen-Les-Essarts	Hans Herrmann	8	Jean Behra	Behra-Porsche	1st	retired	gearbox
			Gerard Laureau	36	Jean Behra	RSK	21th	9th	

Carel Godin de Beaufort, Zandvoort 1959.

Carel de Beaufort, Zandvoort 1959.

July 26	Formula 2	Grand Prix Auvergne/ Clermond-Ferrand	Jean Behra Carel Godin de Beaufort	12 13	Jean Behra Ecurie Maarsbergen	Behra-Porsche RSK	– –	12th	not scored
August 2	Formula-1 WC	German Grand Prix/ Avus/Berlin	Jean Behra	12	Jean Behra	Behra-Porsche			did not start, fatal accident in another race
			Wolfgang Graf Berghe von Trips	14	Dr. Ing. hc F. Porsche KG	718/2-01			did not start after Behra's accident
August 29	Formula 2	Kentish 100/ Brands Hatch	Joakim Bonnier		Dr. Ing. hc F. Porsche KG	718/2-01	–	4th	
September 23	Formula 2	Flugplatzrennen Zeltweg/ Zeltweg	Ernst Vogel Carel Godin de Beaufort Wolfgang Seidel	17 18 19	Porsche Österreich Ecurie Maarsbergen Wolfgang Seidel	RSK RSK RSK	4th 6th –	3rd 6th retired	
December 12	Formula-1 WC	American Grand Prix/ Sebring	Harry Blanchard	17	Harry Blanchard	RSK	16th	7th	

1960

Datum	Wettbewerb	Veranstaltung /Ort	Fahrer	Nr.	Bewerber	Typ	Training	Ergebnis	Bemerkungen
6. Februar	Formel-1-WM	Grand Prix von Argentinien/Buenos Aires	Masten Gregory	2	Camoradi USA	Behra-Porsche	16.	12.	
19. März	Formel 2	Grand Prix von Syrakus/ Syrakus	Stirling Moss Masten Gregory	20 34	Rob Walker Racing Team Camoradi USA	718/2-03 Behra-Porsche	1.	Ausfall	Ventil; schnellste Runde gemeldet, aber nicht am Rennen teilgenommen
8. April	Formel 2	Grand Prix von Brüssel/ Brüssel	Stirling Moss Joakim Bonnier Christian Goethals Masten Gregory	10 12 14 16	Rob Walker Racing Team Dr. Ing. hc F. Porsche KG Ecurie Eperon d'Or Camoradi USA	718/2-03 718/2-02 Porsche RSK Behra-Porsche	2. 1.	2. Ausfall	schnellste Runde Motor nicht qualifiziert gemeldet, nicht teilgenommen
18. April	Formel 2	Grand Prix von Pau/Pau	Olivier Gendebien	6	Equipe Nationale Belge	718/2-02	3.	3.	
18. April	Formel 2	Lavant Cup/Goodwood	Stirling Moss	21	Rob Walker Racing Team	718/2-03	2.	2.	
30. April	Formel 2	B.A.R.C. 200/Aintree	Graham Hill Joakim Bonnier Stirling Moss Masten Gregory	5 6 7 8	Dr. Ing. hc F. Porsche KG Dr. Ing. hc F. Porsche KG Rob Walker Racing Team Scuderia Centro Sud	718/2-01 718/2-02 718/2-03 Behra-Porsche	3. 7. 1. 28.	3. 2. 1. Ausfall	Kupplung
5. Juni	Formel 2	Grand Prix des Frontieres/ Chimay	Hans Herrmann Christian Goethals	17 19	Camoradi USA Ecurie Eperon d'Or	Behra-Porsche Porsche RSK	3.	Ausfall 12.	Getriebe 7.
24. Juli	Formel 2	Großer Preis der Solitude/ Solitude	Joakim Bonnier Hans Herrmann Graham Hill John Surtees Dan Gurney Lloyd Casner	4 5 6 19 22 23	Dr. Ing. hc F. Porsche KG Dr. Ing. hc F. Porsche KG Dr. Ing. hc F. Porsche KG Dr. Ing. hc F. Porsche KG Dr. Ing. hc F. Porsche KG Camoradi USA	718/2-02 718/2-04 718/2-01 718/2-03 718/2-05 Behra-Porsche	5. 3. 7. 8. 4. 22.	3. 2. 4. Ausfall 5.	Dreher nicht gestartet

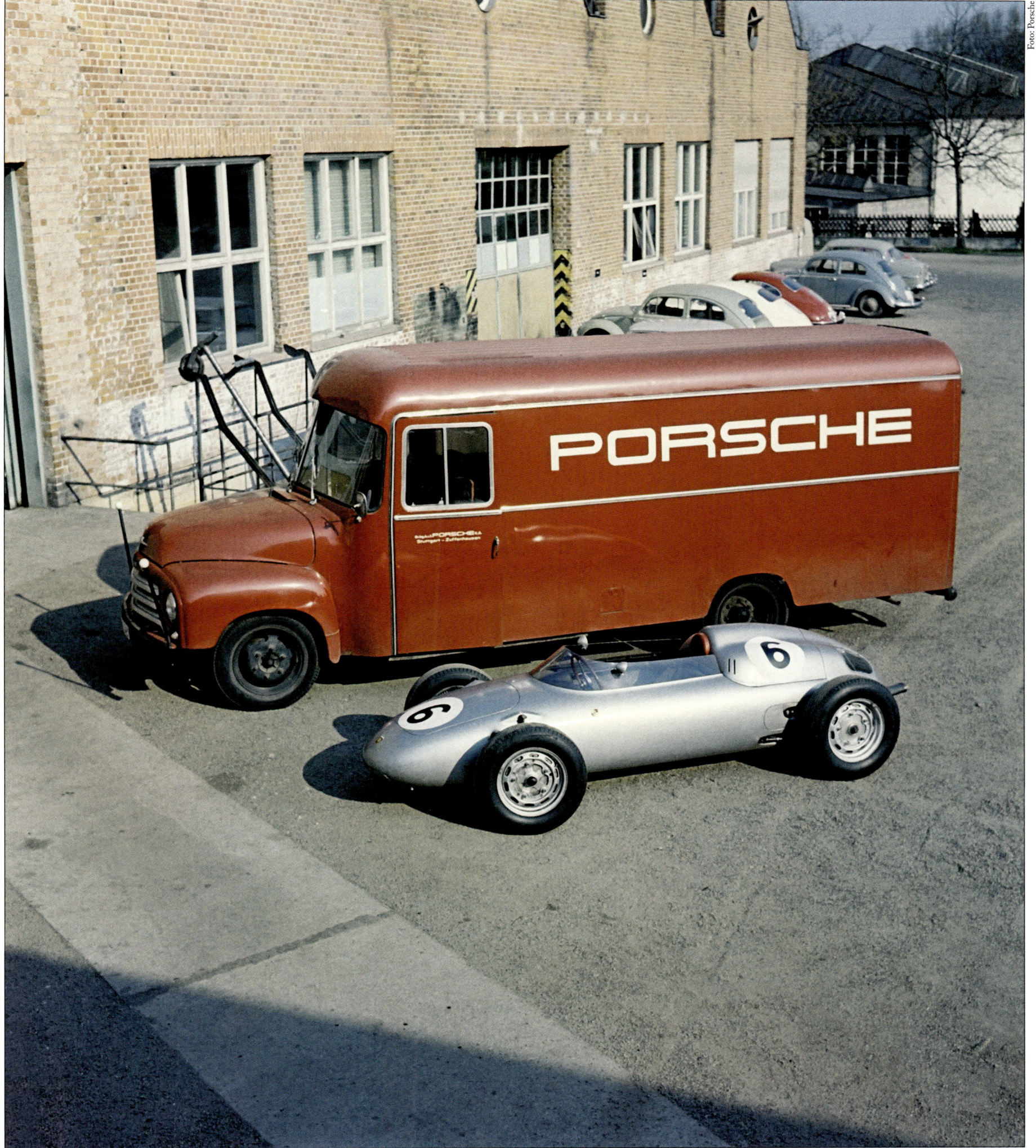

Porsche-Werk Stuttgart, 1960.

Porsche factory Stuttgart, 1960.

Date	Competition	Race	Driver	No.	Entrant	Type	Qualification	Result	Remarks
31. Juli	Formel 2	Großer Preis von Deutschland/Nürburgring-Südschleife	Joakim Bonnier	6	Dr. Ing. hc F. Porsche KG	718/2-02	1.	1.	schnellste Runde
			Edgar Barth	7	Dr. Ing. hc F. Porsche KG	718/2-04	7.	6.	
			Graham Hill	8	Dr. Ing. hc F. Porsche KG	718/2-01	4.	4.	
			Wolfgang Graf Berghe von Trips	9	Dr. Ing. hc F. Porsche KG	718/2-05	2.	2.	
			Hans Herrmann	14	Camoradi USA	718/2-03	5.	5.	zum Einsatz kam der Wagen des Rob-Walker-Teams
28. August	Formel 2	Kentish 100/ Brands Hatch	Graham Hill	2	Dr. Ing. hc F. Porsche KG	718/2-01	6.	4.	
			Joakim Bonnier	4	Dr. Ing. hc F. Porsche KG	718/2-02	4.	3.	
			Stirling Moss	6	Dr. Ing. hc F. Porsche KG	718/2-03	2.	11.	
4. September	Formel-1-WM mit Formel-2-Wertung	Grand Prix von Italien/ Monza	Edgar Barth	24	Dr. Ing. hc F. Porsche KG	718/2-04	12.	7.	Dritter der Formel-2-Wertung
			Hans Herrmann	26	Dr. Ing. hc F. Porsche KG	718/2-05	10.	6.	Zweiter der Formel-2-Wertung
			Fred Gamble	28	Camoradi USA	Behra-Porsche	14.	11.	
			Wolfgang Seidel	32	Scuderia Colonia	718	13.		Der gemeldete 718 kam nicht zum Einsatz. Seidel bestritt das Rennen auf einem Cooper 45
11. September	Formel 2	Grand Prix von Dänemark/Roskildering	Stirling Moss	7	Rob Walker Racing Team	718/2-03	1.	4.	
18. September	Formel 2	Flugplatzrennen Zeltweg/ Zeltweg	Edgar Barth	2	Dr. Ing. hc F. Porsche KG	718/2-04	5.	3.	
			Hans Herrmann	3	Dr. Ing. hc F. Porsche KG	718/2-05	4.	2.	
			Stirling Moss	7	Rob Walker Racing Team	718/2-03	2.	1.	schnellste Runde
2. Oktober	Formel 2	Grand Prix von Modena/ Modena	Edgar Barth	10	Dr. Ing. hc F. Porsche KG	718/2-04	5.	5.	
			Joakim Bonnier	12	Dr. Ing. hc F. Porsche KG	718/2-02	1.	1.	schnellste Runde
			Hans Herrmann	28	Dr. Ing. hc F. Porsche KG	718/2-05	4.	4.	
8. Oktober	Formel 2	Preis von Tirol/ Innsbruck	Hans Herrmann	163	Dr. Ing. hc F. Porsche KG	718/2-05	k. A.	1.	
17. Dezember	Formel 2	Cape Grand Prix/ Killarney	Stirling Moss	7	Dr. Ing. hc F. Porsche KG	718/2	1.	1.	
			Joakim Bonnier	11	Dr. Ing. hc F. Porsche KG	718/2	k. A.	2.	schnellste Runde
27. Dezember	Formel 2	Grand Prix von Südafrika/ East London	Stirling Moss	6	Dr. Ing. hc F. Porsche KG	718/2	2.	1.	schnellste Runde
			Joakim Bonnier	7	Dr. Ing. hc F. Porsche KG	718/2	3.	2.	

Großer Preis von Deutschland, Nürburgring, Südschleife 1960.

German GP 1960, the Südschleife of the Nürburgring.

Date	Competition	Race	Driver	No.	Entrant	Type	Qualification	Result	Remarks
February 6	Formula-1 WC	Argentine Grand Prix/ Buenos Aires	Masten Gregory	2	Camoradi USA	Behra-Porsche	16th	12th	
March 19	Formula 2	Syracuse Grand Prix/ Syracuse	Stirling Moss	20	Rob Walker Racing Team	718/2-03	1st	retired	valve failure; fastest lap
			Masten Gregory	34	Camoradi USA	Behra-Porsche			entered, did not participate
April 8	Formula 2	Brussels Grand Prix/ Brussels	Stirling Moss	10	Rob Walker Racing Team	718/2-03	2nd	2nd	fastest lap
			Joakim Bonnier	12	Dr. Ing. hc F. Porsche KG	718/2-02	1st	retired	engine
			Christian Goethals	14	Ecurie Eperon d'Or	Porsche RSK			did not qaulify
			Masten Gregory	16	Camoradi USA	Behra-Porsche			entered, did not participate
April 18	Formula 2	Pau Grand Prix/Pau	Olivier Gendebien	6	Equipe Nationale Belge	718/2-02	3rd	3rd	
April 18	Formula 2	Lavant Cup/Goodwood	Stirling Moss	21	Rob Walker Racing Team	718/2-03	2nd	2nd	

Date	Category	Race/Location	Driver	No.	Team	Car			Notes
April 30	Formula 2	B.A.R.C. 200/Aintree	Graham Hill	5	Dr. Ing. hc F. Porsche KG	718/2-01	3rd	3rd	
			Joakim Bonnier	6	Dr. Ing. hc F. Porsche KG	718/2-02	7th	2nd	
			Stirling Moss	7	Rob Walker Racing Team	718/2-03	1st	1st	
			Masten Gregory	8	Scuderia Centro Sud	Behra-Porsche	28th	retired	clutch
June 5	Formula 2	Grand Prix des Frontieres/Chimay	Hans Herrmann	17	Camoradi USA	Behra-Porsche	3rd	retired	gearbox
			Christian Goethals	19	Ecurie Eperon d'Or	Porsche RSK	12th	7th	
July 24	Formula 2	Großer Preis der Solitude/Solitude	Joakim Bonnier	4	Dr. Ing. hc F. Porsche KG	718/2-02	5th	3rd	
			Hans Herrmann	5	Dr. Ing. hc F. Porsche KG	718/2-04	3rd	2nd	
			Graham Hill	6	Dr. Ing. hc F. Porsche KG	718/2-01	7th	4th	
			John Surtees	19	Dr. Ing. hc F. Porsche KG	718/2-03	8th	retired	skidded off the track
			Dan Gurney	22	Dr. Ing. hc F. Porsche KG	718/2-05	4th	5th	
			Lloyd Casner	23	Camoradi USA	Behra-Porsche	22th		did not start
July 31	Formula 2	German Grand Prix/Nürburgring-Südschleife	Joakim Bonnier	6	Dr. Ing. hc F. Porsche KG	718/2-02	1st	1st	fastest lap
			Edgar Barth	7	Dr. Ing. hc F. Porsche KG	718/2-04	7th	6th	
			Graham Hill	8	Dr. Ing. hc F. Porsche KG	718/2-01	4th	4th	
			Wolfgang Graf Berghe von Trips	9	Dr. Ing. hc F. Porsche KG	718/2-05	2nd	2nd	
			Hans Herrmann	14	Camoradi USA	718/2-03	5th	5th	car entered came from Rob Walker Team
August 28	Formula 2	Kentish 100/Brands Hatch	Graham Hill	2	Dr. Ing. hc F. Porsche KG	718/2-01	6th	4th	
			Joakim Bonnier	4	Dr. Ing. hc F. Porsche KG	718/2-02	4th	3rd	
			Stirling Moss	6	Dr. Ing. hc F. Porsche KG	718/2-03	2nd	11th	
September 4	Formula-1 WC plus Formula-2 category	Italien Grand Prix/Monza	Edgar Barth	24	Dr. Ing. hc F. Porsche KG	718/2-04	12th	7th	3rd Formula-2 category
			Hans Herrmann	26	Dr. Ing. hc F. Porsche KG	718/2-05	10th	6th	2nd Formula-2 category
			Fred Gamble	28	Camoradi USA	Behra-Porsche	14th	11th	
			Wolfgang Seidel	32	Scuderia Colonia	718	13th		a 718 was entered, but Seidel finally drove a Cooper 45
September 11	Formula 2	Danish Grand Prix/Roskildering	Stirling Moss	7	Rob Walker Racing Team	718/2-03	1st	4th	
September 18	Formula 2	Flugplatzrennen Zeltweg/Zeltweg	Edgar Barth	2	Dr. Ing. hc F. Porsche KG	718/2-04	5th	3rd	
			Hans Herrmann	3	Dr. Ing. hc F. Porsche KG	718/2-05	4th	2nd	
			Stirling Moss	7	Rob Walker Racing Team	718/2-03	2nd	1st	fastest lap
October 2	Formula 2	Modena Grand Prix/Modena	Edgar Barth	10	Dr. Ing. hc F. Porsche KG	718/2-04	5th	5th	
			Joakim Bonnier	12	Dr. Ing. hc F. Porsche KG	718/2-02	1st	1st	fastest lap
			Hans Herrmann	28	Dr. Ing. hc F. Porsche KG	718/2-05	4th	4th	
October 8	Formula 2	Preis von Tirol/Innsbruck	Hans Herrmann	163	Dr. Ing. hc F. Porsche KG	718/2-05	–	1st	
December 17	Formula 2	Cape Grand Prix/Killarney	Stirling Moss	7	Dr. Ing. hc F. Porsche KG	718/2	1st	1st	
			Joakim Bonnier	11	Dr. Ing. hc F. Porsche KG	718/2	–	2nd	fastest lap
December 27	Formula 2	South African Grand Prix/East London	Stirling Moss	6	Dr. Ing. hc F. Porsche KG	718/2	2nd	1st	fastest lap
			Joakim Bonnier	7	Dr. Ing. hc F. Porsche KG	718/2	3rd	2nd	

Foto: Porsche

Joakim Bonnier, Monaco 1961.

Joakim Bonnier, Monaco, 1961.

1961

Datum	Wettbewerb	Veranstaltung /Ort	Fahrer	Nr.	Bewerber	Typ	Training	Ergebnis	Bemerkungen
9. April	Formel 1	Grand Prix von Brüssel/ Brüssel	Joakim Bonnier	38	Dr. Ing. hc F. Porsche KG	718/2-04	1.	Ausfall	Sieg im ersten Lauf; Unfall im zweiten von drei Läufen
			Dan Gurney	32	Dr. Ing. hc F. Porsche KG	718/2-03	3.	Ausfall	Getriebe
25. April	Formel 1	Grand Prix von Syrakus/ Syrakus	Joakim Bonnier	12	Dr. Ing. hc F. Porsche KG	718/2-04	6.	3.	
			Dan Gurney	30	Dr. Ing. hc F. Porsche KG	718/2-03	1.	2.	schnellste Runde
14. Mai	Formel-1-WM	Grand Prix von Monaco/ Monte Carlo	Joakim Bonnier	2	Dr. Ing. hc F. Porsche KG	787/01	9.	Ausfall	Kraftstoffzufuhr
			Dan Gurney	4	Dr. Ing. hc F. Porsche KG	718/2-04	10.	5.	
			Hans Herrmann	6	Dr. Ing. hc F. Porsche KG	718/2-05	12.	9.	
22. Mai	Formel-1-WM	Grand Prix von Holland/ Zandvoort	Joakim Bonnier	6	Dr. Ing. hc F. Porsche KG	787/02	11.	11.	
			Dan Gurney	7	Dr. Ing. hc F. Porsche KG	787/01	6.	10.	
			Carel Godin de Beaufort	8	Ecurie Maarsbergen	718/2-01	15.	14.	
			Hans Herrmann	9	Ecurie Maarsbergen	718/2-05	12.	15.	
18. Juni	Formel-1-WM	Grand Prix von Belgien/ Spa	Joakim Bonnier	18	Dr. Ing. hc F. Porsche KG	718/2-04	9.	7.	
			Dan Gurney	20	Dr. Ing. hc F. Porsche KG	718/2-03	10.	6.	
			Carel Godin de Beaufort	22	Ecurie Maarsbergen	718/2-01	14.	11.	
2. Juli	Formel-1-WM	Grand Prix von Frankreich/ Reims	Joakim Bonnier	10	Dr. Ing. hc F. Porsche KG	718/2-03	13.	7.	
			Dan Gurney	12	Dr. Ing. hc F. Porsche KG	718/2-04	9.	2.	
			Carel Godin de Beaufort	14	Ecurie Maarsbergen	718/2-01	17.	Ausfall	Motor
15. Juli	Formel-1-WM	Grand Prix von England/ Aintree	Joakim Bonnier	8	Dr. Ing. hc F. Porsche KG	718/2-03	3.	5.	
			Dan Gurney	10	Dr. Ing. hc F. Porsche KG	718/2-04	12.	7.	
			Carel Godin de Beaufort	56	Ecurie Maarsbergen	718/2-01	18.	16.	
23. Juli	Formel 1	Großer Preis der Solitude/ Stuttgart	Joakim Bonnier	9	Dr. Ing. hc F. Porsche KG	718/2-04	1.	2.	
			Hans Herrmann	10	Dr. Ing. hc F. Porsche KG	718/2-02	6.	6.	
			Dan Gurney	11	Dr. Ing. hc F. Porsche KG	718/2-03	2.	3.	schnellste Runde
			Edgar Barth	12	Dr. Ing. hc F. Porsche KG	787/02	10.	8.	
			Carel Godin de Beaufort	21	Ecurie Maarsbergen	718/2-01	13.	Ausfall	Motor
6. August	Formel-1-WM	Großer Preis von Deutschland/ Nürburgring	Joakim Bonnier	8	Dr. Ing. hc F. Porsche KG	718/2-04	4.	Ausfall	Motor
			Dan Gurney	9	Dr. Ing. hc F. Porsche KG	718/2-03	7.	7.	
			Edgar Barth	10	Dr. Ing. hc F. Porsche KG	787/02			gemeldet, aber nicht am Rennen teilgenommen
			Hans Herrmann	11	Dr. Ing. hc F. Porsche KG	718/2-02	11.	13.	
			Carel Godin de Beaufort	31	Ecurie Maarsbergen	718/2-01	17.	14.	
20. August	Formel 1	Kannonloppet/ Karlskoga	Joakim Bonnier	4	Dr. Ing. hc F. Porsche KG	718/2-04	2.	2.	
			Ulf Norinder	15	Ecurie Maarsbergen	718/2-01	9.	Ausfall	Dreher
27. August	Formel 1	Grand Prix von Dänemark/Roskilde	Carel Godin de Beaufort	15	Ecurie Maarsbergen	718/2-01	9.	Ausfall	Reifenschaden
3. September	Formel 1	Grand Prix von Modena/ Modena	Joakim Bonnier	10	Dr. Ing. hc F. Porsche KG	718/2-04	2.	2.	
			Dan Gurney	12	Dr. Ing. hc F. Porsche KG	718/2-03	3.	3.	
			Carel Godin de Beaufort	34	Ecurie Maarsbergen	718/2-01			nicht qualifiziert
10. September	Formel-1-WM	Grand Prix von Italien/ Monza	Joakim Bonnier	44	Dr. Ing. hc F. Porsche KG	718/2-04	8.	Ausfall	Hinterradaufhängung
			Dan Gurney	46	Dr. Ing. hc F. Porsche KG	718/2-03	12.	2.	
			Carel Godin de Beaufort	74	Ecurie Maarsbergen	718/2-01	15.	7.	
17. September	Formel 1	Flugplatzrennen Zeltweg/ Zeltweg	Joakim Bonnier	2	Dr. Ing. hc F. Porsche KG	718/2-04	8.	3.	
			Carel Godin de Beaufort	12	Ecurie Maarsbergen	718/2-01	13.	6.	
23. September	Formel 1	International Gold Cup/ Oulton Park	Joakim Bonnier	10	Dr. Ing. hc F. Porsche KG	718/2-04			gemeldet, aber nicht am Rennen teilgenommen
			Dan Gurney	11	Dr. Ing. hc F. Porsche KG	718/2-03			gemeldet, aber nicht am Rennen teilgenommen
8. Oktober	Formel-1-WM	Grand Prix der USA/ Watkins Glen	Joakim Bonnier	11	Dr. Ing. hc F. Porsche KG	718/2-04	10.	6.	
			Dan Gurney	12	Dr. Ing. hc F. Porsche KG	718/2-03	7.	2.	
12. Oktober	Formel 1	Coppa Italia Vallelunga/ Vallelunga	Giancarlo Baghetti	18	Scuderia Sant Ambroeus	718/2-02	2.	1.	
9. Dezember	Formel 1	Rand Grand Prix/ Kyalami	Edgar Barth	4	Dr. Ing. hc F. Porsche KG	718/2-03	9.	4.	
			Joakim Bonnier	5	Dr. Ing. hc F. Porsche KG	718/2-04	4.	3.	schnellste Runde
			Dawie Gous	27	Dawie Gous	RSK			gemeldet, aber nicht am Rennen teilgenommen
17. Dezember	Formel 1	Natal Grand Prix/ Westmead	Joakim Bonnier	4	Dr. Ing. hc F. Porsche KG	718/2-03	2.	3.	
			Edgar Barth	5	Dr. Ing. hc F. Porsche KG	718/2-04	8.	4.	
26. Dezember	Formel 1	Grand Prix von Südafrika/ East London	Edgar Barth	4	Dr. Ing. hc F. Porsche KG	718/2-03	7.	5.	
			Joakim Bonnier	5	Dr. Ing. hc F. Porsche KG	718/2-04	4.	3.	

Dan Gurney (20) und Joakim Bonnier (18), Grand Prix von Belgien, Spa Francorchamps 1961.

Dan Gurney (20) and Joakim Bonnier (18), Belgian Grand Prix, Spa Francorchamps, 1961.

Foto: Porsche

Start Solitude 1961.

Start of the Solitude race, 1961.

1961

Date	Competition	Race	Driver	No.	Entrant	Type	Qualification	Result	Remarks
April 9	Formula 1	Brussels Grand Prix/ Brussels	Joakim Bonnier	38	Dr. Ing. hc F. Porsche KG	718/2-04	1st	retired	1st first heat; accident in 2nd of three heats
			Dan Gurney	32	Dr. Ing. hc F. Porsche KG	718/2-03	3rd	retired	gearbox
April 25	Formula 1	Syracuse Grand Prix/ Syracuse	Joakim Bonnier	12	Dr. Ing. hc F. Porsche KG	718/2-04	6th	3rd	
			Dan Gurney	30	Dr. Ing. hc F. Porsche KG	718/2-03	1st	2nd	fastest lap
May 14	Formula-1 WC	Monaco Grand Prix/ Monte Carlo	Joakim Bonnier	2	Dr. Ing. hc F. Porsche KG	787/01	9th	retired	fuel system
			Dan Gurney	4	Dr. Ing. hc F. Porsche KG	718/2-04	10th	5th	
			Hans Herrmann	6	Dr. Ing. hc F. Porsche KG	718/2-05	12th	9th	
May 22	Formula-1 WC	Dutch Grand Prix/ Zandvoort	Joakim Bonnier	6	Dr. Ing. hc F. Porsche KG	787/02	11th	11th	
			Dan Gurney	7	Dr. Ing. hc F. Porsche KG	787/01	6th	10th	
			Carel Godin de Beaufort	8	Ecurie Maarsbergen	718/2-01	15th	14th	
			Hans Herrmann	9	Ecurie Maarsbergen	718/2-05	12th	15th	
June 18	Formula-1 WC	Belgian Grand Prix/ Spa	Joakim Bonnier	18	Dr. Ing. hc F. Porsche KG	718/2-04	9th	7th	
			Dan Gurney	20	Dr. Ing. hc F. Porsche KG	718/2-03	10th	6th	
			Carel Godin de Beaufort	22	Ecurie Maarsbergen	718/2-01	14th	11th	
July 2	Formula-1 WC	French Grand Prix/ Reims	Joakim Bonnier	10	Dr. Ing. hc F. Porsche KG	718/2-03	13th	7th	
			Dan Gurney	12	Dr. Ing. hc F. Porsche KG	718/2-04	9th	2nd	
			Carel Godin de Beaufort	14	Ecurie Maarsbergen	718/2-01	17th	retired	engine
July 15	Formula-1 WC	British Grand Prix/ Aintree	Joakim Bonnier	8	Dr. Ing. hc F. Porsche KG	718/2-03	3rd	5th	
			Dan Gurney	10	Dr. Ing. hc F. Porsche KG	718/2-04	12th	7th	
			Carel Godin de Beaufort	56	Ecurie Maarsbergen	718/2-01	18th	16th	
July 23	Formula 1	Großer Preis der Solitude/ Stuttgart	Joakim Bonnier	9	Dr. Ing. hc F. Porsche KG	718/2-04	1st	2nd	
			Hans Herrmann	10	Dr. Ing. hc F. Porsche KG	718/2-02	6th	6th	
			Dan Gurney	11	Dr. Ing. hc F. Porsche KG	718/2-03	2nd	3rd	fastest lap
			Edgar Barth	12	Dr. Ing. hc F. Porsche KG	787/02	10th	8th	
			Carel Godin de Beaufort	21	Ecurie Maarsbergen	718/2-01	13th	retired	engine
August 6	Formula-1 WC	German Grand Prix/ Nürburgring	Joakim Bonnier	8	Dr. Ing. hc F. Porsche KG	718/2-04	4th	retired	engine
			Dan Gurney	9	Dr. Ing. hc F. Porsche KG	718/2-03	7th	7th	
			Edgar Barth	10	Dr. Ing. hc F. Porsche KG	787/02			entered, did not participate
			Hans Herrmann	11	Dr. Ing. hc F. Porsche KG	718/2-02	11th	13th	
			Carel Godin de Beaufort	31	Ecurie Maarsbergen	718/2-01	17th	14th	
August 20	Formula 1	Kannonloppet/ Karlskoga	Joakim Bonnier	4	Dr. Ing. hc F. Porsche KG	718/2-04	2nd	2nd	
			Ulf Norinder	15	Ecurie Maarsbergen	718/2-01	9th	retired	skidded off the track
August 27	Formula 1	Danish Grand Prix/ Roskilde	Carel Godin de Beaufort	15	Ecurie Maarsbergen	718/2-01	9th	retired	tyre
September 3	Formula 1	Modena Grand Prix/ Modena	Joakim Bonnier	10	Dr. Ing. hc F. Porsche KG	718/2-04	2nd	2nd	
			Dan Gurney	12	Dr. Ing. hc F. Porsche KG	718/2-03	3rd	3rd	
			Carel Godin de Beaufort	34	Ecurie Maarsbergen	718/2-01			did not qualify
September 10	Formula-1 WC	Italian Grand Prix/ Monza	Joakim Bonnier	44	Dr. Ing. hc F. Porsche KG	718/2-04	8th	retired	rear suspension
			Dan Gurney	46	Dr. Ing. hc F. Porsche KG	718/2-03	12th	2nd	
			Carel Godin de Beaufort	74	Ecurie Maarsbergen	718/2-01	15th	7th	
September 17	Formula 1	Flugplatzrennen Zeltweg/ Zeltweg	Joakim Bonnier	2	Dr. Ing. hc F. Porsche KG	718/2-04	8th	3rd	
			Carel Godin de Beaufort	12	Ecurie Maarsbergen	718/2-01	13th	6th	
September 23	Formula 1	International Gold Cup/ Oulton Park	Joakim Bonnier	10	Dr. Ing. hc F. Porsche KG	718/2-04			entered, did not participate
			Dan Gurney	11	Dr. Ing. hc F. Porsche KG	718/2-03			entered, did not participate
October 8	Formula-1 WC	American Grand Prix/ Watkins Glen	Joakim Bonnier	11	Dr. Ing. hc F. Porsche KG	718/2-04	10th	6th	
			Dan Gurney	12	Dr. Ing. hc F. Porsche KG	718/2-03	7th	2nd	
October 12	Formula 1	Coppa Italia Vallelunga/ Vallelunga	Giancarlo Baghetti	18	Scuderia Sant Ambroeus	718/2-02	2nd	1st	
December 9	Formula 1	Rand Grand Prix/ Kyalami	Edgar Barth	4	Dr. Ing. hc F. Porsche KG	718/2-03	9th	4th	
			Joakim Bonnier	5	Dr. Ing. hc F. Porsche KG	718/2-04	4th	3rd	fastest lap
			Dawie Gous	27	Dawie Gous	RSK			entered, did not participate
December 17	Formula 1	Natal Grand Prix/ Westmead	Joakim Bonnier	4	Dr. Ing. hc F. Porsche KG	718/2-03	2nd	3rd	
			Edgar Barth	5	Dr. Ing. hc F. Porsche KG	718/2-04	8th	4th	
December 26	Formula 1	South African Grand Prix/ East London	Edgar Barth	4	Dr. Ing. hc F. Porsche KG	718/2-03	7th	5th	
			Joakim Bonnier	5	Dr. Ing. hc F. Porsche KG	718/2-04	4th	3rd	

Dan Gurney, Rouen 1962.

Dan Gurney, Rouen 1962.

1962

Datum	Wettbewerb	Veranstaltung /Ort	Fahrer	Nr.	Bewerber	Typ	Training	Ergebnis	Bemerkungen
2. Januar	Formel 1	Cape Grand Prix/ Killarney	Edgar Barth	4	Dr. Ing. hc F. Porsche KG	718/2-03	5.	6.	
			Joakim Bonnier	5	Dr. Ing. hc F. Porsche KG	718/2-04	3.	3.	
1. April	Formel 1	Grand Prix von Brüssel/ Brüssel	Joakim Bonnier	16	Scuderia SSS Rep di Venezia	718/2-03	6.	2.	
			Wolfgang Seidel	17	Autosport Team Wolfgang Seidel	718/2-01	17.	7.	
			Heinz Schiller	18	Ecurie Nationale Suisse	718/2-02	16.	6.	
14. April	Formel 1	Lombank Trophy/ Snetterton	Joakim Bonnier	2	Scuderia SSS Rep di Venezia	718/2-03	8.	3.	
			Wolfgang Seidel	17	Autosport Team Wolfgang Seidel	718/2-01	13.	6.	
23. April	Formel 1	Grand Prix von Pau/Pau	Ludwig Heimrath	14	Dr. Ing. hc F. Porsche KG	718/2-04	12.	Ausfall	Unfall
			Joakim Bonnier	16	Scuderia SSS Rep di Venezia	718/2-03	3.	Ausfall	Getriebeschaden
			Heinz Schiller	34	Autosport Team Wolfgang Seidel	718/2-02	15.	9.	
23. April	Formel 1	Lavant Cup/Goodwood	Wolfgang Seidel	11	Autosport Team Wolfgang Seidel	718/2-01	8.	7.	
23. April	Formel 1	Glover Trophy/Goodwood	Wolfgang Seidel	11	Autosport Team Wolfgang Seidel	718/2-01	13.	10.	
29. April	Formel 1	B.A.R.C. 200/Aintree	Wolfgang Seidel	26	Autosport Team Wolfgang Seidel	718/2-01	14.	Ausfall	Kegel- und Tellerrad
12. Mai	Formel 1	BRDC International Trophy/Silverstone	Joakim Bonnier	17	Scuderia SSS Rep di Venezia	718/2-03	14.	12.	
20. Mai	Formel-1-WM	Grand Prix von Holland/ Zandvoort	Joakim Bonnier	11	Porsche System Engineering	804/01	13.	7.	
			Dan Gurney	12	Porsche System Engineering	804/02	8.	Ausfall	Getriebe
			Carel Godin de Beaufort	14	Ecurie Maarsbergen	718/2-01	14.	6.	
			Ben Pon	15	Ecurie Maarsbergen	787/02	18.	Ausfall	Unfall
20. Mai	Formel 1	Grand Prix von Neapel/ Posillipo	Carlo Abate	32	Scuderia SSS Rep di Venezia	718/2-03	7.	4.	
			Heinz Schiller	40	Ecurie Filipinetti	718/2-02	nicht qualifiziert		

Datum	Klasse	Rennen	Fahrer	Nr.	Team	Chassis			Bemerkung
3. Juni	Formel-1-WM	Grand Prix von Monaco/ Monte Carlo	Joakim Bonnier	2	Porsche System Engineering	718/2-03	15.	5.	
			Dan Gurney	4	Porsche System Engineering	804/02	5.	Ausfall	Unfall
			Carel Godin de Beaufort	44	Ecurie Maarsbergen	718/2-01	nicht qualifiziert		
11. Juni	Formel 1	2000 Guineas/ Mallory Park	Joakim Bonnier	10	Scuderia SSS Rep di Venezia	718/2-03	5.	6.	
			Carel Godin de Beaufort	85	Ecurie Maarsbergen	718/2-01	6.	9.	
17. Juni	Formel-1-WM	Grand Prix von Belgien/ Spa	Carel Godin de Beaufort	7	Ecurie Maarsbergen	718/2-01	13.	7.	
			Heinz Schiller	8	Ecurie Maarsbergen	718/2			gemeldet, aber nicht am Rennen teilgenommen
			Lucien Bianchi	14	Scuderia SSS 718 Rep di Venezia				gemeldet, aber nicht am Rennen teilgenommen
			Joakim Bonnier	24	Porsche System Engineering	804			gemeldet, aber nicht am Rennen teilgenommen
1. Juli	Formel 1	Grand Prix von Reims/ Reims	Joakim Bonnier	36	Scuderia SSS Rep di Venezia	718/2-03	11.	8.	
			Carel Godin de Beaufort	46	Ecurie Maarsbergen	718/2-01	8.	7.	
8. Juli	Formel-1-WM	Grand Prix von Frankreich/ Rouen	Dan Gurney	30	Porsche System Engineering	804/01	6.	1.	
			Joakim Bonnier	32	Porsche System Engineering	804/02	9.	Ausfall	Benzinpumpe
			Carel Godin de Beaufort	38	Ecurie Maarsbergen	718/2-01	17.	6.	
15. Juli	Formel 1	Großer Preis der Solitude/ Solitude	Dan Gurney	10	Porsche System Engineering	804/03	2.	1.	schnellste Runde
			Joakim Bonnier	11	Porsche System Engineering	804/02	3.	2.	
			Carel Godin de Beaufort	18	Ecurie Maarsbergen	718/2-01	8.	5.	
21. Juli	Formel-1-WM	Grand Prix von England/ Aintree	Dan Gurney	8	Porsche System Engineering	804/03	6.	9.	
			Joakim Bonnier	10	Porsche System Engineering	804/02	7.	Ausfall	Kegel- und Tellerrad
			Carel Godin de Beaufort	54	Ecurie Maarsbergen	718/2-01	17.	14.	
5. August	Formel-1-WM	Großer Preis von Deutschland/Nürburgring	Dan Gurney	7	Porsche System Engineering	804/03	1.	3.	
			Joakim Bonnier	8	Porsche System Engineering	804/02	6.	7.	
			Carel Godin de Beaufort	18	Ecurie Maarsbergen	718/2-01	8.	13.	
			Nino Vaccarella	26	Scuderia SSS Rep di Venezia	718/2-03	15.	15.	
			Heini Walter	32	Ecurie Filipinetti	718/2-02	14.	14.	
12. August	Formel 1	Kannonloppet/ Karlskoga	Joakim Bonnier	5	Porsche System Engineering	804/01	3.	3.	
			Carel Godin de Beaufort	6	Ecurie Maarsbergen	718/2-01	8.	6.	
19. August	Formel 1	Großer Preis des Mittelmeeres/Pergusa	Heinz Schiller	24	Ecurie Filipinetti	718/2-02	5.	Ausfall	Ölpumpe
			Carlo Abate	26	Scuderia SSS Rep di Venezia	718/2-03	4.	3.	
26. August	Formel 1	Grand Prix von Dänemark/Roskildering	Carel Godin de Beaufort	14	Ecurie Maarsbergen	718/2-01	9.	7.	

Joakim Bonnier, Solitude 1962.

Joakim Bonnier, Solitude 1962.

1. September	Formel 1	Gold Cup/Oulton Park	Carel Godin de Beaufort 25	Ecurie Maarsbergen	718/2-01	18.	7.	
16. September	Formel-1-WM	Grand Prix von Italien/ Monza	Dan Gurney 16	Porsche System Engineering	804/03	7.	Ausfall	Hinterachse
			Joakim Bonnier 18	Porsche System Engineering	804/02	9.	6.	
			Carel Godin de Beaufort 32	Ecurie Maarsbergen	718/2-01	20.	10.	
7. Oktober	Formel-1-WM	Grand Prix der USA/ Watkins Glen	Dan Gurney 10	Porsche System Engineering	804/03	4.	5.	
			Joakim Bonnier 11	Porsche System Engineering	804/02	9.	nicht gewertet	
			Carel Godin de Beaufort 12	Ecurie Maarsbergen	718/2-01	13.	Ausfall	Unfall
4. November	Formel 1	Grand Prix von Mexiko/ Mexiko City	Carel Godin de Beaufort 12	Ecurie Maarsbergen	718/2-01	12.	7.	
29. Dezember	Formel-1-WM	Grand Prix von Südafrika/ East London	Carel Godin de Beaufort 15	Ecurie Maarsbergen	718/2-01	16.	Ausfall	Benzinpumpe

Date	Competition	Race	Driver	No.	Entrant	Type	Qualification	Result	Remarks
January 2	Formula 1	Cape Grand Prix/ Killarney	Edgar Barth	4	Dr. Ing. hc F. Porsche KG	718/2-03	5th	6th	
			Joakim Bonnier	5	Dr. Ing. hc F. Porsche KG	718/2-04	3rd	3rd	
April 1	Formula 1	Brussels Grand Prix/ Brussels	Joakim Bonnier	16	Scuderia SSS Rep di Venezia	718/2-03	6th	2nd	
			Wolfgang Seidel	17	Autosport Team Wolfgang Seidel	718/2-01	17th	7th	
			Heinz Schiller	18	Ecurie Nationale Suisse	718/2-02	16th	6th	
April 14	Formula 1	Lombank Trophy/ Snetterton	Joakim Bonnier	2	Scuderia SSS Rep di Venezia	718/2-03	8th	3rd	
			Wolfgang Seidel	17	Autosport Team Wolfgang Seidel	718/2-01	13th	6th	
April 23	Formula 1	Pau Grand Prix/Pau	Ludwig Heimrath	14	Dr. Ing. hc F. Porsche KG	718/2-04	12th	retired	accident
			Joakim Bonnier	16	Scuderia SSS Rep di Venezia	718/2-03	3rd	retired	gearbox
			Heinz Schiller	34	Autosport Team Wolfgang Seidel	718/2-02	15th	9th	
April 23	Formula 1	Lavant Cup/Goodwood	Wolfgang Seidel	11	Autosport Team Wolfgang Seidel	718/2-01	8th	7th	
April 23	Formula 1	Glover Trophy/Goodwood	Wolfgang Seidel	11	Autosport Team Wolfgang Seidel	718/2-01	13th	10th	
April 29	Formula 1	B.A.R.C. 200/Aintree	Wolfgang Seidel	26	Autosport Team Wolfgang Seidel	718/2-01	14th	retired	gear train
May 12	Formula 1	BRDC International Trophy/Silverstone	Joakim Bonnier	17	Scuderia SSS Rep di Venezia	718/2-03	14th	12th	
May 20	Formula 1-WC	Dutch Grand Prix/ Zandvoort	Joakim Bonnier	11	Porsche System Engineering	804/01	13th	7th	
			Dan Gurney	12	Porsche System Engineering	804/02	8th	retired	gearbox
			Carel Godin de Beaufort	14	Ecurie Maarsbergen	718/2-01	14th	6th	
			Ben Pon	15	Ecurie Maarsbergen	787/02	18th	retired	accident
May 20	Formula 1	Naples Grand Prix/ Posillipo	Carlo Abate	32	Scuderia SSS Rep di Venezia	718/2-03	7th	4th	
			Heinz Schiller	40	Ecurie Filipinetti	718/2-02	not qualified		
June 3	Formula 1-WM	Monaco Grand Prix/ Monte Carlo	Joakim Bonnier	2	Porsche System Engineering	718/2-03	15th	5th	
			Dan Gurney	4	Porsche System Engineering	804/02	5th	retired	accident
			Carel Godin de Beaufort	44	Ecurie Maarsbergen	718/2-01	not qualified		
June 11	Formula 1	2000 Guineas/ Mallory Park	Joakim Bonnier	10	Scuderia SSS Rep di Venezia	718/2-03	5th	6th	
			Carel Godin de Beaufort	85	Ecurie Maarsbergen	718/2-01	6th	9th	
June 17	Formula 1 WC	Belgian Grand Prix/ Spa	Carel Godin de Beaufort	7	Ecurie Maarsbergen	718/2-01	13th	7th	
			Heinz Schiller	8	Ecurie Maarsbergen	718/2			entered, did not participate
			Lucien Bianchi	14	Scuderia SSS 718 Rep di Venezia				entered, did not participate
			Joakim Bonnier	24	Porsche System Engineering	804			entered, did not participate
July 1	Formula 1	Reims Grand Prix/ Reims	Joakim Bonnier	36	Scuderia SSS Rep di Venezia	718/2-03	11th	8th	
			Carel Godin de Beaufort	46	Ecurie Maarsbergen	718/2-01	8th	7th	
July 8	Formula-1 WC	French Grand Prix/ Rouen	Dan Gurney	30	Porsche System Engineering	804/01	6th	1st	
			Joakim Bonnier	32	Porsche System Engineering	804/02	9th	retired	fuel pump
			Carel Godin de Beaufort	38	Ecurie Maarsbergen	718/2-01	17th	6th	

Foto: Porsche

**Großer Preis von England,
Aintree 1962.**

British Grand Prix, Aintree
1962.

**Großer Preis von Italien,
Monza 1962.**

Italian Grand Prix, Monza
1962.

Date	Competition	Event/Location	Driver	Nr.	Entrant	Typ	Training	Result	Remarks
July 15	Formula 1	Großer Preis der Solitude/ Solitude	Dan Gurney	10	Porsche System Engineering	804/03	2nd	1st	fastest lap
			Joakim Bonnier	11	Porsche System Engineering	804/02	3rd	2nd	
			Carel Godin de Beaufort	18	Ecurie Maarsbergen	718/2-01	8th	5th	
July 21	Formula-1 WC	British Grand Prix/ Aintree	Dan Gurney	8	Porsche System Engineering	804/03	6th	9th	
			Joakim Bonnier	10	Porsche System Engineering	804/02	7th	retired	gear train
			Carel Godin de Beaufort	54	Ecurie Maarsbergen	718/2-01	17th	14th	
August 5	Formula-1 WC	German Grand Prix Nürburgring	Dan Gurney	7	Porsche System Engineering	804/03	1st	3rd	
			Joakim Bonnier	8	Porsche System Engineering	804/02	6th	7th	
			Carel Godin de Beaufort	18	Ecurie Maarsbergen	718/2-01	8th	13th	
			Nino Vaccarella	26	Scuderia SSS Rep di Venezia	718/2-03	15th	15th	
			Heini Walter	32	Ecurie Filipinetti	718/2-02	14th	14th	
August 12	Formula 1	Kannonloppet/ Karlskoga	Joakim Bonnier	5	Porsche System Engineering	804/01	3rd	3rd	
			Carel Godin de Beaufort	6	Ecurie Maarsbergen	718/2-01	8th	6th	
August 19	Formula 1	Grand Prix of the Mediteranean/Pergusa	Heinz Schiller	24	Ecurie Filipinetti	718/2-02	5th	retired	oil pump
			Carlo Abate	26	Scuderia SSS Rep di Venezia	718/2-03	4th	3rd	
August 26	Formula 1	Danish Grand Prix/ Roskildering	Carel Godin de Beaufort	14	Ecurie Maarsbergen	718/2-01	9th	7th	
September 1	Formula 1	Gold Cup/Oulton Park	Carel Godin de Beaufort	25	Ecurie Maarsbergen	718/2-01	18th	7th	
September 16	Formula-1 WC	Italian Grand Prix/ Monza	Dan Gurney	16	Porsche System Engineering	804/03	7th	retired	rear axle
			Joakim Bonnier	18	Porsche System Engineering	804/02	9th	6th	
			Carel Godin de Beaufort	32	Ecurie Maarsbergen	718/2-01	20th	10th	
October 7	Formula-1 WC	American Grand Prix/ Watkins Glen	Dan Gurney	10	Porsche System Engineering	804/03	4th	5th	
			Joakim Bonnier	11	Porsche System Engineering	804/02	9th	not classified	
			Carel Godin de Beaufort	12	Ecurie Maarsbergen	718/2-01	13th	retired	accident
November 4	Formula 1	Mexican Grand Prix/ Mexiko City	Carel Godin de Beaufort	12	Ecurie Maarsbergen	718/2-01	12th	7th	
December 29	Formula-1 WC	South African Grand Prix/ East London	Carel Godin de Beaufort	15	Ecurie Maarsbergen	718/2-01	16th	retired	fuel pump

1963

Datum	Wettbewerb	Veranstaltung /Ort	Fahrer	Nr.	Bewerber	Typ	Training	Ergebnis	Bemerkungen
15. April	Formel 1	Grand Prix von Pau/Pau	Carel Godin de Beaufort	16	Ecurie Maarsbergen	718/2-01	9.	4.	
			Heinz Schiller	24	Scuderia Filipinetti	718/2-02	10.	3.	
21. April	Formel 1	Grand Prix von Imola/ Imola	Carel Godin de Beaufort	12	Ecurie Maarsbergen	718/2-01	8.	6.	
			Jack Fairman	14	Ecurie Maarsbergen	718/2-02	9.	7.	
			Carlo Abate	26	Scuderia Centro Sud	718/2	12.	5.	
25. April	Formel 1	Grand Prix von Syrakus/ Syrakus	Carel Godin de Beaufort	8	Ecurie Maarsbergen	718/2-01	4.	2.	
11. Mai	Formel 1	BRDC International Trophy/Silverstone	Carel Godin de Beaufort	20	Ecurie Maarsbergen	718/2-01	17.	9.	
19. Mai	Formel 1	Grand Prix von Rom / Vallelunga	Carel Godin de Beaufort	40	Ecurie Maarsbergen	718/2-01	1.	2.	
9. Juni	Formel-1-WM	Grand Prix von Belgien/ Spa	Carel Godin de Beaufort	29	Ecurie Maarsbergen	718/2-01	18.	6.	
23. Juni	Formel-1-WM	Grand Prix von Holland/ Zandvoort	Carel Godin de Beaufort	32	Ecurie Maarsbergen	718/2-01	19.	9.	
			Gerhard Mitter	34	Ecurie Maarsbergen	718/2-02	16.	Ausfall	Kupplung
20. Juli	Formel-1-WM	Grand Prix von England/ Silverstone	Carel Godin de Beaufort	23	Ecurie Maarsbergen	718/2-01	21.	10.	
28. Juli	Formel 1	Großer Preis der Solitude/ Solitude	Carel Godin de Beaufort	23	Ecurie Maarsbergen	718/2-01	13.	7.	
			Gerhard Mitter	24	Ecurie Maarsbergen	718/2-02	11.	5.	
4. August	Formel-1-WM	Großer Preis von Deutschland/Nürburgring	Carel Godin de Beaufort	17	Ecurie Maarsbergen	718/2-01	17.	Ausfall	Felgenbruch
			Gerhard Mitter	26	Ecurie Maarsbergen	718/2-02	15.	4.	

Datum	Formel	Rennen	Fahrer	Nr.	Team	Chassis	Start	Ziel	Bemerkung
11. August	Formel 1	Kannonloppet/Karlskoga	Carel Godin de Beaufort	8	Ecurie Maarsbergen	718/2-02	8.	7.	
18. August	Formel 1	Großer Preis des Mittelmeeres/Pergusa	Carel Godin de Beaufort	8	Ecurie Maarsbergen	718/2-01	12.	nicht gestartet	Achsschenkelbruch im Training
			Carlo Abate	14	Graf Volpi	718/2-03	10.	8.	
1. September	Formel 1	Großer Preis von Österreich/Zeltweg	Carel Godin de Beaufort	6	Ecurie Maarsbergen	718/2-01	10.	3.	
			Kurt Bardi-Barry	7	Ecurie Maarsbergen	718/2-02	16.	Ausfall	Fahrer gab auf
8. September	Formel-1-WM	Grand Prix von Italien/Monza	Gerhard Mitter	26	Ecurie Maarsbergen	718/2-02			gemeldet, aber nicht am Start
			Carel Godin de Beaufort	28	Ecurie Maarsbergen	718/2-01	nicht qualifiziert		
21. September	Formel 1	Gold Cup/Oulton Park	Carel Godin de Beaufort	3	Ecurie Maarsbergen	718/2-01	20.	10.	
6. Oktober	Formel-1-WM	Grand Prix der USA/Watkins Glen	Carel Godin de Beaufort	12	Ecurie Maarsbergen	718/2-01	19.	6.	
3. November	Formel-1-WM	Grand Prix von Mexiko/Mexiko City	Carel Godin de Beaufort	12	Ecurie Maarsbergen	718/2-01	18.	10.	
28. Dezember	Formel-1-WM	Grand Prix von Südafrika/Kyalami	Carel Godin de Beaufort	14	Ecurie Maarsbergen	718/2-01	20.	10.	

Mitter und de Beaufort, Großer Preis von Deutschland 1963.

Mitter und de Beaufort, German Grand Prix 1963.

Carel Godin de Beaufort, Nürburgring 1963.

Carel Godin de Beaufort, Nürburgring 1963.

Nino Vaccarella, Großer Preis von Deutschland 1963.

Nino Vaccarella, German Grand Prix 1963.

Date	Competition	Race	Driver	No.	Entrant	Type	Qualification	Result	Remarks
April 15	Formula 1	Pau Grand Prix/Pau	Carel Godin de Beaufort	16	Ecurie Maarsbergen	718/2-01	9th	4th	
			Heinz Schiller	24	Scuderia Filipinetti	718/2-02	10th	3rd	
April 21	Formula 1	Imola Grand Prix/ Imola	Carel Godin de Beaufort	12	Ecurie Maarsbergen	718/2-01	8th	6th	
			Jack Fairman	14	Ecurie Maarsbergen	718/2-02	9th	7th	
			Carlo Abate	26	Scuderia Centro Sud	718/2	12th	5th	
April 25	Formula 1	Syracuse Grand Prix/ Syracuse	Carel Godin de Beaufort	8	Ecurie Maarsbergen	718/2-01	4th	2nd	
May 11	Formula 1	BRDC International Trophy/Silverstone	Carel Godin de Beaufort	20	Ecurie Maarsbergen	718/2-01	17th	9th	
May 19	Formula 1	Rome Grand Prix/ Vallelunga	Carel Godin de Beaufort	40	Ecurie Maarsbergen	718/2-01	1st	2nd	
June 9	Formula-1 WC	Belgian Grand Prix/ Spa	Carel Godin de Beaufort	9	Ecurie Maarsbergen	718/2-01	18th	6th	
June 23	Formula-1 WC	Dutch Grand Prix/ Zandvoort	Carel Godin de Beaufort	32	Ecurie Maarsbergen	718/2-01	19th	9th	
			Gerhard Mitter	34	Ecurie Maarsbergen	718/2-02	16th	retired	clutch
July 20	Formula-1 WC	British Grand Prix/ Silverstone	Carel Godin de Beaufort	23	Ecurie Maarsbergen	718/2-01	21th	10th	
July 28	Formula 1	Großer Preis der Solitude/ Solitude	Carel Godin de Beaufort	23	Ecurie Maarsbergen	718/2-01	13th	7th	
			Gerhard Mitter	24	Ecurie Maarsbergen	718/2-02	11th	5th	
August 4	Formula-1 WC	German Grand Prix/ Nürburgring	Carel Godin de Beaufort	17	Ecurie Maarsbergen	718/2-01	17th	retired	broken rim
			Gerhard Mitter	26	Ecurie Maarsbergen	718/2-02	15th	4th	
August 11	Formula 1	Kannonloppet/Karlskoga	Carel Godin de Beaufort	8	Ecurie Maarsbergen	718/2-02	8th	7th	
August 18	Formula 1	Grand Prix of the Mediterranean/Pergusa	Carel Godin de Beaufort	8	Ecurie Maarsbergen	718/2-01	12th	did not start	axle failure during practice
			Carlo Abate	14	Graf Volpi	718/2-03	10th	8th	
September 1	Formula 1	Austrian Grand Prix/ Zeltweg	Carel Godin de Beaufort	6	Ecurie Maarsbergen	718/2-01	10th	3rd	
			Kurt Bardi-Barry	7	Ecurie Maarsbergen	718/2-02	16th	retired	
September 8	Formula-1 WC	Italian Grand Prix/ Monza	Gerhard Mitter	26	Ecurie Maarsbergen	718/2-02			entered, did not start
			Carel Godin de Beaufort	28	Ecurie Maarsbergen	718/2-01	did not qualify		
September 21	Formula 1	Gold Cup/Oulton Park	Carel Godin de Beaufort	3	Ecurie Maarsbergen	718/2-01	20th	10th	
October 6	Formula-1 WC	American Grand Prix/ Watkins Glen	Carel Godin de Beaufort	12	Ecurie Maarsbergen	718/2-01	19th	6th	
November 3	Formula-1 WC	Mexican Grand Prix/ Mexiko City	Carel Godin de Beaufort	12	Ecurie Maarsbergen	718/2-01	18th	10th	
December 28	Formula-1 WC	South African Grand Prix/ Kyalami	Carel Godin de Beaufort	14	Ecurie Maarsbergen	718/2-01	20th	10th	

Foto: Porsche

Start zum Großen Preis von Deutschland 1963.

German GP 1963: The start.

Carel de Beaufort, Solitude 1964.

Carel de Beaufort, Solitude
1964.

Foto: Porsche

1964

Datum	Wettbewerb	Veranstaltung /Ort	Fahrer	Nr.	Bewerber	Typ	Training	Ergebnis	Bemerkungen
12. April	Formel 1	Grand Prix von Syrakus/ Syrakus	Carel Godin de Beaufort	8	Ecurie Maarsbergen	718/2-01			gemeldet, aber nicht am Start
2. Mai	Formel 1	BRDC International Trophy/Silverstone	Carel Godin de Beaufort	24	Ecurie Maarsbergen	718/2-01	22.	11.	
24. Mai	Formel-1-WM	Grand Prix von Holland/ Zandvoort	Carel Godin de Beaufort	28	Ecurie Maarsbergen	718/2-01	17.	Ausfall	Motorschaden
19. Juli	Formel 1	Großer Preis der Solitude/ Solitude	Carel Godin de Beaufort	9	Ecurie Maarsbergen	718/2-01	16.	8.	
2. August	Formel-1-WM	Großer Preis von Deutschland/Nürburgring	Carel Godin de Beaufort	29	Ecurie Maarsbergen	718/2-01			schwerer Unfall im Training am 1. August, de Beaufort verstarb am Renntag

k. A. = keine Angaben verfügbar

Date	Competition	Race	Driver	No.	Entrant	Type	Qualification	Result	Remarks
April 12	Formula 1	Syracuse Grand Prix/ Syracuse	Carel Godin de Beaufort	8	Ecurie Maarsbergen	718/2-01			entered, did not start
May 2	Formula 1	BRDC International Trophy/Silverstone	Carel Godin de Beaufort	24	Ecurie Maarsbergen	718/2-01	22th	11th	
May 24	Formula-1 WC	Dutch Grand Prix/ Zandvoort	Carel Godin de Beaufort	28	Ecurie Maarsbergen	718/2-01	17th	retired	engine
July 19	Formula 1	Großer Preis der Solitude/ Solitude	Carel Godin de Beaufort	9	Ecurie Maarsbergen	718/2-01	16th	8th	
August 2	Formula-1 WC	German Grand Prix/ Nürburgring	Carel Godin de Beaufort	29	Ecurie Maarsbergen	718/2-01			severe accident on August 1st, de Beaufort died on the day of the race

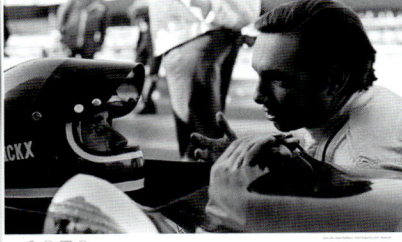

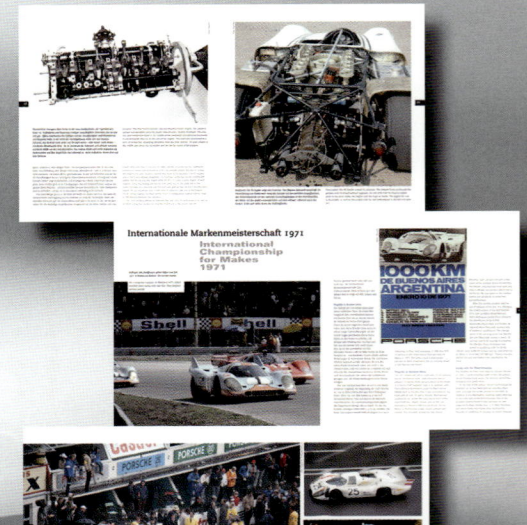
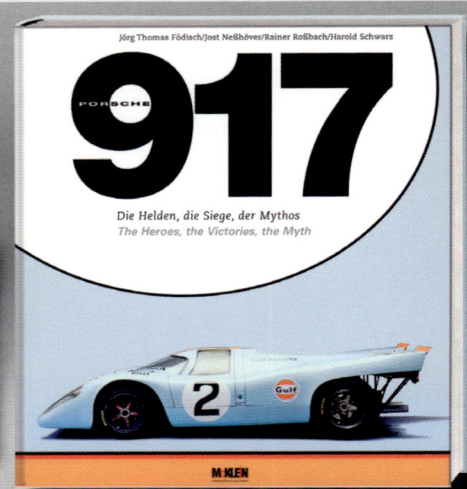